Christ Centered Therapy

The Practical Integration of Theology and Psychology

Christ *Centered* Therapy

The Practical Integration of Theology and Psychology

Neil T. Anderson, D. Min.
Terry E. Zuehlke, Ph.D.
Julianne S. Zuehlke, M.S.

ZondervanPublishingHouse

Grand Rapids, Michigan

A Division of HarperCollinsPublishers

Christ-Centered Therapy
Copyright © 2000 by Neil T. Anderson, Terry E. Zuehlke, and Julianne S. Zuehlke

Requests for information should be addressed to:

ZondervanPublishingHouse
Grand Rapids, Michigan 49530

Library of Congress Cataloging-in-Publication Data

Anderson, Neil T., 1942–
    Christ-centered therapy: the practical integration of theology and psychology / Neil Anderson, Terry Zuehlke, and Julianne Zuehlke.
        p.   cm.
    Includes bibliographical references and index.
    ISBN: 0-310-23113-2
    1. Counseling—Religious aspects—Christianity. 2. Psychotherapy—Religious aspects—Christianity. I. Zuehlke, Terry (Terry E.), 1946– II. Zuehlke, Julianne (Julianne S.) III. Title.
    BR115.C69 A53 2000
    261.5'15—dc21   00-039263

This edition is printed on acid-free paper.

Interior design by Amy E. Langeler
Table and figure designs by Melissa Elenbaas
Form designs by Rob Monacelli

Printed in the United States of America

---

01 02 03 04 05 /❖ DC/ 10 9 8 7 6 5 4 3 2

Contents

Cognitive-Behavioral Therapy
Bonding
Early Recollections
Eating Disorders
Grief and Loss
Physical, Emotional, and Sexual Abuse
Parenting
TheoPhostics

Anxiety Disorders
Depression
Boundaries
Dissociative Identity Disorder
Marriage Communications
Sexual Addiction
Chemical Addictions
Who I Am in Christ
The Overcomer's Covenant in Christ

TABLES

FIGURES

ACKNOWLEDGMENTS

All three authors wish to thank our publisher and the staff with whom we have been associated—in particular, John Sloan, Dirk Buursma, Jonathan Petersen, and the many support persons who were professional and superlative in all aspects! We also want to thank the contributing "Tool Kit" authors who have shared from their clinical experiences. Dr. Stephen and Judy King were dreamers with us in this project from the beginning. Their contributions in the "Tool Kit" are especially valued.

Neil, Terry, and Julie

Terry and Julie also wish to express gratitude to Neil Anderson and several others:

We were greatly influenced when we first heard Dr. Anderson's empowering message of claiming our identity in Christ and of achieving personal victory over the lies of the enemy. We were born-again Christian counselors in private practice, working with clients from a secular humanistic perspective. A great thirst arose within us to integrate the spiritual truths of the inerrant Word of God in our work with clients. We realized that withholding the Truth from clients would stunt their healing and reveal a double-mindedness on our part. How could we worship and pray to the true and living God who heals, comforts, gives peace, and forgives our sins through the death of Jesus Christ, and not integrate those truths into our counseling with clients? Due to the empowering of the Holy Spirit, we were challenged in this regard, and we gradually began to alter our counseling. The results have been wonderful, and the blessings in clients' lives have been remarkable. When Neil gave us the opportunity to join with him in assisting counselors with the integration of theology and psychology, we jumped at the chance. This book is the result of our collaboration. Thank you, Neil.

We also want to thank our many clients for seeking our counsel and providing their real-life experiences as templates for integration. We thank staff members at our clinic who ventured forth with integration as we modeled it for them. We thank our prayer warriors, namely, Dr. John and Carolyn Fugate, Tim and Kathy White, and Bob and Barbara Francis. We thank readers of the rough-draft manuscript: Dr. Bruce Roselle, Dr. Carl Haugen, and Linda Wismer. We also thank the Lord for our cabin on Lake of the Woods in Ontario, Canada, where we wrote the majority of our sections during times away from the rigors of clinical practice and ministry.

We are aware that others have written about integration with clarity and excellence. In this postmodern era of relativism and pragmatism, we trust this book will help remind counselors of the biblical absolutes wherein true healing occurs. To God be the glory!

Terry and Julie

INTRODUCTION

Since the cultural revolution of the 1960s, the mental and emotional needs of the American people have increased dramatically. According to the National Institute of Mental Health, more than 19 million people in America will suffer from depression in any given year. The number of doctor visits in which patients received prescriptions for mental problems rose from 32.7 million to 45.6 million between 1985 and 1994. Visits in which depression was diagnosed almost doubled over this ten-year period, increasing from 11 million to more than 20.4 million.[1] Clearly we are experiencing a "blues epidemic."

We are also living in an age of anxiety. In fact, the number one mental health problem in America today is no longer depression but anxiety disorders, with chemical addiction ranking third. Adding to this mix of mental and emotional problems are the disintegration of the nuclear family and the struggles of interpersonal relationships. If anyone doubts that our problems are not serious, the recent rash of school and business shootings should signal loudly and clearly that all is not well in America. There is an underlying rage set to explode at the slightest provocation.

Fortunately, the last three decades have seen a tremendous increase of Christians entering the mental health profession. Some do so to find answers for themselves, but many are responding to God's call to search for biblical answers that will help desperately hurting people. Of course, in order to legally practice their profession as therapists, they must be licensed by the state, which involves extensive education in psychology, social work, marriage and family studies, and psychiatric nursing. In addition, most states require candidates to undergo a supervised intern program for at least one year. In the end, most therapists who meet these varied requirements enjoy a clinical comfort level with the psychological principles they have learned.

Many Christian therapists who have met the preceding requirements also experience a spiritual comfort level with regard to their personal faith. Often coming from sound evangelical churches, they practice the disciplines of the Christian life, such as worship, Bible study, prayer, and evangelism. Many, however, have lacked the opportunity or the expertise to integrate these spiritual principles into their counseling practices. Although they feel comfortable within each area separately, they have a number of questions and insecurities about combining psychological principles and spiritual principles within their practice.

Consider, for example, the struggles of two different Christian therapists. The first, a relatively inexperienced psychologist, was uncertain how to introduce prayer into a session. He explained, "It feels so strange to be praying with my client. I never had any experience like this in school!" His education and training did not include anything about the role of the Holy Spirit or about the interference of evil spirits. As a result, he didn't know how to integrate a basic spiritual discipline such as prayer into his practice.

By way of contrast, a licensed counselor who was trained as a pastor had a difficult time trying to apply principles from the American Psychiatric Association's *Diagnostic and Statistical Manual of Mental Disorders,* 4th ed. (DSM-IV). Although well equipped to address the spiritual aspect of emotional problems, he lacked clinical skills of diagnosis and struggled with case management decision making. Like the psychologist, the pastor-therapist needed to learn basic principles for integrating the Christian faith with therapy and then to put those principles into practice through application exercises.

THE NEED FOR INTEGRATION

We are not the first to recognize the need for integration principles and application exercises. Christian psychologist and author Gary Collins, for example, explains that the key current area of need when we think of integration is not theoretical but practical. How do we do integration? What skills and methods are involved? Collins concludes that practice-focused, training-oriented books and articles are needed.[2]

Our hope is that this book will meet this need by integrating the truth of God's Word with the tools of psychological assessment and treatment. As evangelical Christians, we believe that the Bible is the only authoritative source for faith and practice. Therefore, we have sought to develop a biblical worldview, to demonstrate the relevancy of the gospel, including the reality of our identity in Christ, and to set forth biblical principles and techniques in the area of Christian counseling. If we say that Jesus Christ is the answer and that the truth of God's Word sets people free, then such core beliefs must be fully integrated into the practice of the Christian therapist.

We are painfully aware of the ongoing controversy in Christian circles regarding the relevance of psychotherapeutic practices and of psychology in general. In the broad scope of history, psychology is a relatively new area of scientific study, as are computer science and microbiology. And although we cannot accept a secular psychology any more than we can accept a liberal theology, we cannot reject psychology as a disciplined science. In a narrow sense, psychology is simply the study of the human mind and how it functions. A broader definition includes related matters such as emotions, identity, personality, and relationships. Because humans are complex beings, it is vital for members of the helping professions to understand not only how the brain functions (neurology) but also how the mind works (psychology). To that end, our goal in this book is to bring the psychiatrist, the professional counselor, and the practical theologian together in order to present to the Christian community a unified answer from a biblical-Christian worldview.

We believe there is such a thing as biblical psychology. The Bible speaks with authority about thinking and feeling and about pathological problems such as anxiety disorders, depression, anger, and bitterness. Moreover, since we are transformed by the renewing of our minds (see Romans 12:2), we must, if we are to be conformed to the image of God, understand how the mind functions. And this kind of awareness is also an essential part of the sanctification process, as Neil Anderson and Robert Saucy explain in *The Common Made Holy*.[3] Sanctification is God's will for our lives (see 1 Thessalonians 4:3), so Christian counselors need a comprehensive understanding not only of psychological principles but also of positional and progressive sanctification.

We do not intend to address every possible issue related to Christian counseling. Volumes have been written on such topics as counseling techniques, the integration of psychology and religion, counseling ethics, what it means to be a Christian counselor, spiritual warfare, and managed care. We suggest that readers consult the works referenced in the notes for in-depth study of these issues. What this book will provide is a framework of principles for integrating counseling and Christian faith as well as application exercises to help the Christian counselor put these principles into action in his or her counseling practice. We have seen these principles and exercises work in our own practices, so we know they can work for other Christian counselors committed to meeting the emotional and psychological needs of our day.

ORIGIN AND OVERVIEW OF OUR INTEGRATIVE APPROACH

Terry and Julie Zuehlke first met Neil Anderson when he conducted a "Living Free in Christ" conference at their church several years ago. After seeing many people resolve psychological and spiritual conflicts and find their freedom and identity in Christ, the Zuehlkes began to integrate the biblical principles taught at the conference into their work at their professional counseling center. Key to this work of integration was understanding the full gospel based on the finished work of Jesus Christ as well as the present ministry of the Holy Spirit. They began to regard every Christian client as a child of God who is a new creation in Christ. Instead of simply teaching coping skills, they encouraged genuine repentance that led to freedom in Christ. They also began to apply spiritual warfare principles in a form suitable for a counseling context.

Eventually, Julie reduced her time at the clinic in order to serve on the senior staff at their church, overseeing the pastoral care ministries. Terry continued to direct their Christ-centered professional counseling center. This is the model we hope to share: a practical theologian and two experienced therapists (one of whom is also a pastoral care director at a large church) working together to provide a comprehensive, biblical answer for a world that desperately needs to know the truth that will set them free.

We firmly believe every church can be equipped to help its people resolve their personal and spiritual conflicts. That is the purpose of Neil Anderson's ministry, as he seeks to offer churches and mission groups resources that will enable them to establish their people, marriages, and ministries alive and free in Christ. But we also believe there is a need for professional Christian counselors who are uniquely trained to help both church members with specific needs and people who would not be inclined to seek help from the church. For the latter, the professional Christian counselor offers a bridge from the world to the church.

To equip church leaders and Christian counselors to meet these needs, we begin in chapter one by discussing the need to clarify the values and worldview of the therapist as well as the client. Then, in chapter two, we work toward establishing a biblical worldview. We review the historical interplay between psychology and religion as it relates to mental illness diagnosis and treatment, and we discuss the question of disturbing psychological conditions as "symptoms" or "sin." In chapter three we provide an overview of four conceptualizations of Christian counseling, as outlined by prominent writers, as well as our own operational paradigm. In chapter four we attempt to establish a biblical integration between theology and psychology. The goal of this chapter is to lay the biblical basis for personal and spiritual conflict resolution rather than simply symptom reduction. Having an adequate "theology of resolution" is of paramount importance for the Christian counselor. In chapter five we explore the roles and responsibilities of God, the therapist, and the client as they relate to the counseling process.

Chapter six lays out the theological underpinnings for an emphatically biblical strategy for Christian counseling. Chapter seven integrates theology with strategic methodology and provides spiritual and psychological assessment for the therapist as well as the client. Chapter eight shows how root spiritual issues can be addressed in the marketplace using psychological impairment language, an approach that enables the Christian client to be firmly rooted in Christ. Chapter nine contains a therapist's tool kit. Here we share approaches proven to be effective in resolving a variety of problems.

Chapter ten discusses how the professional therapist and the church community can and should work together. We outline both mutual and individual responsibilities of the Christian professional and the church, then present a flowchart depicting counselor and church cooperation. This chapter provides a picture of how clients can move between the two environments to achieve freedom and attain resolution to their conflicts. Finally, chapter eleven talks about the accountability and integrity of Christian counseling in the marketplace. We also discuss the relationship professional counselors have with state licensing boards, as well as the need for proper documentation.

Our desire throughout is to integrate the truth from God's Word with compatible methodology from the science of psychology. We want to help Christian counselors deepen their personal relationship with Jesus Christ, improve their clinical skills, practice with freedom in the context of a biblical worldview, and navigate the third-party-payer environment in the marketplace. These competencies will assist counselors as they deal with the wounded emotions of believers in the Lord Jesus Christ who are seeking healing, restoration, and the truth about their identity. It will also equip Christian counselors to graciously work with nonbelievers who may, as a result of loving exposure to the Truth within the counseling context, decide to put their trust in Jesus Christ as Lord and Savior.

1

Values and Worldview Clarification

Just because so many lies flourish in the realm of psychology does not mean Christians should abandon it. Instead, Christians must bring God's truth to a deceived discipline.

DAVID A. NOEBEL

Psychology as a disciplined study did not originate from Christian sources. Moreover, psychology entered the curriculum of Christian education in a significant way only in the last half of the twentieth century, no doubt because the historical and prevalent stance taken by the field of psychology has been that spiritual values have little or no place in counseling—a position caused by, among other factors, a competing worldview, political correctness, a liberal church, and an inaccurate understanding of science. In contrast to the historical view, we maintain that the spiritual values reflected in worldviews play an indispensable role in the clinical decisions made by therapists and in the lives of clients who come for treatment. Psychotherapy is not, in fact, devoid of a worldview but embraces either a Christian or an alternative spiritual perspective.

Thus, current trends to acknowledge the presence of conflicting worldviews within the professional community reflect a welcome change. For example, the American Psychological Association (APA) mandates that psychologists take an informed view of religion as one of the several significant dimensions of human differences or diversity—or else make appropriate referrals.[1] In addition, the American Psychiatric Association's Committee on Religion and Psychiatry recommends that the religiosity of an individual be addressed in clinical practice.[2] Both ethical guidelines require the development of a knowledge base and a competency at all levels of mental health provision: education, training, research, and clinical practice.

The truth that religious values have a crucial place in the ethical practice of mental health counseling is beginning to gain official recognition. Fuller Theological Seminary psychology professor Siang-Yang Tan observes, "A biblical approach to counseling ... that explicitly utilizes Christian religious values or perspectives and interventions (prayer, use of Scripture) and relies on appropriate spiritual gifts and the power and ministry of the Holy Spirit, makes unique contributions to counseling effectiveness, especially with religious, Christian clients."[3]

BIG BROTHER AND THE HEALTH CARE ENVIRONMENT

Clearly these are changing times for the mental health profession, which is resulting in a significant amount of confusion. On the one hand, the United States government is starting to limit the establishment of bureaucratic structures around many aspects of its citizens' lives and is turning matters of private and family concern over to individual citizens. To compensate for its shrinking involvement, the government is looking to churches and private-sector organizations to provide for the needs of the people in their respective communities.

The health care system, on the other hand, is not shrinking but rather expanding its regulatory control. It manages care through cost controls and by "rationing" health care services. Managed care's influence in the mental health field has established bureaucratic structures that regulate practices in counseling. In addition, the actions of state licensing boards, professional practitioner organizations, and the court system serve to maintain a politically correct stranglehold on Christian practitioners. Consequently, the community of Christian mental health consumers and practitioners has been limited in its ability to mutually determine its values and spiritual approaches. Although secular, humanistic, atheistic, agnostic, and Eastern forms of spirituality are accepted because they are regarded as "politically correct," the values and worldview of biblical Christianity on which this culture and its freedoms are based have been increasingly met with hostility.

THE ROLE OF THE CHURCH

This turn of events should not surprise us, for Scripture warns of a coming apostasy (see Matthew 24:24, 37–38; 1 Timothy 4:1). In simple terms, an apostate is anyone who has the form and function of religion but who lacks the supernatural power of the Holy Spirit and a commitment to absolute truth. Similarly, apostate churches are those that endorse the cultural misbeliefs and practices of our morally backslidden culture. Instead of righteously influencing society, such churches have become its prey, for whenever we abandon the authority of Scripture we lose our moral compass.

The apostle Paul encourages us to "preach the Word; be prepared in season and out of season; correct, rebuke and encourage—with great patience and careful instruction. For the time will come when men will not put up with sound doctrine. Instead, to suit their own desires, they will gather around them a great number of teachers to say what their itching ears want to hear. They will turn their ears away from the truth and turn aside to myths" (2 Timothy 4:2–4). Sadly, all too many churches today have become at best irrelevant or at worst proclaimers of a false Christianity that fails to address issues such as public and personal morality.

Adverse legal decisions have also contributed to ushering the Christian influence out of the public arena. Examples of such decisions include the banning of school prayer, of Christian symbols on public property at Christmas, and of prayer at graduation ceremonies or sports events. Through the political and legal processes in this country, we are being pressured to practice our religion within our four walls, to stay out of politics, and to stop interfering with society.

The church, however, must inform the culture by means of a compassionate voice of truth and empower its members to take righteous stands in the marketplace. The church is supposed to be "the pillar and foundation of the truth" (1 Timothy 3:15), but if we fail to proclaim that truth in love, we will cease to be the salt and light of our culture (see Matthew 5:13–16). Law, education, and politics will function in a vacuum without Judeo-Christian principles influencing their actions. The church is not the executor of the state, but it should be the conscience of the state; to do so demands that the church remain true to God's Word. For example, it is difficult, if not impossible, for the conscientious Christian counselor to encourage a client to abandon a homosexual lifestyle when the "church" is vigorously debating whether to ordain homosexuals into ministry.

THE COUNSELOR AS ETHICIST AND SCIENTIST

The decreasing role of pastoral counseling and discipleship training, as well as the phenomenal growth of clinical psychology in the past thirty years, signal another critical shift in our culture. Prior to 1960, the local pastor was the primary choice for those seeking personal help and guidance. Since then, however, discipleship training has functionally been replaced by professional counseling. Compare the number of people helpers who have been trained as disciplers or pastors with the number of those who have been trained to be psychotherapists. From a biblical perspective, disciplers and counselors are essentially identical. A good Christian counselor is a good discipler and vice versa; the primary difference between pastors and professional Christian counselors relates to the amount of theological or psychological training they receive. Yet today people are more prone to seek help for a personal problem from a psychotherapist than from a pastor.

Because of these spiritual, legal, and social changes, psychotherapists and other mental health professionals have become the primary caregivers and dispensers of moral guidance in our society. Psychology as a discipline allows the powerful mantle of modern science to be placed on the counselor's shoulders. Therefore, practitioners not only have taken on implicit roles as experts in the area of morality but also explicit roles as experts in science. Since, moreover, science often opposes God and promotes "values-neutrality" (which is itself a value), many professionally trained mental health practitioners share a commitment to "objectivity" and "neutrality." Consequently, practicing mental health professionals generally harbor a high degree of antitheistic sentiment, which, in turn, typically promotes non-Christian values in the name of objective science and values-neutrality.

Researchers and educators have long argued that spiritual values can and should be kept out of psychological theory, research, and practice. As a result, most therapists are trained to believe they can be a blank slate, an objective and scientific technician, a nonjudgmental listener and evaluator, and an embodiment of clinical pragmatism and humanistic idealism.[4] A closer look, however, reveals that spiritual values are hidden beneath theoretical language. The language of psychological theories invariably speaks of humanity's search for meaning, self-actualization, and the realization of one's own human potential. These psychological orientations contain the spirituality of secular, humanistic, agnostic, and New Age worldviews, which are erroneously seen as "scientific." Because these orientations differ from the monotheistic spiritual perspective, they are not regarded as being related to spiritual values.

As noted above, the field of psychology has a historical bias against theistic spiritual perspectives, a bias that has remained largely unrecognized and unchallenged. Despite compelling evidence that it does in fact embrace identifiable values, psychology still presents itself as holding to an objective, scientific, and valueless stance. German philosopher Karl Marx (1818–1883) called monotheistic religion the "opium of the people," thus relegating its value to that of a mere anesthetic for the uncritical mind. Yet the system he was proposing was most assuredly driven by spiritual values, even though it presented itself as scientific.

To make matters worse, psychology has not only erroneously claimed values-neutrality but has openly discriminated against practitioners whose values differ from those of institutionalized psychology. For example, Terry recalls a member of a state board of psychology stating that any therapist who prays with a client is engaging in unethical behavior. Terry and Julie also know of a psychologist in private practice who was reprimanded when he prayed with a particular client. Even though the client claimed to be a Christian and had consented to prayer in the sessions, the client complained to the board of psychology that this psychologist had prayed with her!

In 1980, Brigham Young University psychology professor Allen Bergin ignited open discussion about psychology's historical bias against theistic and spiritual approaches. In his bombshell article Dr. Bergin

- stated that interest in values issues has been increasing among health professionals.
- challenged therapists to make their values explicit. Therapists who are theistic should openly disclose this orientation, as should humanists (atheists and agnostics), utopianists, and New Agers.
- revealed the value assumptions that had been covertly advanced in the major schools of thought in the profession.
- described openly theistic and spiritual belief systems.
- showed that humanistic and behavioristic ideals were in opposition to monotheistic values.
- confronted the profession with its negative bias toward monotheistic values.
- encouraged all therapists to be open about their values and less subtly coercive with clients.

- challenged non-Christian therapists to be culturally sensitive and respectful of monotheistic clients.
- called for the infusion of monotheistic spiritual values into mainstream psychology on the basis of careful scholarship, just as infusion of other values bases needs to be studied and examined.[5]

More than a thousand professional people are reported to have responded to this article, and many leading individuals endorsed its general themes without necessarily agreeing with every specific value. Their support served as the impetus to move forward with the exploration of the relevance of spiritual content in counseling.

As we ponder the roles of psychology, the church, the government, and managed care in the delivery of mental health care, we can draw one dominant conclusion: The question is not *whether* spiritual values are operational in counseling practice but rather *which values* are operational. Nothing is valueless, since that position is in itself a value! Those who promote the idea that counseling is valueless and nonreligious are advocating a value system of valuelessness. Similarly, those who hold to an atheistic worldview are promoting a religious belief of godlessness and antitheism.

Managed care can be ethical only when it recognizes the legitimacy of monotheistic religious values and stops pretending that alternative religious beliefs are neutral and valueless. A value-free approach to psychotherapy is impossible; therefore, any claim to be value-free should be supplanted by a more open and complete value-informed perspective. Fortunately, long-term and entrenched biases, stereotypes, and taboos are slowly giving way to empirical findings that show positive relationships between mental health and committed religiosity.[6] While the prevalence of religious and spiritual beliefs is high among the American public, the predominant exposure to other worldviews during the typical counselor's higher education and the absence of equal instruction in a Christian worldview has produced two generations of largely nontheistic practitioners. Thus, the values of the American public and those of the average counselor may very well stand in opposition to one another. Moreover, research shows that clients move their values toward their therapists' values, which means that nontheistic values generally prevail.[7]

One example of counseling being influenced by the values orientation of a therapist is seen in the issue of divorce. The predominant Christian perspective on divorce is that it is only permissible when adultery or physical abandonment is present or when an unbelieving spouse decides to divorce a believer. When clients speak to us of their marital difficulties, they will find us working very diligently to preserve these marriages. Even when the biblical grounds for divorce are present, we still seek repentance and reconciliation. We work patiently with one or both parties because of our commitment to the biblical value that marriage is a reflection of the relationship between Christ and his church, whom he will never leave or forsake (see Ephesians 5:22–33).

Secular therapists by and large do not hold to the same value system. Clients have shared with us their experiences with non-Christian therapists who, when hearing that one spouse wants out, will assume the marriage is unredeemable. They typically then recommend divorce as the best option and proceed with divorce counseling. The overriding value seems to be whatever it takes to make each person individually happy and self-fulfilled. If one spouse cannot be happy in the marriage, secular therapists think it best to terminate the marriage. Individual happiness becomes the ultimate value.

This case example reveals that both groups of therapists — the Christian and the non-Christian — are working on the basis of a worldview and a set of values. Does each of these approaches have a significant impact on the client and the outcome? Emphatically, yes! Is one approach value-free and the other value-laden? Emphatically, no! Both are based on implicit as well as explicit values orientations to which the therapists ascribe. The real issue is whether it is better to work from a biblically based, value-informed perspective or to blissfully maintain that values are not part of the equation. Psychologists P. Scott Richards and Allen Bergin state that "persons have spiritual issues that are inextricably intertwined with their presenting problems. Their treatments cannot be completely successful if their therapists do not appropriately address these beliefs and issues."[8]

PSYCHOTHERAPY: THE PROMOTION OF A WORLDVIEW

The delightful children's story called *The Emperor's New Clothes* has fascinated and entertained readers of all ages for years. In the story, a pompous emperor is fooled into believing he is wearing grand and glorious clothing as he parades before his people. Of course, the emperor soon hears the snickers of the crowd, for he is actually wearing nothing at all. Such is the state of secular psychology today — self-inflated and self-deceived. The professional pride that so readily accompanies titles and degrees often contributes to this self-deception. In the words of the apostle Paul, "Although they claimed to be wise, they became fools and exchanged the glory of the immortal God for images made to look like mortal man" (Romans 1:22 – 23).

The present belief that it is possible to treat persons psychologically in a values-neutral manner is a myth. Equally false is the belief that psychology is only about instincts, motivations, emotional states, and life situations that can be studied scientifically apart from values. Unfortunately, treatment approaches, funding allocations, and disciplinary actions are regulated by the "emperors" of a worldview blind to the truth that values are the very lifeblood of all we do as counselors with our clients.

For example, when Terry submitted to a managed care provider a *Diagnostic and Statistical Manual of Mental Disorders IV* (DSM-IV) diagnosis of Religious or Spiritual Problem (V-Code 62.89) secondary to a primary diagnosis of Major Depressive Disorder, the claim was rejected as unacceptable for reimbursement. The case reviewer believed a focus on spiritual problems would overshadow the client's other areas of impaired function. We who observe these discriminatory stances and see this myth in action do not snicker on the emperor's sidelines; we grieve deeply over the destruction caused by this fallacy that values do not impact counseling.

Others also recognize the problem. For example, the American Psychological Association recently published a groundbreaking book titled *Religion and the Clinical Practice of Psychology*, edited by Pepperdine Graduate School of Education and Psychology professor Edward P. Shafranske. This work is the result of an ongoing dialogue within APA Division 36 (Psychology of Religion) among colleagues who acknowledge the absurdity of attempts at valuelessness and religion-free counseling. The volume, which we cite frequently in this book, includes a number of chapters written by scholars and clinicians who share the recognition that values, religion, and faith are an integral part of persons as whole human beings as well as integral to the successful outcome of therapy.[9]

In this monumental work, contributors Allen Bergin, I. Reed Payne, and P. Scott Richards cite the conclusion of G. Owen, who states, "Secularization of psychotherapy can no longer be promoted without question. Value-free therapy is no longer viable."[10] To draw this conclusion does not imply, however, the promotion of a particular set of values, merely the ethical imperative of dealing openly with one's own values as a therapist and those of the client. Thus, Bergin, Payne, and Richards add:

> Professional malaise and lassitude, or even the hostility sometimes encountered when addressing these issues, cannot be explained by an elitist or condescending pronouncement that these aspects of human nature are not scientific. Science is defined by methodology, not by content, and many of these areas have been studied scientifically. No, the reason for this neglect lies elsewhere. Among the reasons is the clear but discomforting factor of value judgment—the preferencing process. Aside from the investigative problems, which are numerous, the fact remains that a large number of influential psychologists have chosen (for one reason or another) to exclude issues of purpose, meaning, values, and spiritual and religious constructs or experiences from their theorizing about human behavior.[11]

Others, such as W. Bevan, W. O'Donohue, James Olthuis, and Nicholas Wolterstorff, have recognized the profound influence of "control beliefs" within every area of life.[12] These control beliefs are foundational commitments, a set worldview, a preferred ideology that affect creative thought, scientific inquiry, and ultimate answers.[13] These scholars acknowledge that valuelessness is in reality the imposition of a values position. Why then the hostility toward the inclusion of values and monotheistic religious interventions in therapy? Apparently some influential psychologists are choosing to exclude the worldviews and spiritual experiences of their clients from their theorizing because of their own worldviews and their desire to control or at least influence the worldviews of others!

Psychology has had a long-standing history of hostility toward monotheistic spiritual perspectives.[14] Some mental health professionals view Christian values and beliefs as advocating unhealthy behaviors, such as misperceiving biblical submission as promoting spouse abuse and biblical discipline as promoting child abuse. They also interpret Christian beliefs to be based on superstitious, nonscientific myths (for example, creation and resurrection from the dead).

Some have even argued that Christians are more emotionally disturbed, rigid, and unhealthy than the general population. This view among many of the major theoreticians in psychology matches the belief expressed in a 1997 *New York Times* article that labeled Christians "poor, uneducated, and easily led."[15] Psychologist Wendell Watters likewise speculates that Christian beliefs may promote a form of mental illness. "A true Christian," he writes, "must always be in a state of torment, since he or she can never really be certain that God has forgiven him or her."[16] And well-known humanist and psychologist Albert Ellis calls Christians "emotionally disturbed, usually neurotic but sometimes psychotic."[17] Such stereotyping of a class of people is taboo in our politically correct world when it comes to women, African-Americans, homosexuals, Jews, and others, but stereotypes against Christians seem to abound in the psychological and political communities today. This hostility against monotheistic spiritual perspectives in general and Christianity in particular derives from a values base rather than from a science base, from the content of a certain worldview rather than from a scientific methodology, from belief instead of from fact.

The review of all quantitative articles in two major psychiatric journals over the course of a twelve-year period revealed that seventy-two percent of religious commitment variables studied were beneficial to mental health; in addition, four of the religious dimensions studied were beneficial to mental health in ninety-two percent of the reported findings.[18] The research certainly depicts a different picture from the one painted by those who see "psychological instability" in religious persons!

Psychologist Edward Shafranske notes that the vast majority of individuals in Western society are raised within some religious tradition.[19] Recent surveys found that ninety-three percent of Americans identified with a religious group; over eighty percent regard religion as "fairly" or "very important" in their lives.[20] By way of contrast, psychologist and professor Stanton Jones discovered that religion plays a minimal role in the lives of most academic psychologists in the United States. A 1984 survey revealed that fifty percent of academic psychologists had no religious preference, compared with only ten percent of the general population. Among psychotherapists, only thirty-three percent of clinical psychologists describe religious faith as the most important influence in their lives, while seventy-two percent of the general population claim that their faith is important.[21]

These statistics indicate rather clearly that psychologists are an atypical subpopulation within our country, possessing much higher levels of agnosticism, skepticism, and atheism than their client base. In light of these differences, it seems quite likely that psychologists will misunderstand client religiosity, inappropriately evaluate the role of faith within clients' lives, and neglect to integrate religious elements into clinical practice.[22]

As we lay out a biblical framework for counseling in the general marketplace, it may be helpful to keep in mind the impact that similarity or dissimilarity between a client's and therapist's religious values has on the therapeutic outcome in counseling. Evidence demonstrates that religious clients respond better to therapy that is adapted to their religious values.[23] T. Kelly and Hans Strupp discovered that the only variable in which a similarity between the patient and therapist is significant in predicting the outcome of therapy is "salvation" agreement between the therapist and client.[24] This research supports the conclusion that patient-therapist similarity with regard to religious values may be one of our best predictors of successful outcome. Thus, it should be one variable in deciding how clients and therapists are matched. In fact, Edward Shafranske boldly asserts that this "values match" must be taken into account, not only as a matter of ethical practice, but especially because religious involvement has the potential to be a significant influencer in a person's mental health.[25] A person's beliefs, practices, and affiliations work together to create motivations that propel the individual into behavior.

Therapists must acknowledge they are change agents who should endorse values and lifestyles that are, on the basis of evidence and honest debate, shown to enhance mental health; they should adopt an explicit and nonrelativistic stance about values, not an implicit and relativistic therapeutic stance.[26] Of course, every therapist needs to tolerate differences, but a relativistic stance holds that no values are universal, that all values are merely cultural- or situation-specific. This pluralistic trend in therapy is problematic, not only because it suggests that all worldviews are equally true and entirely relative (which is itself a worldview), but also because it is logically inconsistent with the goal of therapy, which is to induce change in the client. Whenever therapists advocate a specific goal, which all therapists do, they cease to be relativists! In addition, when client values carry the potential for negative emotional, physical, or spiritual consequences, relativistic therapists cannot logically challenge these destructive client values and still stay true to their worldview.[27]

For example, because certain cultures regard cannibalism as normal human behavior, a therapist dealing with a cannibal would have no basis for suggesting change in the client's behavioral choice without illogically abandoning his or her commitment to relativism. In a similar way, men in some cultures take two or more wives and sense no impropriety or illegality in doing so. Therefore, a counselor dealing with a polygamous individual who is harboring wives in several states would have no ground for suggesting change in that person's behavior as long as the counselor maintained a relativism in values. The only situation in which relativistic counselors might feel justified in setting aside their relativism is when illegal activities are involved. But as a whole, the idea of relativism in therapy is absurd, as can be seen in the extremes to which it can lead.

This leads to the question of whether or not there are universal absolutes on which we can base our values in mental health. If we look over the course of history, we can see there are basic values that, if a culture embraces them, will promote its survival. When such values have been neglected and violated, the culture has disintegrated. Furthermore, if we compare the testimony of history to the claims of various religious stances, we may find we can draw clear conclusions about what these absolutes are. For example, we see that cultures where homosexuality flourished have crumbled, that societies where murder and sexuality were unrestrained have failed, and that nations where the family unit was decimated have not survived.[28]

We must examine closely the "civil war of values" (a phrase coined by Dr. James Dobson) going on not only in our culture in general but in the discipline of psychology in particular. As we formulate principles for integrating spiritual truths with the practice of counseling, we are doing so not in a vacuum but in the context of our current time in history, with competing views of culture, humanity, and religion influencing the process. If counselors who read this book end up believing they cannot apply its principles unless they are in a church setting, we will have lost the "civil war." The cultural mind-set that religion and culture should not interact, that the Christian faith should be left out of the marketplace, and that only "secular" values can play a role in counseling is misguided and wrong. We believe that biblical principles of counseling are superior to the counseling beliefs promoted in our culture, not only because they have demonstrated their superiority in the counseling room, but also because they are based on the absolute truth of God's Word.

EXPLICIT VALUES IN PSYCHOTHERAPY: FOUR COMPETING WORLDVIEWS

No therapist is values-neutral. Inevitably, a therapist's worldview will be revealed in his or her methodology. Clients come to therapy sessions with preconceived notions about themselves, the world they live in, and God — and so do therapists. So what types of worldviews are at work here?

In *Understanding the Times,* renowned worldview expert David Noebel lists four worldviews that exert the most influence over people in Western society. According to Noebel, the dominant worldviews include humanism, utopianism, New Age, and biblical Christianity. He writes, "The term worldview refers to any ideology, philosophy, theology, movement, or religion that provides an overarching approach to understanding God, the world, and man's relations to God and the world."[29]

Four Western Worldview Models[30]

	HUMANISM	UTOPIANISM	NEW AGE	BIBLICAL CHRISTIANITY
SOURCES	Humanist Manifestos I and II	Writings of Marx and Lenin	Writings of Spangler, Ferguson, and the like	Bible
THEOLOGY	Atheism	Atheism	Pantheism	Theism
PHILOSOPHY	Naturalism	Dialectical Materialism	Nonnaturalism	Supernaturalism
ETHICS	Relativism	Proletariat Morality	Relativism	Absolutes
BIOLOGY	Darwinian Evolution	Darwinian/Punctuated Evolution	Darwinian/Punctuated Evolution	Creation
PSYCHOLOGY	Self-actualization	Behaviorism	Collective Consciousness	Mind/Body
SOCIOLOGY	Nontraditional Family	Abolition of Home, Church, and State	Nontraditional Home, Church, and State	Traditional Home, Church, and State
LAW	Positive Law	Positive Law	Self-law	Biblical and Natural Law
POLITICS	World Government (Globalism)	New World Order (New Civilization)	New Age Order	Justice, Freedom, and Order
ECONOMICS	Socialism	Socialism	Universal Enlightened Production	Stewardship of Property
HISTORY	Historical Evolution	Historical Materialism	Evolutionary Godhood	Historical Resurrection

TABLE 1.1

Noebel contends that every worldview contains distinct perspectives in ten areas: theology, philosophy, ethics, biology, psychology, sociology, law, politics, economics, and history (see Table 1.1). All ten disciplines are interrelated, which means that in each case psychology is intertwined with one or more of the other disciplines, including theology!

Ironically enough, prominent humanist Bertrand Russell (1872–1970) inadvertently supported the idea that one cannot separate religion and philosophy. Regarding utopianists (communists), Russell wrote, "They have all the characteristics of religions. They advocate a way of life on the basis of irrational dogmas; they have a sacred history, a Messiah, and a priesthood. I do not see what more could be demanded to qualify a doctrine as religion."[31] Indeed, Russell is right about the utopianists, but the context of his comments implies that he views his own humanist position as nonreligious, which is simply not true. Russell's worldview is vulnerable to the same criticism.

Every philosophy assumes some view of God, a view we can fit loosely into one of the following categories:

- There is one God (Christianity, Judaism, Islam).
- There is no God (humanism, utopianism).
- There are many gods (pantheism).
- All is god (New Age).[32]

Clarifying one's worldview is critical for the counselor as well as for the client, since both have a controlling belief regarding the world in which they live. Every worldview has some explanation for the client's problem and what is required to resolve it. Based on their particular worldview, therapists will use certain methodologies and sources to develop a treatment plan and, as they participate in case consultation sessions, present case management plans to managed care providers and converse with professional licensing boards.

From our experience we can say that these environments often are not open to the Christian worldview. However, if the Christian voice of truth is silenced, we are waving a white flag rather than maintaining our position in Christ until our precious Bridegroom comes. If, because of intimidation from the surrounding culture, Christian counselors are afraid to tell believing and unbelieving clients the truth of God's Word in love, then those counselors will have failed themselves and their clients. We must follow the example of Paul, who testified in his letter to Timothy:

For God did not give us a spirit of timidity, but a spirit of power, of love and of self-discipline. So do not be ashamed to testify about our Lord, or ashamed of me his prisoner. But join with me in suffering for the gospel, by the power of God, who has saved us and called us to a holy life — not because of anything we have done but because of his own purpose and grace. This grace was given us in Christ Jesus before the beginning of time, but it has now been revealed through the appearing of our Savior, Christ Jesus, who has destroyed death and has brought life and immortality to light through the gospel. And of this gospel I was appointed a herald and an apostle and a teacher. That is why I am suffering as I am. Yet I am not ashamed, because I know whom I have believed, and am convinced that he is able to guard what I have entrusted to him for that day. What you heard from me, keep as the pattern of sound teaching, with faith and love in Christ Jesus. Guard the good deposit that was entrusted to you — guard it with the help of the Holy Spirit who lives in us.

—2 TIMOTHY 1:7 – 14

This is a convicting passage for any Christian therapist who knows the prevailing climate, the fierce opposition, and the competing worldviews that exist in our culture. But we also know the truth that will set people free, and we are commissioned by God to share this truth in love. Therefore, we joyfully stand in the righteousness of Christ and minister to those who are struggling.

But to minister effectively, we must understand not only the biblical worldview but also the worldviews prevalent in contemporary psychology. With that in mind, we'll briefly consider how these four major worldviews influence the counseling process.

HUMANIST PSYCHOLOGY

According to David Noebel, humanist psychology adheres to three major assumptions: "Man is good by nature and therefore perfectible; society and its social institutions are responsible for man's evil acts; and mental health can be restored to everyone who gets in touch with his inner 'good' self."[33] This brand of psychology denies the existence of the supernatural and focuses on strictly material entities such as the brain or stimuli and responses to stimuli (that is, behaviorism). Behaviorists believe that human thoughts and personality are determined solely by biological processes in the brain. In their view, "psychology is understanding how physical stimuli encourage our physical brains and bodies to behave."[34] They argue that the supernatural does not exist, only the natural, and that all of human experience is mechanical. Historically, modern psychology has been derived primarily from this concept of Western rationalism and naturalism. Erich Fromm (1900–1980), Abraham Maslow (1908–1970), Carl Rogers (1902–1987), and Rollo May (1909–1994) were well-known proponents of this worldview.

Generally these psychologists believe that humans are innately good and that evil occurs because of society's influence on humanity's thinking. Individuals need to be true to their feelings and innermost natures; the good is defined in terms of what is good for the individual (self-centeredness). Humanists believe their psychology is superior in explaining why people act the way they do, because it is "scientific." For example, Carl Rogers states that true science explores the private worlds of "inner personal meanings."[35] He thus suggests a redefinition of science that omits the standard scientific method: repeatable, observable, structured phenomena in the objective world. By his definition, all the major religions are scientific because they all have inner personal meaning. In reality, humanism is not a pure natural science but a religious worldview.

As Cornell University professor Richard Baer observes with regard to humanism's entrenchment in the American public school system, "Education never takes place in a moral and philosophical vacuum. If the larger questions about human beings and their destiny are not being asked and answered within a predominantly Judeo-Christian framework [worldview], they will be addressed with another philosophical or religious framework — but hardly one that is 'neutral.'"[36]

Dr. Baer's quote applies equally well to modern psychology and the therapeutic process. Psychology and counseling do not take place in a vacuum but within the context of the therapist's worldview. The question is not if a worldview or certain set of values is being promoted but which ones are predominating.

Humanism is a religious system, as many of its own publications admit.[37] Also, the United States Supreme Court in the 1961 case of *Torcaso v Watkins* declared, "Among *religions* in this country which do not teach what would generally be considered a belief in the existence of God are Buddhism, Taoism, Ethical Culture, Secular Humanism, and others" (emphasis added).[38]

Some humanists reveal quite clearly their distaste for other religious systems. Ted Turner, for example, 1990 Humanist of the Year and founder of Turner Broadcasting System (which owns TBS Superstation, CNN, CNN Headline News, and Turner Network Television), has been remarkably candid about his views regarding Christianity. In 1985 Turner founded the Better World Society and a few years later established a $500,000 prize to be given to anyone able to invent a new worldview suitable for the new, peaceful earth he imagined. National columnist Cal Thomas made the following observation in *The Washington Times*: "According to Turner, Christianity is a 'religion for losers'; 'Christ should not have bothered dying on the cross. I don't want anybody to die for me,' said Turner. 'I've had a few drinks and a few girlfriends, and if that's gonna put me in hell, so be it.'"[39]

UTOPIANISM PSYCHOLOGY

Like humanists, utopianists view the mind as material and comprised of merely a series of physical brain activities. Human development is a march toward the perfect social order (which is utopianism) and away from free will. Human beings can be educated and controlled so that they only do good, leading to the perfection of the human race. Proponents of this view take some of the teachings of B. F. Skinner (1904–1990), Ivan P. Pavlov (1849–1936), and John B. Watson (1878–1958), but modify them as they synthesize behaviorism with free will.

In the utopianist worldview, there is no acknowledgment of personal responsibility for sin; tragic events in life are due, rather, to society's structures. The cure for humanity's ills is to increase education, remove poverty, and eliminate oppression. When all those problems are solved, so the thinking goes, society and humanity will be perfected. Utopianists believe capitalism has failed to positively influence the mental health of individuals; they are convinced that only utopianism can provide the optimal setting for psychological health. Even though utopianist systems have collapsed in eastern Europe, this viewpoint lives on there as well as in China, in smaller communist countries, in South America, and in Africa—and even in the higher educational, legal, judicial, social, and political systems of the United States.

In this psychological system, freedom does not mean selecting one's own behavior but choosing what type of society will regulate and control one's behavior. "This is at best," notes David Noebel, "a stunted concept of freedom—man is free to select the society that will determine his every action."[40] Freedom as we typically understand the word is meaningless. It is redefined into another framework. Neil Anderson saw the results of this when he conducted a conference for pastors in Croatia. Years of communism had stripped them of any sense of self; it was as though they had no individual identity or autonomy. They all ended up being puppets in an autocratic state.

The contemporary notion of "political correctness" is one example of the way society determines the individual response and the expression of freedom differently from what we have traditionally understood in our Judeo-Christian legacy. The practice of political correctness reflects a utopianist worldview. Society condones or disapproves of certain language because of the perceived effect on certain classes of people. For example, it is politically correct to use the terms "abortion opponents" rather than "pro-life advocates"; or "African-American" rather than "black"; or "right-wing fundamentalist" but not "left-wing liberal"; or "gay" but not "sexually deviant." The state determines and controls the thought patterns and language of its people in the utopianist worldview.

NEW AGE PSYCHOLOGY

The fastest-growing philosophy/religion in America is the one known as New Age. The goal of New Age psychology is to achieve higher consciousness, thereby speeding up the work of evolution toward a collective God-consciousness. You don't need a messiah to die for your sins and give you life—you simply need enlightenment. This view is a Westernized version of Eastern mysticism in which God is impersonal and part of everything. A rock is God, an ant is God, a person is God, and the earth is God. The radical segment of the environmental movement is spurred on by this belief when it regards humans to be of no more value than other entities, such as trees, animals, and the elements of nature. A rock is a tree is a human.

In the New Age worldview, the resolving of health problems is a process of achieving mind over matter. People suffer illnesses because they haven't attained higher consciousness. To this way of thinking, the inability to contact the "god within" can also lead to criminal behaviors. Instead of being incarcerated, criminals need wise guidance in reaching inward.[41] Furthermore, not only does higher consciousness guarantee health, but it provides answers for the world and paves the way for ultimate unity and peace on earth.[42]

Proponents of this worldview are varied in their background, featuring such individuals as Shirley MacLaine, Marianne Williamson, Marilyn Ferguson, and the late John Denver. New Age defenders declare that humanism failed because it taught that humanity is finite and thus has limits to what it can accomplish. But if you really are God and only need to realize it, then you can accomplish anything you dare to believe.

Meditation is one of the primary methods used in New Age psychology to induce higher levels of consciousness, usually aided by crystals or mantras and one or more spirit guides (demons). Meditation opens up a person's ability to channel spirits.[43] New Age psychologists often use and recommend channeling, as well as other practices such as astrology, fire walking, Ouija boards, and aura readings, to augment meditation and achieve higher consciousness. They also commonly use visualization, which is the practice of imagining events in the future and willing them to come true.

New Age meditation focuses on the "god within," while Christian meditation focuses on the God without. Christian meditation involves Bible reading and reflection, as well as prayer. Thus, it is nothing less than religious discrimination when professional boards and managed care organizations both allow and endorse New Age meditation in clinical practice while censoring Christian therapists or challenging payment for Christians who use biblical interventions such as prayer.

A BIBLICAL WORLDVIEW

The public is inundated with conflicting worldviews in the name of cultural diversity; it is reported daily by the media and self-evident in our educational, political, and economic systems. Even in religious circles the pure beauty of what we possess in Jesus Christ and in the revelation of God's Word escapes many who consider themselves children of God. Commenting on these conflicting worldviews, David Noebel puts the biblical perspective in words too profound to omit from this discussion. Thus we quote, with permission, his detailed presentation of the biblical worldview in relationship to the other worldviews:

> Many people believe that when Christians confront other worldviews and attempt to speak to such "worldly" disciplines as politics, economics, biology, and law [we add psychology], they are overstepping their bounds. "Mind your own business," we are told. Jesus taught his followers, "you do not belong to the world, but I have chosen you out of the world" (John 15:19).

How, then, can the Christian justify his claim to a worldview that speaks to every facet of life? Shouldn't he stick to spiritual matters and allow non-Christians to concentrate on the practical matters of running the world?

In short, isn't there a difference between the secular and the sacred? Not according to Dietrich Bonhoeffer, who says we should not distinguish between the two: "There are not two realities, but only one reality, and that is the reality of God, which has become manifest in Christ in the reality of the world."

From the biblical Christian perspective, the ten disciplines addressed in this text reflect various aspects of God and his creative or redemptive order. God created mankind with theological, philosophical, ethical, biological, etc. dimensions. We live and move and have our being (our very essence and existence) within and about these categories. Why? Because that is the way God created us.

Such being the case, these categories are, from the Christian perspective, sacred and not secular. They are sacred because they are imprinted in the creative order. Both the early record of Genesis and the life of Jesus Christ reflect this truth.

For example, Genesis 1:1, "In the beginning God created the heavens and the earth" — is value-laden with theological and philosophical ramifications. Genesis 2:9, "knowledge of good and evil" — contains ethical ramifications; Genesis 1:21, "after their kind" — biological; Genesis 2:7, "a living soul" — psychological; Genesis 1:28, "be fruitful, and multiply, and fill the earth" — sociological and ecological; Genesis 3:11, "I commanded thee" — legal; Genesis 9:6, "whoso sheddeth man's blood" — political and legal; Genesis 1:29. "it shall be for food" — economic; Genesis 3:15, "enmity between thee and the woman" — historical. All ten disciplines are addressed in just the first few chapters of the Bible because they manifest and accent certain aspects of the creative order.

Further, God manifests himself in the form of Christ in such a way as to underline the significance of each discipline. In theology, for example, Jesus Christ is "the fullness of the Godhead" (Colossians 2:9); in philosophy, Christ is the Logos of God (John 1:1); in ethics, Christ is "the true light" (John 1:9; 3:19–20); in biology, Christ is "the life" (John 1:4; 11:25; Colossians 1:16); in psychology, Christ is "Savior" (Luke 1:46–47; Titus 2:13); in sociology, Christ is "Son" (Luke 1:30–31; Isaiah 9:6); in law, Christ is lawgiver (Genesis 49:10; Isaiah 9:7); in politics, Christ is "King of kings and Lord of lords" (Revelation 19:16; 1 Timothy 6:15; Isaiah 9:6; Luke 1:33); in economics, Christ is Owner of all things (Psalm 24:1; 50:10–12; 1 Corinthians 10:26); and in history, Christ is the Alpha and Omega (Revelation 1:8). The integration of these various categories into society has come to be known as Western Civilization.

The Bible and the life of Jesus Christ provide the Christian with the basis for a complete worldview. Indeed, the Christian gains a perspective so comprehensive that he is commanded to "take captive every thought to make it obedient to Christ" (2 Corinthians 10:5).

Once we have captured all thoughts and made them obedient to Christ, we are to use these thoughts to "demolish arguments and every pretension that sets itself up against the knowledge of God" (2 Corinthians 10:4–5). When nations and men forget God (see Psalm 2) they experience what mankind has experienced in the twentieth century. Nazism and communism, two major movements bereft of the knowledge of God, cost the human race millions of lives. Whittaker Chambers says that communism's problem is not a problem of economics, but of atheism: "Faith is the central problem of this age." Alexander Solzhenitsyn echoes him: "Men have forgotten God."

The apostle Paul insists in Colossians 2 that those who have "received Christ Jesus the Lord" (Colossians 2:6) are to be rooted and built up in him, strengthened in the faith as they were taught (Colossians 2:7). While the Christian works to strengthen his faith or worldview, he must see to it that no one takes him "captive through hollow and deceptive philosophy, which depends on human tradition and the basic principles of this world rather than on Christ" (Colossians 2:8). From the Christian point of view, humanism, utopianism, and New Age represent "the basic principles of this world." They are based on the wisdom of this world, and not on Christ.

This wasn't mere doctrine for Paul. He practiced what he preached. In Acts 17, Paul confronted the vain and deceitful philosophies of the atheistic Epicureans and pantheistic Stoics — the professional Humanists of his day. The apostle countered their ideas with Christian ideas, he reasoned and preached, and he accented three Christian truths — the resurrection of Jesus Christ (Acts 17:18), the creation of the universe by God (Acts 17:14), and the judgment to come (Acts 17:31).

Can we do less? We, too, must fearlessly proclaim the good news of the gospel (God created the universe and all things in it, mankind rebelliously smashed the image of God by sin, Jesus Christ died for our sin, was raised from the dead, and is alive forevermore — 1 Corinthians 15:1–4), and we must stand fast in the context of the same worldview as Paul — creation, resurrection, and judgment.[44]

The next chapter, "Reclaiming a Biblical Psychology," will consider the biblical worldview in greater depth.

Reclaiming a Biblical Psychology

The very essence of religion is to adjust the mind and soul of man. Healing means bringing the person into a right relationship with the physical, mental, and spiritual laws of God.

CHARLES ALLEN

Psychology is a study of the mind, so there can be no better place to begin this study than with what the Creator has revealed about how body, soul, and spirit were intended to function in harmony with him. We are not a random collection of molecules. We are created in the image of God. God breathed into Adam, and "the man became a living being" (Genesis 2:7). This combination of divine breath and dust makes up the created nature of humankind living in harmony with God.

According to Sir John Eccles (1903–1997), who was a world-renowned neurophysiologist, this dualism is the only explanation for consciousness. We have a "unity of identity," a sense of who we are that persists throughout our entire lives, even though all our brain molecules continually change. Human memory exists independently of specific nerve cells in which memory is supposedly encoded. Humanists and utopianists cannot explain this phenomenon, since they have no concept of the brain and the mind as separate entities. They also have no concept of free will apart from environmental manipulation.[1]

All psychological problems that are not organic malfunctions arise from humanity's basic sinful nature—from our rebellion against God. The recognition of sin introduces personal responsibility for change and for facing the problem of guilt resulting from sin. Society is the result of individual actions, so individuals must be seen as responsible for the evils in society. The individual must change for the better before society can change. Instead of putting ourselves at the center of the universe or making society responsible or viewing personhood as mechanical, we must "think after God and will after God," the God who is revealed in the Bible.[2]

WORLDVIEWS IN CONFLICT

The English poet Samuel Taylor Coleridge (1772–1834) in *Fears in Solitude* gives poetic expression to the unbelief that can occur among educated men and women:

Forth from his dark and lonely hiding place,
(Portentous sight!) the owlet Atheism,
Sailing on obscene wings athwart the noon,
Drops his blue-fringed lids, and holds them close,
And hooting at the glorious sun in Heaven,
Cries out, "Where is it?[3]

The apostle Paul wrote, "For since the creation of the world God's invisible qualities—his eternal power and divine nature—have been clearly seen, being understood from what has been made, so that men are without excuse" (Romans 1:20). Since God has so clearly revealed himself in nature, why hasn't the world embraced him as Creator and Lord? Why haven't we acknowledged his Word as the only authoritative source of truth? Even when God revealed himself in the person of Jesus Christ, who is the Truth, people rejected him. Paul explains, "Although they claimed to be wise, they became fools and exchanged the glory of the immortal God for images made to look like mortal man and birds and animals and reptiles" (Romans 1:22–23).

Similarly, the psalmist wrote, "The heavens declare the glory of God; the skies proclaim the work of his hands" (Psalm 19:1). Statements such as this are referring to general revelation. Empirical research is a form of general revelation, but it does not bear the same authority as special revelation, which includes the Word of God and God's ultimate revelation of himself in Jesus Christ. Conducting empirical research is an important part of higher education, because it helps us understand the condition of the present world and its inhabitants. Empirical research is helpful when it is simply *descriptive*, but it lacks *prescriptive* authority. The purpose of special revelation is to explain and interpret general revelation. We must interpret all of our observations through the grid of Scripture. In other words, "what is" (general) must be understood by "why it is" (special) from God's perspective.

In the practice of counseling a Christian therapist will confidently and respectfully reference and use the Bible as the basis of his or her worldview. Wisdom is seeing life from God's perspective. We must learn to think scripturally and help our clients come to know the truth that will set them free. Merely possessing knowledge about Scripture is not enough. Likewise, applying a verse now and then is Band-Aid methodology. As we'll discuss later, coming to know this truth is far more than an intellectual exercise. The words of Jesus are insufficient to set one free without the life of Jesus, who *is* the Word.

SECULAR OR SACRED?

The word *secular* implies the absence of a religious foundation. As we have seen, this absence of a religious foundation in and of itself implies a religious belief (namely, there is no God) that becomes part of one's worldview. Because one's worldview influences every major area of life (including psychology), there is no such thing as counseling apart from a religious perspective of one kind or another. What transpires in the counseling environment says volumes about what the counselor and client believe about God. Thus David Noebel rightly concludes, "Trying to separate the sacred from the secular is like trying to sear the soul from the body — a deadly experiment. We must recognize that all worldviews have religious implications."[4]

The problem is similar to saying, "You can't legislate morality." We would judge this statement to be total nonsense! We legislate morality every day. Every bill signed into law reflects some moral judgment; if it were impossible to legislate morality, we wouldn't have any laws identifying crimes. What the proponents of amoral legislation are really saying is, "You can't legislate *your* morality." They don't want to be held accountable for a right or wrong standard from a religious perspective other than their own.

According to David Noebel, to maintain that nonreligious secularism exists in counseling is a calculated political maneuver.[5] All non-Christian worldviews reflect a religious belief, but secularists typically choose to believe that their god (or gods) is impersonal and thus does not have to be served. The crux of the matter is that they do not want to be accountable to some higher being — to have Jesus as Lord of their lives. Rather, they want to be the lord of their own lives. It's the ultimate issue of life and what separates Christian from non-Christian counseling — namely, the issue of who is God, or who is playing God?

THE NEED FOR INFORMED CONSENT

Because every counseling session is values-based and promotes a religious agenda, we need to explicitly state and practice our value system with honesty. As we'll discuss later in more detail, clients should make their choice of therapist on the basis of a full disclosure of the therapist's values orientation. To disclose one's values orientation leads to informed consent by the client to continue or to decide not to continue. It is unethical according to professional care standards for counselors and state licensing boards to discriminate against one religious perspective while elevating and honoring others. Furthermore, clients have the freedom to choose whether they want to play God, submit to an impersonal God, or submit to the one true and personal God. Christian counseling is unique because it relies not only on divinely revealed truth but also on the presence of God. God is the One from whom secularists want to separate themselves.

It is problematic that professional organizations send mixed messages and practice double standards in this area. It is unethical for these groups to advocate values-neutrality and tolerance for cultural and individual differences while promoting value positions (for example, proabortion and deviant sexual behavior) that are insensitive to the cultural beliefs and values of many. It is dishonest for therapists to say they are value-free and relativistic yet promote specific values and absolutes at the same time! Professional integrity requires therapists to state their values openly and clearly, to practice within those parameters, and to inform clients of those values so as to facilitate informed consent. Instead of being helped, a client who is already confused about how to achieve satisfaction in life will very likely become more confused by a therapist who is hostile to the values that are central to the client's existence.[6]

A therapist must be open to the assessment of religious and spiritual needs, even if the client does not initiate the topic. Avoiding religious issues or routinely redirecting spiritual concerns elsewhere is no more justifiable than refusing to deal with the death of a client's family member or with his or her fears of social encounters. Stanton Jones explains: "Rather than recommitting ourselves to an impossible value neutrality, we should instead recognize that one cannot intervene in the fabric of human life without getting deeply involved in moral and religious matters. It thus seems incumbent on practitioners in our field to press for greater explicitness about this as we present our profession to the public."[7]

In our own practice, we often hear complaints from former clients about non-Christian practitioners. The clients assumed that their counselors were neutral, only to discover a blatant religious and moral agenda being advanced that was opposed to their own worldview! By the same token, Christian therapists who are religiously zealous and possess their own self-righteous agendas of how everyone should believe are misguided as well. As Allen Bergin, I. Reed Payne, and P. Scott Richards observe, there is "a sensitive line ... between exploring and even critiquing values, faith, beliefs, and spiritual constructs while pursuing psychological integrity."[8]

COUNSELING IN THE MARKETPLACE

An article titled "Christian Counselors in Secular Settings" offers keen insight into how Christian counselors can walk that sensitive line. In the article, a school counselor, a military psychologist, and a prison psychologist discuss the role of Christian values and worldview within their work settings. They agree that they should seek to demonstrate Christlike compassion in counseling, use psychological interventions that are consistent with Scripture, and conduct an open initial evaluation of a client's religious background. When a client acknowledges a religious orientation, the counselor would then assess the impact of the client's beliefs on the presenting problem. If the spiritual issues are relevant and the worldview matches the therapist's, the spiritual issues are addressed as part of the treatment, if the client so desires. If the client adheres to another faith, the importance of spiritual issues is acknowledged and he or she is encouraged to seek spiritual counsel from trusted and qualified individuals who share his or her worldview. One of the counselors interviewed states the following:

> In essence, I only do "Christian counseling" with patients of the Christian faith who have expressed a desire to address such issues. Additionally, the extent of the Christian focus will depend on the relevance of these issues to their presenting problem.... I believe this type of practice is within any restrictions imposed by professional ethics and organization regulations. Essentially, it is my understanding that secular

institutions do not want us evangelizing our patients or imposing our belief systems on them. However, this does not mean that spiritual issues are ignored.... To ignore these issues is to miss an important part of understanding why our patients believe and behave as they do.[9]

We can empathize with the struggle these professionals encounter. There is a clear difference between those who are paid employees of a public school, a state prison, and a military institution and those who work in the private sector. The former often face different restrictions than those who are counseling in private practice. We agree that Christian therapists in those nonprivate domains have the right, even the obligation, to counsel Christian clients from a biblical perspective; this is (or should be) congruent with the ethical standards of state licensing boards.

However, we disagree with their views on evangelism. Certain counselors have judged evangelism in a stereotypical way, and the gospel is therefore not made available to those who need to hear about Jesus. According to these counselors, evangelism is tantamount to pushing the gospel on colleagues or patients against their will, which leads in turn to antagonism against these attempts. While some Christian counselors undoubtedly have pressed their own self-centered agendas, to do so is unnecessary and unethical. Speaking the truth in love includes "the good news." Sharing the good news appropriately has to be a component for every Christian counselor in the context of therapy, whether in the public or private sector. If counselors genuinely believe that Jesus Christ is the answer and that there is a literal heaven and hell, then failing to share the gospel is unethical and in conflict with their worldview.

Biblical Christianity's validity as a worldview relevant for counseling practice has not been adequately examined in the past. For example, a recent study revealed that out of 2,348 research articles in four prominent psychiatry journals, only 2.5 percent included one or more religious variables. In only three studies was religion the central study variable.[10] Why, then, do the psychological and social sciences fail to integrate historical Christianity into their disciplines? Research psychiatrist David Larson explains: "Many see Christianity or any religious commitment as outdated, anti-intellectual, and harmful to emotional health."[11]

Terry experienced this kind of bias when he worked as a staff psychologist for a managed health care system. A circular had been distributed, asking all clinicians to identify whether they were able to counsel clients who desired a Christian counselor (requests for this "values base" had been increasing). Terry was one of only two counselors with this competency among a staff of fifty. Later, after an increase in requests for his services from Christian parents, Terry proposed starting a parenting group based on biblical values. This request was rejected by clinic management, who explained, "The clinic must not be seen as endorsing a particular belief system." The next week, however, clinic management circulated a request asking therapists to indicate their willingness to lead a gay/lesbian support group for those desiring assistance in handling their lifestyle choice. It seems that biblical-Christian support in counseling was "out," while unbiblical humanist support was "in." Obviously, this turn of events caused Terry to wonder about the purpose of trying to identify Christian therapists, since he was apparently not going to be empowered to practice within that values base. One belief system clearly was being preferred over another, despite the formal assertion that such was not the case.

This kind of discrimination is repeated countless times across North America. Confusion in our culture in general and in the psychological culture in particular is inevitable as long as the witness of the Christian community remains within the walls of church buildings. We must learn to express our message clearly and respectfully, in a language the non-Christian world can understand. The guiding principle is given by Peter in his first letter:

> Who is going to harm you if you are eager to do good? But even if you should suffer for what is right, you are blessed. "Do not fear what they fear; do not be frightened." But in your hearts set apart Christ as Lord. Always be prepared to give an answer to everyone who asks you to give the reason for the hope that you have. But do this with gentleness and respect, keeping a clear conscience, so that those who speak maliciously against your good behavior in Christ may be ashamed of their slander.
>
> —1 PETER 3:13–16

In their review of articles published between 1978 and 1989, researchers David Larson and Susan Larson discovered that of the religious commitment variables that were researched, ninety-two percent positively advanced mental health, which led them to conclude that religious beliefs and practices can aid physical and mental health.[12] In a 1994 study to determine the effectiveness of bringing spiritual aspects into therapy, psychologists learned that religious patients who received treatment with religious content had better outcomes than patients, religious or not, with whom religious content was omitted.[13] In a September 1999 speech to attendees at the American Association of Christian Counselors conference, David Larson called attention to emerging research revealing that religion benefits eighty-four percent of the people in their mental and physical health. The ratio of benefit to harm was thirty to one in mental health and twenty to one in physical health.

In light of all the evidence that religion plays a positive role in counseling, we would do well to heed Gary Collins's words regarding the purpose of Christian counseling:

> Counseling books often include similar lists of counseling goals: to help counselees change behavior, attitudes, values, and/or perceptions; to teach skills, including social, interpersonal, and communication skills; to encourage the recognition and expression of emotion; to give support in times of need; to teach responsibility; to instill insights; to face emotional trauma and scars from the past; to guide as decisions are made; to clear away misconceptions about oneself, other people, therapy, Christianity, or any additional area of misperception; to help counselees mobilize inner and environmental resources in times of crisis; to teach problem-solving methods; and to increase counselee competence and self-awareness ... among others.
>
> Christian counselors might be involved in helping counselees pursue any of these goals, but do we also have unique purposes because we are followers of Jesus Christ? Does the Christian counselor seek to
>
> - present the gospel message and encourage counselees to commit their lives to Jesus Christ?
> - stimulate spiritual growth?
> - encourage counselees to confess sin and to experience divine forgiveness?
> - model Christian standards, attitudes, and lifestyle?
> - stimulate counselees to develop values and to live lives that are based on biblical teaching, instead of living in accordance with relativistic humanistic standards?
>
> The Christian who makes these issues a part of counseling is in danger of being criticized for not respecting counselee values, violating ethical principles, or bringing religion into counseling. These can be valid criticisms, especially when the Christian works with nonbelievers.... Apparently, many Christian counselors choose to keep their beliefs hidden behind a professional facade, choosing to say nothing about religion unless the client raises the issue.[14]

We do need to recognize that clients have come primarily for therapy and not for evangelism and that introducing Christ is just one component of counseling. Integration of biblical values is yet another important component. Avoiding manipulation and treating others with respect are two foundational principles for effective counseling from a biblical worldview.

On the other hand, if Christian therapists fail to introduce their worldview, they are basing their counseling on some other religion such as humanism, stifling their own beliefs, and compartmentalizing life into the sacred and secular. If we are convinced that belief in Jesus Christ makes a difference both now and for eternity, is it right before God to withhold such information? If we see clients engaging in immoral behavior or reaching conclusions that are clearly inconsistent with biblical teaching, are we not being harmful, hypocritical, and cowardly if we observe the struggles and say nothing about Jesus Christ? If we claim to be Christian counselors, are we not acting unethically if we never mention Jesus or bring up Christian issues during our counseling? Albert Ellis, one of the world's most influential psychotherapists, does not hesitate to proclaim his particular brand of humanism,[15] while professional conventions and journals are increasingly introducing New Age and Eastern religious concepts into therapy. Do we observe these developments and say nothing about Christian principles, essentially simply because our professions are so intolerant of anything Christian?

If truth be told, much depends on how Christian concepts are introduced in therapy. No one would propose that we pressure, indoctrinate, or intimidate clients into considering Christian teachings and values. But counselors whose lives reflect the indwelling presence of Christ have every right to present God's Word gently and lovingly, as they are led by the Holy Spirit in his timing. Like the rich young man who walked away from Jesus (see Matthew 19:16 – 30), our clients may reject the message. We should not force them to do what they choose not to do. But neither does the committed Christian counselor keep his or her beliefs hidden under a bushel where they are never seen and never allowed to make an impact.

In their standard textbook on counseling ethics, Gerald Corey, Marianne Schneider Corey, and Patrick Callanan conclude that it is "neither possible nor desirable for counselors to be scrupulously neutral with respect to values in the counseling relationship."[16] Counseling is not indoctrination, they assert, but because counselor values do influence therapy, "it is important for counselors to be willing to express their values openly when they are relevant to the questions that come up in their sessions with clients."[17] Committed people, including those who are not believers, have values that are unlikely to remain hidden; our most cherished values do indeed permeate our lives and influence almost everything we do.

Christian counselors recognize the importance of Christian values and of a personal and growing relationship with Jesus Christ. No person can or should be forced to accept Christian ways of thinking, but a good counselor is constantly aware of the spiritual needs of his or her clients. One purpose of Christian counseling is to deal, at least in brief, with these spiritual issues. Psychologists Edward Shafranske and H. Newton Malony contend that religious matters are integral to the fabric of psychotherapy and should be included because of

- the professional ideal of cultural inclusion and a respect for diversity (a value)
- the substantial evidence of religion as a cultural fact
- the developing body of theoretical, clinical, and empirical research literature concerning religion as a positive variable in mental health
- the appreciation of psychological treatment as a value-based form of intervention[18]

We cannot avoid transmitting values in counseling; the question is which values we transmit. In a 1980 article, Allen Bergin concluded that "blank slate" therapy was a misnomer and that values were indeed embedded, either explicitly or implicitly, in all practice.[19] Bergin, Payne, and Richards offer the following summary: "It can be stated that the therapy relationship inevitably includes the transmission of values.... It has been shown that values are an essential aspect of the therapeutic enterprise."[20] Any reader interested in the vast amount of research and inquiry supporting these conclusions is encouraged to obtain the works by Shafranske, Richards and Bergin, and Miller and to study the excellent contributions by highly qualified professionals in the field.[21]

In summary, the entire psychological community needs to be more honest, both in its public relations and in its practices, with regard to the value bases of the mental health enterprise. The argument for greater honesty is really quite simple:

SINCE therapy is influenced by the values of practitioners;

SINCE mental heath practitioners are largely non-Christian, as compared with the general public; and

SINCE therapy is values-based and involves changing clients' values, both moral and religious;

THEN presenting therapy as values-neutral is a misrepresentation of reality.[22]

Therefore, we conclude that it is impossible, unethical, and dishonest to attempt values-neutral counseling. A therapist's values base needs to be presented honestly and factually during the initial intake session — which is as important a way to communicate to the client the therapist's qualifications as the educational degrees behind his or her name. For example, we routinely tell our clients the following:

All counseling is values-based. There are many values in our society: New Age, Eastern (such as Hindu or Buddhist), secular, humanistic, agnostic, atheistic. Mine is Christian-based. I process the decisions I make, the suggestions I offer, and the assignments I give through that particular worldview. I use that grid to guide my recommendations, just as therapists with other grids use theirs to guide their counseling.

This is an example of informed consent. In addition, Terry and Julie's clinic includes this values information on the intake sheet that a client signs, which indicates informed consent for our stated values base (see the Professional Counseling Agreement form, point 9, in Appendix D).

We know that many Christian therapists practice in secular settings. These clinics will typically not include values information on their intake sheets because they generally disregard the fact that they operate from a religious worldview. We suggest that Christian therapists in this situation speak with their supervisors about their own values base and their intent to relay it to clients; we'd recommend that therapists reassure their supervisors that they will respect their clients' worldviews as well. If the supervisor will not permit such informed consent, we'd advise the therapist to contact one of the cutting-edge Christian legal groups, such as the American Center for Law and Justice (P.O. Box 64429, Virginia Beach, VA 23467-4429, 804-579-2489), The Rutherford Institute (www.rutherford.org), and the Christian Legal Society (4208 Evergreen Land, Suite 222, Annandale, VA 22003, 703-642-1070) for consideration of a legal remedy.

SPIRITUALITY AND PSYCHOTHERAPY

Because psychotherapy is a spiritual process, psychotherapy and spiritual direction are related. Redeemer College psychology professor David Benner notes that a therapist who is well trained or experienced in both psychotherapy and spiritual direction can provide an integrated psychospiritual therapy to clients who desire such an explicit integration approach. By doing so, counselors can offer both effective psychotherapeutic help as well as spiritual guidance to clients so they can grow as whole persons.[23]

Spiritual issues arise frequently in psychotherapy. Suppose a client asks, "Should I vent my anger at my wife?" This is not just a question pertaining to psychological health. Many psychologists have observed that clients do not separate moral from religious issues but tend to intertwine them. An appropriate answer to this question considers the value of the husband-wife relationship as well as the boundary between emotional honesty and sin. Therapists should also acknowledge that their reaction to this question will be interpreted by the client in a positive or negative sense. Therapists embody value assumptions about human life that are "good" (healthy, whole, adaptive, realistic, rational) and "bad" (abnormal, pathological, immature, stunted, self-deceived). Psychologist W. O'Donohue makes the following observation: "That psychologists view a certain state of affairs as problematic is influenced by our own metaphysical views concerning such issues as what constitutes the good life, human nature, and morality."[24] In short, one cannot separate psychotherapy from spirituality, either in theory or in practice.

For example, a client of Julie's had an affair because of his predominantly passive-aggressive stance in life. He had failed to confront his own family of origin's pathology due to fear and their intimidation of him. When a conflict in his current family situation called for him to take an assertive stand toward his family of origin, he acted out and fled into the arms of another woman for "comfort." A humanist psychologist might applaud him for meeting his personal needs for affirmation and love. A utopianist psychologist might view the affair as indulgent, since this man was part of the upper class. If he had had to labor like the worker, this would not have happened. Moreover, the corrupt system of capitalism promoted this self-indulgence. A New Age psychologist might conclude that this man's sexual experimentation could help him get him in touch with his cosmic self. He, his wife, and the affair partner are all really part of god, so this experience could reveal his inner self more clearly. A biblically based Christian psychologist, however, would understand this man's behavior as sinful, encourage him to seek repentance and reconciliation, and help him to understand how his legitimate needs can be met in Jesus Christ. Each of these therapists would intertwine spiritual beliefs and psychotherapy in the treatment, but only the Christian psychologist could offer guidance based on the truth God reveals in his Word.

THE EXCLUDED MIDDLE

In order to formulate a biblical worldview, we must consider both the kingdom of Satan and the kingdom of God. The fundamental battle is between the father of lies and the Spirit of truth, between the ruler of this world and the Creator of all there is, between the accuser of God's people and the author and perfecter of our faith, between the tempter and the only way of escape. The Bible speaks of the spiritual battle being waged in the heavenly realms between Christ and the antichrist (see Ephesians 6:12). The term *heavenly realms* does not refer to some distant place but to the spiritual realm that is continuously present in our time-and-space world.

The tendency of the Western world is to exclude the spiritual realm from everyday experience. Dr. Paul Hiebert of Trinity Evangelical Divinity School characterizes this as the "excluded middle,"[25] as Figure 2.1 portrays.

The Western world generally sees reality in two tiers. The upper tier, where God and the spiritual forces reside, can be understood through religion and mysticism; the lower tier is the empirical, material, natural world, and it can be examined and scientifically understood. The two tiers are regarded as separate, with the spiritual seen as having little or no impact on the material world. Non-Western cultures, however, understand the spiritual realm to be on a par with and even more influential than the material realm. This spiritual realm is very real for the two-thirds of the world who live in non-Western cultures and reject the strict materialism of the West. In their worldview they see an interaction with spiritual forces in almost every dimension of life. They worship their gods with peace offerings, hoping to ward off evil spirits. Their holy men (sorcerers, shamans, and witch doctors) attempt to manipulate the spiritual world through charms and rituals — practices that are as relevant to them as science is to us.[26] In most Western cultures, agnostics and deists loosely acknowledge the upper tier yet live exclusively in the lower. They

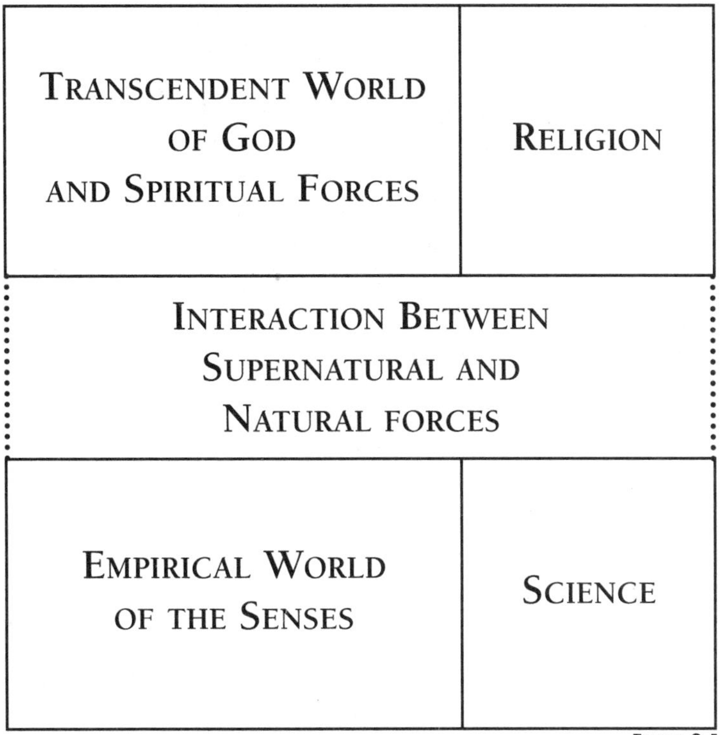

TRANSCENDENT WORLD OF GOD AND SPIRITUAL FORCES	**RELIGION**
INTERACTION BETWEEN SUPERNATURAL AND NATURAL FORCES	
EMPIRICAL WORLD OF THE SENSES	**SCIENCE**

FIGURE 2.1

see little, if any, interaction between the two. Atheists and behaviorists, however, sanction only the lower material tier, believing allegiance to the spiritual to be a crutch for weak-willed people.

The Bible does not teach a separation between the natural and spiritual worlds. First, the Bible teaches that the unseen world is just as real, or even more real, than the seen world. Paul writes in 2 Corinthians 4:18, "So we fix our eyes not on what is seen, but on what is unseen. For what is seen is temporary, but what is unseen is eternal." This truth is why we are instructed to "live by faith, not by sight" (2 Corinthians 5:7). Second, an omnipresent God is never distant, and his Son sustains "all things by his powerful word" (Hebrews 1:3). Third, Paul reminds us that "our struggle is not against flesh and blood, but against the rulers, against the authorities, against the powers of this dark world and against the spiritual forces of evil in the heavenly realms" (Ephesians 6:12). We must never forget that the world, the flesh, and the devil form a three-stranded braid always acting in opposition to our sanctification (see Ephesians 2:1 – 3).

Students of personality and therapeutic change have encountered obstacles in their attempts to apply a Western, two-tiered way of thinking to observed clinical phenomena with clients. P. Scott Richards and Allen Bergin describe it this way:

> Dozens of great people have grappled with the gap between modernist psychological models or methods and the need to understand the spiritual in the personal and clinical phenomena with which they were dealing. Pioneers broke off, venturing into humanistic, existential, cognitive themes, and even further into courageous creators of a theistic, spiritual perspective in human personality and psychotherapy.[27]

Christian therapists have expended considerable effort to develop and implement spiritual interventions in their therapeutic work; many other therapists want to include spiritual perspectives and interventions but don't know how to go about implementing it. Meanwhile, spiritual therapy is growing at a phenomenal rate in New Age circles. Unfortunately, these counselors have no understanding of biblical revelation to guide them through the heavenly realms. They believe that everything is spiritual, that everyone is god; they change the names of demons to spirit guides, and the names of mediums to channelers.

Psychologists Richards and Bergin observe that leading minds in the development of the sciences, including psychology, excluded explicit spiritual content from their theories, laws, principles, and technical procedures, even though many were professing Christians. Many of these scientists assumed a Christian worldview and viewed the scientific project itself as a way of revealing God's designs in nature and humanity. They intentionally excluded the spiritual in order to differentiate the observable realm from the supernatural and therefore to more effectively study and predict natural processes.[28] Yet, to do so was unnecessary, because science and divine revelation are not at odds. God created this world and everything in it. Science can only discover, make intelligent observations about, and attempt to manipulate in a meaningful way that which already exists. We would suggest that science, as it is with politics and any other human endeavor, lacks meaningful direction without divine guidance.

THE ORIGIN OF PSYCHOLOGICAL PROBLEMS: NATURAL OR DEMONIC?

Some of humanity's earliest writings have addressed the problem of mental distress and how to help those who are struggling.[29] History has alternated between a belief that spiritual forces were the predominant cause to a belief that primarily physical causes were responsible. In general, those who studied the etiology of mental duress have also been dualistic in outlook, emphasizing either one cause or the other; only seldom were spiritual and physical explanations for mental problems integrated.

The early writings of the Chinese, Egyptians, Greeks, and Hebrews disclosed their belief that unusual behavior deviating from expected conduct is the result of demonic possession. Both good and evil demons were thought to exist. The conclusion as to whether the person's possession was beneficial (demonstration of extraordinary strength or magical powers) or negative (cutting oneself, screaming, acting bizarrely) depended on the particular behavior of the individual. Of course, these secular opinions of positive and negative demonic influence are contrary to what the Bible teaches about demons. Every fallen spirit under the lordship of Satan is in opposition to God and therefore is not beneficial to possess.

Consider the mental state of Saul, the first king of Israel. Those who point exclusively to natural causation would say that he appeared to have suffered from major depression. He demonstrated withdrawal, irritability, and a melancholy mood, and he relied on music therapy administered by David, the shepherd boy, to lift his spirits. The physical and mental stress of being king created a chemical imbalance in serotonin and dopamine, which in turn caused a biological depression. In this case, these counselors would have misdiagnosed the problem — a problem clearly revealed in Scripture: "An evil spirit from the LORD came upon Saul as he was sitting in his house" (1 Samuel 19:9).

Even if one correctly diagnosed the presence of an evil spirit, how would one deal with it effectively? Early approaches attempted to placate the spirits. If that proved unsuccessful, the spirits were to be exorcised or driven out of the body. If none of these treatments proved effective, practitioners performed a primitive surgery known as trephining, a procedure in which a small hole was chipped in a patient's skull so as to allow the demon to escape. In short, as James Coleman and William Broen observe, the practitioners in these cultures "were apparently a curious mixture of priest, physician, psychologist, and magician."[30]

The Gospel of Mark describes an encounter Jesus had with a man who was inhabited by a group of demons named Legion (see Mark 5:1 – 15). Jesus sent the demons out of the man into a herd of pigs, who "rushed down the steep bank into the lake and were drowned" (5:13).

Those who later saw the man who had formerly been possessed "sitting there, dressed and in his right mind" (5:15) became afraid of Jesus and asked him to leave. Even in the presence of the Son of God, the reality of causation and healing of abnormal behavior from a spiritual perspective was not understood or accepted. The observation that the man was now "in his right mind" shows the connection between psychology and spiritual warfare. He was physically functional after the demonic influence was removed.

Three of the Gospels (Matthew 17:14–18, Mark 9:14–27, and Luke 9:37–42) record the restoration of a child with epileptic-type seizures. A demon-possessed boy was brought to Jesus for healing after the disciples had failed to drive out the demon. Scripture adds that the demon had attempted to kill the child by causing him to fall into fire and into water. Other symptoms included foaming at the mouth, gnashing of teeth, being thrown to the ground, and becoming rigid. These verses clearly reveal that epileptic-type seizures and suicidal actions can be caused by evil spirits and may not be attributable to natural causes. Therapists routinely see similar symptoms in their counseling, but unfortunately relatively few consider a spiritual cause and cure.

During Greece's golden age, Hippocrates (c. 460–c. 377 B.C.), known as the "father of modern medicine," shifted the idea of causation for mental illness away from spirituality and to natural causes. Demons and gods were discounted as causes of psychopathology. Hippocrates remarked, "For my own part, I do not believe that the human body is ever befouled by a god."[31] According to Hippocrates, since the brain is the seat of intellectual functioning, brain malfunction is the source of mental illness. Hippocrates also advocated physical methods of treatment for the emotionally disturbed. His prescriptions included diet, exercise, and peaceful living. He also recommended marriage for a woman suffering from hysteria caused, so he suggested, by her uterus wandering throughout her body seeking a place to have children. Since Hippocrates also considered environment an important source of pathological behavior, people were sometimes removed from their homes.

This polarization of thinking as to the cause and appropriate treatment of mental illness was again reversed during the dark times of the Middle Ages. Treatment of the mentally ill was performed largely by the clergy. Monasteries took in the mentally ill and employed prayer, diet, the sprinkling of holy water, visits to religious sites, and the laying on of hands in order to remove the disturbing spirit. Unfortunately, since it was also widely believed that the demon or spirit was punished if those in whom he resided were poorly treated, mentally disturbed persons were also at times subjected to harsh therapy. Whipping, starvation, immersion in hot water, and other means of torture were used to punish Satan and thus, as the thinking went, make his host's body such an unpleasant place to dwell that he would leave. The former recognition of the naturalistic causes of mental illness and its humane treatment were displaced by beliefs about demonology as the sole cause and the resulting harsh treatment of patients.

The fall of the Roman empire (A.D. 476) led to significant disruption of social, political, economic, and educational ways of life. Occurrences of epidemic manias, known in Europe as St. Vitus's Dance, led to the conviction that the destitute were the cause of the terrible and chaotic events of the time. Eminent personality theorist Theodore Millon notes, "As the turmoil of natural calamity continued, mental disorders were equated increasingly with sin and satanic influence."[32] Perhaps the darkest hour for the church in the fifteenth century came when Pope Innocent VIII issued his *Summis Desiderantes Affectibus (Desiring with the Greatest Ardor)* in 1484. Based on Exodus 22:18, "Do not allow a sorceress to live," the directive led clergy to use every means possible to identify and destroy witches. Shortly after the publication of *Summis,* yet another manual, *Malleus Maleficarum (The Hammer of Witches),* appeared. This "divinely inspired" text set out to prove the existence of witchcraft, to describe methods of identifying witches, and to specify examination procedures and the legal consequences of being judged a witch. Given such sanction, witch-hunters persecuted thousands. Torture was recommended as a means of obtaining confession. The inevitable consequence for most was the penalty of strangulation, beheading, and burning at the stake.[33]

Based on the *Malleus* manual, the church developed the institution of the Inquisition to examine those suspected of witchcraft and other types of "heretical" behavior. These horrible procedures were applied equally in both Protestant and Catholic countries and even in several American colonies in the sixteenth and seventeenth centuries. Although the actual torture and execution of alleged witches ended in 1782, the belief that mental illness represents either punishment from God or deliberate involvement with the devil persisted.

Not everyone in the days of Pope Innocent VIII and the Inquisition agreed with the process for dealing with the mentally ill. For example,

German physician Johann Weyer (1515–1588), often cited as the father of modern psychiatry, argued for a return to the naturalistic view of causation of emotional disturbances. Weyer also harshly criticized the torture of alleged witches, calling instead for more humane treatment. Unfortunately, the organized church was not ready to accept his view that some of those being burned as witches were mentally ill.

Other important figures advocating a more humane approach to treatment include Philippe Pinel in France (1745–1826) and Dorthea Dix in the United States (1802–1887). Both were influential in their efforts to improve the treatment approach toward and the living conditions of the mentally ill. Like Weyer, these pioneers championed the view that the mentally ill are in reality just normal individuals who need help in a religiously friendly environment. What was best for those who exhibited some form of psychopathology remained, however, the topic of heated debate. Commenting on the vacation-like atmosphere of some treatment facilities, British evangelist John Wesley wrote in 1768 that "the giving up of witchcraft is in effect the giving up of the Bible."[34]

Like a pendulum, arguments over the causation and treatment of mental disturbances had shifted from a predominantly demonic point of view in the early days of the Greeks and Romans to explanations of naturalistic, physical causes and more humane treatment advocated by Hippocrates, then back again to a view of satanic influences and witchcraft during the Middle Ages, and finally back to the more humane treatment of Philippe Pinel and Dorthea Dix in the eighteenth and nineteenth centuries.

In the last half of the twentieth century, the use of medication has taken center stage as the primary approach to mental illness. However, this "medical model" has also been challenged on the grounds that most abnormal behavior does not involve some type of brain pathology. Psychiatrist Thomas Szasz, who popularized the controversial phrase *the myth of mental illness,* has questioned this emphasis on medication. Writing from a humanistic orientation, Szasz argued that people diagnosed as mentally ill are not really "sick" in the medical sense; rather, they are struggling with daily problems in living and need help learning more effective stress-management techniques and coping strategies.[35]

The dichotomous approach that placed the causes and treatment of psychopathology either in the organic or the spiritual realm was dramatically reconfigured by Austrian physician Sigmund Freud (1856-1939) and his psychoanalytic model of personality, mental disease, and psychotherapy. At the risk of oversimplification, one can say that Freud was the first to express the belief that mental disorders have both a psychological and a natural (organic) basis. Freud did not believe that mental disturbances stemmed either from demons or from physiological factors. Rather, psychoanalytic psychotherapy (psychoanalysis) suggested that painful thoughts and feelings were repressed into an unconscious force that exerted powerful pressures within a patient. The pressure expressed itself in symptoms that symbolically represented these repressed thoughts and feelings. Emotional catharsis, also known as abreaction, relieved the unconscious pressure and, in turn, eliminated the symptom that the pressure created.[36]

Dr. Freud, an agnostic and pessimist, rejected the inclusion of spiritual concepts in his approach and considered religion to be a neurotic illusion people turn to for help with their infantile dependency needs. Although we do not endorse his psychoanalytic theory, we recognize its role in moving mental health's understanding out of the dualistic realm of "either-or" by pointing to other contributing factors.

Freud's teaching opened the door for other psychological schools of thought, each attempting to determine both the causes of maladaptive behavior and the most realistic techniques for treating people with disturbed emotions and aberrant behavior. Behaviorism, humanism, existentialism, cognitive-behavioral approaches, and the interpersonal model have all addressed these issues, with varying degrees of acceptability and effectiveness.

ORIGIN OF PSYCHOLOGICAL PROBLEMS: SICKNESS OR SIN?

There is yet another key question that must be asked: What is the cause of the mental distress that affects individuals? Is it sickness or sin? This is no minor issue, to be sure, since a counselor's belief concerning the causation of mental illness will determine his or her approach to a client's presenting problem. Consider the following two scenarios, both of which represent extreme approaches we do not endorse. They reflect the excessive spiritual and psychological approaches that lack an appreciation for the important integration a Christ-centered approach provides.

First scenario:

> A client admits to a pastor that he hit his wife, and the pastor focuses on the moral error and the need for confession. He assists the husband in seeking forgiveness from his wife and refers the client to relevant biblical passages that deal with anger, such as James 1:19 ("Everyone should be quick to listen, slow to speak and slow to become angry"). The client is encouraged to meditate on this passage and memorize it for recall when conflict begins to emerge. The pastor also recommends a men's accountability group for the husband—a setting where Christian men can pray for him, model healthy masculine behavior in the home, and hold him accountable for his behavior. The client and his wife are encouraged to prioritize a quiet time together where they can pray for each other and strengthen the marriage through Bible study.

The second scenario depicts the same situation, but in this case the counselor takes a secular approach to analyzing the issues:

> This counselor focuses on exploring the sources of the anger, such as possible childhood physical abuse, gender-role misconceptions, and any struggles for control that exist in his marriage. The therapist looks for the presence of depression underlying the irritability and explosive outbursts in the client and refers to a psychiatrist for a medication evaluation. The therapist also administers a psychological test to determine a differential diagnosis, teaches him assertive communication styles and anger-management techniques, and engages him in role-playing conflictual situations that may emerge in his marriage. He invites the wife to counseling sessions and encourages her to call 911 the next time her husband strikes her, explaining that research has demonstrated that to do so serves as a deterrent against future abusive behavior.

Both the pastor and the counselor are concerned with *behavioral* change, but their methods differ. The pastor identifies the sinful components of the behavior and takes steps to address the *moral* dimension; the secular counselor addresses the *psychological* context of the man's behavior, assigning the subsequent steps. The pastor focuses on the need for *confession* of the moral violation; the counselor establishes a position of *moral neutrality* toward the offense. The pastor sees the root problem as *sin;* the non-Christian counselor views it as *sickness.*

Wheaton College psychology professor Mark McMinn suggests that the etiological question (Is it sickness or sin?) may be answered by considering the concept of "attributional style," that is, how we view the misfortunes, consequences, and pain in people's lives.[37] This concept relates to what we identify as the causes of such events in our lives — causes that may be internal (for example, organic problems, ignorance, immaturity, or willful sin) or external (for example, negative circumstances, broken relationships, or environmental problems).

In the field of psychology, this perspective on causation is represented by what psychologist and social learning theorist Julian Rotter labels "the locus of control." Those holding to an *external* locus of control believe that luck or some outside force determines what happens to them. Thus, getting a good job depends on being in the right place at the right time. Those with an *internal* locus of control look to themselves to control what happens to them.

We maintain that a biblical worldview is wholistic and thus includes both internal and external factors. The whole world has been polluted by the Fall (see Genesis 3). We have all sinned and fall short of God's glory (see Romans 3:23). We all have bodies that are destined to die (see Romans 5:12 – 14). Every day we face the reality of original sin, the passions and desires of the flesh, dysfunctional families, diseases, and unfortunate circumstances beyond our ability to control. We also live in a polluted atmosphere and a world governed by the one Jesus called "the prince of this world" (John 16:11); in fact, writes John, "the whole world is under the control of the evil one" (1 John 5:19). Thus, the concepts of sin, sickness, and spiritual warfare are connected in the biblical worldview.

Suppose that a tired executive struggles to cope with mounting pressures at work. He stops at the local watering hole for "happy hour" to relieve the pressures of the day by drinking himself into a stupor. It is a sin to yield to that temptation of abusing alcohol, but it also becomes a pattern of behavior that begins to affect him physically (a sickness). He starts developing a tolerance for alcohol and "needs" more and more to feed his chemical addiction. Shame, fear, and guilt lead to further bondage and despair. Which is it? Sin or sickness?

Or consider the woman living in the fast lane, working fifty to sixty hours a week, volunteering on two community boards, driving in three carpools for her children, leading a church fellowship group several times a year. Eventually this woman becomes depressed. She has been doing good things but struggles with post-adrenaline exhaustion. The diagnosis of her problem is Major Depressive Disorder, Single Episode. Is this sickness or sin? Is this woman unwittingly and innocently stressing her physiological makeup, thereby creating neurotransmitter deficiencies, or is she engaging in sinful behaviors of narcissism (seeing self as indispensable), pride (valuing accomplishments more than she does other people), self-reliance (independence from God), and neglect of family (putting personal desires ahead of family needs)? Should she be counseled to employ stress-management techniques of relaxation, prioritizing, and pacing (that is, symptom-based interventions)? Should she be presented with the need to confess her self-idolatry as sin, make restitution with her family, and engage in spiritual disciplines of reliance on the Lord rather than on the self (that is, sin-based interventions)?

Herein lies the difference between internal and external attribution. Those who focus on *internal attribution* would contend that the alcohol abuser and the depressed woman made choices and are responsible for the consequences of those choices. The inclination is to admonish them for their sinful behavior and encourage them to live in a better, more health-producing way. Advocates of *external attribution,* however, would argue that the physiological problems of the addiction and the serotonin depletion plus adrenal exhaustion were leading the victims to their sickened state. The inclination here is to feel sympathy for the sufferers.

These two perspectives—admonishment for sin and sympathy for sickness—need to be reconciled in the Christian counseling worldview. The two explanations of the causes of the problem—willful disobedience to God's law and an inevitable demise to the power of illness—need to be balanced. So how can the Christian counselor accomplish this?[38]

The place to begin is with an adequate understanding of sin. Theology professor Millard Erickson observes, "Sin is any lack of conformity, active or passive, to the moral will of God. This may be a matter of act, of thought, or of inner disposition or state."[39] Here outward acts and thoughts (sickness) are intertwined with inner sin (depravity). A Christian worldview does not merely equate sin with bad behavior, which can be resolved by confession, but recognizes sin as an innate part of the human condition inherited from the first man, Adam (see Genesis

1 – 3). Only this understanding of sin offers real hope for positive mental health, as Mark McMinn perceptively explains:

> The ubiquity of sin is both bad news and good news. It is bad because we are indeed sick, burdened by sin that affects every attitude, behavior, relationship, and thought in our lives. We are bundles of mixed motives, constantly fighting to yield more control to God and less to our sin nature. It is good because this view of sin disqualifies the objections of psychologists who claim Christians are destined to be emotionally sick. Christians who understand sin properly view themselves as part of a universal community of sinners. If sin is a sickness, something that affects all people and interferes constantly with our capacity to make good choices, then our attributions no longer need to be internal and shame producing. We are all pilgrims together, struggling with common temptations and burdens. Those who understand sin most accurately are able to make both internal (personal) and external (universal) attributions for the causes of their problems.[40]

A BALANCED WORLDVIEW

In formulating a biblical worldview, it is helpful to consider the balance between the natural and the spiritual, between the true nature of humanity (anthropology) and the true nature of God (theology), as well as their respective roles and responsibilities. The following diagram (Figure 2.2) represents a balanced and biblical view of these elements as well as their relation to one another.

It is important to understand that we are not pitting the natural and the spiritual against each other; we only wish to show what happens when one realm is emphasized at the expense of the other. Jesus Christ, the God-Man, is the center. Christ possessed both the divine and human nature (see Philippians 2:5 – 8); he also lived in a spiritual and a natural world. Christ is the only one who is perfectly balanced. The problem is that we all think we are balanced. If we had enough self-awareness to recognize that we are seriously out of balance — either up or down, left or right — we would be motivated to make serious efforts to correct it. We also interpret the world from the viewpoint of our own education and experiences. The circle around Christ represents the tolerance of belief within Christian orthodoxy. Anything outside the circle is wrong and needs to be confessed and renounced.

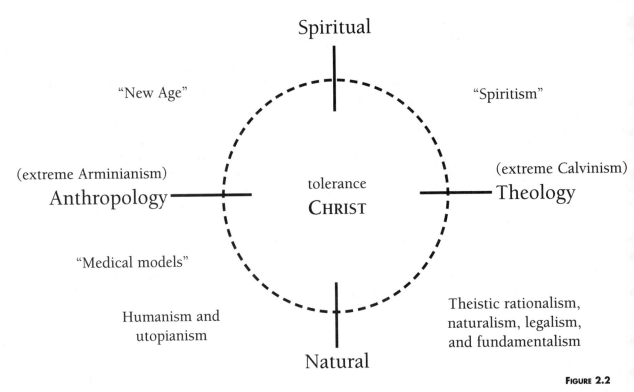

Spiritual

"New Age"   "Spiritism"

(extreme Arminianism)   (extreme Calvinism)
Anthropology   tolerance   Theology
                                CHRIST

"Medical models"

Humanism and   Theistic rationalism,
utopianism   naturalism, legalism,
                               and fundamentalism

Natural

FIGURE 2.2

Compared with the rest of the world's perspectives, the Western worldview has been significantly skewed toward the natural. Humanism (and to a lesser extent, utopianism) has been the dominant worldview shaping the development of psychology. Advocates of these views typically consider only natural persons living in a materialistic world. In keeping with this stance, all public mental health services keep a strict separation between church and state. The past growth of Christian counseling, represented by the "medical model," has caused a movement in the lower-left quadrant (see Figure 2.2). Most contemporary counselors, including Christians, have learned their counseling techniques in this quadrant. Liberal and neo-orthodox churches who have lost their commitment to absolute truth also occupy this quadrant.

In recent years, Western culture has begun to shift upward into the upper-left quadrant (see Figure 2.2). Unfortunately, the spiritual direction of this shift is not predominately Christian but New Age, whose practitioners have little or no sense of biblical theology. We cannot overstate how profoundly their impact is being felt in education, business, medicine, and psychotherapy. It is safe to say that the prevailing religion in America (especially in our colleges and universities) is no longer Christianity but is instead New Age.

Many of our churches have typically resided in the lower-right quadrant (see Figure 2.2). Western rationalism and naturalism have significantly influenced our theology. Moreover, many of our seminaries have emphasized scholarship over godliness and spiritual formation, reducing our walk with God to an intellectual exercise. We know all about God but hardly know him at all. In addition, legalism and dead orthodoxy have plagued the church. We have captured the letter of the law but seem to know little of the Spirit of the law.

All this is changing as well. Fundamentalism as a movement appears to be fading in America. The fundamentals of our faith have not changed, and they never will, but many traditions and customs that were formed more from our culture than from the Bible are being thrown off. People will no longer commit themselves to institutions or even denominations, but they will commit themselves to Jesus Christ and his kingdom. Thus, the church is also shifting upward toward the upper-right quadrant (see Figure 2.2.). Like any other movement, the outcome contains both good news and bad news. The good news is that people are discovering their spiritual identity in Christ and learning to live by faith and in the power of the Holy Spirit; they are also discovering the reality of the spiritual world.

The bad news is that some have adopted a subjective form of spirituality that has no objective base in Scripture. The Word has been replaced by the spirit, but which spirit? Without discernment, people can easily be deceived into thinking they are being led by the Holy Spirit when in reality they are paying attention to a deceiving spirit (see 1 Timothy 4:1). Others have become demon-chasers who proceed to spiritualize almost everything. Theistic naturalism is, in some cases, being replaced by theistic spiritism.

One example of the intricate and intriguing questions that accompany this movement upward can be seen in the ongoing debate between certain theological Calvinists and theological Arminians. Does our victory in Jesus Christ depend fully on God (extreme Calvinism), or does it rest fully on humans (extreme Arminianism)? How many Christian counselors are prepared to help their clients sort it all out? To equip Christian counselors to do just that, we'll turn our attention in the next chapter to diverse strategies in Christian counseling.

3

Diverse Strategies in Christian Counseling

There is more diversity in counseling style and theory among counselors who are Christians than there is unity of style and theory.

EVERETT L. WORTHINGTON JR. AND S. R. GASCOYNE

Discussions with clients who seek a biblical approach to psychotherapy as well as with therapists who identify themselves as Christians reveal widely divergent beliefs and values about integration. To some, the term *Christian counselor* denotes a person who uses only the Bible in counseling sessions; others envision a therapist who goes to church on Sunday but practices secular counseling Monday through Friday; still others use the term only for born-again believers who integrate biblical and psychological principles into the practice of psychotherapy.

The spectrum is broad, which only serves to confuse a needy society. Without a clear understanding of client and therapist definitions, such diversity is not only confusing but potentially harmful. Research by Everett L. Worthington and S. R. Gascoyne has demonstrated that this problem of defining *Christian counselor* is widespread.[1] Christian psychologist and author Larry Crabb has called this "the thorny, hotly debated, and far from resolved problem of integrating Christianity and psychology."[2]

To confuse matters further, beliefs about what it means to be a Christian vary from school to school. Thus, we believe it is necessary to establish our definitions at the outset. We regard as Christians only those who have a *personal relationship with God.* By faith they have received Jesus Christ into their lives and are now children of God (see John 1:12). Christians have made a personal choice to trust only in the finished work of Jesus Christ for their salvation. Since we were all born spiritually dead in our sins, we all have a need to be born again (see John 3:5 – 8). But all born-again believers (Christians) are forgiven because Christ died for their sins, and they are now spiritually alive in Christ because of his resurrection.

The evangelical Christian community is defined by several nonnegotiable core beliefs, including the authority of the Bible; a monotheistic view of God, who is revealed as Father, Son, and Holy Spirit; justification by faith; and the commitment to live a holy life in the process of being conformed to the image of God. Beyond these essential beliefs, which are a matter of conviction, are secondary beliefs that are more a matter of preference. These generally come to light in denominational differences. In these we agree to disagree, just as Paul and Barnabas disagreed over taking Mark along on their mission trip (see Acts 15:36 – 40). They went their separate ways but were joyfully reunited. We recognize there will always be these kinds of differences among Christian counselors.

We have already discussed in length how important it is for client and therapist to establish a mutually clear understanding of their respective value systems and worldviews. We have judged that "informed consent and open agreement between client and therapist about the relevance of values and religious issues in the therapy transaction are foundational and crucial to an effective therapeutic alliance."[3] The therapeutic relationship must embody a process whereby the parties involved talk the same language with respect to worldviews, lifestyle choices, and values orientations.

When applicable, beliefs and attitudes about issues such as homosexuality, abortion, divorce, and cohabitation need to be mutually understood within the therapeutic alliance. Thus K. E. Kudlac states, "From a languaging perspective, it is not necessary for the therapist to subscribe to the same beliefs held by the client; however, to be able to fully enter into a conversation, these beliefs must be addressed."[4] When client and therapist share similar worldviews, therapy may proceed. *Agreement* is not mandatory, however, in order for therapy to move on, only full *understanding* of each other's worldview. Two people can work together when they disagree, but they cannot work together if they misunderstand each other.

If the client does not wish to continue after the therapist's value system has been disclosed, the therapist should refer the client to other appropriate therapeutic resources. Alternatively, if a therapist does not accept the spiritual orientation requested by the client, counseling may or may not proceed. Whether or not a referral is necessary in this case depends on the clinician's judgment as to the likelihood of attaining a client's therapeutic goals. Thus we read in the American Psychological Association's "Ethical Principles of Psychologists and Code of Conduct," Standard 1.08, Human Differences:

> Where differences of age, gender, race, ethnicity, national origin, religion, sexual orientation, disability, language, or socioeconomic status significantly affect psychologists' work concerning particular individuals or groups, psychologists obtain the training, experience, consultation, or supervision necessary to ensure the competence of their services, or they make appropriate referrals.[5]

This APA standard requires the therapist to fully understand his or her value system so as to avoid any negative impact on a client if value differences do exist. It also indicates that psychologists may work with clients with a different religious orientation as long as the quality of the therapy is not compromised. Research has clearly established that a therapist's awareness of his or her views on spiritual issues is an important component of clinical expertise.[6]

Having established the importance of values clarification first for the therapist and then in conjunction with the client, it is important to address conceptual categories that apply to the therapist's approach to spiritual case formulation. The following sections will briefly summarize the conceptualizations of Drs. Everett Worthington, Larry Crabb, Gary Collins, and Siang-Yang Tan. We will then present our own formulation of the clinical approaches to Christian counseling.

EVERETT WORTHINGTON'S FRAMEWORK

Researchers David Larson and Susan Larson have reviewed research studies involving the degree to which spiritual values are integrated into psychotherapy sessions by nonreligious and religious counselors. Referring to the framework of psychology professor Everett Worthington, they identify the following stances of therapists who treat religiously committed patients:

1. Across the Gap: Therapists who personally do not value religious commitment and ignore it or see it primarily as harmful for their patients.

2. The Collaborative: Therapists who personally are not religiously committed but respect and deal positively with religious commitment in therapy.

3. Behind the Door: Therapists who personally hold religious values but ignore or refrain from dealing with religious commitment and religious values in therapy.

4. The Conjoint: Therapists who personally are religiously committed and who deal positively with religious commitment in therapy.

After presenting this paradigm, Dr. Larson and Ms. Larson include in their material the following challenges to therapists:

- Where are you presently on this matrix?
- What steps "across the gap" can mental health professionals take to become "collaborative" and sensitive to their patients' religious commitment? Or how might they pave the way to refer patients to a "conjoint" therapist if they feel uncomfortable dealing with religious issues?
- What steps from "behind the door" can mental health professionals take to become "conjoint"?[7]

These are valid questions for all counselors to consider, yet the issue is even more vital for Christian counselors who recognize how one's worldview affects one's practice. To that end, the following three clinicians address their models to the Christian counseling community and do not include non-Christian therapists in their framework. The model we present will do the same.

LARRY CRABB'S FRAMEWORK

Early in his career Dr. Larry Crabb identified four distinct approaches for counselors in determining what they believe to be a truly biblical counseling strategy. Briefly, they are described as follows:

1. *Separate But Equal.* This position is maintained by those who believe Scripture deals with spiritual and theological problems only; all other issues should be referred to other qualified professionals. "If a person has pneumonia, send him to the physician, not the pastor ... if he has psychological problems, if he is mentally ill, have the wisdom to refer him to a trained professional counselor."[8]

Diverse Strategies in Christian Counseling

The weakness of this approach, in Dr. Crabb's view, is that its advocates fail to recognize the ability of Scripture to address psychological problems such as depression, anxiety, codependency, addiction, infidelity, anger, and family conflicts. Such a position evidences a failure to understand the Bible's approach to the whole gamut of emotional disorders. Does not Scripture address forgiveness, marital faithfulness, parenting, alcoholism, mood disorders, and fears? Of course it does!

2. Tossed Salad. Representatives of this approach to integration adopt the strategy followed in preparing a tossed salad: Mix several ingredients together into a single bowl to create a tasty blend. Crabb suggests this sort of thinking is characteristic of most Christian counselors. Proponents of this construct believe that if we "combine the insights and resources of Scripture with the wisdom of psychology ... a truly effective and sophisticated Christian psychotherapy will emerge."[9]

Such thinking makes sense but is too superficial. Dr. Crabb correctly points out that the field of psychology is basically agnostic and humanistic. Therefore, great care must be exercised before psychological principles are unabashedly integrated with Christian beliefs. An unwitting Christian counselor trained in a secular graduate program could be vulnerable to New Age tenets or other schemes of the devil and thus offer them to a client without ever realizing the mistake. This approach "correctly assumes that secular psychology has something to offer but does not pay enough attention to a possible mingling of contradictory presuppositions."[10] It also places empirical research on a par with divine revelation.

3. Nothing Buttery. According to Dr. Crabb, "Nothing Butterists ... neatly handle the problem of integration by disregarding psychology altogether. Their basic tenet is Nothing But Grace, Nothing But Christ, Nothing But Faith, Nothing But the Word."[11] While favoring this approach's emphasis on the authority and importance of Scripture, Crabb disagrees with the orientation because he views it as too narrow.

To argue that counseling is simply a matter of identifying sin and exhorting change betrays a simplistic understanding of Christianity and a failure to fully appreciate the real demands of counseling. Therefore, Crabb questions this approach in two areas: "(1) it discredits all knowledge from secular sources as tainted and unneeded and (2) it tends to reduce the complex interaction of two persons to a simplistic 'identify-confront-change' model."[12]

Yet, advocates of this view do make a valid point when they caution mental health professionals about mixing psychology with biblical principles. For the last fifty years Gallup polls have found that ninety-five percent of the general population claim a belief in God. However, by the time psychotherapists who come from theistic homes complete their professional training, only seventy-one percent retain a belief in God. Almost one-fourth of the psychotherapists end up as atheists or agnostics, or hold no beliefs whatsoever![13]

4. *Spoiling the Egyptians.* Crabb describes this approach as an attempt to screen secular psychological concepts in order to determine their compatibility with Christian presuppositions. The goal here is to select concepts and research data from the field of psychology that support a biblical approach to understanding and relating to God and humans.

During the Exodus, the Israelites left Egypt with the goods of the Egyptians to sustain them, an act approved by God (see Exodus 11:2–3; 12:35–36). Likewise, a psychologist can use principles that are effective in dealing with human emotions and behaviors as long as those principles are compatible with the Bible. The key "is to look at psychology through the glasses of Scripture."[14]

Christian counselors seeking to integrate the Bible's teachings with psychological constructs should hold themselves to high standards of professionalism. Dr. Crabb proposes four specific qualifications, which we paraphrase as follows:[15]

1. Christian counselors should accept psychological insights only if these insights are completely consistent with biblical truth.
2. They should regard the Bible as the infallible Word of God.
3. They should agree to give Scripture "functional control" over their thinking, with the result that biblical principles take priority over contrary nonbiblical opinion and are put into practice thoroughly and consistently.
4. They should demonstrate serious interest in the content of Scripture by engaging in regular and systematic Bible study, spending at least as much time in Bible study as in the study of psychology, so that they gain both an overall grasp of the Bible's structure and content and a working knowledge of basic biblical doctrines. Finally, they should benefit from the Spirit's gifts by enjoying regular fellowship in a Bible-believing church.

Dr. Crabb concludes that "a Christian who has spoiled [taken from] the Egyptians of secular psychology, carefully weeding out the elements which oppose his commitment to the revelation of Scripture, will be better equipped to counsel than either the Tossed Salad counselor who mixes concepts as they seem called for or the Nothing Butterist counselor who refuses to benefit from the insights of secular study."[16]

GARY COLLINS'S FRAMEWORK

Psychiatrists Frank Minirth and Walter Byrd have reviewed psychologist Gary Collins's five categories of Christian counselors and the varying ways each approaches spiritual case formulation.[17] The five categories are as follows:

1. *Mainstream.* Counselors in this category are largely associated with the Clinical Pastoral Education movement. Although their writings have been valuable, their approach has been criticized by some conservative Christian counselors as too liberal, with human experience and psychology being given priority over Scripture. Fuller Theological Seminary psychology professor Hendrika Vande Kemp elaborates: "Generally, the pastoral psychological literature has been derivative, constituting little more than adaptations of Freud, Rogers, and other popular clinical approaches."[18]

2. *Evangelical Pastor.* Included in this category are ministers who provide a biblical counseling orientation from a preaching-teaching perspective. Drs. Minirth and Byrd suggest that representatives of this category would include Charles Swindoll, Charles Stanley, D. James Kennedy, and John MacArthur. Jay Adams is one of the forerunners in this group, and, although perceived by some as antagonistic toward M.D. and Ph.D. professionals in Christian counseling, Adams has reminded Christian counselors of the profound importance of the Word of God.[19]

3. *Christian Professional.* Professionally trained therapists such as Bruce Narramore, James Dobson, Chris Thurman, Larry Crabb, Gary Collins, Robert Hemfelt, Paul Meier, and Dave Carder constitute the third category. At times members of this category have been criticized for underutilizing God's Word when dealing with emotional or mental problems.

4. *Theoretician-Researcher.* Members of this group "have studied and researched the field of theology and psychology as they have attempted

to provide an apologetic to face the anti-Christian challenge."[20] Austrian psychiatrist Sigmund Freud, for example, referred to religion as nothing more than an illusion caused by a universal human need to be accepted by a powerful father figure. Theoretician-Researchers believe that Christian counselors should be able to give biblical answers to such challenges to the basic tenets of the Bible; they also believe scientific data is of much more importance when dealing with non-Christians.

5. *Evangelical Popularizers.* Members of this category usually have minimal formal training in psychology but are able to articulate scriptural principles in a clear and practical manner. According to Drs. Minirth and Byrd, the popular writers and speakers in this group include Bill Gothard, Keith Miller, and Tim LaHaye.[21]

SIANG-YANG TAN'S FRAMEWORK

One final classification system we cite is that of psychologist and professor Siang-Yang Tan. He describes an implicit and explicit integration model for the blending of scriptural and psychological theories and methodologies. "*Implicit integration* of religion in clinical practice refers to a more covert approach that does not . . . openly, directly, or systematically use spiritual resources like prayer and Scripture . . . in therapy."[22] In this approach, religious issues may be addressed periodically in the psychotherapy session, but only if the client initiates the discussion. An implicit integrationist would not be comfortable with open attention on spiritual issues in an ongoing manner and would probably refer the client to a therapist who would practice a clearer and more deliberate integration of spiritual concerns and psychological principles.

Explicit integration of religion in clinical practice refers to a more overt approach that directly and systematically deals with spiritual issues in therapy. It uses spiritual resources such as prayer, Scripture, and referrals to churches, parachurch organizations, or lay counselors. This approach emphasizes the spirituality of both therapist and client as foundational to effective therapy and human growth and healing. It integrates psychological therapy with some degree of spiritual guidance in the therapeutic context. Therapists practicing from an explicit integration perspective are usually religious themselves and thus are comfortable with not simply praying *for* clients but praying *with* clients aloud and systematically in therapy sessions where appropriate.[23]

OUR PROPOSED FRAMEWORK

Building on the strengths of the preceding frameworks, we have formulated a four-category description of the various approaches to Christian counseling. In doing so, we assume the therapists we describe are born-again Christians who are simply choosing differing strategies in their integration of theology and psychology in the therapy setting. These categories are not meant to be comprehensive or exclusive but are presented to help the reader clarify his or her orientation in the psychotherapy setting.

Our categories are *nomothetic*—simply put, they are concerned with approaches to Christian psychotherapy in the *general* and *abstract* sense, not with any one point of view. In some instances there will be thematic overlap between our constructs and those previously discussed, which is acceptable because none of these systems is intended to be entirely distinct. Moreover, we believe it is permissible to formulate approaches with different points of emphasis. We agree with Mark McMinn when he states, "Intradisciplinary integration is a recently emerging frontier for Christian counselors. The question is not how we understand the relationship between psychology and theology but how we practically use the Christian faith in our counseling."[24]

Figure 3.1 illustrates our conceptual model of the clinical approaches to psychotherapy. We have used the concepts of implicit and explicit disclosure of spiritual principles and resources as one way to describe a Christian counselor. In addition, the vertical axis reflects a continuum of integration of psychological and spiritual techniques in the treatment approach.

This matrix illustrates four categories of Christian counselors. Before discussing the categories in detail, we'll briefly outline the chief characteristics of each.

1. *Bible-Only Counselors.* These Christian counselors see the integration of psychological principles as unwise at best, and these principles are not used when religious concerns are addressed in the therapy hour.

2. *Closed Counselors.* This therapist is a Christian in private or personal life but believes that open expression of and attention to spiritual issues should not occur in a psychotherapy session.

3. *Closet Counselors.* Counselors who adopt this approach may have integrated their expressions of faith with psychological principles but for various reasons do not openly demonstrate this fact in the therapy session.

4. *Conjoint Counselors.* Therapists in this category are most likely to accomplish the multidimensional goals for counseling in a Christian setting; they utilize explicit expression of the spiritual aspects of life in a treatment plan, along with psychological assessment and treatment techniques. These therapists take a balanced approach to counseling.

A brief glance at the matrix reveals two blank fields (see Figure 3.1). One is blank because it is not possible to integrate spiritual considerations explicitly and openly if a therapist believes psychological techniques are the only elements available for a treatment session; the other

	Implicit Disclosure	Explicit Disclosure
Only Psychological	Closed	
Integrated	Closet	Conjoint
Only Spiritual		Bible Only

FIGURE 3.1

71

is blank because it is likewise impossible for a counselor who believes spiritual approaches are the only options for addressing mental health problems to employ psychological techniques simultaneously.

BIBLE-ONLY COUNSELORS

These Christian counselors are like those identified as Nothing Butterists in Larry Crabb's model. Counselors in the *Bible-Only* category may or may not acknowledge the validity of the various therapy approaches of psychology, but they see no need to integrate such techniques into a counseling session. The thinking of these counselors is exclusively spiritual, both in orientation and methodology. Sin is viewed as the source of all psychopathology — and thus condemned. Counselors who possess this orientation rely heavily in their treatment, if not exclusively, on the message of the Bible, the power of the Holy Spirit, and the fellowship of God's people. They may or may not be ordained ministers. Some Bible-Only adherents train laypeople to provide Christian counseling; others believe ordination is necessary. Some would not even endorse unordained counselors who, by virtue of academic training, are licensed to practice as therapists.

In *The Christian Counselor's Manual*, pastoral counseling expert Jay Adams explains, "The authority of Christ, given to 'Those who have the rule' (Hebrews 13:7, 17; 1 Thessalonians 5:13) must not be despised. The unordained Christian counselor, working outside the organized church of Christ, has not received and cannot exercise such authority."[25] Therefore, Adams concludes, "Theological and biblical training ... is the essential background for a counselor; not training in psychology or psychiatry."[26]

Members of this group generally view the integration of psychological principles and biblical teachings as an impossibility or as a watering down of theology. In fact, attempts to integrate the two are often viewed as heretical. Author and pastor John MacArthur states that "'Christian psychology' is an attempt to harmonize two inherently contradictory systems of thought. Modern psychology and the Bible cannot be blended without serious compromise to or utter abandonment of the principle of Scripture's sufficiency."[27]

Larry Crabb disagrees, explaining that "without question the kinds of problems which constitute the substance of emotional disorders are difficulties to which the Bible speaks. To create a wall between Scripture and psychology and to assume that the two disciplines are Separate But Equal, each dealing with different problem areas, must be rejected firmly as an inaccurate reflection of biblical content."[28]

In philosophy professor Gary Habermas's exploration of spiritual and psychological integration, he uncovered four recurring objections that Bible-Only practitioners use against others who want to integrate psychological theory and methodology with biblical principles.[29] First, most Christian psychologists are often deficient in their knowledge of biblical principles. Dr. Habermas notes, "Sophistication in the social sciences does not automatically prepare one for a Bible-based counseling ministry, and neither does sitting under the teaching of a gifted preacher generally equip the psychologist in these areas. As a result, the Bible and theology often are viewed as being irrelevant, or there is proof-texting and pulling verses out of context."[30] Habermas quotes John MacArthur as saying, "There are even those psychologists who claim to perform a therapeutic technique they call 'Christian counseling' but in reality are using secular theory to treat spiritual problems with biblical references tacked on."[31]

Second, Bible-Only advocates claim that the teaching of sin as the source of all trouble is treated too casually and that the significance of repentance is minimized. This same criticism has been leveled at Crabb's Tossed Salad group, in which basic Christian principles are said to be compromised. Practitioners in the Bible-Only category believe that counselors who address spiritual problems with psychological concepts and methods do not adequately hold individuals accountable for their behavior. The incorporation of psychological principles is believed to provide an escape route for the client, giving that person the opportunity to develop the belief that he or she is a helpless victim of "uncontrollable factors, such as those found in one's childhood or environment. Then therapy, rather than repentance, is prescribed."[32]

Furthermore, using psychological concepts opens up the possibility for abdicating responsibility and shifting the blame for the problem. Comedian Flip Wilson's famous quote, "The devil made me do it," illustrates this point of view. The charge is this: If time is spent focusing on the *cause* of difficulties, then there is an implicit message that accountability is reduced. Christian counselors in the Bible-Only category are firmly convinced that they already know why a problem has arisen. Every person is a sinner — and that's all the explanation necessary to identify why a client gets into trouble and needs help. To address past or present causes is seen as a waste of time.

The third criticism identified by Dr. Habermas is that "many counselors seem to imply that humans have the power to control their lives by proper thinking, actions, and/or emotions. This is the assumption that happiness is within our grasp, and that view, in turn, further promotes a self-centered outlook."[33] Abraham Lincoln's famous statement that "most people are about as happy as they choose to be" would be seen as unbiblical by proponents of the Bible-Only perspective. They would take issue with the implication that humans are capable of healing themselves without placing their faith in Jesus Christ; Lincoln's remark would be interpreted as an example of a person leaning on his or her own understanding. As Master's College professor Jim Owen explains, "The fundamental error of 'Christian' psychology is that it turns away from the authority of Scripture. It attempts to ground the believer's walk, not in faith in Christ, but rather in knowledge."[34]

Even further, Bible-Only counselors view psychological theories and methods as a psychotherapeutic "Tower of Babel" in which humans attempt to achieve the status of "Wonderful Counselor" (Isaiah 9:6). Writing about this self-sufficient attitude, Jim Owen criticizes the utilization of methodologies that are dependent on human power and derived from human wisdom. He observes the following:

> Despite the scriptural warnings that our weapons of war are not those of this world (2 Corinthians 10:3, 4), and despite our Lord's admonition that we can do nothing apart from abiding in Him (John 15:5), believers continue to build their faith and God's church upon wood, hay, and straw. The appearance is often deceptively imposing and persuasive, but the end result is that our faith comes to rest on man's wisdom and not God's power. The edifices we build are misleading and carnal. Thus, they are without eternal significance.[35]

A fourth concern of Bible-Only proponents relates to their detection of an "ivory tower" attitude taken by many secularly trained Christian therapists. The latter often suggest that Bible-Only counselors rely too heavily on Scripture and virtually exclude secular diagnosis and treatment methodology; Bible-Only advocates "put the shoe on the other foot" and "resist the idea that only those with graduate degrees and/or professional licenses are capable of counseling effectively."[36] They further maintain that an academic-scientific-secular orientation is too superficial and omits important biblical assistance and guidance. Bible-Only proponents are vulnerable to a similar charge, however, when their graduate-training programs demonstrate a decided imbalance. For example, a seminary catalog we've seen lists no courses on psychodiagnosis or psychopathology in its Pastoral Care curriculum.

In short, Bible-Only counselors regard secular methodology as superficial at best, and inane, irrelevant, and possibly dangerous at worst. To bridge the gap, some have developed their own treatment approaches that rely solely on the Scriptures. Jay Adams, for example, formulated a system he called *nouthetic confrontation* (from the Greek *noutheteo*, meaning "to warn or admonish"), which he calls for all members of the body of Christ, not just pastors, to use. Using 2 Timothy 3:16 as a foundational passage ("All Scripture is God-breathed and is useful for teaching, rebuking, correcting and training in righteousness"), Adams states that "nouthetic confrontation is, in short, confrontation with the principles and practices of the Scriptures."[37] Simply put, Bible-Only counselors tend to bring Bible passages to bear on people's lives "in order to expose sinful patterns, to correct what is wrong, and to establish new ways of life of which God approves."[38]

This approach to Christian therapy can be illustrated by the following vignettes that describe actual experiences in our caseloads. In one situation, a Christian couple came in for marriage counseling. They struggled with a poor sense of worth and had a codependent relationship. The husband was verbally abusive, complained of lack of support from family members (especially his wife), and had a long-standing stronghold of self-doubt and feelings of inadequacy. The wife was extremely passive and dependent, and she lacked an awareness of and the ability to set healthy boundaries.

Even after a number of therapy sessions, the husband continued to be verbally and physically abusive. After one such incident the wife placed an emergency call to Terry, asking for guidance. The ensuing telephone discussion led to the husband's decision to remove himself temporarily from their home. After another incident, the wife made a 911 call to the police; the husband again left the home without charges being filed. Several months later Terry received another emergency call. The wife reported that her husband was being verbally abusive and physically intimidating both to her and to one of their teenage children. The police were again summoned, but this time the teenage child had to decide whether to file charges of fifth-degree domestic assault against the father.

The wife contacted Terry and their pastor. Terry advised the mother and teen to file charges, observing that abuse is not to be tolerated; the pastor, in contrast, only advised the mother and teen to "pray through it," explaining, "God will deal with this in his own way." This pastor did not understand the need for the family to set boundaries for their protection, nor did he sense the deterrent to abusive behavior that calling in the police provides. In fact, the pastor overlooked clear biblical teaching about the divinely established role of the state (Romans 13:1–5). Clearly not all pastors would respond in the same way, but if they do not grasp the totality of the problem, they could too easily apply Scripture in a superficial way.

Like the Bible-Only advocates, we hold to Scripture as the only authority for faith and practice. But we also believe we cannot ignore the valuable contribution that science is making to the mental health profession. Nor can we fully discount the value of the experience that comes from studying human behavior and related fields. Suppose a closet alcoholic went to a pastor for help with related problems. How many pastors have enough experience to recognize the signs of alcoholism? Even if they did, how many have enough understanding of alcoholism to provide a comprehensive solution that would lead to complete recovery? In the majority of cases, pointing out Scripture passages that condemn drinking, asking for honest confession, and seeking a commitment never to do it again would probably not be enough to overcome the addiction. Most alcoholics are aware that what they're doing is wrong and that they've been in the *sin-confess-sin-confess-sin* cycle for years.

Important as it is, knowing the Bible is not always enough. For example, in spite of years of pastoral experience and extensive seminary education, Neil Anderson knew he couldn't write *Freedom From Addiction* without coauthor Mike Quarles. Mike had learned how to overcome a powerful addiction in his own life. Mike had struggled with alcoholism before and after ministry. Although he had graduated from a Reformed seminary and had pastored a Presbyterian church for seven years, his theology was not adequate to resolve his addiction. Eventually, however, Mike did find the truth that set him free.

How many pastors do you know who experience marriage and family difficulties in spite of their theological training? How many well-known and highly educated pastors do you know who have fallen sexually? Why wasn't their theology adequate to help them overcome their struggle with lust?

Actually, we believe Scripture *does* have an adequate answer for these bondages. However, for some reason, to know the Scriptures has not been personally liberating for many who have dedicated themselves to full-time ministry. Neil has a burden to tackle these issues, and he has addressed in the following books most of the major problems with which Christians struggle — each book written after a period of brokenness in Neil's own life and after many years of experience:

Sexual addiction: *A Way of Escape*

Chemical addiction: *Freedom From Addiction*

Depression: *Finding Hope Again*

Anxiety disorders: *Freedom From Fear*

Marriage problems: *The Christ Centered Marriage*

Corporate bondage: *Setting Your Church Free*

Perhaps an illustration will help make our point. Like pastors, missionaries usually receive theological education before they enter ministry. But in most instances, preparation for the mission field also requires *additional* training in cross-cultural work. One hopes that the theological education would give missionaries an adequate grid by which to evaluate further training, but few would challenge the fact that they need this additional training. The research of anthropologists and sociologists can offer valuable insight into people groups and cultures. Anthropology and sociology do not provide a fully adequate answer, but they do help us understand the issues and problems. So it is with psychology as well. It does not offer completely adequate answers to the problems we face, but it can help a discerning Christian counselor address those difficulties in an informed way.

CLOSED COUNSELORS

Closed counselors reside at the opposite end of the continuum from Bible-Only counselors. A Closed counselor is a Christian who practices an exclusively secular psychological methodology in the office. Just as Jay Adams's claim that effective counseling can be done only by ordained clergy may seem rather extreme, so it is with those clinicians in this category who maintain that effective counseling can only be done by those with graduate degrees and professional licenses. Members of this classification would fit most closely with Larry Crabb's Separate But Equal group.

In *Our Sufficiency in Christ*, John MacArthur criticizes practitioners of humanistic psychology who advocate a closed approach. Challenging ivory tower mental health professionals, MacArthur denounces the contention that "only those who are trained in psychology — those with the secret knowledge — are qualified to help people with serious spiritual and emotional problems. The acceptance of that attitude is misleading millions and crippling church ministry."[39] He also observes that psychology is limited to a study of the natural aspect of humans and thus has no business trying to help clients address their spiritual needs. Dr. MacArthur explains:

> Outside of the Word and the Spirit there are no solutions to any of the problems of the human soul. Only God knows the soul and only God can change it. Yet the widely accepted ideas of modern psychology are theories originally developed by atheists on the assumption that there is no God and the individual alone has the power to change himself into a better person through certain techniques.[40]

As noted above, the predominant psychotherapeutic techniques used in the Closed counselor's office stem largely from a humanistic training experience. Take Christ out of the office of a Closed therapist and virtually nothing changes. These Christian counselors are closely aligned with psychology in general, as revealed in the survey of professional psychotherapists conducted by Edward Shafranske and H. Newton Malony. Reporting on the results of their research, Siang-Yang Tan noted, "Seventy-one percent of the clinical psychologists they surveyed were affiliated with an organized religion, with forty-one percent attending religious services regularly. However, about eighty-five percent of them indicated that they had little or no training in the area of psychology and religion. It is not surprising, therefore, that sixty-eight percent of them felt it was inappropriate for a psychologist to pray with a client, and fifty-five percent said it was inappropriate to use religious scripture or texts in therapy."[41] Addressing this point of view, Allen Bergin and J. P. Jensen call for "a careful reeducation of therapists whose conceptual/clinical frameworks have room only for secular and naturalistic constructs."[42] Larry Crabb holds a similar opinion regarding the shortcomings of Closed advocates. Therapists who "value technique above conviction and theory above character ... will not adequately shepherd their clients."[43]

Referring to the opposite positions of Bible-Only and Closed proponents and their views on the devil's influence in the world, psychologist and professor Dan Allender writes, "It seems we have reached a point where Satan is either seen as the sole cause of human misery or an embarrassment to those who see psychological symptoms as a by-product of dysfunctional human interaction. Both views create an atmosphere where evil's work progresses due to the myopia of extremism."[44]

In reality, professionals who take the Closed approach are Christian counselors doing secular counseling instead of Christian counselors who have a biblical worldview and understand how divine revelation shapes the understanding of the causation and the treatment of mental illness. Their Christian faith does, one would hope, make them better people, which can help facilitate the counseling process, to be sure, but this is about all that can be positively said of them. Their worldview is so thickly veiled that the client is unlikely to be aware of it. Consider the client who is emotionally distressed because of a recent diagnosis of breast cancer. A Closed therapist would empathize with her feelings of anxiety and depression and teach her certain coping skills, but is that enough? Does the client know how to cast her anxiety on Christ? Does she understand how the God of all hope is the answer to depression? Does she understand how the fear of the Lord is the beginning of wisdom and is, in fact, the only fear that can dispel all other fears—including the fear of death? Does she understand the role suffering plays in the sanctifying process? The Closed therapist misses opportunities to help people draw closer to God.

Christian therapists who leave their faith at the office door, either overtly or covertly, should ponder the remarks of psychologist and professor Kenneth Pargament:

> Psychologists have much to gain from looking beyond their own borders to the broader world around them. When they do, they find that religious beliefs, practices, and institutions are more alive and well than they might have guessed on the basis of their own religious commitments. Furthermore, they find that religion has the capacity to build, sustain, and rebuild human lives, individually and collectively, in many ways. And, finally, they discover a number of new opportunities for intervention between psychological and religious communities.[45]

Pastor John MacArthur has "no quarrel" with therapists who use "common sense or social sciences as a helpful observer's platform to look on human conduct and develop tools to assist people in getting some external controls in their behavior. That may be useful as a first step for getting to the real spiritual cure."[46] He does believe, however, that secular psychological counseling can, at best, only be superficial and incapable of providing actual solutions to the real needs of the soul, which are resolved only in Jesus Christ. He observes, "I have no tolerance for those who exalt psychology above the Scripture, intercession, and the perfect sufficiency of our God."[47] Finally, citing Job's response to his friends (see Job 12:17–20), Dr. MacArthur concludes, "God's wisdom is so vastly superior to man's that the greatest human counselors are made into a spectacle.... If anyone had to endure the folly of well-intentioned human counselors it was Job. Their irrelevant, useless advice was as much a grief to him as the satanic afflictions he suffered."[48]

CLOSET COUNSELORS

Therapists in the *Closet* classification are aware that biblical principles apply to the psychotherapeutic process, but for a variety of reasons they limit their application in therapy. Avoidance of spiritual treatment procedures is generally due to unresolved issues related to personal insecurities or professional inexperience. Therapists may fear rejection, failure, or embarrassment. Others limit their approach because they are afraid the client will be offended by the introduction of religious values and will choose to leave psychotherapy. Finally, others lack confidence in their ability to articulate Christian beliefs in a biblically accurate and meaningful way. What if clients ask biblically related questions? Do therapists have enough theological training to answer correctly? Exposure of their own uncertainties might make it appear that their own spiritual awareness is a mile wide but only an inch deep. This kind of self-doubt is a favorite strategy of the evil one. Sadly, the result is a failed opportunity to share the good news of salvation and introduce Christian approaches into the healing process.

Their relationship with their professional licensure board is an understandable concern for the Closet therapists. Fears of malpractice lawsuits, loss of license to practice, loss of respect by professional peers, and removal from provider panels also concern them. Some Christian counselors also have an inordinate fear of the devil; they are intimidated by the thought of spiritual warfare and feel inadequately trained to deal with this in the therapeutic setting.

Finally, Closet therapists may fail to raise religious issues with a client because of apathy or ignorance. Yet, for a psychologist to disregard religion as one of a client's significant dimensions of differences or diversity is a violation of the American Psychological Association's "Ethical Principles of Psychologists and Code of Conduct," Standard 1.08.[49] Fear, insecurity, ignorance, and apathy must be overcome by those identifying themselves as Christian therapists, because those very same feelings are what they should be helping their clients overcome.

CONJOINT COUNSELORS

The fourth and final category of Christian therapists represented in our matrix are *Conjoint* counselors. These therapists work diligently to integrate Christian principles into their therapy. The comparable approach in Larry Crabb's scheme is Spoiling the Egyptians. Therapists who adopt this approach accept or reject psychological truths based on their consistency with the Bible. As Dr. Crabb explains, "If psychology offers insights which will sharpen our counseling skills and increase our effectiveness, we want to know them. If all problems are at core spiritual matters we don't want to neglect the critically necessary resources available through the Lord by a wrong emphasis on psychological theory."[50]

A Conjoint therapist counsels from a Christian worldview and embraces both spiritual resources and compatible insights and methodologies from the sciences of mental health. Conjoint therapists believe that mentally healthy people are "those who have a true knowledge of God, a true knowledge of who they are as children of God, and a balanced biblical worldview that includes the reality of the spiritual world."[51] Implementation of this counseling approach incorporates physical, psychological, and spiritual aspects of the whole person.

A Conjoint approach combines the ministries of counseling and discipleship. We help clients understand how unresolved issues from their past are contributing to their present struggles. We also help them resolve their personal and spiritual conflicts and establish them alive and free in Jesus Christ. We cannot undo or fix the past, but we believe that by the grace of God people can be set free from the hurts of their past; when they realize their freedom in Christ, they can be all that God has created them to be. Finally, we help clients understand how to walk by faith and in the power of the Holy Spirit, so they can live responsible lives and be conformed to the image of God.

Conjoint therapists do not set up polarities between the psychological and the spiritual. They understand that "our struggle is not against flesh and blood, but against the rulers, against the authorities, against the powers of this dark world and against the spiritual forces of evil in the heavenly realms" (Ephesians 6:12). Conjoint counselors believe that problems arise ultimately from sin in humanity and from sin in the counselee's own life. Thus, they do not compromise the truth that will set their clients free, and they clearly acknowledge the presence of God as Wonderful Counselor and Great Physician. Conjoint therapists pray for healing but also see the value of medication and close cooperation with doctors.

A growing body of research demonstrates that the inclusion of monotheistic, spiritual counseling adds an important dimension to the psychotherapeutic process. After studying research on the importance of using "religious forms of coping," Kenneth Pargament draws this conclusion: "These studies suggest that the sacred is particularly helpful in the worst of times. Vested with unlimited strength and compassion, the sacred offers a source of solace, hope, and power when other resources have been exhausted and people must look beyond themselves for help."[52] Pargament thus reminds psychologists of the vital importance of integrating religious concepts with traditional psychological approaches: "The extraordinary power of religion lies in the melding of the sacred with the human in the search for significance."[53]

We are fully aware that not every Christian counselor supports this approach or is willing to test it out. There are both psychologists and pastors who are strongly opposed to the suggestion that spiritual and psychological healing can be achieved in the office of the psychotherapist. Pastor John MacArthur offers "no encouragement for people who wish to mix psychology with the divine resources and sell the mixture as a spiritual elixir. Their methodology amounts to a tacit admission that what God has given us in Christ is not really adequate to meet our deepest needs and salve our troubled lives."[54]

The arguments for and against these views often resort to generalities and stereotypes. Counselors have had to work with clients who have been spiritually abused by their pastors; at the same time pastors have been appalled by the advice and methodology of counselors. Let's not be afraid to admit it: There are bad counselors who profess to be Christians, but there are also bad pastors who claim the authority of Scripture as a way to promulgate their own beliefs. Pastors also have the luxury of generally seeing only those people who agree with their worldview and who share their belief in the authority of Scripture—people who would very likely not consult with the pastor if they didn't agree on basic worldview. Offering services to those who do not hold to a biblical worldview is not as cut-and-dried for the professional counselor. It may take several sessions to get a client to a place where he or she would be open to biblical instruction.

Another issue that should be considered by the Conjoint counselor is the timing of godly advice and the appropriateness of direct intervention. We are supposed to *weep* with those who weep, not *instruct* those who weep. It is easy as psychologists to dispense advice, but it is much more pastoral to listen, to empathize, and to enter into the client's experience. The tendency for many of us is to become too confrontational and too focused on behavior. The presenting problem is seldom the root issue. Conjoint therapists use counseling techniques to get to the root issues and then help bring resolution in Christ.

In our experience, there are times when the initial use of Christian concepts in therapy is not helpful or appropriate. We must start with the mind-set of the client. Some are not believers, while others have been deeply hurt by spiritual leaders in the past. We know of a respected Christian Conjoint therapist who offers group sessions for severely damaged Christians. It can take months to overcome the spiritual damage inflicted by church leaders and to prepare those who have been abused to receive Christian counsel. Many Christian clients begin therapy with a professional counselor instead of with a pastor because they feel that the church has not provided an adequate answer for their problems or a compassionate response to their pain.

Few Christians who come to see us express surprise at our introductory discussion of our biblical strategy for therapy. However, nonbelievers often raise their eyebrows when we explain our theistic worldview. To this very day not one has withdrawn from therapy because we have clarified our value system. A therapist's Christian counseling strategy is not offensive, even to those who come for reasons other than desiring a spiritual approach to their problems, as long as it is introduced to but not imposed on them. Some of our clients, for example, come to us for counseling because of name recognition or because of a referral from another client; others have come because of the convenient location. Terry even had one client explain that she made an appointment because she liked the name of our clinic; another liked the way our ad looked in the Yellow Pages! Yet, these can be viewed as divine appointments directed by the Holy Spirit, similar to the woman at the well in John 4:4–26. This Samaritan woman came to the well because she needed water, not knowing that *God* was behind this divine appointment to bring her to Jesus Christ!

Therefore, these differences in orientation, regardless of how significant they may seem, do not preclude counseling. As noted earlier, clarification and mutual understanding of differences should take place as necessary elements of informed consent. In such situations where there are significant differences, the therapist could proceed with psychotherapy but should, out of respect for the value system of the client, use wisdom in addressing spiritual concepts and implementing spiritual treatment approaches. The counselor could engage in private prayer for the client before, during, and after sessions. Recommendations would flow out of a biblical worldview, and opportunities for discussion of spiritual issues would be observed.

If a good rapport has been established with a client and therapeutic goals are open to revision during the course of counseling, life's spiritual dimension may become an acceptable consideration for the client. During the treatment process, we look for opportunities to obtain client approval to introduce religious considerations. A typical comment might go something like this:

> I'm sure you recall our discussion about our differing worldviews when you initially sought our services. So far we have been dealing with your treatment goals in terms of things you can change in the physical and psychological areas of life. I'm wondering if you've given any more thought to the spiritual dimension of your life?

We try hard to stay in step with God's timing in the lives of our clients, not wanting to run ahead of him or lag behind him. By the same token, we do not want to violate our clients' wishes. Should they consent to pursue the spiritual dimension, we can proceed to discuss their relationship with God. Attention can be given to the core issues of salvation, one's identity in Christ, and growth in spiritual maturity. If there is any indication of reluctance, the issue is not pressed. We choose, like Jesus, to be gentle, not forcing ourselves on others against their will. We remain expectant, prayerful, and ready to share the love of God when the window of opportunity is opened.

4

The Integration of Theology and Psychology

What a chimera, then, is man! What a novelty! What a monster, what a chaos, what a contradiction, what a prodigy! Judge of all things, feeble worm of the earth, depository of truth, a sink of uncertainty and error, the glory and the shame of the universe.

BLAISE PASCAL

French scientist and philosopher Blaise Pascal's (1623–1662) portrayal of humankind as a bundle of contradictions would not solicit much disagreement from even the most casual observer of fallen humanity. We love and hate one another with the same intensity. "With the tongue we praise our Lord and Father, and with it we curse men, who have been made in God's likeness. Out of the same mouth come praise and cursing" (James 3:9–10). But in the beginning it was not so. Who is this creature the Bible calls *man*? Israel's great king and poet David pondered that question in Psalm 8:

> When I consider your heavens,
>   the work of your fingers,
> the moon and the stars,
>   which you have set in place,
> what is man that you are mindful of him,
>   the son of man that you care for him?
> You made him a little lower than the heavenly beings
>   and crowned him with glory and honor.
> You made him ruler over the works of your hands;
>   you put everything under his feet.
>
> —*PSALM 8:3–6*

The first book of the Bible contains these words: "So God created man in his own image, in the image of God he created him; male and

85

female he created them (Genesis 1:27). Being created in the image of God is what sets us apart from the animal kingdom. Our soul has the ability to think, feel, and choose. Consequently, we have the capacity to participate with God in the shaping of our own lives. The temptation we must continually battle is to act independently of God and determine for ourselves who we are and what we shall become.

The creation account also declares, "The LORD God formed the man from the dust of the ground and breathed into his nostrils the breath of life, and the man became a living being" (Genesis 2:7). This combination of dust (natural) and divine breath (spiritual) constitutes the nature of humans created in God's image. The original creation of humanity can be depicted as follows (see Figure 4.1):

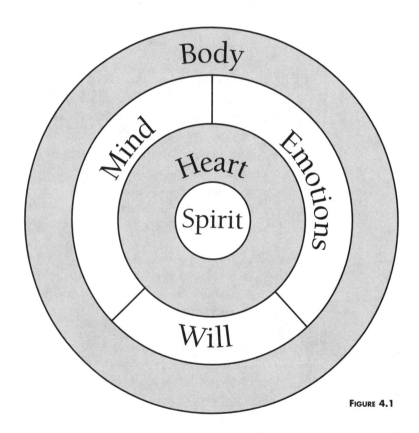

FIGURE 4.1

Theologians have not come to complete agreement regarding the basic nature of humanity. Those adopting a trichotomous view believe we are composed of body, soul, and spirit. In this view, the soul includes mind, will, and emotions. Others take a dichotomous perspective and understand the soul and the spirit to be essentially the same. Those who incline toward this approach appeal to the fact that we are essentially material and immaterial, possessing an inner person and an outer person. A growing number of Bible scholars and therapists support a wholistic approach to the integration of the components of human nature.

The human heart is even more difficult to define. It seems to be the core of our inner being. Consider the proverb of Solomon: "As water reflects a face, so a man's heart reflects the man" (Proverbs 27:19). New Testament professor Robert Jewett gives further explanation: "A characteristic of the heart as the center of man is its inherent openness to outside impulses, its directionality, its propensity to give itself to a master and to live toward some desired goal."[1] There is truth in this description, because we are not the source of our own life. Rather, we are dependent creatures who by nature look outside ourselves for life. What the heart takes in also becomes its master, stamping the heart with its character. In the original creation, God was at the center of Adam and Eve's life, and they naturally took on his character. The heart of humankind was never designed by God to function as master.

Adam was created to be both physically and spiritually alive. In the Bible, the idea of being alive means "to be in union with"; to die means "to be separated from." Thus, to be physically alive means that one's soul/spirit is in union with one's body. Spiritual life means that one's soul/spirit is in union with God. When Christians die physically, they will be absent from their bodies and present with the Lord (see 2 Corinthians 5:6).

Living in the presence of God, Adam and Eve had all of their needs provided for. They did not have to search for significance. Their divine purpose was to rule over the birds of the sky, the beasts of the field, and the fish of the sea (see Genesis 1:28). They had a sense of belonging, not only to God but also to each other. They lived safely and securely in God's presence and could have done so forever had they not chosen to live independently of him. God said that they would surely die on the day they disobeyed him (see Genesis 2:17). Eve was deceived by the devil, she and Adam sinned, and both died — that is, they died spiritually, and their souls were instantly separated from God (see Genesis 3:6–19). Physical death would also be a consequence for sin, but that didn't come for over nine hundred years for Adam (see Genesis 5:4).

Before the Fall Adam and Eve were naked and unashamed. God had created them to be sexual beings, so there was nothing sinful about having a sexual relationship with each other and nothing to give them shame. But after they died spiritually, their insecurity was immediately evident. Frightened to death that someone might find out what was going on inside, they now tried to cover up and hide. Adam explained, "I was afraid because I was naked; so I hid" (Genesis 3:10). Fear was the first negative emotion expressed by Adam.

Something also happened to the human mind. For some reason Adam thought he could hide from an omnipresent and omniscient God. Rebellion against God had left Adam a natural man, unable to discern the things of God. The apostle Paul says of such unregenerate people, "They are darkened in their understanding and separated from the life of God because of the ignorance that is in them due to the hardening of their hearts" (Ephesians 4:18). Elsewhere Paul observes, "The man without the Spirit does not accept the things that come from the Spirit of God, for they are foolishness to him, and he cannot understand them, because they are spiritually discerned" (1 Corinthians 2:14).

From the time of Adam every single person on earth has been born dead in transgressions and sins (see Ephesians 2:1). We are all born physically alive but spiritually dead. Sin separates us from God. Left on our own we try to make a name for ourselves and derive our purpose in life from the natural order. The Bible tells us that the sinful heart is deceitful and desperately sick (see Jeremiah 17:9), and indeed it is, for it is radically influenced by the nature of the fallen world. Satan became the rebellious holder of temporal authority, the "prince of this world" (John 12:31). All this was set in motion when Adam and Eve forfeited their spiritual position and calling through their fall into sin.

THE GOSPEL

However, God had an immediate plan for redemption, which was revealed when he cursed the devil: "And I will put enmity between you and the woman, and between your offspring and hers; he will crush your head, and you will strike his heel" (Genesis 3:15). God said there would be a struggle between satanic forces and humanity. The offspring of the woman began with Cain and his natural descendants, but out of this offspring would come the Christ—the Messiah. Satan would cripple humans ("strike his heel"), but Christ would deliver the fatal blow ("crush your head"). The offspring of the serpent would include his demons and anyone who serves in the kingdom of darkness, those whose spiritual "father" is the devil (see John 8:44).

In preparation for Christ's coming, God made a conditional covenant with humanity based on the Mosaic law. The law, which was ceremonial, civil, and moral, provided for a temporal means by which humans could relate to God and each other. But the law was powerless to give life; therefore, righteousness could not be based on the law (see Galatians 3:21). Moses' law was a tutor that would eventually lead us to Jesus Christ, who is the only name under heaven given to us by which we can be saved (see Acts 4:12; Galatians 3:24). The Old Testament prophet Ezekiel prophesied what God was going to do in order to save his fallen people:

> I will give them an undivided heart and put a new spirit in them; I will remove from them their heart of stone and give them a heart of flesh. Then they will follow my decrees and be careful to keep my laws. They will be my people, and I will be their God.
>
> —*Ezekiel 11:19–20*

The gospel is far more than just the proclamation of forgiveness of sins. "The wages of sin is death, but the gift of God is eternal life in Christ Jesus our Lord" (Romans 6:23). Thank God for Good Friday, because Jesus had to die on the cross in order for us to be forgiven. "Without the shedding of blood," states the author of the letter to the Hebrews, "there is no forgiveness" (Hebrews 9:22). And we celebrate Easter Sunday with unrestrained joy and gratitude, because without the resurrection there would be no new life. Jesus came to give us life and to put a new heart and a new spirit within us. When we are born again spiritually, our soul/spirit is in union with God — a reality often conveyed in Scripture as being "in Christ," or "in him," which is one of the most frequent prepositional phrases found in the New Testament. Referring to Timothy the apostle Paul said, "He will remind you of my way of life *in Christ Jesus,* which agrees with what I teach everywhere in every church" (1 Corinthians 4:17, emphasis added).

What Adam and Eve lost in the Fall was life — spiritual life. What Jesus came to give us was life (see John 10:10). Eternal life is not merely something we get when we physically die. John writes, "He who has the Son has life; he who does not have the Son of God does not have life"

(1 John 5:12). If you do not have eternal (spiritual) life before you physically die, all you have to look forward to is hell. Jesus explains, "I am the resurrection and the life. He who believes in me will live, even though he dies; and whoever lives and believes in me will never die" (John 11:25–26). In other words, every born-again believer is spiritually alive and will continue to be so when he or she physically dies. Jesus is the "bread of *life*" (John 6:35), "the way and the truth and the *life*" (John 14:6), and every Christian has his or her name written in the Lamb's "book of *life*" (Revelation 13:8, emphases added).

A NEW IDENTITY

The gospel also answers the question of who we are: "Yet to all who received [Jesus], to those who believed in his name, he gave the right to become children of God — children born not of natural descent, nor of human decision or a husband's will, but born of God" (John 1:12–13). Before life in Christ, we had no option but to make a name for ourselves or grasp some identity from our culture or work. But now we "have put on the new self, which is being renewed in knowledge in the image of its Creator. Here there is no Greek or Jew, circumcised or uncircumcised, barbarian, Scythian, slave or free, but Christ is all, and is in all" (Colossians 3:10–11). The apostle John writes, "How great is the love the Father has lavished on us, that we should be called children of God! And that is what we are!" (1 John 3:1).

Understanding what it means to be a child of God is essential for every Christian. We've had the privilege of helping people all over the world resolve their personal and spiritual conflicts and find their freedom in Christ. Every defeated Christian had one thing in common: None of them knew who they were "in Christ" or understood what it meant to be a child of God. If the "Spirit himself testifies with our spirit that we are God's children" (Romans 8:16), why were these defeated Christians not sensing this reality? Paul says, "Because you are sons, God sent the Spirit of his Son into our hearts, the Spirit who calls out, '*Abba*, Father'" (Galatians 4:6). Nevertheless, these Christians did experience the presence of their heavenly Father after we helped them resolve their personal and spiritual conflicts through genuine repentance, submitting to God, and resisting the devil (James 4:7). As we move on in this book, we'll explain how professional therapists can accomplish this result in their interactions with clients.

The recognition that our identity is in Christ has profound implications for Christian counseling. Consider this startling truth: Who we are is not determined by what we do. What we do is determined by who we are and by the beliefs we have of ourselves and others. Notice how Peter applies this new identity to the marriage relationship: "Husbands, in the same way be considerate as you live with your wives, and treat them with respect as the weaker partner and as heirs with you of the gracious gift of life, so that nothing will hinder your prayers" (1 Peter 3:7). In a Christian marriage, both husband and wife are children of God and should be respected as such and treated accordingly. When Paul led the runaway slave Onesimus to a relationship with Christ and sent him back to his earthly master, Onesimus was to be received as a "brother in the Lord" (Philemon 16).

Whether we consider ourselves *saints* or *sinners* is another important biblical truth related to identity. In the King James Version of the Bible, believers are called "saints," "holy ones," or "righteous ones" more than 240 times. By way of contrast, unbelievers are called "sinners" over 340 times. Clearly, Scripture uses the term *saint* to refer to the believer and *sinner* in reference to the unbeliever.[2] Therefore, it is counterproductive to refer to Christians as sinners and then expect them to act as saints. People cannot consistently behave in a way that is inconsistent with how they perceive themselves. As Christians we are not trying to *become* children of God (saints); we *are* children of God who are becoming like Jesus Christ. We are not working *for* our salvation; we are *working it out* (see Philippians 2:12). This reality is why it is so important to understand *positional sanctification* (what God has already accomplished for us and who we already are in Christ) and *progressive sanctification* (making real in our experience what is already true about us).

Our position and identity in Christ is not just positional truth; rather, it is the basis for living and growing "in Christ." Scottish theologian Sinclair Ferguson defines sanctification as "the consistent practical out-working of what it means to belong to the new creation in Christ."[3] Similarly, distinguished British theologian John Stott writes:

> So, in practice we should constantly be reminding ourselves who we are. We need to learn to talk to ourselves, and ask ourselves questions: "Don't you know? Don't you know the meaning of conversion and baptism? Don't you know that you have been united to Christ in his death and resurrection? Don't you know that you have been enslaved to God and have committed yourself to His obedience? Don't you know

these things? Don't you know who you are?" We must go on pressing ourselves with such questions, until we reply to ourselves: "Yes, I do know who I am, a new person in Christ, and by the grace of God I shall live accordingly."[4]

Knowing who we are in Christ and what it truly means to be a child of God makes an incredible difference as we work with struggling Christians. For instance, certainly there are Christians who have chemical addictions, who struggle with alcohol and drugs, but that is not who they are. Thus, sitting in a circle repeating a failure identity is counterproductive to their recovery. It is correct and necessary to say, "I am a child of God who struggles with alcohol." Recovery in Christ requires them to walk in the light (see 1 John 1:7) and speak the truth in love (see Ephesians 4:15). The only thing we ever have to admit to is the truth, which is the first step in recovery. Granted, "If we claim to be without sin, we deceive ourselves and the truth is not in us" (1 John 1:8), but be careful how you understand this passage. *Having sin* and *being sin* are two totally different concepts. God had to change who we are; we have to assume our responsibility to live as children of God: "For you were once darkness, but now you are light in the Lord. Live as children of light" (Ephesians 5:8).

All Christians struggle in the process of growing and maturing. Helping them as they work though the process requires us to separate *them* from their acts of immaturity or indiscretions. For instance, there is a significant difference between saying, "I have a problem child," and saying, "My child has a problem." If you have a problem child, the only way to get rid of the problem is to get rid of the child. But if your child has a problem, it is surely possible to help him or her resolve the problem. In order to overcome addictive behavior, we need to realize that we are alive in Christ and dead to sin (see Romans 6:11), resolve our personal and spiritual conflicts, find our identity and freedom in Christ, have our needs met in Christ, and learn how to live our lives through faith and in the power of the Holy Spirit—only then will we no longer gratify the desires of the flesh (see Galatians 5:16). Only then will the truth set us free (see John 8:32).

The same reasoning holds true for homosexuality. God created us male and female. Some people have, to be sure, homosexual behaviors, feelings, and tendencies, but that is not who they are. Establishing a true identity is the first step in overcoming homosexuality. The adage "Once a sinner, always a sinner" is not true if you understand and believe the gospel, nor is "Once an alcoholic, always an alcoholic" or "Once a homosexual, always a homosexual." Those are the conclusions drawn by a world that has no gospel. Without the gospel, we would all remain an ill-fated product of our past. No one can fix our past. Not even God does that. Rather, he sets us free from it by making us new creations in Christ (see 2 Corinthians 5:17). Our spiritual heritage takes precedence over a physical and natural heritage, which is why Paul can pray "that the eyes of [our] heart may be enlightened in order that [we] may know the hope to which he has called [us], the riches of his glorious inheritance in the saints" (Ephesians 1:18).

Apart from the gospel, the best we can do is to help those with mental health problems learn to cope, live more responsibly, and abstain from addictive behaviors. Secular encouragement consists of the mantra "Work the program, the program works." But the best programs in the world, including Christian ones, cannot set anyone free, nor can good deeds. Only Christ can set us free. The goal in recovery has to be more than abstinence, for, you see, if abstinence were the goal, then Ephesians 5:18 would read, "Do not get drunk on wine; therefore, stop drinking." The answer is to "be filled with the Spirit," because "where the Spirit of the Lord is, there is freedom" (2 Corinthians 3:17).

We are not saved by how we *behave* but by how we *believe*. Therefore, changing a client's behavior without changing what he or she believes can only lead in the end to legalism and drivenness or rebellion. Rules without relationships lead to rebellion. Any message that advocates only a change in behavior with external accountability will fall far short in the end. It may allow people to cope better in society temporarily, but it cannot and will not liberate them.

There's another reason why merely abstaining from aberrant behavior isn't enough. People without Christ choose sinful behaviors as a means of coping, of dealing with their pain, of getting rid of their inhibitions, or of having their own needs met. Take alcohol away from an alcoholic, and all you've done is create a dry drunk. Alcoholics and those who struggle with other addictions have legitimate needs that are the basis for most temptations. Every temptation is an attempt to convince us to live our lives independently of God. But for every temptation God has provided a way of escape (see 1 Corinthians 10:13). It is much easier to find the way of escape if you know who you are in Christ and if you recognize how God "will meet all your needs according to his glorious riches *in Christ Jesus*" (Philippians 4:19, emphasis added).

Everyone has needs, the most critical of which are associated with *being* (life, identity, acceptance, security, and significance). Only Jesus Christ can meet these needs. Take a moment to study the following list, taken from Neil Anderson's book *Living Free in Christ*,[5] to learn exactly who you are as a Christian and to discover how all your *being* needs are met in Christ.

WHO I AM IN CHRIST

I AM ACCEPTED IN CHRIST

I am God's child (John 1:12)

I am Christ's friend (John 15:15)

I have been justified (Romans 5:1)

I am united with the Lord and one with him in spirit (1 Corinthians 6:17)

I have been bought with a price; I belong to God (1 Corinthians 6:20)

I am a member of Christ's body (1 Corinthians 12:27)

I am a saint (Ephesians 1:1)

I have been adopted as God's child (Ephesians 1:5)

I have direct access to God through the Holy Spirit (Ephesians 2:18)

I have been redeemed and forgiven of all my sins (Colossians 1:14)

I am complete in Christ (Colossians 2:10)

I AM SECURE IN CHRIST

I am free forever from condemnation (Romans 8:1–2)

I am assured that all things work together for good (Romans 8:28)

I am free from any condemning charges against me (Romans 8:33–34)

I cannot be separated from the love of God (Romans 8:35, 38–39)

I have been established, anointed, and sealed by God (2 Corinthians 1:21–22)

I am confident that the good work God has begun in me will be perfected (Philippians 1:6)

I am a citizen of heaven (Philippians 3:20)

I am hidden with Christ in God (Colossians 3:3)

I have not been given a spirit of fear, but of power, love, and a sound mind (2 Timothy 1:7)

I can find grace and mercy to help me in time of need (Hebrews 4:16)

I am born of God, and the evil one cannot touch me (1 John 5:18)

I Am Significant in Christ

I am the salt and light of the earth (Matthew 5:13 – 14)

I am a branch of the true vine, a channel of his life (John 15:1, 5)

I have been chosen and appointed to bear fruit (John 15:16)

I am a personal witness of Christ (Acts 1:8)

I am God's temple (1 Corinthians 3:16)

I am a minister of reconciliation (2 Corinthians 5:17 – 20)

I am God's coworker (2 Corinthians 6:1)

I am seated with Christ in the heavenly realms (Ephesians 2:6)

I am God's workmanship (Ephesians 2:10)

I may approach God with freedom and confidence (Ephesians 3:12)

I can do all things through Christ who gives me strength (Philippians 4:13)

ESTABLISHING THE RIGHT CAUSE

Why do people do what they do, and why do they feel the way they feel? Establishing causation may be the most difficult task facing a counselor—and the one requiring the greatest need for the integration of theology and psychology. For example, one often hears the following explanation of why Christians continue to struggle: "Of course we're going to sin; we're all sinners, and our hearts are deceitful and desperately sick." We would contend that this is a false explanation and that verbalizing it makes the possibility of living a righteous life even more hopeless.

We recognize that this claim may be new to many readers and that you may need more explanation in order to be convinced. For readers who want to consider the issue in greater depth, we urge you to examine *The Common Made Holy,* by Neil Anderson and Robert Saucy. You'll also benefit from reading two other books by Neil, *Victory Over the Darkness* and *The Bondage Breaker* (Neil has recorded the message of these two books in audio and video formats as well); we use these books in our interactions with our clients, because both books apply the gospel message of who we are in Christ to issues of everyday life.

In giving us a new heart, God has changed the very core nature of who we are in the inner person. We are no longer "in Adam" or "in the flesh," but "in Christ." Paul writes, "You are not in the flesh but in the Spirit, if indeed the Spirit of God dwells in you. But if anyone does not have the Spirit of Christ, he does not belong to Him" (Romans 8:9 New American Standard Bible). Paul also teaches, "Therefore, if anyone is *in Christ,* he is a new creation; the old has gone, the new has come!" (2 Corinthians 5:17, emphasis added). Again, "For he has rescued us from the dominion of darkness and brought us into the kingdom of the Son he loves, in whom we have redemption, the forgiveness of sins" (Colossians 1:13–14). If all this is true (and it most assuredly is), then why do we still struggle with the same thoughts, feelings, and behaviors?

Because we were all born dead in our transgressions and sins (see Ephesians 2:1), we had neither the presence of God in our lives nor knowledge of his ways. Therefore, we all learned to live our lives independently of God. From the very first our minds were programmed by the external world, which is why the heart of an unregenerate person is deceitful and desperately sick (see Jeremiah 17:9). But when we came to Christ, everything we have explained so far concerning our identity and position in Christ became instantly true. We became children of God who are alive and free in Christ, but no one pushed the "Clear" button in our memory bank. In fact there is no "Delete" button on the computer operation going on between our ears. Everything we previously learned and experienced before salvation is still recorded in our minds. The apostle Paul recognized the importance of what goes on in our minds, as he writes to the Romans, "Do not conform any longer to the pattern of this world, but be transformed by the *renewing of your mind*. Then you will be able to test and approve what God's will is — his good, pleasing and perfect will" (Romans 12:2, emphasis added).

HOW WE GOT OUR WORLDVIEW

Before we came to Christ we all were conformed to this world, and we can continue to be if we allow ourselves to be influenced by it. Messages from this world are constantly being received by our brains and interpreted by our minds. Prior to birth, the only world an infant has seen is the inside of his or her mother's womb. Newborn children have just enough preprogramming to sustain life. Other than that, their minds are a blank slate. They have no vocabulary and no understanding of the world around them. Their worldview is shaped by the environment in which they are raised. Values and attitudes about life are formed in their minds in primarily two ways. First, *prevailing experiences,* such as the homes in which they are raised, the neighborhoods in which they play, the friends they have, and the churches they attend (or do not attend), make a significant impact on people's worldviews. Values are more caught than taught, however. Formal education is another vital experience that shapes our worldview. It's important to understand that all children will interpret the data they receive differently — which is one reason why two children raised in the same home can respond so differently to life's situations and circumstances.

Second, *traumatic experiences,* such as the death of a family member, the divorce of one's parents, and emotional, sexual, or physical abuse, make the other primary contribution to attitude formation. Traumatic experiences are deeply etched in people's minds, and they shape their beliefs about God, themselves, and the world in which they live. These deeply rooted beliefs are what keep people in bondage to the past, not the traumatic experience itself. Suppose, for example, a husband/father abandoned his family. The wife and children would each process this loss differently. Their questions might range from "Where was God?" to "What's wrong with me?" Their responses might include "all men are sick and untrustworthy"; "I will never get married [or remarried]"; "he didn't love us, so there must be something wrong with me"; and "from now on I'm going to ..."

These impressions are burned into our minds over time through repetition (prevailing experiences) or through the intensity of powerful experiences, both good and bad (traumatic experiences). We live according to what we have chosen to believe about ourselves and about the world around us. Moreover, we are not always aware that we are continuously gathering information that forms, alters, or intensifies our beliefs. Many people cruise through life with a carefree attitude, unaware of how they are being influenced by the world in which they live.

The external sources of information vary greatly from one culture to another, and none of them is completely value-neutral. We all receive safe and healthy input from our surroundings, but we also encounter contaminated and unhealthy external stimuli that affect our worldview and our perception of ourselves. Our belief system is constantly changing as we process positive and negative information and experiences. Unfortunately, not every piece of information we receive comes clearly marked as productive or unproductive, good or evil, true or false!

DEFENSE MECHANISMS

During our early, formative years, we learned how to cope, succeed, or simply survive independently of God. Psychologists call these coping or survival strategies *defense mechanisms*. There are potentially an infinite variety of ways people can use to defend themselves. The more common defense mechanisms include lying, denial, projection, fantasy, emotional insulation, regression, displacement, and rationalization. For example, when children are aware of the consequences of telling the truth, they will often lie to protect themselves or will blame someone else. If they repeat this behavior for several weeks, it will become a habit; if it persists, it will become an established part of their temperament.

In some ways defense mechanisms are similar to what the Bible calls *strongholds*, which Paul refers to in his second letter to the Corinthians: "The weapons we fight with are not the weapons of the world. On the contrary, they have divine power to demolish strongholds. We demolish arguments and every pretension that sets itself up against the knowledge of God, and we take captive every thought to make it obedient to Christ" (2 Corinthians 10:4–5).

Strongholds can be our habitual patterns of thought. They can be memory traces burned into our minds over time by the trauma of certain experiences. Some Christian groups call them "flesh patterns" because they represent the old nature, namely, how we learned to live our lives independently of God. A mental stronghold is like the grooves worn in a dirt road over the course of time. If someone were to drive in that manner long enough, it wouldn't even become necessary to steer the car down the road. The car would naturally follow those grooves, and any attempt to steer out of the grooves would be met with great resistance.

An inferiority complex, for example, is a stronghold. We were not born inferior to anyone else, but many people began to believe they were inferior because of the environment in which they were raised. Someone always got higher scores on exams, ran faster, looked prettier, and played better, or had more money, a better job, a bigger house, more education, and so on. In our competitive culture, how could anyone not develop some sense of inferiority or struggle with personal identity and sense of worth?

The world has recognized that most people do not have a healthy sense of who they are. Some people respond by trying to be prettier, stronger, wealthier, and more popular than anyone else. They are going to beat the system, no matter what. Other people employ more humane approaches and try to build up the self-esteem of those who have been beaten down by the system. However, stroking one another's egos and picking ourselves up by our bootstraps simply does not and will not work. Others rebel against the system and become part of a counterculture. In the end, everyone loses in the kingdom of self-effort and darkness.

For instance, adult children of alcoholics often develop sophisticated mental strongholds or defense mechanisms in order to survive. Suppose a father of three boys is an alcoholic. All three boys choose to respond to their father in different ways. The older boy stands up to his father and physically defends himself if necessary. The middle son chooses to accommodate his father, while the younger son runs and hides whenever his father comes home drunk. Thirty years later, the father has disappeared from the picture, and the three boys are now adult men. When confronted with hostile situations, how will they respond? Chances are the older one will fight, the middle son will accommodate, and the younger son will run and hide.

Do we have to live with old defense mechanisms the rest of our lives? Can these mental strongholds be torn down in Christ? Can our temperaments be transformed by the renewing of our minds? If we have been trained wrongly, can we be retrained? If we have been taught wrongly, can we be retaught? If we have believed lies, can we renounce those lies and choose the truth? Yes, yes, yes! The treatment technique called *cognitive-behavioral therapy* (CBT) specifically seeks to address these issues, and later in this chapter we'll discuss this technique in more detail (see also the tool kit discussion in chapter nine).

INTEGRATING THE BODY, SOUL, AND SPIRIT

Because we desire a wholistic answer, we need to understand the part our physical bodies play in the forming of our identity. God created us to have an outer (material) person and an inner (immaterial) person. Since we are "fearfully and wonderfully made" (Psalm 139:14), it only makes sense that God created the outer person to correlate with the inner person. Please refer to Figure 4.2 as we discuss the relationship between the inner and the outer person:

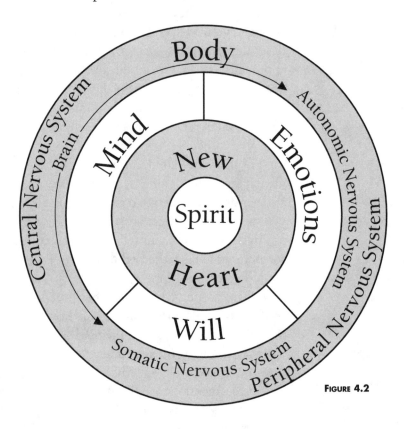

FIGURE 4.2

The correlation between the mind and the brain is obvious, but we must not ignore the fundamental difference between the two. The brain came from the dust of this earth and will return to dust when we physically die. At that moment we will be absent from our bodies and present with the Lord (see 2 Corinthians 5:6–9; Philippians 1:21–24); however, we will not be mindless. The brain-mind combination is similar to that of a computer. Every computer system is made up of two distinct components—hardware and software. In this analogy, the hardware (the physical computer) is obviously the brain.

The brain functions much like a digital computer, which has millions of switching transistors and all its information coded in a binary numbering system of zeroes and ones. Whereas a personal computer is mechanical, our brains are living organisms composed of approximately 100 billion neurons (the fundamental functional unit of nervous tissue). Each neuron is a living organism that in and of itself is a microcomputer; each is composed of a brain cell, an axon (impulse conductor), and many dendrites (inputs to the brain cell) as follows (see Figure 4.3):

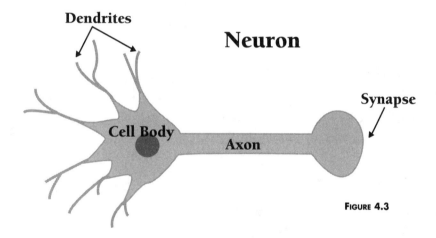

FIGURE 4.3

Each brain cell has many inputs (dendrites) and only one output through the axon, which channels neurotransmitters to other dendrites. The axon is covered by a myelin sheath for insulation because the cell sends electrochemical messages along the axon. Every neuron is connected to tens of thousands of other neurons. Bearing in mind that there are some 100 billion neurons, the potential number of combinations is mind-boggling! The junction between the axon of one neuron and the dendrites of another is called a synapse. Every brain cell receives information through its dendrites—information that it processes, integrates, and sends on to other neurons.

In the axon there exist many mitochondria, which produce neurotransmitters. When a signal from the cell reaches the axon, it releases neurotransmitters, which cross the synapse to other dendrites. There are numerous types of neurotransmitters, of which norepinephrine, dopamine, serotonin, and acetylcholine are the best known and the most important for our discussion.

The brain and the spinal cord make up the nervous system, which splits off into a peripheral nervous system and a central nervous system. The peripheral nervous system has two channels — the autonomic nervous system and the somatic nervous system. The somatic nervous system regulates muscular and skeletal movements, such as speech and gestures, and correlates with our will. We do not carry out an action without first thinking it. The thought-action response is normally so rapid that one is scarcely aware of the sequence, but it always comes into play. When the system breaks down, involuntary muscular movements can occur, as with Parkinson's disease (shaking palsy), where there is a progressive degeneration of nerve cells in the part of the brain that controls muscle movements.

Our autonomic nervous system regulates our internal organs. We do not have direct volitional control over our glands, nor do we consciously regulate the beat of our heart or the functioning of our endocrine system. They function "automatically." In a general sense, we do not have volitional control over our emotions either. That is to say, we cannot will ourselves to feel good or like someone we hate. We do, however, have control of what we think, and we can decide to believe that what God says is true. Just as our glands are regulated by our nervous system, our emotions are primarily a by-product of our thoughts. It is not the circumstances of life that determine how we feel; rather, how we feel is principally determined by how we interpret the events of life (what we choose to think and believe) and secondarily by how we choose to behave. Between the external stimulus and the emotional response is the brain (receiver) and the mind (interpreter).

WHEN STRESS BECOMES DISTRESS

Let's apply these lessons to the problem of stress. When external pressures put demands on our physical system, our adrenal glands respond by secreting cortisone-like hormones (adrenaline) into our physical bodies. Thus, our bodies automatically respond to external pressures. This adrenaline rush is the natural fight-or-flight response to the pressures of life. However, if the pressures persist for too long, our adrenal glands can't keep up, and stress becomes distress. The result can be physical illness or intense irritation with things that would not bother us physically or emotionally in less-stressful times.

Why, then, do two people respond differently to the same stressful situation? One actually seizes the opportunity and thrives under the pressure, while another falls apart. Does this mean that one person has superior adrenal glands? Although certainly we may differ considerably in our physical condition, the major difference lies in our perceptions. It's not just the external factors that determine the degree of stress we feel, for we all face the pressures of deadlines, schedules, trauma, and temptations. The major difference is how we mentally interpret the external world and process the data our brain is receiving.

It's important to understand that the adrenal glands do not initiate the release of adrenaline. They are the responders, not the initiators. The hormone is released into the bloodstream after the brain has recorded the external inputs and the mind interprets them. The brain itself can only function in the way in which it has been programmed.

Our bodies also generate a natural and normal production of neurotransmitters that allows the brain to function. If we lacked this ability, physical life could not be sustained in infancy. In other words, we are preprogrammed from birth to physically exist. There is a natural will to live and to seek food, clothing, shelter, and safety. Of course, this raises a key question: Could how we choose to think affect how the brain operates, either in keeping with or in opposition to this natural will to live? If the secretion of adrenaline is triggered by how we think or perceive reality, could serotonin or other neurotransmitters be affected by how we think and choose to believe? Apparently so, for researchers such as psychologist Martin Seligman are beginning to demonstrate that learned helplessness and hopelessness can change our neurological system.[6]

How, then, does the presence of the "Wonderful Counselor" (Isaiah 9:6), the "God of all hope" (Romans 15:13), transform us? Does his presence transform our outer self or inner self? In other words, is there anything that physically changed in our lives the moment we were born again? Nothing that was observable to the naked eye; our bodies stayed the same. In this respect, it is much like loading a new program on a computer. Nothing looks different. However, although the same number of hardware components exist in the computer, the screen will begin to show a different output, and the electronic flow through the computer will change. Similarly, if a new program is loaded on our "computer," we should start to live differently. Certainly we have the potential to do so, because we've had our eyes opened to the truth and because the power of the Holy Spirit enables us to live by faith. The flow of neurotransmitters will surely change, even though the number of brain cells remains the same.

Now this kind of thinking leads to the raising of yet another critical question. What is the primary cause of our mental and emotional problems? Is it the hardware, or is it the software? Is the cause of our difficulties primarily neurological, or psycho-spiritual? From a biblical perspective, we must conclude that the "software" is primarily at fault. Of course, some of us can and do experience neurological and biochemical problems, such as organic brain syndrome, Alzheimer's disease, and strokes, but Scripture's emphasis is on renewing our minds and living by faith. By all means, Christian counselors should work in harmony with the medical professions, who have the power to prescribe medication; however, we must not forget that, although taking a pill to cure one's body is commendable, taking a pill in an effort to cure one's soul is deplorable.

BIBLICAL FAITH LEADS TO WHOLENESS

God's presence in our lives will gradually affect even our physical being. According to Paul, "He who raised Christ from the dead will also give life to your mortal bodies through his Spirit, who lives in you" (Romans 8:11). This reality is evident when we walk by the Spirit, for the fruit of the Spirit includes love (the character of God), joy (the antithesis of depression), peace (the opposite of anxiety), patience (the antithesis of anger), self-control, and a number of other characteristics of a healthy, mature person (see Galatians 5:22–23). The connection between the initiating cause (the Spirit of truth working in our lives) and the end result (love, joy, peace, patience, self-control) is the mind, which directs the brain, which in turn regulates all our glands and muscular movements.

For example, when Jesus was here on earth, he asked two blind men, "'Do you believe that I am able to do this [have mercy on you and heal you]?' 'Yes Lord,' they replied. Then he touched their eyes and said, 'According to your faith will it be done to you'" (Matthew 9:28–29). The external power of Jesus was made effective by their choice to believe.

In other words, the Lord chose to bring about a physical healing through the channel of their belief. Is this not true in every other aspect of life? We are saved by faith (see Ephesians 2:8) and sanctified by faith (see Galatians 3:3–5); we also walk, or live, by faith (see 2 Corinthians 5:7). God never bypasses the mind; rather, he works through it, transforming us by the renewing of our minds (see Romans 12:2). God makes possible the renewing of our minds by his very presence in our lives. We respond in faith by choosing to believe the truth and to live by the power of the Holy Spirit so that we do not gratify the desires of the flesh (see Galatians 5:16). Jesus is not only "the way" (how we should live) and "the life" (our spiritual union with God) but also "the truth" (what we should believe—see John 14:6). Even the operation of spiritual gifts incorporates the use of our minds. Note how the apostle Paul determines to exercise his gifts: "I will pray with my spirit, but I will also pray with my mind; I will sing with my spirit, but I will also sing with my mind" (1 Corinthians 14:15).

COGNITIVE-BEHAVIORAL THERAPY

We noted earlier that we have very little direct control of our emotions, but we can change how we think and we can choose what we believe. Many secular psychologists, such as Albert Ellis and Aaron T. Beck, have been saying for years that our emotions are essentially a product of our thoughts. Christian counselors such as William Backus, the author of *Telling Yourself the Truth*, and David Stoop, the author of *Self-Talk*, say essentially the same thing.[7] Cognitive-behavioral therapy will be discussed in more detail in chapter nine as part of our tool kit for counselors, but it's appropriate to introduce it here.

The essential premise of cognitive-behavioral therapy is that certain "precipitating" events do not cause an emotional response; rather, the emotional response is determined by how the mind *interprets* the events. Recall that our brains receive the external data through our five senses and that our minds interpret the data, which in turn determines our volitional and emotional response. For instance, if two people hear the sound of a slamming door in their house at night, one might become afraid while the other ignores it. Why the difference? The first person thought they were alone and concluded that someone was breaking in. The second person, however, had previously invited a relative to enter the house (thus the noise created no fear) but had failed to tell the first person. If what a person believes or thinks does not conform to the truth, then what that person feels will not conform to reality.

Cognitive-behavioral therapy is perhaps the fastest-growing and most widely accepted approach to counseling at the present time. Psychologist Albert Ellis describes this treatment as the replacement of irrational beliefs with "a number of realistic, flexible, effective new philosophies."[8] The process of helping others or yourself would typically follow this sequence:

1. First, the client is helped to see the connection between negative thoughts, the emotions they create, and the behaviors that follow.
2. Then the client is taught to recognize and monitor negative thoughts or distortions of reality. Thoughts or beliefs leading to negative feelings and improper responses to life are identified as ineffective or dysfunctional.
3. Next, the client examines the evidence for and against such distorted thinking or perceptions of reality. What does the evidence indicate? Is this thinking true or false, rational or irrational, biblical or unbiblical? Is the client going to continue to think in this way, to believe what is being thought, and to act accordingly — or will the client change? This is decision time.
4. If the client concludes that what has been believed is not true and that his or her perception of reality was not right, then the client must substitute new ways of thinking and responding.
5. Finally, the client is helped to identify and change the inappropriate assumptions that predisposed him or her to distort the experiences in the first place.

The description of this process is about as close to the description of the concept of Christian repentance as one can get. Still, we would add one crucial element to this list. If you have distorted, false, and negative beliefs about God, yourself, and the world, then you are in disagreement with what God said about himself, yourself, and the world in which live. This disagreement can be described as "missing the mark," which is a common way to describe sin. Paul writes, "Everything that does not come from faith is sin" (Romans 14:23). Christians repent when they *agree* with God that what they have believed is not true and that what they have done is not right, then *turn* from those false beliefs and destructive behaviors. Confession is simply agreeing with God. If the old, world-based beliefs are substituted with Christian beliefs based on the eternal Word of God, then this is true repentance. The word *repentance* in the original Greek language (*metanoia*) literally means "a change of mind," a change that must take place within us if we are going to live a truly liberated Christian life.

TAKE CAPTIVE EVERY THOUGHT

Since we are called to repent and be transformed by the renewing of our minds, we are in essential agreement with the cognitive approach to therapy. Likewise, since we are saved and sanctified by faith, we must learn to know and choose to believe the truth. There are, however, two other critical issues often overlooked in our Western world — issues that, if ignored, will leave us short of a complete answer. The first is to understand the spiritual battle for our minds; the second is to understand the need to abide in Christ.

Computer programmers coined the acronym *GIGO*, which means "Garbage in, garbage out." Jesus said, "The good man brings good things out of the good stored up in his heart, and the evil man brings evil things out of the evil stored up in his heart. For out of the overflow of his heart his mouth speaks" (Luke 6:45). We have to be very careful what we put into our minds, hence the need to "take captive every thought to make it obedient to Christ" (2 Corinthians 10:5). It makes no difference where the thought originates, whether from the television set, the radio, a book, a speaker, our memory bank, one of our own original thoughts, or the father of lies. We are to take captive every thought to make it obedient to Christ.

If what we are thinking is not true according to God's Word, then we should not pay attention to it. Rather, we must follow Paul's advice: "Whatever is true, whatever is noble, whatever is right, whatever is pure, whatever is lovely, whatever is admirable — if anything is excellent or praiseworthy — think about such things" (Philippians 4:8). In short, we do not get rid of negative thoughts by trying not to think of them; we overcome them by choosing the truth and continuing to choose it until the negative thoughts are drowned out or are completely replaced by the truth. We let Christ's peace rule in our hearts by letting the words of Christ dwell richly within us (see Colossians 3:15 – 16). If we want to experience the freedom that Christ purchased for us (see Romans 8:2; Galatians 5:1) and have a peace of mind that transcends all understanding (see Philippians 4:7), then we must choose to think only those thoughts that perfectly align with the Word of God.

Every computer owner knows the potential of a computer to contract a "virus." A virus may be a harmless irritation, or it may cause severe damage to programs residing on the computer. Computer viruses are often not accidents but intentional creations — some from commercial software contaminated by disgruntled employees, some from programs created by devious people who aim to introduce a killer virus into any system that accesses them. Therefore, most computer systems have programs that scan for viruses — and so should we.

It's not always easy to detect a virus in our own belief system, because the primary strategy of the enemy is *deception*. Every Christian is subject to tempting, accusing, and deceiving thoughts, which is exactly why we are instructed to put on the armor of God and to take up the shield of faith and stand against the flaming arrows Satan aims at our minds (see Ephesians 6:10–18). Why is deception the most devious of his schemes? If you were tempted, you would know it. If you were accused, you would know it. But if you were deceived, you wouldn't know it. In the Garden of Eden, Eve was deceived and believed a lie. It's hard to stand against deception, and that's why Jesus prays for his followers: "My prayer is not that you take them out of the world but that you protect them from the evil one.... Sanctify them by the truth; your word is truth" (John 17:15, 17). The apostle Paul shared with the Corinthians his fear of deception: "But I am afraid that just as Eve was deceived by the serpent's cunning, your minds may somehow be led astray from your sincere and pure devotion to Christ" (2 Corinthians 11:3). Later, writing to Timothy, Paul observes, "The Spirit clearly says that in later times some will abandon the faith and follow deceiving spirits and things taught by demons" (1 Timothy 4:1).

We've seen evidence of this all over the world: People struggle with their thoughts, have difficulty concentrating, and hear "voices." These "voices" or negative thoughts are usually self-condemning, suicidal, delusional, and phobic, with the result that these people contend with feelings of guilt, fear, hopelessness, sadness, and deep despair. Therapists typically associate such symptoms with diagnoses of depression, anxiety disorders, or psychosis. If a client communicated these symptoms to a secular therapist or doctor, chemical imbalance would typically be identified as the cause, and the client would probably be prescribed some kind of tranquilizer, antipsychotic medication, or antidepressant drug.

It's important to consider the possibility of a neurological problem, to be sure, but earnest and thoughtful questions need to be asked. How can a chemical produce a thought that is personal, and how can our neurotransmitters randomly fire in such a way as to produce a thought that one is opposed to thinking? Is this an organically based mental illness, or is it a battle for the mind? Is mental illness primarily a hardware problem, or a software problem? Why is it difficult for a committed Christian to believe that these negative thoughts are either patterns of the sinful flesh learned from living in a fallen world or flaming arrows from Satan — situations that Scripture clearly warns us about (see Ephesians 6:16; 1 Peter 5:8)? If truth be told, therapists with a secular worldview would very likely not even consider such possibilities.

A person is generally considered to be mentally healthy if he or she is in touch with reality and relatively free from anxiety. Thus, people who hear voices or see things therapists cannot hear or see would be considered mentally ill according to conventional wisdom. However, ironically, the one who may be out of touch with reality is the secular therapist. What people are hearing and seeing is very real and can be dealt with by submitting to God and resisting the devil (see James 4:7). We get unsolicited testimonies from people all over the world who have been set free from these condemning thoughts and voices. They are now experiencing the peace of God that guards their hearts and minds (see Philippians 4:7), and they are emotionally free. Therapists could not hear or see what their clients were hearing and seeing, because the battle was in the mind. There was no physical sound or material object present that would reflect light. Christian therapists must remember that our battle may not be against flesh and blood but rather against the dark forces of evil (see Ephesians 6:12).

THE PRESENCE OF GOD

Not only have secular psychologists and many Christian therapists overlooked the kingdom of darkness and the possibility that spiritual warfare could be part of the counseling process, they have also completely overlooked the real presence of Jesus Christ. To understand the reality of the spiritual world requires biblical faith. However, contemporary secular psychology has not consulted the only authoritative source of truth about God, humans, and the world in which we live. Moreover, some Christian therapists live out a practical dichotomy, holding to "psychology only" in the office and "Christ only" in their religious practices.

While conducting research for his book on anxiety disorders, Neil Anderson came across the testimony of psychologist Edmund Bourne, a highly credible practitioner who specialized in helping those who were struggling with anxiety disorders. Bourne is the author of *The Anxiety & Phobia Workbook,*[9] which won the Benjamin Franklin Book Award for Excellence in Psychology. Dr. Bourne entered this field of study because he struggled personally with anxiety disorders. Five years after the publication of the first edition of his workbook, his own anxiety disorder took a turn for the worse — a circumstance that caused him to reevaluate his own life as well as his approach to treatment. In 1998 he published a new book called *Healing Fear*. In the foreword he writes:

> The guiding metaphor for this book is "healing" as an approach to overcoming anxiety, in contrast to "applied technology." I feel it's important to introduce this perspective into the field of anxiety treatment since the vast majority of self-help books available (including my first book) utilize the applied technology approach. These books present — in a variety of ways — the mainstream cognitive behavioral methodology for treating anxiety disorders. Cognitive behavioral therapy reflects the dominant zeitgeist of Western society — a worldview that has primary faith in scientifically validated technologies that give humans knowledge and power to overcome obstacles to successful adaptation.... I don't want to diminish the importance of cognitive behavioral therapy (CBT) and the applied technology approach. Such an approach produces effective results in many cases, and I use it in my professional practice every day. In the past few years, though, I feel that the cognitive behavior strategy has reached its limits. CBT and medication can produce results quickly and are very compatible with the brief therapy, managed-care environment in the mental health profession at present. When follow-up is done over one-to three-year intervals, however, some of the gains are lost. Relapses occur rather often, and people seem to get themselves back into the same difficulties that precipitated the original anxiety disorder.[10]

Dr. Bourne seems to be saying a similar thing to what was communicated by the prophet Jeremiah over 2,500 years ago: "They dress the wound of my people as though it were not serious. 'Peace, peace,' they say, when there is no peace" (Jeremiah 6:14). In a sense, Bourne's words read like a modern-day commentary on Paul's admonition in Colossians 2:8 as well: "See to it that no one takes you captive through hollow and deceptive philosophy, which depends on human tradition and the basic principles of this world rather than on Christ." After carefully evaluating the issues, Dr. Bourne draws the conclusion that "anxiety arises from a state of disconnection."[11] We agree — and we would add that the primary disconnection is from God.

From a Christian perspective, cognitive-behavioral therapy is a valuable part of the repentance process, as long as it is biblically based. Repentance begins by admitting I was wrong, that what I believed was not true. I choose not to believe that anymore, and I choose to believe the truth according to God's Word and live accordingly from this day on. In a secular clinical setting, the outcome typically involves realizing one's error in thinking and disputing it; in a Christian clinical setting, however, it is crucial to remember that God grants repentance, and the Holy Spirit guides a client into all truth. Renewing our minds is essential for sanctification, and the truth will set us free — without a doubt. But if all we do is have our minds renewed, living the Christian life can become nothing more than carrying out an intellectual exercise. Freedom cannot be fully accomplished without the presence of God and fellowship in the body of Christ. Thus, when Jesus was asked by a law expert what the greatest commandment is, he stated, " 'Love the Lord your God with all your heart and with all your soul and with all your mind.' This is the first and greatest commandment. And the second is like it: 'Love your neighbor as yourself' " (Matthew 22:37 – 39). We absolutely need God and we need each other in order to live free and productive lives. Furthermore, in order to live and walk by faith, we must know the truth. Jesus is the truth (see John 14:6), his word is truth (see John 17:17), the Holy Spirit has come to guide us into all truth (see John 16:13), and that truth will set us free (see John 8:32).

We don't know for sure whether Edmund Bourne has a saving knowledge of Jesus Christ, but in his own search for answers he came to the following conclusion — a conclusion with which we heartily concur:

> In my own experience, spirituality has been important, and I believe it will come to play an increasingly important role in the psychology of the future. Holistic medicine, with its interest in meditation, prayer, and the role of spiritual healing in recovery from serious illness, has become a mainstream movement in the nineties. I believe there will be a "holistic psychology" in the not too distant future, like holistic medicine, [that] integrates scientifically based treatment approaches with alternative, more spiritually based modalities.[12]

5

God, Client, and Therapist in Christian Counseling

The most important thought that ever occupied my mind is that of my individual responsibility to God.

DANIEL WEBSTER

If you can explain every good thing that happens in your life in terms of hard work and good old-fashioned human ingenuity, then where is God? If your education has taught you how to help a person by using skillful techniques, effective support groups, and other human props, then where is God? If you believe you can help people resolve all their conflicts, find purpose and meaning in life, and see that their needs are met without God, then you are in league with the god of this world. For, you see, that's exactly what Satan is trying to do. Enticing us to think and act independently of God is the goal of every temptation. So it is that the apostle Paul warns us, "See to it that no one takes you captive through hollow and deceptive philosophy, which depends on human tradition and the basic principles of this world rather than on Christ" (Colossians 2:8).

Integrating God into the therapeutic process is what sets Christian counseling apart from secular counseling. Christian counselors know that apart from Christ they can do nothing (see John 15:5), that while they may be able to help a person cope for a season, in the end they can only postpone the inevitable. Successful Christian therapists are alive and free in Christ and will not be tempted to minister independently of God. They seek to be filled with and led by God's Spirit. They also realize they are not the ultimate answer for their clients, nor can they fill the role of the Holy Spirit in their clients' lives.

ROLE RESPONSIBILITIES

A great deal of psychological literature discusses the role relationship between the therapist and client. Most therapists have been trained not to be rescuers or enablers, and they know the boundaries in the therapist-client relationship. However, relatively few have received training on how to view the role that only God can play in the therapeutic relationship. Moreover, there may be certain Christian therapists who think it unnecessary to invite God's presence, because they know that God is omnipresent. Nevertheless, every Christian therapy session includes three participants, as illustrated below (see Figure 5.1):

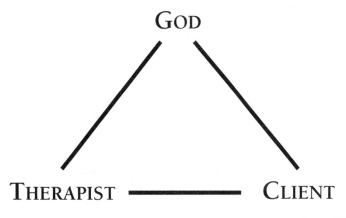

FIGURE 5.1

In the case of Christian counselors, one hopes there exists an intimate relationship between the therapist and God. What remains to be established is a right relationship between the therapist and the client and a right relationship between the client and God. All three participants have an important role to play — a role that cannot be played by either of the other two without hindering the process. We'll first discuss God's sovereign role, which is something we often take time to explain to our Christian clients. In the course of living there is a very precise line between divine sovereignty and human responsibility, as shown in Figure 5.2.

Christians may place the line in different places, depending on our theology, but we all agree that there is a line. Everything on the left side of the line is God's responsibility, and if we try to do what only God can do, we will invariably become frustrated and ultimately fail. We are not

GOD'S SOVEREIGNTY

MAN'S RESPONSIBILITY

FIGURE 5.2

the Creator, and we cannot save ourselves; we should not try to be someone else's conscience, and we cannot change another person. Nothing will interfere more with therapy than attempting to play the role of God in another person's life. The truth of the matter is that God will always be faithful to his Word and to his covenant relationship with us.

The key to successful Christian therapy is to know God and to understand his ways. The prophet Jeremiah describes God as declaring, "Let not the wise man boast of his wisdom or the strong man boast of his strength or the rich man boast of his riches, but let him who boasts boast about this: that he understands and knows me, that I am the LORD, who exercises kindness, justice and righteousness on earth, for in these I delight" (Jeremiah 9:23 – 24). Jesus is "the way and the truth and the life" (John 14:6). There is no other way that works for all eternity. Jesus is the absolute truth, and by virtue of his life we can live accordingly by faith. Anyone can choose to live another way, and many will at their own peril. God's Word teaches us, "There is a way that seems right to a man, but in the end it leads to death" (Proverbs 14:12).

The Creator designed us to live a certain way. When we rebel against God and live another way, it leads to death. To make this declaration always invites scorn from non-Christians and pricks the pride of the self-sufficient. Perhaps an analogy will illustrate why it's easy to react so strongly against the Creator's design. Suppose you purchase a new computer that is formatted differently from your old one. You want so badly to use this new computer in the same way you used your old one, but you can't. You will have to learn an entirely new way. The company designed this new computer to work "one way." If you want to produce any good work at all, you're going to have to learn to use it the way the designer created it to work.

The right side of the line in Figure 5.2 depicts our responsibility — a responsibility revealed to us in Scripture. God will not do for us what he has instructed us to do; in fact, he cannot. God can only do that which is consistent with his nature and his word. For example, God cannot lie, and he will not deviate from his word or his way: "The grass withers and the flowers fall, but the word of our God stands forever" (Isaiah 40:8). The truth that God is immutable is what gives consistency to our life. Because "Jesus Christ is the same yesterday and today and forever" (Hebrews 13:8), we can count on him. It would do us no good to pray and ask God to think for us, when he instructed us to think for ourselves (see 1 Corinthians 14:20; Philippians 4:8). He will not believe for us, repent for us, forgive others for us, and so on, but he will enable us to do all he has commanded us to do.

The devil has a field day when we fail to understand this simple truth. We expect God to act a certain way, and when he doesn't we're disappointed with him. Or perhaps we pray, and nothing happens. Could it be that "when you ask, you do not receive, because you ask with wrong motives" (James 4:3)? Not recognizing who is responsible for what is even more devastating when it comes to spiritual conflicts. For example, suppose a child suddenly becomes aware of some spiritual presence in his room, pulls the covers over his head, and cries out, "God, do something!" But God doesn't seem to do anything. So he wonders, "Why don't you do something, God? You're all-powerful. You can make it go away. Maybe you don't care, or maybe I'm not a Christian. Maybe that's why you won't help me!"

By the time people caught in these kinds of struggles seek help, they're typically questioning God and their own salvation. They assume God didn't do anything — but they're wrong. God defeated the devil decisively and positioned the church with Christ's authority over the kingdom of darkness. Whose responsibility is it to resist the devil, to put on the armor of God, and to take captive every thought to make it obedient to Christ? But what if we don't meet our own responsibilities? Will God meet them for us? Defeated Christians often ask God to take their responsibility for them, or they ask him to change just this one time in order to accommodate them. Yet, if he did, he would no longer be God. God will always stay true to his character and will always keep his word. Therefore, we can claim his promises and rest in the finished work of Jesus Christ.

THE CLIENT'S RESPONSIBILITY

To our knowledge there is only one place in Scripture that explains what the sick or suffering are supposed to do. Take note of these words from the book of James:

> Is any one of you in trouble? He should pray. Is anyone happy? Let him sing songs of praise. Is any one of you sick? He should call the elders of the church to pray over him and anoint him with oil in the name of the Lord. And the prayer offered in faith will make the sick person well; the Lord will raise him up. If he has sinned, he will be forgiven. Therefore confess your sins to each other and pray for each other so that you may be healed. The prayer of a righteous man is powerful and effective.
>
> —JAMES 5:13–16

The focus of this passage is usually on the role of the elders, while the responsibility and role of the suffering and the sick are often overlooked. The righteous man's prayer will not be very effective if the following three principles are overlooked:

First, we cannot do other people's praying for them. Initially, the one who is suffering is the one who should be praying. We believe in intercessory prayer, to be sure, but such prayer is never intended to supercede another person's responsibility to pray. The point is that I cannot do your praying for you: "For there is one God and one mediator between God and men, the man Christ Jesus" (1 Timothy 2:5). We can never play the role of a mediator in another person's life. We believe in the priesthood of the believer. Thus, every child of God has the same access to our heavenly Father, and no therapist or pastor can step between the two and ask God on behalf of the other. If one of two children came to their father and said, "Johnny wants to know if he can go to the movie," a wise parent would say, "Go back and tell Johnny he needs to ask me himself." The relationship between father and son is far more important than the movie.

Neil recalls the time a pastor came to his office with a young man who was hearing voices. Three hours later the young man left with a clear mind. The pastor was amazed, not with the results but with the process. "What a trap I have gotten myself into," the pastor proclaimed. "People come to me all the time and ask me to pray for them. Of course I do, but not once have I shown them how to pray for themselves—and I have seen little or no results from doing their praying for them." Nor has any other pastor or therapist, for that matter.

The only effective prayer at this stage is the prayer of a repentant heart. Chances are, the suffering person's own prayer hasn't been effective, and the psalmist explains why: "If I regard iniquity in my heart, the Lord will not hear me" (Psalm 66:18 King James Version). The answer is to deal with the iniquity, not to ask someone else to do your praying for you. We cannot have a secondhand relationship with God. Expecting the therapist or pastor to petition God for us is abdicating our responsibility—and it will not work.

After Neil participated in a Christian recovery conference, a licensed therapist asked for Neil's help. Three hours later she walked out free. At the door she paused and said, "I always thought someone else had to pray for me." That perception is common among pastoral counselors and clients. We've learned to put that responsibility back where it belongs—on the client. Conviction of sin and divine guidance come directly from God to all his children. *We* do not pray and ask God to show us, so we in turn can tell the client. In our process, *the client* prays, and God reveals what he wants to reveal to the client.

The same is true for testing the spirits. John wrote, "Dear friends, do not believe every spirit, but test the spirits to see whether they are from God" (1 John 4:1). The passage does not say, "Have your pastor or somebody more spiritual than you test the spirits for you." One young man said, "This voice in my head says it wants to go to heaven with me." Neil instructed him to pray and to ask God to show him the true nature of the voice. The young man did so, and immediately he knew it was a filthy spirit. When he told it to leave in the name of Jesus, it left. It was his responsibility to test the spirit and to tell it to depart.

The second principle taught in this passage is this: Christians will never experience victory, wholeness, or mental, emotional, and spiritual health until they assume their own responsibility for doing their part. This principle relates to who it is that God holds responsible for taking the initiative to call the elders of the church. No one can be healthy for someone else. Good health is not contagious; only sickness is. No one can eat right and get enough exercise and enough rest for another person. The same holds true for spiritual maturity and victory in Christ. No one can practice Christian spiritual disciplines for another person. Some clients will come with the attitude, "Fix me!" If you are moved by love for them, you will help them understand that you cannot fix them. Only God can change who they are, and if any lasting change is to take place in their lives, it will be directly related to what they have chosen to believe and to do in response to God.

Once, when Neil conducted a conference at a church, he was greeted by the pastor, who said, "I have fifty lay prayer-counselors to help you." They were wonderful intercessors who had been taught to pray for others. Routinely at every worship service at this church, people were invited to come forward for prayer, and they did so, making all kinds of requests. The prayer-counselors would anoint them with oil and intercede on their behalf. Interestingly, there was also a professional counseling center operated by the church; after the conference, Neil met with the professional counselors and asked, "Does what you do in the church service create problems for you in counseling?" They all agreed that people from their own church were the hardest to counsel. Why would that be?

Obviously, there is nothing wrong with praying for people's needs, and what these prayer-counselors were doing revealed that this was a caring church. It willingly allotted time in the worship service to address people's individual needs; most churches make no provision for such an opportunity. The problem was with the subtle message being conveyed to the congregation: If someone's marriage was going to be saved, if some rebellious child was to come home, God was the only one who had to do something.

Thus, when members of that congregation sought personal counseling, they expected the counselor to anoint them with oil and pray over them. What was being overlooked was *their own responsibility*. What more does God need to do in order for us to live a victorious life in Christ? He defeated the devil, forgave our sins, set us free from our past, made us new creations in Christ, empowered us with his Holy Spirit, gave us his rule book for life, and told us to repent and walk by faith in accordance with the truth. The only missing ingredient is our response to him with a heart of repentance and faith.

The third principle is this: Confession, which is honest and open agreement with God, must come before healing. This principle derives from the order of Scripture: "Therefore confess your sins to each other and pray for each other so that you may be healed. The prayer of a righteous man is powerful and effective" (James 5:16). If there is any one principle that is uniformly believed in the field of recovery (secular or Christian), it is the need to get out of denial and start facing the truth. Confession comes before healing.

Suppose you have a rebellious son with whom you have a strained relationship. One day you tell him to mow the lawn, but he doesn't obey.

Later he comes with a request. "Dad, I have a hot date tonight. I need the keys to the car and twenty dollars." Would you give it to him? Would God? We don't think so. We think a righteous heavenly Father would say, "Son, you have many unresolved issues in your life that are seriously affecting your relationship with me. Why don't you seek reconciliation with me; then we'll see if the money and car are really what is best for you."

All too often elders are called to pray for sick people, only to discover later that these people were living in bondage to sin, bitterness, pride, and rebellion. Many may very well be sick for psychosomatic reasons. If you love them, you will help them resolve their personal and spiritual conflicts first. If the sick and the suffering are truly repentant, then the prayers of the righteous will be effective. Since healing follows confession in this Scripture passage, one could conclude that James is addressing only those who are sick because they are living outside of God's will.

THE THERAPIST'S RESPONSIBILITY

THE TRUTH ENCOUNTER

While it is crucial that we help our clients learn to submit to God, James says we must also "resist the devil" (4:7). If you try to resist the devil without first submitting to God, you may end up with a very unpleasant experience; on the other hand, you can submit to God but not resist the devil — and stay in bondage. The tragedy is that many recovery ministries and Christian counselors do not advocate both submitting to God and resisting the devil.

This raises a question: How do we know whether a problem is spiritual or psychological? The question implies a false dichotomy. Personal problems are never not psychological — that is, our mind, emotions, and will are always a part of the problem as well as a part of the solution. On this side of eternity, our humanity is never excluded from the process. God works through our minds and does not bypass them. On the other hand, our problems are never not spiritual. There is no time when God is not present, for Christ sustains "all things by his powerful word" (Hebrews 1:3). There is also no time when one can safely take off the armor of God (see Ephesians 6:10–18). The possibility of being tempted, accused, and deceived by the enemy is ever-present.

If we accept both realities, we will stop polarizing our responses to problems. We will not utilize psychotherapeutic marketplace practices that ignore the reality of the spiritual world, nor will we focus exclusively on a deliverance ministry that overlooks the personal responsibility of the client. Neither paradigm is sufficient. We have a whole, perfect God who takes into account every reality and who relates to whole persons. So it must be with the Christian therapist as well.

How can we recognize when and how demons may be implicated in a problem, and, when they are, what we can do about it? To answer these questions, we must understand the whole gospel and the historical progression from the Old Testament (the old covenant) to the New Testament (the new covenant).

In the last chapter we discussed two-thirds of the gospel message. First, Jesus died for our sins, and we are forgiven if we put our trust in him. Second, Jesus was resurrected, which gave us new life "in him." If we omit the resurrection from our gospel presentation, we end up with forgiven sinners instead of redeemed saints. The final third of the gospel has to do with spiritual warfare. Thus John writes, "The reason the Son of God appeared was to destroy the devil's work" (1 John 3:8) — which is just as much a part of the gospel message as the truth that our sins are forgiven.

In preparation for the day of Pentecost (Acts 2), which ushered in the church age, Jesus trained his twelve disciples by sending them out to minister: "When Jesus had called the Twelve together, he gave them power and authority to drive out all demons" (Luke 9:1). When he trained the seventy-two, they "returned with joy and said, 'Lord, even the demons submit to us in your name'" (10:17). Notice how the Lord responded to their joyful report: "He replied, 'I saw Satan fall like lightning from heaven. I have given you authority to trample on snakes and scorpions and to overcome all the power of the enemy; nothing will harm you. However, do not rejoice that the spirits submit to you, but rejoice that your names are written in heaven'" (10:18–20).

Several intervention principles can be discerned. First, the church has authority and power over the kingdom of darkness. Authority is the right to rule; power is the ability to rule. As members of the body of Christ, Christian therapists have this delegated authority because of their position in Christ; they have power when they are filled with the Holy Spirit. Therefore, we are admonished to "be strong in the Lord and in his mighty power" (Ephesians 6:10). In the Great Commission Jesus said,

"All authority in heaven and on earth has been given to me. Therefore go and make disciples of all nations" (Matthew 28:18–19). We minister by virtue of Christ's authority and power. We cannot use either one at our own discretion. The moment we do so we are operating according to the flesh instead of according to the Spirit. We have the authority to do God's will — nothing more, nothing less.

Second, this authority is what the church and the born-again therapist have over the kingdom of darkness, but not over each other. In the Luke 10 passage, "snakes and scorpions" refer to the devil and his demons; slimy snakes and bugs are not our enemy. By all means we are to resist the kingdom of darkness, but the Bible teaches that we are to submit to the governing authorities that God in his grace and wisdom has given us to guide our societal relationships (home, school, work, and state).

Third, we must not let the devil set the agenda. God sets the agenda, and we must remember that he is in control. As Jesus declares, we are to rejoice that our names "are written in heaven" (Luke 10:20), that we are "children of God" (John 1:12). Paul offers a similar warning against letting the devil set the agenda: "But I am afraid that just as Eve was deceived by the serpent's cunning, your minds may somehow be led astray from your sincere and pure devotion to Christ" (2 Corinthians 11:3).

Before the cross, Satan was not a defeated foe. It took a special, endowed authority-agent to drive out demons. After the cross, Satan and his demons are defeated, and the church has been raised up to be seated with Christ in the heavenly realms (see Ephesians 2:6). We are "heirs of God and co-heirs with Christ" (Romans 8:17). Every child of God, and thus every Christian therapist, possesses the same spiritual position and therefore the same authority over the kingdom of darkness. Paul declares this gospel message in his letter to the Colossian church:

> When you were dead in your sins and in the uncircumcision of your sinful nature, God made you alive with Christ. He forgave us all our sins, having canceled the written code, with its regulations, that was against us and that stood opposed to us; he took it away, nailing it to the cross. And having disarmed the powers and authorities, he made a public spectacle of them, triumphing over them by the cross.
>
> —*COLOSSIANS 2:13–15*

The following incident illustrates how this authority works in practice. Once Neil was counseling a woman who was struggling with a dissociative identity disorder (DID) due to ritual abuse. She suddenly got out of her chair with glazed eyes and began walking toward him. What would you do as a therapist? Neil calmly took his place in Christ and said, "I am a child of God; the evil one cannot touch me. Sit down" (see 1 John 5:18). The woman immediately stopped her forward motion and returned to her chair. You see, authority does not increase with volume. We do not shout out the devil. (The same holds true, by the way, for parental authority. If you are shouting at your children in an attempt to control them, you are not properly exercising your God-given authority; in fact, you are undermining it.)

Exercising our authority in psychotherapeutic sessions requires us to speak the truth in love (see Ephesians 4:15). For example, our children have no obligation to obey our thoughts, and neither does the devil. Only God is omniscient; only he knows the thoughts and attitudes of the heart (see Hebrews 4:12). Although it may seem that Satan knows our thoughts perfectly, he does not. He does, however, have the advantage of observing us twenty-four hours of each day (therapists as well as clients), so he can fairly well determine what we are thinking—for we typically "will out" our thought life at some time or another. Moreover, it's easy for Satan to know what we're thinking if he is the one who has given us the thought.

Both therapist and client can be spiritually deceived, which is why we are called to make our profession of faith public. We do this in our counseling sessions by setting forth our biblical worldview both verbally and in writing. As Paul declares, "For it is with your heart that you believe and are justified, and it is with your mouth that you confess and are saved" (Romans 10:10).

Every occult practice dabbles either with the mind or the future, and in reality it's often both. Satan wants us to believe he knows our minds and the future, but he does not. Many of our clients have visited fortune-tellers, consulted New Age mediums, and read their horoscopes in an effort to discern the future; even in Christian circles the desire to know the future has led many to be caught up in prophetic movements. We have to learn to trust God for tomorrow and to live responsible lives today by seeking the power of revealed truth, not the hidden, esoteric "knowledge" of gurus, psychics, New Age mediums, and false prophets.

Many therapists avoid dealing with spiritual issues out of fear. They're afraid that clients will report them to the professional board, that clients will be offended, that they as therapists will violate the value of political correctness, or that they will encounter disapproval from managed care authorities. This kind of fear plays right into Satan's hand. He wants to be feared, because he wants to be worshiped. But there is not a single Bible verse that tells us to fear Satan. The only legitimate object of fear is God, and the fear of God is the beginning of wisdom (see Proverbs 1:7). Thus the apostle Paul explains, "For God did not give us a spirit of timidity, but a spirit of power, of love and of self-discipline" (2 Timothy 1:7).

Moreover, some therapists and pastors feel insecure about dealing with spiritual issues. They are not sure what they would do if they detected spiritual opposition—a concern that usually disappears when they understand how to maintain control in the counseling session by placing the responsibility where it belongs, namely, back on the client. For example, whenever we suspect demonic interference, we ask the client to do one significant thing: to share with us what is going on in his or her mind. The mind is the control center, so if a client does not lose control, we do not have to fear losing control either. The power for the Christian therapist lies in the truth; the power of the devil is in the lie. If you expose the lie, the power is broken, because Jesus has already "disarmed the powers and authorities" (Colossians 2:15).

People's lives are often like houses in which spills haven't been cleaned up and the garbage hasn't been taken out for weeks—which, of course, attracts a lot of flies. The natural tendency is to focus on getting rid of the flies because they are so irritating. Consequently, some deliverance ministries study the flight patterns of flies, determine their rank structure, and learn all their names in order to cast them out. They are swatting flies instead of getting rid of the garbage. Even if they do get rid of the flies, there is nothing to keep them from coming back, maybe even seven times worse (see Luke 11:26). A better answer is to ignore the flies and to get rid of the garbage. Repentance and faith in God are, have been, and will continue to be the answer in this present age. Once the client has submitted to God, it is no problem to resist the devil; he no longer has any right to be there!

Some therapists interpret spiritual problems to represent a power encounter between the spiritual forces of good and the spiritual forces of evil. Whenever a spiritual problem is discerned, they call in the missionary, pastor, or counselor, who will then do battle with the evil one. These helpers will attempt to call up the demons and proceed to drive them out. In this kind of deliverance ministry, the deliverer is the *pastoral agent*, who is getting information from the demons. But why should we believe the demons? Whenever the devil or his demons speak, they do so from their own nature, and it is their nature to lie, because Satan is "the father of lies" (John 8:44).

We believe the Epistles tell a different story. The deliverer is *Jesus Christ,* and he has already come. What's more, therapists should be getting their information from the Holy Spirit, the Spirit of truth, who will then guide clients into all truth (see John 16:13), a truth that will set them free (see John 8:32). Setting a captive free is better understood as a truth encounter, because it is the truth that sets captives free. It is never our responsibility to defeat the devil; Jesus has already done that (see Hebrews 2:14). Rather, the therapist has the privilege of facilitating this truth encounter, either in the counseling office or through collaboration with the church.

It's important to note that the Epistles contain no instructions to drive out demons. Satan was defeated at the cross, and every believer possesses the same authority over the devil and his angels. The responsibility has shifted from the outside pastoral agent to the individual. The therapist cannot put on the armor of God for the client, resist the devil for the client, or take captive every thought to make it obedient to Christ for the client. No therapist can repent, believe, confess, or forgive others for the client; the therapist can only help the client. All a therapist can do is what Paul describes in his second letter to Timothy:

> The Lord's servant must not quarrel; instead, he must be kind to everyone, able to teach, not resentful. Those who oppose him he must gently instruct, in the hope that God will grant them repentance leading them to a knowledge of the truth, and that they will come to their senses and escape from the trap of the devil, who has taken them captive to do his will.
>
> —2 TIMOTHY 2:24–26

THE THERAPIST'S CHARACTER

Thus far we have seen that we cannot "play God" in someone else's life, that we cannot do for others what God requires them to do. The role of a Christian therapist is more like that of a facilitator who carries out "the ministry of reconciliation" (2 Corinthians 5:18). Let's look a bit more carefully at the qualifications of the person described in 2 Timothy 2:24–26, the person God will use to liberate his people:

First, the Christian therapist must be the Lord's servant. Christian therapists must be people who are totally dependent on God. The Lord's servants begin every therapy session recognizing that they cannot bind up a client's broken heart; only God can do that. They know they cannot set anyone free; only God can do that. They cannot change their clients or make them whole; only Christ can change them and make them complete. They can share the gospel, but they remember that Jesus said, "No one can come to me unless the Father who sent me draws him" (John 6:44). Christian therapy is not just a counseling technique we learn; rather, it is a dynamic, living encounter with God, who is the "Wonderful Counselor" (Isaiah 9:6).

Second, the Christian therapist must not quarrel. Quarreling will usually put you, your client, or both of you on the defensive, which is not where you want to be. It is not the therapist's role to convince clients of anything. If they do not want to believe the truth, you have no choice but to let them. Even God would undoubtedly say to them, in essence, "Let it be done to you in accordance with how you believe." If they don't want to deal with their issues, you can't make them. It is not the role of the therapist to bring conviction; it is our role to share the truth in love.

It's clear that some clients don't want to resolve anything; they simply want to argue. We cannot yield to the temptation of trying to win the argument. An old proverb states, "A man convinced against his will is of the same opinion still." Be aware too that the devil will take a deceived client down a thousand and one rabbit trails; we must not go down these trails with a deceived client. He or she will also set up smoke screens to keep us from addressing the real issue; we must have enough discernment to see through the deception. Effective counselors know how to stay focused and keep the session moving in a meaningful direction.

Third, the Christian therapist must be kind to everyone. From the Wisdom Literature, we read, "What is desirable in a man is his kindness" (Proverbs 19:22 New American Standard Bible). Likewise, Jesus said, "Go and learn what this means: 'I desire mercy, not sacrifice'" (Matthew 9:13, quoting Hosea 6:6). In Hosea 6:6, *mercy* is the rendering of the Hebrew word *hesed*, which is translated "love," "kindness," or "unfailing love" in other passages. It's a word that typically refers to the character of God. Kindness is the one essential character trait that is a prerequisite for Christian therapy, because people will generally not be vulnerable and share openly with an unkind person.

When Neil taught pastoral counseling at Talbot School of Theology, he asked students to write on a piece of paper the most offensive thing they had ever done, that is, the one sin they would like to keep hidden from others. He watched as the anxiety level peaked, and then he said, "You don't have to do that." Do you really think they would have? Don't you think they would have put the sixth or seventh most offensive sin, and then only with great reluctance. Can you imagine what was going on in their minds? "What's he going to have us do with this piece of paper? Share it with our neighbors? Hand it in?"

Neil wanted them to experience how a client must feel when faced with the same prospect. Does the therapist really need to hear that deep, dark, awful secret? In most cases, yes — because it is often the root issue of the client's problem. For instance, a client once confessed, "I made a lunch appointment three times with a psychologist friend for the purpose of telling him about my problem with lust, but I never did. Instead I talked about marriage and family problems that were just symptoms of the real issue." These deep moral issues are what keep many from experiencing their freedom in Christ.

After Neil told his relieved students they didn't have to write down their sin, he asked them another question. "If you had to confess this information to someone, who would you tell?" He didn't want names; he wanted them to ponder what kind of person this would be and what kinds of actions this person would have to do in order to merit their trust. He had students share the number one item on their lists, which he then recorded on the board. These lists invariably included these characteristics: compassionate, loving, trustworthy, confidential, competent, godly, nonjudgmental, good listener, accepting, and someone who had an answer. Then he asked, "Who does this list describe?" With one voice they answered, "God!"

Here is the central issue in Christian therapeutic practice: If you haven't committed yourself to become a compassionate, trustworthy person, would you now? If you're not that kind of a person, no one will share root issues with you, and you'll be treating symptoms and not the underlying cause. To become a kind and loving person is God's plan for every therapist's life: "It is God's will that you should be sanctified" (1 Thessalonians 4:3). In later chapters we'll look more closely at the issue of a therapist's self-assessment.

Bear in mind, however, that there are limits to what we can accomplish by exhibiting these character traits — traits that are enhanced by training programs that help prospective counselors develop skills of congruence, accurate empathy, genuineness, concreteness, and various types of listening and probing techniques. These are good pastoral skills every Christian counselor should learn in order to draw all the necessary information out of the client so they can get at the root issues and make the right diagnosis.

Suppose a secular therapist is highly skilled and able to establish trusting relationships so that clients fully disclose their past. The therapist is able to reconstruct their past and explain with great precision why they are struggling. At this juncture, a cognitive therapist would help them understand how their thinking affects them emotionally and contributes to irresponsible behavior. Clients would very likely leave with a clearer understanding of what has been happening to them, and they may even know how to cope better in the future. However, they are still the same persons — still a product of their past on a journey of self-improvement.

Few people would be willing to share all the dirt in their lives just for the purpose of sharing it; more might be willing to share it in order to gain some understanding of why they are so dysfunctional, but that is typically as far as secular counseling can take them. You see, secular therapists have no gospel to proclaim. Christian therapy, on the other hand, is radically different. A Christian can share with God all the dirt in his or her life for the purpose of resolving it. Christianity has a theology of resolution that sets us free from our past. We cannot undo or fix anyone's past — God does not even do that — but we can be free from it. Because of the gospel, we are not primarily a product of our past; we are new creations in Christ (see 2 Corinthians 5:17).

In other words, all the intimate details do not come out when we simply listen to our clients' stories. They come out when clients are confessing and repenting before God. The Holy Spirit brings conviction (see John 16:8) and guides into all truth (see John 16:13); this is not something Christian therapists can do. As Paul notes, "Godly sorrow brings repentance that leads to salvation and leaves no regret, but worldly sorrow brings death" (2 Corinthians 7:10). Judas betrayed Jesus, experienced the sorrow of the world, and committed suicide (see Matthew 27:1 – 10). On the other hand, Peter disowned Jesus three times, came under the conviction of the Holy Spirit, and became the first spokesperson for the church (see John 18:15 – 18, 25 – 27; 21:15 – 19).

People often feel sorry when they are caught or express sorrow when confronted, but this sorrow does not always lead to repentance. People can experience a moment of catharsis with another person, then later deeply regret doing so. They leave thinking, "I cannot believe I told that person all those intimate details! What must she think of me?" But we have never seen anyone genuinely repent and regret finding his or her freedom in Christ. We frequently hear clients say, "I have never shared this with anyone before" — not because we are such good therapists, for in actuality it has little to do with us. They are sharing this for the first time with God in our presence for the purpose of resolving it, and that makes all the difference in the world.

The fourth characteristic listed by Paul in 2 Timothy 2:24–25 is this: The Christian therapist should be able to teach. The emphasis here is not on one's ability to communicate but on one's ability to apply the truth. Teaching and applying the truth is a therapist's major function in Christian therapy, for people are living in bondage to the lies they believe. Cognitive therapy will produce no liberating results if we do not know the truth. On the other hand, Jesus said, "If you hold to my teaching, you are really my disciples. Then you will know the truth, and the truth will set you free" (John 8:31–32). In order to liberate clients, the truth has to penetrate their hearts. It is not enough for a client to give mental assent, because if that's all there is, it's highly likely that nothing will change. When David came under conviction for his sin with Bathsheba, he wrote, "Surely you desire truth in the inner parts; you teach me wisdom in the inmost place" (Psalm 51:6).

Contrary to popular thinking, the dominant function of the heart is not an emotional one. The heart, according to Scripture, is first of all the place where we think, secondly where we will, and thirdly where we feel. Bible scholar H. Wheeler Robinson (1872–1945) counted in the Bible 822 uses of the word *heart* for some aspect of human personality. "According to his categorization, 204 of the 822 uses refer to intellectual activity, 195 to the volitional aspect, and 166 to an emotional state."[1] Rather than understanding the heart to be the seat of our emotions, it is better to understand it as the seat of reflection. Only in the heart do the mind, will, and emotions come together. Our emotional core is influenced the moment truth enters the heart, and together they drive the will. There is a huge difference between intellectual knowledge and experiential truth.

Every therapist has had clients who mentally nod in agreement with his or her teaching yet show no emotional response and little if any change in behavior. The truth was never "owned" by them. Clients can harden their own hearts by the deceitfulness of sin; they can be trapped in the lie that John warns us about: "If we claim to be without sin, we deceive ourselves and the truth is not in us" (1 John 1:8).

God, Client, and Therapist in Christian Counseling

The teaching of Paul articulates another reason why some clients cannot seem to process the truth:

> Brothers, I could not address you as spiritual but as worldly—mere infants in Christ. I gave you milk, not solid food, for *you were not yet ready for it*. Indeed, *you are still not ready*. You are still worldly. For since there is jealousy and quarreling among you, are you not worldly? Are you not acting like mere men?
>
> —*1 CORINTHIANS 3:1–3, EMPHASIS ADDED*

These are people who are not yet able to receive the full counsel of God (the "solid food"). We have to help them resolve their personal and spiritual conflicts first, for only then they will be able to receive the truth. David did not come to repentance until God sent Nathan to confront him with his sin. First he repented, then he knew the truth in his inner person.

We see this frequently in our counseling. For example, a father came to Neil to ask him to counsel his unmarried, sexually active daughter. Her opening statement was, "I don't want to get right with God or anything like that." Neil responded, "That's fine, but since you're here, could I help you in any way? Why don't you start by telling me your story." It turned out that the girl had been active in church until the night she was date-raped. Sexual promiscuity followed this unfortunate experience. After listening to her troubles, Neil asked, "Would you like to resolve these difficulties?" She responded affirmatively, so Neil walked her through the "Steps to Freedom in Christ." She left his office free. Her opening statement had just been a smoke screen. The joy on her face revealed the truth in her heart.

Fifth, Christian therapists must not be resentful; rather they must be patient when wronged. It's not uncommon for clients to turn on their therapists in a moment of despair. The grace of God is never more evident than when we show patience under fire. The degree of our own security in Christ will be revealed. Let clients have their emotional catharsis, even if it is momentarily very pointedly directed at you. Remember: These are hurting people who are responding out of a position of weakness. If we refrain from becoming defensive, it may very well open the door for ministry.

Not wanting to read too much into Paul's teaching in 2 Timothy 2:24–25, one might yet observe that patience is needed for another reason. It may take several hours to help a person resolve his or her conflicts. Ideally, we do not want to open a wound without closing it in the same session. In addition, knowing that some wounds can be difficult to get to and to resolve, we discuss this reality with clients and let them know we will patiently work with them for as many sessions as it takes to accomplish their treatment goals. If finances pose a problem, we work with our clients to craft a suitable payment schedule.

When people seek help, does their problem initially get worse, or better? In the vast majority of cases it will get worse for a time. So your clients may reason, "It was bad before, but now it's worse. I think I'll go back to where I was" — which is exactly what happened when the Israelites left Egypt. It was bad in Egypt but worse in the desert. So they all wanted to go back into bondage (see Numbers 14:1–4), but Moses encouraged them to press on to the Promised Land. We must do the same for our clients.

Finally, Paul's words to Timothy in 2 Timothy 2:25 teach us that Christian therapists should be gentle. Jesus described himself so memorably when he said to the crowd gathered to hear him, "Come to me, all you who are weary and burdened, and I will give you rest. Take my yoke upon you and learn from me, for I am gentle and humble in heart, and you will find rest for your souls. For my yoke is easy and my burden is light" (Matthew 11:28–30). We have been invited to walk with the gentle Jesus. Gentleness is a fruit of the Spirit (see Galatians 5:23). Being a gentle person is a cherished "Christ-value" that keeps us from running roughshod over people. We should not press ahead of God's timing or pressure people to respond. The Christian therapist is yoked with Jesus. Apart from Christ, we can do nothing (see John 15:5). God is the One who grants "repentance leading them to a knowledge of the truth" (2 Timothy 2:25), but he has chosen to work through us, his servants, to bring freedom to his people. May every Christian therapist be one of them.

The following poem, written by one of Neil's counselees, captures the need for kindness, patience, and gentleness as character traits for God's servants:

The Wreath

A friend of mine whose grapevine died, had put it out for trash.
I said to her, "I'll take that vine and make something of that."
At home the bag of dead, dry vines looked nothing but a mess,
but as I gently bent one vine, entwining 'round and 'round,
A rustic wreath began to form, potential did abound.
One vine would not go where it should, and anxious as I was,
I forced it so to change its shape, it broke — and what the cause?
If I had taken precious time to slowly change its form,
It would have made a lovely wreath, not a dead vine, broken,
   torn.
As I finished bending, adding blooms, applying trim,
I realized how that rustic wreath is like my life within.
You see, so many in my life have tried to make me change.
They've forced my spirit anxiously, I tried to rearrange.
But when the pain was far too great, they forced my fragile
   form,
I plunged far deeper in despair, my spirit broken, torn.
Then God allowed a gentle one that knew of dying vines,
To kindly, patiently allow the Lord to take his time.
And though the vine has not yet formed a decorative wreath,
I know that with God's servants' help, one day when Christ I
   meet,
He'll see a finished circle, a perfect gift to him.
It will be a final product, a wreath with all the trim.
So as you look upon this gift, the vine round and complete,
Remember God is using you to gently shape his wreath.

6

A Biblical Strategy for Christian Counseling

The theological problems of original sin, origin of evil, predestination, and the like are the soul's mumps, and measles, and whooping cough.

RALPH WALDO EMERSON

God is the author of life, not death. He formed the universe and all that is in it by the word of his mouth. He spoke matter and time into existence and uniquely created Adam and Eve in his own image. Adam and Eve had perfect communion with their Creator and with each other. All their needs were provided for in the Garden of Eden. They were without flaw in body, soul, and spirit. God even gave them dominion over the birds of the sky, the beasts of the field, and the fish of the sea (see Genesis 1:28).

But there was another presence in the Garden—a spiritual being who defied God in eternity past (see Isaiah 14:12–15). This being tried to dethrone God and set himself up to be God's equal. Such arrogance and pride caused Lucifer to lose his position, and this "model of perfection" (Ezekiel 28:12) became Satan, the accuser, evil personified. In the Garden this "father of lies" (John 8:44) whispered to Eve, "For God knows that when you eat of [the fruit] your eyes will be opened, and you will be like God, knowing good and evil" (Genesis 3:5).

Deceived into believing that God was denying her of the wisdom he alone possessed (which Eve thought was "rightfully" hers), Eve ate the forbidden fruit. Adam, who was the first in creation, failed in his leadership and willingly chose to sin (see 1 Timothy 2:14). God's new creation fell into the same rebellion as Satan, and judgment likewise fell on them. This sin of rebellion exacted a penalty—death. Just as Satan lost his honored position with God, Adam and Eve lost their position and dominion over the earth, not only for themselves but also for all their descendants. Satan became the rebel holder of spiritual authority by default; he became "the prince of this world" (John 14:30), "the ruler of the kingdom of the air, the spirit who is now at work in those who are disobedient" (Ephesians 2:2). John says, "We know that we are children of God, and that the whole world is under the control of the evil one" (1 John 5:19). Every Christian therapist needs to understand these teachings and how they permeate every counseling session.

The once-perfect creation became corrupt. Entropy and death entered time and space. Adam and Eve, who had been perfect in body, soul, and spirit, were now imperfect. Their bodies, which had been free from disease and susceptibility to trauma, now became subject to both. They had been created spiritually alive with the ability to communicate openly with God, but after the Fall they were spiritually dead, unable to receive truth from God. The apostle Paul explains why: "The man without the Spirit does not accept the things that come from the Spirit of God, for they are foolishness to him, and he cannot understand them, because they are spiritually discerned" (1 Corinthians 2:14). Elsewhere he observes, "They are darkened in their understanding and separated from the life of God because of the ignorance that is in them due to the hardening of their hearts" (Ephesians 4:18). Their hearts were hardened by the deceitfulness of this world, and their minds became the target for every kind of deception. According to Paul, even as believers we retain a degree of this mental vulnerability: "I am afraid that just as Eve was deceived by the serpent's cunning, your minds may somehow be led astray from your sincere and pure devotion to Christ" (2 Corinthians 11:3).

Adam and Eve experienced an overwhelming sense of guilt and shame. Their newly birthed sin nature was evident when God questioned them about their abrupt change in behavior. The fact that they were "darkened in their understanding" became immediately evident when they tried to hide from an omnipresent God. Furthermore, Adam blamed Eve, who blamed the serpent. This shifting of blame is the first recorded use of defense mechanisms. Look at Table 6.1 to see how the Fall affected the total nature of humankind.

Yet God had a plan to restore fallen humanity. He would send his Son Jesus to die for our sins and defeat the devil at the cross (John specifically mentions that "the reason the Son of God appeared was to destroy the devil's work" — 1 John 3:8), and, through Jesus' resurrection, to give new life to all who believe in him. Consequently, every believer is

	PRE-FALL MAN	POST-FALL MAN
NATURE	righteous	"by nature objects of wrath" (Ephesians 2:3)
MIND	truthful, right	"darkened in their understanding" (Ephesians 4:18)
SPIRIT	alive	"separated from the life of God" (Ephesians 4:18)
EMOTION	safe, secure, and free	"the hardening of their hearts… having lost all sensitivity" (Ephesians 4:18, 19)
WILL	free to choose	"given themselves over to sensuality so as to indulge in every kind of impurity, with a continual lust for more" (Ephesians 4:19)

TABLE 6.1

positionally alive and free "in Christ," able to grow "in Christ." The apostle Paul reveals how this entire process of growth is dependent on who we are "in Christ":

> So then, just as you received Christ Jesus as Lord, continue to live *in him,* rooted and built up *in him,* strengthened in the faith as you were taught, and overflowing with thankfulness.
> See to it that no one takes you captive through hollow and deceptive philosophy, which depends on human tradition and the basic principles of this world rather than on Christ.
> For *in Christ* all the fullness of the Deity lives in bodily form, and you have been given fullness *in Christ,* who is the head over every power and authority.
>
> —*COLOSSIANS 2:6–10, EMPHASIS ADDED*

This passage reveals the fundamental difference between Christian and non-Christian counseling—one is carried out in accordance with Christ, and the other in accordance with "human tradition and the basic principles of this world." Salvation brings forgiveness of sins and a new spiritual life "in Christ," which means that our soul is once again in

UNITED WITH CHRIST

IN CHRIST'S DEATH	Romans 6:3; Galatians 2:20; Colossians 3:1-3
IN CHRIST'S BURIAL	Romans 6:4
IN CHRIST'S RESURRECTION	Romans 6:5, 8, 11
IN CHRIST'S ASCENSION	Ephesians 2:6
IN CHRIST'S LIFE	Romans 5:10-11
IN CHRIST'S POWER	Ephesians 1:19-20
IN CHRIST'S INHERITANCE	Romans 8:16-17; Ephesians 1:11-14

TABLE 6.2

union with God. Every born-again believer is spiritually alive "in Christ" and thus united with him (see Table 6.2).

According to Paul, we first have to be rooted "in Christ," then we can be built up "in him," and finally we will be able to walk, or live, "in him" (see Colossians 2:6 – 7). This progression of growth is completely dependent on our life in Christ. If there is nothing living, then nothing will grow. Jesus explained, "I am the vine; you are the branches. If a man remains in me and I in him, he will bear much fruit; apart from me you can do nothing" (John 15:5).

In order to develop a strategy for Christian counseling, we must assess where a client is having conflict. Table 6.3 defines levels of conflict; Table 6.4 shows what would happen at each level if resolution is accomplished.[1] Level 1 relates to root issues (being firmly rooted in Christ). There are definable root issues that need to be resolved before any growth can take place. Level 2 relates to growth issues (being built up in Christ). Most of these conflicts reveal immaturity. Level 3 relates to living issues (walking in Christ). Recall that positional sanctification (Level 1) is the basis for progressive sanctification (Levels 2 and 3). We believe there are certain identifiable spiritual and psychological conflicts at every level. Growth and productivity will be impeded in people unless there is some resolution of these conflicts.

To be sure, no one can be divided up in little squares like the charts indicate. Rather, we believe there are definable spiritual and psychological

Levels of Conflict

	LEVEL 1	LEVEL 2	LEVEL 3
	"rooted … in [Christ Jesus]" (Colossians 2:10)	"built up in him" (Colossians 2:7)	"as you received Christ Jesus as Lord, continue to [walk] in him" (Colossians 2:6)
SPIRITUAL	Lack of salvation or lack of assurance of salvation (Ephesians 2:1-3)	Walking according to the flesh (Romans 8:4-5, 12-14; Galatians 5:19-21)	Insensitivity to the Holy Spirit's leading (Hebrews 5:11-14)
RATIONAL	Puffed up in pride and darkened in their understanding (1 Corinthians 8:1; Ephesians 4:18)	Wrong belief or philosophy of life (Colossians 2:8)	Lack of knowledge (Hosea 4:6)
EMOTIONAL	Fear, guilt, and shame (Matthew 10:26-33; Romans 8:1-2)	Anger, anxiety, and depression (Ephesians 4:31; 1 Peter 5:7; 2 Corinthians 4:1-18)	Discouragement and sorrow (Galatians 6:9)
VOLITIONAL	Rebellion (1 Timothy 1:9)	Compulsive behavior and lack of self-control (1 Corinthians 3:1-3)	Lack of discipline (2 Thessalonians 3:7, 11)
RELATIONAL	Rejection (Ephesians 2:1-3)	Bitterness and unforgiveness (Colossians 3:13)	Selfishness (1 Corinthians 10:24; Philippians 2:1-5)

TABLE 6.3

(that is, rational, emotional, volitional, and relational) hurdles that must be overcome in order to begin or to continue growing in Christ. We are not suggesting a tidy order that every counseling session follows. With some clients it may take several sessions simply to develop trust, and others may not be open to Christian therapy at all. We need to accept clients where they are in their present relationship to Christ. For instance, consider the spiritual category on the Levels of Conflict chart (see Table 6.3). The Level 1 spiritual conflict is lack of salvation or the lack of assurance of salvation. We cannot help people mature "in Christ" if they are not

Levels of Resolution

	LEVEL 1	LEVEL 2	LEVEL 3
	"rooted ... in [Christ Jesus]" (Colossians 2:10)	"built up in him" (Colossians 2:7)	"as you received Christ Jesus as Lord, continue to [walk] in him" (Colossians 2:6)
SPIRITUAL	Child of God (Romans 8:16; 1 John 5:13)	Walking according to the Spirit (Romans 8:4-5, 12-13; Galatians 5:22-23)	Led by the Holy Spirit (Romans 8:14)
RATIONAL	Truth (John 8:32)	Correctly handling the word of truth (2 Timothy 2:15)	Adequate and equipped for every good work (2 Timothy 3:16-17)
EMOTIONAL	Freedom (Galatians 5:1)	Joy, peace, and patience (Galatians 5:22)	Contentment (Philippians 4:11)
VOLITIONAL	Submissive (Romans 13:1-2)	Self-controlled (Galatians 5:23)	Disciplined (1 Timothy 4:7-8)
RELATIONAL	Acceptance (Romans 5:8; 15:7)	Forgiveness (Ephesians 4:32)	Devoted to one another in brotherly love and looking to the interests of others (Romans 12:10; Philippians 2:1-5)

TABLE 6.4

rooted "in Christ." To resolve the conflict at this level, we would have to lead them to Christ and point them to the assurance of salvation.

LEVEL 1 CONFLICT RESOLUTION

... continue to [walk] in him, *rooted* and built up *in him.*

—*COLOSSIANS 2:10, EMPHASIS ADDED*

In order to be free from the past and live a productive life in Christ, Christian clients need to change from their old ways of thinking and living to a new way of thinking and living in a righteous relationship with

God. The first step for new believers is to repent of their old sinful ways and to put their trust in God by believing the truth. The word *repent* (Greek *metanoia*) literally means "to change one's mind." Christian cognitive therapists help clients see the lies they have been believing and encourage them to choose the truth.

Clients who are not firmly rooted in Christ need to know who they are in Christ and what it means to be a child of God. In other words, they need to know their new spiritual heritage. This vision is at the core of what Paul shares in his beautiful prayer for the Ephesian Christians: "I pray also that the eyes of your heart may be enlightened in order that you may know the hope to which he has called you, the riches of his glorious inheritance in the saints, and his incomparably great power for us who believe" (Ephesians 1:18–19). If we are saved by faith and are instructed to walk by faith, then we must know the *object* of our faith: God and his Word. If what we believe is not true, our walk of faith will not be fruitful. The foundation on which believers build their lives is grounded in three biblical assurances:

1. the finished work of Christ (Colossians 2:14–15)
2. the believer's union with Christ (Colossians 2:9–10, 13)
3. the present work of the Spirit of Christ (Colossians 2:6; 3:15; 2 Thessalonians 2:13)

Having a true knowledge of God and of who we are in Christ significantly impacts how we perceive ourselves and how we live. We noted earlier that defeated clients consistently seem to demonstrate one thing in common: None of them knows who they are in Christ or understands what it means to be a child of God. In order to sense God's intimate presence, they must resolve their psychological and spiritual conflicts first by submitting to God and resisting the devil (see James 4:7); they need to resolve those issues that are critical between themselves and their heavenly Father, then eliminate any deceptive influences by the devil on their minds. To do so accomplishes two critical objectives. First, it enables them to appropriate the power of God for Christian living, and, second, it gives them a clear mind by which to make conscious choices. We will share how we resolve these conflicts later. For now, we want to emphasize that people who know who they are in Christ have established the essential foundation for being all that God wants them to be in Christ. Level 1 counseling is where most Christian therapists should begin their work. As Table 6.3 shows, conflicts at Level 1 include

- lack of salvation or lack of assurance of salvation
- pride and darkened understanding
- fear, guilt, and shame
- rebellion
- rejection

The Level 1 spiritual conflict is the lack of salvation or the lack of assurance of salvation. In chapter eight we'll talk about appropriate ways of sharing the gospel with clients. Certainly therapists can offer the opportunity to receive Christ, but the gift of eternal life comes from God. However, therapists can help clients resolve their psychological and spiritual conflicts. As a result, clients' fears and feelings of rejection will dissipate when they become firmly rooted in Christ. The assurance of one's salvation comes when "the Spirit himself testifies with our spirit that we are God's children" (Romans 8:16).

While there are challenges in each of these areas of conflict, it can be particularly difficult to work with rebellious (volitional) people. Chances are good they will not volunteer for counseling in the first place. Thus, we agree with tough-love advocates who recommend strict programs of behavior modification that admit that people make choices and are responsible for those choices — seeking to orchestrate negative consequences for a person's rebellious behavior. Such a process is called an intervention.

Whether the consequences are natural or orchestrated, rebellious people must come to their own conclusion or inner conviction that they no longer want to live as they have been living. Some people must be severely beaten up by life before they are broken enough to ask for help. About this type of person Paul wrote, "I have decided to deliver such a one to Satan for the destruction of his flesh, so that his spirit may be saved in the day of the Lord Jesus" (1 Corinthians 5:6 New American Standard Bible). In other words, commit these persons to Satan's domain — the world. *Destruction* does not mean annihilation, but ruin, and *flesh* refers to the physical body in this passage.

Every counselor experiences a measure of resistance in almost every client they see. Virtually all clients have finely honed defense mechanisms they use to protect themselves. One of the goals of therapy is to help clients evaluate whether these defenses are healthy or not. The skillful therapist copes with this natural resistance and patiently guides a client to good conclusions — a much easier process to handle if the Lord has already convicted someone of the need to examine his or her own attitudes and behaviors.

Most clients are broken people or they would not even be asking for help. The Christian counselor should relate to them with the unconditional love and acceptance of the heavenly Father. This understanding stance by the counselor helps alleviate two other Level 1 conflicts, namely, fear (emotional) and rejection (relational). Helping a client to feel safe and accepted lays a very important foundation for further growth. Overcoming the Level 1 conflict of pride and darkened understanding (rational) will require instruction and maybe some reading assignments as determined by the therapist for a particular need. God said, "My people are destroyed from lack of knowledge" (Hosea 4:6). In sum, the goal for Level 1 counseling is to establish the client alive and free in Christ, which entails the following:

- establishing sufficient rapport so that the client begins to share openly, root issues are identified, and resolution is initiated
- leading a client to Christ, who provides the assurance of salvation
- breaking down the defenses that have been erected to protect a client from fear and rejection (this may continue throughout the therapeutic process)
- guiding a client to a true knowledge of who he or she is in Christ
- exploring ways in which a client may be "playing God" or rebelling against God's authority
- helping a client understand the unconditional love and acceptance of the heavenly Father

LEVEL 2 CONFLICT RESOLUTION

... continue to [walk] in him, rooted and *built up in him.*

—COLOSSIANS 2:7, EMPHASIS ADDED

The key to understanding Level 2 Christian counseling is to adopt the same goal that God has for every one of his children, namely, their sanctification (that is, the process of becoming conformed to the image of God). If you don't believe that sanctification is important, consider the following verses:

It is God's will that you should be sanctified.

—1 THESSALONIANS 4:3

But just as he who called you is holy, so be holy in all you do; for it is written: "Be holy, because I am holy."

—*1 PETER 1:15 – 16*

For those God foreknew he also predestined to be conformed to the likeness of his Son.

—*ROMANS 8:29*

The goal of this command is love, which comes from a pure heart and a good conscience and a sincere faith.

—*1 TIMOTHY 1:5*

What, then, stands in the way of our sanctification? As we have seen in Table 6.3, Level 2 conflicts include

- walking according to the flesh
- wrong belief or philosophy of life
- anger, anxiety, and depression
- compulsive behavior and lack of self-control
- bitterness and unforgiveness

Resolving Level 2 conflicts should help clients solidify their true identity in Christ and provide them with a biblical sense of purpose in life. Our sense of worth is found in our identity as children of God and is joyfully experienced as we grow in grace. Our sense of worth is not found in performance, appearance, or status, or even through the spiritual gifts, talents, or intelligence that God distributes in different measure to his children. What God has uniformly distributed is *himself*, because every Christian is his child and he loves them all the same. Any Christian who genuinely understands who he or she is and whose life is characterized by the fruit of the Spirit (see Galatians 5:22 – 23) will feel a true sense of self and experience mental health — provided, of course, there are no biochemical problems. The fact that all Christians have the same opportunity to be all that God calls them to be is the good news we are privileged to share. The purpose of the therapist's tool kit in chapter nine is to resolve Level 2 and Level 3 conflicts.

LEVEL 3 CONFLICT RESOLUTION

As you received Christ Jesus as Lord, continue to *[walk]* in him.

—*COLOSSIANS 2:6, EMPHASIS ADDED*

Christian counseling takes into account every level of conflict (see again Tables 6.3 and 6.4). If the root issues are resolved (Level 1), then nothing should impede a person's progress toward goal attainment. In our experience, Christians who find their identity and freedom in Christ do heal from their wounds rather rapidly. They are teachable and have a hunger for the Word of God.

Scripture teaches the priorities of maturity before ministry, character before career, and being before doing. Recall that it is not what we do that determines who we are, but who we are that determines what we do. Many Christians have falsely asserted that a woman gains her identity from her family and her role as a mother, while a man receives his identity from his career or his role as a provider. If this were true, then what would happen when a woman experiences the empty nest or a man loses his job? Do they lose their identities? Some have tried to support this claim by pointing to verses 16 and 19 of Genesis 3 (the woman will bear her child in pain, and a man will work by the sweat of his brow), but what is described there is a *fallen* identity and an expression of the curse. Being separated from God, Adam and Eve had no choice but to seek their identity and purpose in the physical realm. But God offers us more, as long as we recognize it. We cannot expect people to behave in a way inconsistent with who they are (both in perception and in maturity). The order taught in God's Word is first *knowing* (cognitive), then *being* (affective), and finally *doing* (volitional).

God works in our lives primarily in the context of committed relationships for two reasons. First, it is not possible, in the long run, to be phonies at home; our children and spouse will see through us. Our true character always reveals itself at home. Second, in committed relationships we cannot easily walk away from our responsibility to become mature in the Lord. The home is where we grow up spiritually, psychologically, and physically. Thus, Paul's words to the Colossian church apply equally in the home:

> Therefore, as God's chosen people, holy and dearly loved, clothe yourselves with compassion, kindness, humility, gentleness and patience. Bear with each other and forgive whatever grievances you may have

against one another. Forgive as the Lord forgave you. And over all these virtues put on love, which binds them all together in perfect unity.

—*Colossians 3:12 – 14*

Level 3 counseling helps clients function in their homes, on their jobs, and in all their relationships in society in a responsible way as children of God. The goal is that clients would become mature enough to live a righteous life by the grace of God. Level 3 counseling is wisdom counseling, based on Scripture and on common sense. Conflict resolution in these situations involves the proper use of one's spiritual gifts, God-given talents and intellect to serve one another and to be a positive witness in the world. As described in Table 6.3, Level 3 conflicts include

- insensitivity to the Holy Spirit's leading
- lack of knowledge
- discouragement and sorrow
- lack of discipline
- selfishness

CONFLICT RESOLUTION FROM JOHN'S PERSPECTIVE

The apostle John provides additional insight into these three levels of conflict:

I write to you, dear children,
  because your sins have been forgiven on account of his name.
I write to you, fathers,
  because you have known him who is from the beginning.
I write to you, young men,
  because you have overcome the evil one.
I write to you, dear children,
  because you have known the Father.
I write to you, fathers,
  because you have known him who is from the beginning.
I write to you, young men,
  because you are strong,
  and the word of God lives in you,
  and you have overcome the evil one.

—*1 John 2:12 – 14*

It can be inferred from this passage that progressing from the spiritual maturity of little children to that of young men and fathers will be spiritually contested. A well-reasoned, wise understanding of the spiritual battle for the mind has been strangely lacking in the counseling strategies of Christian therapists. The truth is this: "Our struggle is not against flesh and blood, but against the rulers, against the authorities, against the powers of this dark world and against the spiritual forces of evil in the heavenly realms" (Ephesians 6:12). If all we are doing is listening to our clients, explaining to them their pathology, and suggesting changes of behavior, we will never expose and bring to the forefront the battle going on for their minds. Why should the devil reveal himself if we are doing nothing to free the client? It is only when we seek to help our clients resolve their conflicts through interventions in the conflict stage, including issuing the call to genuine repentance, that the battle will be exposed.

Some clients will not reveal what is going on in their minds unless they are sure we will believe them. They may tell us what happened to them but be very hesitant to share their true feelings and thoughts; it also happens that clients attempt to explain the negative thoughts or voices in their heads, but their therapists do not have the spiritual insight to understand what is going on. When Neil was teaching at Talbot School of Theology, three undergraduate students at Biola University were referred to a local clinic that specialized in eating disorders. All three tried to communicate their mental struggles to the therapist. The counselor asked each of the young women to write a paper explaining why "blaming the devil" was absolving them from their responsibility to get well.

Bear in mind, they were *not* blaming the devil; they were simply trying to share with the therapist their mental struggle. Apparently the counselor didn't believe them or had no idea how to help them find freedom from such mental torment; perhaps the therapist was afraid to counsel them from the Christian worldview. Because Neil wasn't restricted by those barriers, he was able to help the three students resolve their conflicts and experience the peace of God that transcends all understanding, which is now guarding their hearts and their minds in Christ Jesus (see Philippians 4:6 – 7).

With some clients, conflict resolution may stretch out over an extended period of time. To explain why, Neil uses the illustration of "bananas and onions." *Bananas* are people with only one layer to remove. They have virtually total recall of their past and have experienced few or no major traumas. Bananas have been raised well and taught to live responsibly. They can potentially resolve all known conflicts in a single lengthy session. Most clients, however, are *onions*. They have many layers of conflicts, which peel off one thin layer at a time. Addicts commonly fit into this category. Therapist and client alike may feel flushed with success after removing a layer of deception, only to be confronted with another layer.

There are two reasons why all the onion's layers are not exposed at once. First, God is gracious and typically reveals one major problem at a time. Exposing them all at once could overwhelm some clients. Second, each of us has limited self-knowledge: "Augustine spoke of God revealing the things of a man's heart of which he is unconscious and unaware. The early church father Irenaeus referred to the Spirit revealing in a beneficial way the hidden things of human hearts. . . . Scripture teaches a conception of an unconscious dimension within the human being. Within this dimension lie not only repressed unconscious deeds but also unconscious plans and motives."[2]

The key to recovery in Christ is to resolve all known conflicts first. What, then, do you do if a client has no recall of past experiences? Follow Paul's example: "I do not consider myself yet to have taken hold of it. But one thing I do: Forgetting what is behind and straining toward what is ahead, I press on toward the goal to win the prize for which God has called me heavenward in Christ Jesus" (Philippians 3:13–14). If clients have unresolved conflicts from their past that need to be resolved, the Lord will reveal them at the right time. Until then, help clients get firmly rooted in Christ so they have the strength and resources to repent when the time comes.

FIRST THINGS FIRST

In our battle to live consistently the Christian life, we have sought to apply personal disciplines based on the life of Jesus Christ. In Luke 2:52, we read, "Jesus grew in wisdom and stature, and in favor with God and men." In other words, he grew mentally, physically, spiritually, and socially. The diagram on page 147 (Figure 6.1) illustrates these spiritual disciplines.

When pastors and Christian psychologists turn to their concordances to find out what God has to say about each of these disciplines, by and large they are directed to certain Old Testament passages and to the second half of Paul's letters. New Testament professors tell us that Paul's letters are almost evenly divided — in general the first half of each book is theological, and the second half is practical. Now suppose we were to accurately interpret every practical passage and encourage our clients to live according to these principles. Would they be able to do it? Most would fail, and many churchgoing Christians with no obvious mental health problems would also struggle in successfully using such an approach. Yet too often our counseling goals and the behavioral criteria for discharge we present to clients and third-party payers fall into this category!

To take this approach is, in reality, a subtle form of Christian behaviorism. Such advice sounds something like this: "That isn't the best way to live; here's a better way that's more biblically accurate. Do this and that, and you'll be rewarded." In many cases we have replaced negative legalism (don't do this or that) with positive legalism (do this and that). Yet, if truth be told, this attempt at external conformity to biblical principles seldom produces any lasting fruit. There must be an inner transformation before any lasting external conformity takes place — or we're only playing the role of actors in a stage drama.

Consider, for example, the reaction to the disintegration of the nuclear family since the cultural revolution of the 1960s. Never in the history of humankind has there been such a concerted effort to save the family. Graduate programs have sprung up in Bible colleges and seminaries. Books, videotapes, and radio programs all address the number one "felt need" in America every day. So how are we doing? Not very well! Then what's wrong? There is obviously nothing wrong with biblically based material instructing us to live in keeping with Christian principles. Telling a husband to love his wife as Christ loved the church and suggesting several ways he could do so is certainly biblical. Likewise, telling a wife to submit to her husband so that the Word of God is not dishonored and suggesting some ways she can show him more respect without becoming a doormat is appropriate. These husbands and wives may even go home and try those things for a few days — but it won't work in the long run if husbands and wives are all torn up on the inside with unresolved Level 1 (root issues) conflicts.

The problem is so subtle it could be easily overlooked. Principles explaining every spoke in the wheel (see Figure 6.1) could be biblically accurate. The problem is that these spokes may not be functionally connected to the hub. We can easily put our confidence in ourselves, our biblical programs, and our psychological strategies instead of in Christ and

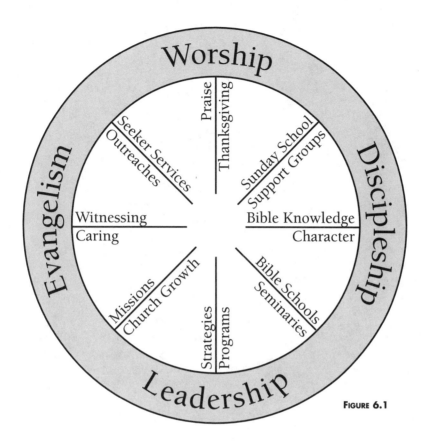

Worship
Praise
Thanksgiving

Discipleship
Sunday School
Support Groups
Bible Knowledge
Character
Bible Schools
Seminaries

Evangelism
Seeker Services
Outreaches
Witnessing
Caring
Missions
Church Growth

Leadership
Strategies
Programs

FIGURE 6.1

his Word. We can too easily misunderstand Jesus' teaching about fruit — "This is to my Father's glory, that you bear much fruit, showing yourselves to be my disciples" (John 15:8) — and conclude that we have to bear fruit. No, we don't! We have to abide (remain) in Christ (see John 15:4–5). Bearing fruit is merely the evidence that we are abiding in Christ. No life can flow to the branches unless we are connected to the vine. If there is no life, there will be no growth. Figure 6.2 shows the need for this spiritually organic connection.

The first half of Paul's letters (the "theological" part) establishes us *in Christ*. It is our contention that if we can help our clients be connected to God in a living and liberated way, they will naturally (or better to say, supernaturally) learn to live out the second half of the letters (the "practical" part). We have told many clients to temporarily set aside their concern for marriage and family and concentrate on their relationship with God. If we can individually help them resolve their psychological and

FIGURE 6.2

spiritual conflicts, then we can begin to bring the family together in a meaningful way. Why? Because no one or nothing on earth (including Satan) can keep them from being the spouse, parent, or family member God has called them to be — and being who God has called them to be is God's will for their lives.

CONNECTING PEOPLE TO GOD

Bob was brought up in a physically abusive and chaotic home. His counselor determined his Axis I diagnosis to be Dysthymic Disorder (chronic depression of mild to moderate severity), according to DSM-IV categories.[3] When Bob's parents and siblings became angry, they would express the anger by hitting each other and throwing chairs, food, and anything not attached to floors, walls, or ceilings. After Bob married, he found that the abusive behavior followed him into his relationship with his wife. He knew the negative impact these violent behaviors had had on him personally, and he detested seeing them being reproduced in him, knowing how much it was frightening and terrorizing his wife. Still, whenever the pressure mounted, he would erupt. Afterwards, he would be torn up with guilt and remorse, vow never again to behave in such a way, then find the pattern repeating itself again and again. Bob became a Christian six years ago, and he had hoped those behaviors would finally cease. They have subsided somewhat but have not gone away. Bob has found the struggle to gain victory to still be intense, and he sees himself repeating the destructive behaviors periodically.

Terri, a twenty-eight-year-old single woman, carried deep wounds from her parents' divorce. In counseling she spoke of issues of male dependency, shame, and a promiscuous relationship pattern with multiple partners. Terri's Axis I diagnosis was Major Depressive Disorder, in partial remission. Her Axis II diagnosis was Histrionic Personality Disorder. She had made a decision for Christ at age twenty but was perplexed by the continuation of these sinful behavior patterns. At one point, she dated and slept with a married man "because he loved me and needed me." She experienced tremendous guilt and remorse afterwards. She desired not to sin, yet she continued to sin. She admitted that she felt a force coming from somewhere that weakened her resolve to flee from dependency on sex.

When considering such cases, where does one start? Both have made a profession of faith in God, so we will assume for the sake of discussion that they are born-again. From our experience, we can reasonably well assume that they have a distorted concept of God and themselves, that they lack a healthy sense of worth and have not experienced mental peace, and that they question God's love and don't have assurance of their salvation. Their personal relationship with God is not very intimate or personal; consequently, their devotional and prayer life is virtually nonexistent.

A person's relationship with God is personal, and, as in any relationship, there are certain issues that need to be resolved in order for the relationship to work. We cannot expect God to bless us if we are living in open rebellion against him: "Rebellion is like the sin of divination, and arrogance like the evil of idolatry" (1 Samuel 15:23). If we are proud, God is opposed to us (see James 4:6). If we are bitter or unwilling to forgive, God will turn us over to the torturers (see Matthew 18:34). These issues must be resolved first, for only God can bind up the brokenhearted and set the captive free.

Perhaps a testimony from a veteran missionary will illustrate the point. This woman received counseling from her psychiatrist, psychologist, and pastor once a week simply to hold her life together. The next step would have been hospitalization. Neil spent one Friday afternoon with her and later received this letter:

I've been wanting to write to you for some time, but I've waited this long to confirm to myself that this is truly "for reals" (as my four-year-old daughter says). I'd like to share an entry from my journal that I wrote two days after our meeting:

Since Friday afternoon I have felt like a different person. The fits of rage and anger are gone. My spirit is so calm and full of joy. I wake up singing praise to God in my heart.

That edge of tension and irritation is gone. I feel so free. The Bible has been really exciting and stimulating and more understandable than ever before. There was nothing "dramatic" that happened during the session on Friday, yet I know in the deepest part of my being that something has changed. I am no longer bound by accusations, doubts, and thoughts of suicide, murder, or other harm that come straight from hell into my head. There is a serenity in my mind and spirit, a clarity of consciousness that is profound.

I've been set free!

I'm excited and expectant about my future now. I know that I'll be growing spiritually again and will be developing in other ways as well. I look forward happily to the discovery of the person God has created and redeemed me to be, as well as the transformation of my marriage.

It is so wonderful to have joy after so long a darkness.

It's been two-and-a-half months since I wrote that, and I'm firmly convinced of the significant benefits of finding freedom in Christ. I've been in therapy for several months, and while I was making progress, there is no comparison with the steps I'm able to make now. My ability to "process" things has increased many-fold. Not only is my spirit more serene, my head is actually clearer! It's easier to make connections and integrate things now. It seems like everything is easier to understand now.

My relationship with God has changed significantly. For eight years I felt that he was distant from me. Shortly before I met you, I was desperately crying out to him to set me free – to release me from this bondage I was in. I wanted so badly to meet with him again, to know his presence was with me again. I needed to know him as friend, as companion, not as the distant authority figure he had become in my mind and experience. Since that day two-and-a-half months ago, I have seen my trust in him grow. I've seen my ability to be honest with him increase greatly. I really have been experiencing that spiritual growth I'd anticipated in my journal. It's great!

This woman had had all the symptoms of severe depression and was being treated as such. Her thoughts went from scrambled to clear after resolving her personal and spiritual conflicts. She could now mentally process issues she hadn't been able to process before. Her perception of God and herself changed dramatically. It was God who granted the repentance and brought the change.

We do not believe in instant maturity, for it will take us the rest of our lives to renew our minds and be conformed to the image of God's Son. Part of the assessment process in our counseling must take into account the layers of deception and bondage that clients possess. If many layers are present (the "onion" principle), we can anticipate it will take a longer period of time to resolve conflicts. But if clients have experienced fewer complexities in life (the "banana" principle), it does not or should not take very long to help those clients be free in Christ.

For years the authors and the staff at Freedom in Christ Ministries have helped people like this missionary resolve their psychological and spiritual conflicts so they can be alive and free in Christ. Neil's book *Helping Others Find Freedom In Christ*[4] shares this process and lays out the theological and practical foundation for using the "Steps to Freedom in Christ" (see Appendix E). During the process, both the client and counselor have a printed copy of the Steps to Freedom. The client asks God to lead him or her to repentance at every Step. At times Terry and Julie will refer a client to their church for a "Freedom Appointment," while at other times they will take their clients through the process in their office, working through each Step one by one. We want to briefly introduce these Steps and note how they can be utilized in the therapeutic process. For a more detailed explanation on how a licensed professional counselor has integrated these Steps into her counseling practice, see Appendix A. For more explanation about the Steps, see Appendix E.

STEP 1: COUNTERFEIT VERSUS REAL

In making a public profession of faith, the early church would stand, face the west, and say, "I renounce you, Satan, and all your works and all your ways." This generic declaration was the first step in repentance. (The Roman Catholic church and most liturgical churches still require this renunciation to be stated at confirmation.) More specifically, the early church would renounce every counterfeit religious experience they had, every false vow or pledge they made, and every false teacher or doctrine in which they believed. We encourage each person we counsel to do that as well. Renunciation involves giving up a claim or right. When we renounce, we are making a definite decision to let go of any past commitments, pledges, vows, pacts, and beliefs that are not Christian. For this practice we find solid biblical support: "He who conceals his sins does not prosper, but whoever confesses and renounces them finds mercy" (Proverbs 28:13).

Some people commit themselves to Christ and choose to believe the Word of God, but they hold on to past commitments and still believe what they have always believed. Yet to do so makes salvation additional instead of transformational—the addition of something to what we already have. On the contrary, every believer must decisively let go of the past; to do this is the first step to genuine repentance. If we have totally embraced the truth, we have also clearly understood what is not true. All this is possible because of Jesus' crucifixion and resurrection. Our sins are forgiven and we possess new life in Jesus Christ the moment we are born-again. However, no one pushed the "Clear" button, and our minds were not instantly transformed to be receptive to the truth of God's Word. By renouncing counterfeit practices and choosing the truth, our minds will be renewed. As new believers we can repent by the grace of God.

The apostle Paul reveals the close link between renouncing and not losing heart (that is, not being depressed or discouraged) when he writes, "Therefore, since through God's mercy we have this ministry, we do not lose heart. Rather, we have renounced secret and shameful ways; we do not use deception, nor do we distort the word of God. On the contrary, by setting forth the truth plainly we commend ourselves to every man's conscience in the sight of God" (2 Corinthians 4:1–2). Paul is contrasting the truth of divine revelation with the deceptions of false teachers and prophets. Knowing God's holiness and his call for purity, Paul exhorts us to renounce every immoral practice, every distortion of the truth, and every deceitfulness of the heart.

God does not take lightly false teachers and false guidance. False teachers were to be put to death (see Deuteronomy 13:5), and there were also serious consequences for those who consulted them: "I will set my face against the person who turns to mediums and spiritists to prostitute himself by following them, and I will cut him off from his people" (Leviticus 20:6). There are similar warnings in the New Testament about false teachers and false prophets. These warnings demonstrate the necessity of renouncing any and all involvement with false guidance, false teachers, false prophets, and all cultic and occultic practices. We do not want to be cut off by God; we want to be connected to him.

Bill reported a history of dabbling in Ouija boards, New Age beliefs, and other occult practices prior to his conversion. His Axis I diagnosis was Dysthymic Disorder. Following a decision for Christ, he experienced continued difficulty with anger and physical abuse in his marriage, despite severe conviction concerning this carnality. Then he was led through the "Steps to Freedom in Christ" at his church. Renouncing every involvement with false teachers brought him tremendous relief. We continued to work on his outbursts of anger, using an aftercare approach of an anger-management group, assertiveness exercises, and spousal commitment to signal escalation when she observed it. Bill and his wife are now communicating much better. Bill's outbursts did not magically disappear, but his healing began when he renounced his sinful past.

STEP 2: DECEPTION VERSUS TRUTH

In order to live free in Christ, we must sort out the lies and choose the truth. We must speak the truth in love (see Ephesians 4:15), walk in the light, and have fellowship with one another (see 1 John 1:7). But people living in bondage believe lies, walk in darkness, and avoid intimate contact with others. There are several ways we can deceive ourselves:

- hearing God's Word but not doing it (James 1:22; 4:17)
- saying we have no sin (1 John 1:8)
- thinking we are something when we are not (Galatians 6:3)
- thinking we are wise by this world's standards (1 Corinthians 3:18–19)
- thinking we will not reap what we sow (Galatians 6:7)
- thinking the unrighteous will inherit the kingdom (1 Corinthians 6:9)
- thinking we can associate with bad company and not be corrupted (1 Corinthians 15:33)

The first step in recovery is to admit we have a problem and find at least one person with whom we can be totally honest. Clients cannot instantly change long-established patterns of the flesh that have become a habitual part of their daily lives, but they can make a determined decision to change the flesh patterns and confess them as wrong. As we work through this Step we also deal with primary defense mechanisms. As Christians, we no longer have to rely on maladaptive defense mechanisms, because we are loved and accepted for who we are. Jesus Christ is our defense. In addition to lying and blaming others, the major defense mechanisms that must be addressed in this Step include

- denial (conscious or subconscious refusal to face the truth)
- fantasy (escaping from the real world)
- emotional insulation (withdrawing to avoid rejection)
- regression (reverting back to a less-threatening time)
- displacement (taking out frustration on others)
- projection (attributing one's own impulses to someone else)
- rationalization (making excuses for poor behavior)

Jody was in her second marriage, this time to a sexually addicted husband. Her first husband had been verbally abusive. Her mother and father had divorced when she was in elementary school, and Jody had been allowed to choose the custodial parent. She chose her father, who was frequently absent because of a job that required considerable travel. Jody essentially raised herself in her father's home, with a neighbor serving as a guardian during the week. She developed strong defenses of independence, a critical spirit, projection, emotional insulation, denial, help rejecting/complaining, and blaming—defenses that she carried with her into both marriages. Her Axis I diagnosis was Dysthymic Disorder; her Axis II diagnosis was Passive-Aggressive Personality Disorder with Paranoid Personality features.

Jody assumed no responsibility for any emotional or behavioral problems in either marriage, adamantly maintaining that her childhood and marriage experiences had not caused her any pain. She sincerely believed that if her two husbands could only have been treated and cured, the problems caused by them would have vanished. She consistently attempted to make the therapist angry and to portray the therapist as the incompetent person in the therapeutic relationship. She even tried to control the therapy process, confirming through it all her own self-sufficiency. Eventually Jody was led through the "Steps to Freedom in Christ" in a church ministry, and as a result she became amenable to aftercare counseling. We doubt that Jody would have consented to seek aftercare counseling if she had not obtained a degree of freedom as a result of these Steps. Continued work on Step 2 remains a goal for Jody, with explicit boundary setting and firmness in the therapeutic relationship a necessity.

STEP 3: BITTERNESS VERSUS FORGIVENESS

It is rare to see clients who do not struggle with bitterness. They carry the emotional scars and bear the pain of wounds inflicted on them by others. Most do not know how to let go of the past and forgive from the heart; some have simply chosen not to. They hang on to their anger as a means of protecting themselves from being hurt again, but in reality they are only hurting themselves. To forgive is to set a captive free, and only when we forgive do we discover that we are the captive. No one can be free from the past and emotionally free in the present without forgiving from the heart. If we do not forgive from our heart, God will turn us over to the torturers (see Matthew 18:34).

God is not out to get us; he's out to restore us. He knows that if we hang on to our bitterness, we will only hurt ourselves and others (see Hebrews 12:15). Thus Paul urges us, "Get rid of all bitterness, rage and anger, brawling and slander, along with every form of malice. Be kind and compassionate to one another, forgiving each other, just as in Christ God forgave you" (Ephesians 4:31–32). We forgive others for our sake and for the sake of our relationship with God. What is gained in forgiving others is spiritual and psychological freedom. Paul also observes that we need to forgive others so that Satan does not take advantage of us (see 2 Corinthians 2:10–11).

June, a fifty-two-year-old divorced woman with an Axis I diagnosis of Schizoaffective Disorder, was dealing with the effects of a domineering but attentive mother who had died after years of taking care of June during June's initial schizophrenic break and then following her divorce. The grieving process was delayed due to June's ambivalence over the helpful but intrusive role her mother had played.

We worked on Step 3 in individual counseling with June. She listed the positive and negative aspects of her mother's role in her life, working on each negative by using the process outlined in Step 3 to forgive and to release the memories to God. She experienced significant symptom relief, and her relationship with her mother was put in proper perspective, which facilitated the expression of grief and the further movement into acceptance.

It's important to understand that we do not heal in order to forgive; we forgive in order to heal. Essentially all forgiveness is efficacious, that is, it produces its desired effect. If we are going to forgive as Christ has forgiven us, then we need to consider what he did. He took all the sins of the world upon himself — choosing to take the consequences of our sins on himself. Forgiveness is agreeing to live with the consequences of someone else's sins. We cry out, "That isn't fair!" because it goes against the grain of our sense of justice. Of course it's not fair, but we must do it anyway. The reality is that everyone is living with the consequences of someone else's sin. We have only one real choice: We can live with those consequences in the bondage of bitterness, or we can live in the freedom of forgiveness. We will never see our clients find freedom in Christ if we cannot help them forgive from the heart.

STEP 4: REBELLION VERSUS SUBMISSION

We live in a rebellious age. It seems as though almost everyone thinks it is his or her right to criticize and sit in judgment on those in authority. But when sown, the seeds of rebellion reap anarchy and spiritual defeat. If we have a rebellion problem, we may in fact have the worst problem in the world. Scripture instructs us to submit to and pray for those who are in authority over us (see 1 Timothy 2:2; Hebrews 13:17). Honoring one's mother and father is the first of the Ten Commandments that ends in a promise (see Deuteronomy 5:16). And consider this teaching from the New Testament:

Everyone must submit himself to the governing authorities, for there is no authority except that which God has established. The authorities that exist have been established by God. Consequently, he who rebels against the authority is rebelling against what God has instituted, and those who do so will bring judgment on themselves. For rulers hold no terror for those who do right, but for those who do wrong. Do you want to be free from fear of the one in authority? Then do what is right and he will commend you.

—ROMANS 13:1–3

There are times when we must obey God rather than humans (see Acts 5:29), but they are generally rare exceptions. When a human authority requires us to do something that is forbidden by God or restricts us from doing what God has called us to do, then we must obey God rather than the authority. The same applies when a person tries to exercise control over us that exceeds the scope of his or her authority. A police officer can give us a ticket for breaking a traffic law but cannot tell us what to believe or prevent us from going to church.

Living under the influence of repressive political regimes, critical bosses, or abusive parents can be oppressive, but they do not determine who we are unless we let them. At times it is surely legitimate and necessary to set up scriptural boundaries to protect ourselves from further abuse. For instance, a battered wife can and should report an abusive husband to the authorities. Moreover, we should righteously assert ourselves by confronting any unbiblical behavior that is abusive.

It takes a great act of faith to trust God to work through less-than-perfect authority figures, but that's what he asks us to do. To have a right relationship with God, we must be submissive both to him and to all the governing authorities who are not violating biblical boundaries. Our commanding General, the Lord Jesus Christ, is saying, "Trust me; be submissive to my authority and follow me!" He will *not* lead us into temptation but will deliver us from evil (see Matthew 6:13).

Dana had been married to Dave for twelve years; they had two children. Her diagnosis was Adjustment Disorder with Mixed Anxiety and Depressed Mood, Chronic. In counseling she shared feelings of emptiness, loneliness, tension, unhappiness, and marital dissatisfaction. Dave, a committed Christian, had turned over every stone to try to figure out how to help Dana with her feelings of discontent. Nothing he did seemed to make any difference. Dave was a devoted husband and father, they had no financial worries, and he lavished Dana with compliments, vacations, flowers, and attention; yet Dana chose to fill the empty spaces in her life by partying with girlfriends and seeking a "good time" dancing in bars with men she didn't know. Dave confronted her with the dangers this posed for her, but she ignored his warnings. She subsequently chose to have an affair with someone at work — a sin for which Dave was willing to forgive her when she confessed. Yet her rebellion against the marital covenant and her continual partying against his will was ripping the fabric of their relationship. In an attempt to fill the void of an unstable and emotionally distant family of origin, Dana set herself up, through her rebellious behavior, to lose the security she had possessed in her marriage.

Unfortunately, this vignette does not end with a satisfactory resolution, for Dana discontinued therapy, choosing not to address the rebellion either psychologically or spiritually. In a sense, she continued the rebellion by refusing to submit to the process of counseling and spiritual resolution in order to resolve her pain. Dana sorely needed a sense of who she was in Christ. She needed to recognize that she was accepted, significant, and secure as a child of the King. Instead, she willingly rebelled against God's established authority.

STEP 5: PRIDE VERSUS HUMILITY

Pride often keeps us locked into false thinking patterns and prevents us from seeking the help we need. The attitude expressed in the statement "I should be able to work this out myself!" is tragic indeed, for we were never meant to live life alone. God created Adam and Eve to live dependently on him. All temptation is an attempt to get us to live our lives independently of God. Pride is an independent spirit that wants to exalt self. But the Bible says, "God opposes the proud but gives grace to the humble" (James 4:6, quoting Proverbs 3:34). Pride says, "I can do this; I can get out of this myself." Reality says, "Oh no you can't!" Such arrogant thinking sets us up for a fall, because "pride goes before destruction, a haughty spirit before a fall" (Proverbs 16:18). We absolutely need God, and we necessarily need each other. Paul states, "For it is we who are the circumcision, we who worship by the Spirit of God, who glory in Christ Jesus, and who *put no confidence in the flesh*" (Philippians 3:3, emphasis added).

Shame and self-deprecation are not the same thing as humility. Humility is confidence properly placed — a confidence we put not in our flesh but in God alone. Self-sufficiency robs us of our sufficiency in Christ, because only *in Christ* can we do all things through him who gives us strength (see Philippians 4:13). God intended for his children to live victoriously through placing great confidence in Christ: "Not that we are competent in ourselves to claim anything for ourselves, but our competence comes from God. He has made us competent as ministers of a new covenant — not of the letter but of the Spirit; for the letter kills, but the Spirit gives life" (2 Corinthians 3:5–6).

There are many ways pride can express itself. In the Steps we list the following possibilities. Pride is

- having a stronger desire to do my will than God's will
- being more dependent on my own strength and resources than on God's
- believing too often that my ideas and opinions are better than others'
- being more concerned about controlling others than developing self-control
- sometimes considering myself more important than others
- tending to think that I have no needs

- finding it difficult to admit that I was wrong
- tending to be more of a people pleaser than a God pleaser
- being overly concerned about getting the credit I deserve
- being driven to obtain the recognition that comes from degrees, titles, and positions
- often thinking that I am more humble than others
- revealed in many other ways as God convicts us

Mark's wife of ten years was involved in an ongoing affair with her boss at work. Both Mark and his wife were Christians. They had married young and now had four small children. Mark had assumed a position of control and dominance in the relationship, giving his wife little room to grow as an individual. When the affair was disclosed, Mark became puffed up with his own righteousness and his own record of sexual purity. He began hurling Scripture verses at his wife, demanding that she repent, grovel, and submit to counseling in order to "get straightened out." In counseling, he refused to examine his own controlling behavior as something that may have contributed to the lack of intimacy in the marriage relationship (the Step 2 issue of Deception Versus Truth). Mark refused to submit to a church intervention when it was recommended he go through the "Steps to Freedom in Christ" (the Step 4 issue of Rebellion Versus Submission). Mark felt he was justified in throwing the first stone (and many subsequent stones) at his wife rather than examining his own heart to see if there was any sin (see John 8:1–11). After ten sessions, he left therapy and proceeded with a technically biblical divorce on the grounds of adultery.

STEP 6: BONDAGE VERSUS FREEDOM

Habitual sin will keep us in bondage, which can be a depressing situation for those who want to live free in Christ. Consider Paul's exhortation to the church at Rome:

> The night is nearly over; the day is almost here. So let us put aside the deeds of darkness and put on the armor of light. Let us behave decently, as in the daytime, not in orgies and drunkenness, not in sexual immorality and debauchery, not in dissension and jealousy. Rather, clothe yourselves with the Lord Jesus Christ, and do not think about how to gratify the desires of the sinful nature.
>
> —*ROMANS 13:12–14*

The only answer for breaking bondage to the sin that so easily entangles (see Hebrews 12:1) is repentance and faith in God. We can be free from bondage to sin because every believer is alive in Christ and dead to sin (see Romans 6:11).

People who have been caught in the *sin-confess-sin-confess-sin* cycle may need to follow the instructions of James 5:16: "Confess your sins to each other and pray for each other so that you may be healed." Confession is not simply saying, "I'm sorry"; rather, it is admitting, "I did it." The Christian counselor can give clients the assurance of God's pardoning grace: "If we confess our sins, [God] is faithful and just and will forgive us our sins and purify us from all unrighteousness" (1 John 1:9); the counselor can also lead clients down the road to the genuine repentance that comes to expression in a change of mind and behavior.

Sexual sins play a dominant role in Step 6. Confession alone will not break the cycle of sexual sin. Paul spells it out for us in his letter to the Romans:

> In the same way, count yourselves dead to sin but alive to God in Christ Jesus. Therefore do not let sin reign in your mortal body so that you obey its evil desires. Do not offer the parts of your body to sin, as instruments of wickedness, but rather offer yourselves to God, as those who have been brought from death to life; and offer the parts of your body to him as instruments of righteousness.
>
> —*ROMANS 6:11 – 13*

In addition to confession, therefore, we must intentionally break the reign of sin in our bodies. Paul declares that our bodies are temples of God, that if we sexually join ourselves with a prostitute we will become one flesh (see 1 Corinthians 6:15 – 20). If we commit a sexual sin, we are using our bodies as instruments not of righteousness but of wickedness. If the sexual sin was with someone other than a marital partner, we will bond together in the flesh. Therefore, we have clients ask the heavenly Father to reveal to their minds every sexual use of their bodies as an instrument of unrighteousness — and God does reveal those occasions. As each incident comes to mind, clients renounce that specific misuse of their bodies and ask God to break that bond. Finally, clients finish the Step by submitting their bodies to God as instruments of righteousness, which brings enormous freedom for those who have been sexually promiscuous or sexually violated.[5]

Tammy is a single, twenty-eight-year-old woman and the only child of her biological parents, who divorced when she was young. Tammy's mother had been sexually active with boyfriends in front of Tammy and was pregnant with Tammy when she wed. The client presented with an Axis I diagnosis of Dysthymic Disorder, an Axis II diagnosis of Histrionic Personality Disorder. She demonstrated mood lability (continual mood changes), promiscuity, flirtatiousness, superficiality, sporadic concentration, memory and appetite problems, middle insomnia, a fifteen-pound weight loss, depression, and tearfulness. Tammy had promiscuous relationships with multiple boyfriends. Due to her Christian commitment, these relationships were egodystonic (something that causes emotional distress and feels abhorrent or alien). Intellectually she knew she was trying to feed the father hunger in her life, that she craved love and affection.

She was rebellious in her teen years and was now exhibiting a lack of submissiveness to youth leaders who had asked her to resign from a sponsor role with teenage girls because of her unrepentant attitude and continuing sexual promiscuity. In counseling, we successfully worked through Step 4 (Rebellion Versus Submission).

During a subsequent session, she blurted out a confession of sexual intercourse with another boyfriend at a time she was feeling particularly vulnerable. She capitulated to his pressuring for sex and experienced self-loathing afterwards. We prayed through Step 6, with significant abreaction (expression of repressed emotions) taking place. At the end of the session, she stated, "I recognized the unlawful bonding as real for the first time; I now know how I am setting myself up for bondage." She continued to work through Step 6 on her own as a homework assignment.

STEP 7: ACQUIESCENCE VERSUS RENUNCIATION

The last step in helping others find freedom in Christ is guiding them to renounce the sins of their ancestors and actively take their place in Christ and resist the devil. The Ten Commandments reveal that the sins of fathers can affect the third and fourth generations (see Exodus 20:5). This reality is evident in our society in the well-known cycles of abuse that continue from generation to generation. Jesus declares the following in his message against the religious leaders of his day:

> Woe to you, teachers of the law and Pharisees, you hypocrites! You build tombs for the prophets and decorate the graves of the righteous.

> And you say, "If we had lived in the days of our forefathers, we would not have taken part with them in shedding the blood of the prophets." So you testify against yourselves that you are the descendants of those who murdered the prophets. Fill up, then, the measure of the sin of your forefathers!
>
> —MATTHEW 23:29–32

Although we are not personally guilty of our ancestors' sins (see Jeremiah 31:29–30; Ezekiel 18:2–32), we do live with the consequences of their sin—and we will continue to live in the way we were taught unless we repent. As Jesus notes, "A student is not above his teacher, but everyone who is fully trained will be like his teacher" (Luke 6:40). The primary teachers in the first five years of our lives are our parents, and much of our personality and temperament becomes established in those early and formative years of our lives.

When people repented in the Old Testament, they confessed their sins *and* the sins of their ancestors (see Nehemiah 1:6–7; 9:2; Jeremiah 14:20; Daniel 9:10–11), and, by inference they refused to follow their forefathers' lead any further. We have the same responsibility today to recognize our own sins and the sins of our ancestors, to confess them, and to refuse to be held in bondage to living these sins out in our lives. We can claim the power of Christ's work on the cross, stated so eloquently by Peter, who wrote, "For you know that it was not with perishable things such as silver or gold that you were redeemed from the empty way of life handed down to you from your forefathers, but with the precious blood of Christ, a lamb without blemish or defect" (1 Peter 1:18–19).

Praying the closing prayers of Step 7 (see Appendix E, pages 407-408) can produce surprising results that are almost always related to a client's ancestors. One client had an apparition of what she believed to be her father. After sharing what she saw, she declared, "I am responsible for my father." She was set free after she renounced that lie and finished the "Steps to Freedom in Christ."

Renouncing the sins of one's parents is also needed in unexpected times and places. For example, Neil counseled a denominational leader's wife who began the session by saying, "I was raised in a good Christian home." During the session certain realities of what life had been like for this woman as she was growing up were brought to the surface. When the session concluded, she remarked, "It wasn't a particularly good Christian home after all, was it?" She sent the following letter to Neil, which illustrates why we believe every Christian client needs to be firmly rooted in Christ:

How can I say thanks? The Lord allowed me to spend time with you just when I was concluding that there was no hope for me to ever break free from the downward spiral of continual defeat, depression, and guilt.

Since I literally grew up in church and had been a pastor's wife for twenty-three years, everyone thought I was as put together on the inside as I was on the outside. On the contrary, I knew that there was no infrastructure on the inside and often wondered when the weight of trying to hold myself together would cause my life to fall apart and come crumbling down. It seemed as if sheer determination was the only thing that kept me going.

When I left your office last Thursday it was a beautiful, crystal-clear day with the snow visible on the mountains. It felt like a film had been lifted from over my eyes. The tape player was playing a piano arrangement of "It Is Well With My Soul." The words of the song fairly exploded in my mind with the realization that it was well in my soul for the first time in years.

The next day in the office my immediate response to "How are you today?" was, "I'm doing great! How about you?" In the past I would have mumbled something about being almost alive. The next comment I heard was, "Boy, something must have happened to you yesterday."

I hear the same songs and read the same Bible verses as before, but it is as if I'm really hearing them for the first time. There is an underlying joy and peace in the midst of the same circumstances that used to bring defeat and discouragement. For the first time I have wanted to read my Bible and pray. It is hard to contain myself. I want to shout from the rooftops what has taken place in my life, but my real desire is for my life to do the shouting.

Already the deceiver has tried to plant thoughts in my mind and tell me that this won't last. It's just another gimmick that won't work. The difference is, now I know those are lies from Satan and not the truth. What a difference freedom in Christ makes!

Practitioner and Client Assessment

I believe that problems can be dissolved by grace, like a mist that is dissipated by the sunshine. One sees the Christian Gospel of salvation quite concretely at work in the gradual dissolution of tangled problems, without any of them being solved in the usual sense of the word.

PAUL TOURNIER

When we walk into our outpatient mental health practice on a given morning, we realize we are about to minister to persons who are entrusting their stories, their pain, and their problems to us. When we pick up the "Day Sheet" that lists the names of our clients and times of appointments, we are struck by the importance of what we do. This is not an assembly line where one part fits all, a fast-food operation in which speed is the primary goal, or a department store where the customer is looking for the best buys. This is a place where people come to grieve, find symptom relief, refute lies, be encouraged, rebuild relationships, find hope in the midst of suffering, and be restored. Many clients hope we'll be able to explain how Jesus Christ is the answer for them.

We realize these individuals are typically in states of crises and that the present events of their lives will have serious implications for their future. In a real sense our offices are psychological emergency rooms. We also realize that what is said and done during their crisis will stick with the client more intensely than what transpires during noncrisis times. The words we speak, the suggestions we offer, and the strategies we employ will be seared into their hearts, minds, and souls as at no other time. The practice of counseling resembles movements made by surgeons. "Incisions" made by the words and strategies employed during these appointment times can be precise, or they can be jagged. These incisions may be right on the mark, or regrettably they may follow along a wrong track. The aftermath of these interventions will lead to post-session healing that continues after the "abscess" or "cancer" is excised, or there will be an "infection and relapse" because of a misdiagnosed condition and subsequent inaccurate intervention.

Our Christian clients are children of God and the apple of his eye. We are the human tools the Lord uses to minister his grace and healing to those in distress. We have the privilege to minister truth to our clients from a foundation of love and concern for them as unique, eternal, image-bearing souls.

PRACTITIONER COMPREHENSIVE SELF-ASSESSMENT

In order to be an effective instrument in God's hands, the counselor must have a full appreciation of his or her own growth issues, as well as a client's personal struggle with sin. The therapist who sits in the counselor's chair is by no means a perfect human being. He or she is also in the process of being conformed to the image of God. The therapist and the client bring into the office the scars of original sin — scars that would surely disqualify both if not for the grace of God. We all stand on one particular rung of the recovery ladder and reach down to help the one below. We cannot model perfection; we can only model growth.

To describe this spiritual struggle, Julie often uses an example from the biology laboratory. She starts with the biblical truth that "all have sinned and fall short of the glory of God" (Romans 3:23). Sin is any departure from God's nature, laws, or principles, either by commission or omission. Heaven is like a sterile petri dish, with no microorganisms growing inside it. However, if even one foreign bacteria enters the petri dish, the entire sterile surface will be overrun with invaders, spoiling the perfection of the sterile environment. James teaches us this truth: "For whoever keeps the whole law and yet stumbles at just one point is guilty of breaking all of it" (James 2:10). The New Living Translation's rendering of this verse reads, "And the person who keeps all of the laws except one is as guilty as the person who has broken all of God's laws."

Taking this truth to heart could result in incredible guilt if it were not for the fact that Jesus dealt with our sin. We are forgiven but not yet perfect. When our redeemed inner person is separated from our mortal bodies at physical death, we will receive a resurrected body and be fully sanctified. Only then will we be able to live in the perfect presence of God.

Until then we must strive to live a righteous life, because God can only work through clean instruments for noble purposes (see 2 Timothy 2:21).

It is imperative that we resolve our own personal and spiritual conflicts before we try to help others. Consider the words of Jesus:

> Why do you look at the speck of sawdust in your brother's eye and pay no attention to the plank in your own eye? How can you say to your brother, "Let me take the speck out of your eye," when all the time there is a plank in your own eye? You hypocrite, first take the plank out of your own eye, and then you will see clearly to remove the speck from your brother's eye.
>
> —MATTHEW 7:3–5

Our clients come to us with specks in their eyes. But it is prideful and arrogant to view their problems as planks and our own imperfections as specks!

Christian psychologist Mark McMinn writes, "Christian spirituality does not begin merely in our quest for understanding. It begins in our understanding that something is deeply wrong within us — a realization that can lead to a renewed dedication to the values of the gospel."[1] In other words, the practice of Christian psychotherapy begins with the awareness of the plank in our own eyes. Both the personal and professional lives of counselors intersect in the realm of spiritual formation. The presence of spiritual disciplines, or lack of them, affects the process behind closed doors. Dr. McMinn observes, "The kind of therapeutic relationships that foster healing are not formed merely from well-chosen techniques, but grow out of the inner life."[2] In short, counseling is both professional and personal, both theoretical and personal, both theological and personal.

How can a client mature in the Lord beyond the level of the counselor's spiritual maturity in the therapeutic relationship? Jesus made the following observation: "Can a blind man lead a blind man? Will they not both fall into a pit? A student is not above his teacher, but everyone who is fully trained will be like his teacher" (Luke 6:39–40). We as therapists can only counsel out of our fullness, for there can be no water fetched out of an empty well! The prophet Jeremiah records a vivid declaration by the Lord: "My people have committed two sins: They have forsaken me, the spring of living water, and have dug their own cisterns, broken cisterns that cannot hold water" (Jeremiah 2:13–14).

Terry was raised in Iowa, where his father planted a large garden every spring. He fertilized the garden, watered it, and pulled the weeds, which enabled the plants to thrive in the rich soil. The harvested beans, peas, tomatoes, carrots, peppers, and onions were the "fruit" of the garden that blessed the family with food in the winter. After Terry and Julie married, they rented a suburban apartment that had a balcony facing west. Eager to have a touch of Iowa in that eastern metropolitan city, Terry built a large wooden box, filled it with dirt, and planted flowers and vegetables.

Everything looked great as Terry watered, weeded, and tended his large window-box garden. After he and Julie traveled out of town for a four-day weekend, they returned to find all the plants wilted and half dead. They had neglected to arrange for watering during their absence, and the intensity of the hot sun had sapped the plants' vitality and stunted their growth. Terry had a choice to make: He could pull up the wilted plants and throw them away, or he could try to save them with a little tender loving care. He chose the latter and made sure he arranged for someone to water the plants whenever they were gone — and the garden survived.

Christian therapy for our clients is like pulling the weeds and nurturing the root system that brings life to the plant. The Latin derivation of the word *nurture* means "to feed, to suckle, to provide the necessary ingredients for growth and well-being." Although we counselors desire growth in our clients, we must understand our limitations. We have the privilege to plant and to water, but *God* makes it grow (see 1 Corinthians 3:7). Jesus states, "I am the true vine, and my Father is the gardener. He cuts off every branch in me that bears no fruit, while every branch that does bear fruit he prunes so that it will be even more fruitful" (John 15:1 – 2).

THERAPY FOR THE CHRISTIAN COUNSELOR

Mark McMinn recommends personal therapy for those who want to become effective counselors.[3] First, to do so gives the therapist a perspective of what it's like to be in the chair of the client. We have no right to expect our clients to do what we are unwilling to do. Second, to do so provides an objective understanding of our own mental health and spiritual maturity. We can use the words of the apostle John as the underlying basis for Christian therapists and their practices: "If we walk in the light, as [God] is in the light, we have fellowship with one another, and the blood of Jesus, his Son, purifies us from all sin" (1 John 1:7). When we expose ourselves to the light, sin loses its power to control us. It is no longer the dark, hovering force that easily crushes us with guilt and shame. In the light, sin is exposed for what it is: a wrong behavior or attitude. The very act of telling someone what we have done or what we have failed to do is the first step in genuine repentance and recovery in Christ. We can do this because we are already forgiven and there is "no condemnation for those who are in Christ Jesus" (Romans 8:1). *Confession* literally means "to agree with God"; it is essentially the same thing as "walking in the light."

If we follow Dr. McMinn's advice and go to a Christian counselor, the therapist can help us to be transparent and vulnerable with God. As Siang-Yang Tan and Douglas Gregg observe, "In reacting to us as God does, without condemnation or reproach, but with grace, wisdom, and counsel, these confessors proclaim the mercy and forgiveness of God."[4] It is personally valuable for us to walk in the light with another counselor and experience the blessing that comes from it. It will also sensitize us to our clients' vulnerability so we can respond with the same mercy and grace, and it ensures congruence in therapy as well as professional integrity.

The "Steps to Freedom in Christ" (see Appendix E) can be used as a means to do some of our own necessary spiritual "housecleaning." We as counselors can get alone with God and work through the process by ourselves. Neil has received unsolicited testimonies of people who are finding their freedom in Christ by working through these issues on their own in the presence of God. At the same time he has received thousands of letters from people who have been assisted through the process by laypersons, pastors, and counselors. We recommend that you work through the Steps with another person whenever possible. We will probably receive a more satisfying resolution if we allow ourselves to be led through the process by a trusted spiritual leader. But we cannot lead someone else to freedom in Christ if we are not free ourselves, and we cannot impart to others what we ourselves do not possess.

INVOLVEMENT IN AN ACCOUNTABILITY GROUP

Involvement in an accountability group in which tough, revealing questions can be asked is another growth strategy to consider. Julie is in an accountability group that has been meeting monthly over the course of the past seven years. The meeting time consists of thirty-minute segments where each group member shares concerns, asks for feedback, and receives prayer support for current life issues. Psychologist Stanton Jones agrees that accountability relationships are crucial. However, he goes beyond the personal accountability group just described and expands it to accountability for the ways counselors represent their differing religious traditions. Jones asserts that we spend too much time on the technical aspects of applied science and too little on the moral-religious dimensions of our work. He believes that psychologists who identify with a particular religious tradition should establish formal accountability relationships with like-minded people in order to articulate that tradition more responsibly.[5] This commitment goes beyond a casual (that is, church school level) understanding of a denomination's doctrines to a deeper, more comprehensive grasp of one's faith, which will in turn facilitate the accurate integration of theology and psychology.

BALANCED READING OF BOTH BIBLICAL AND SECULAR SOURCES

Mark McMinn suggests the following challenge for counselors: For every page we read in contemporary counseling books (including self-help books), we ought to read at least one page in the spiritual classics and one chapter of Scripture.[6] There are, as we have noted, competing worldviews in modern culture, so it is wise to balance our exposure to them with time spent sharpening our biblical-Christian worldview. It is an undeniable fact that our diet affects our health. What we read in the professional psychology journals is very likely being influenced by the utopianist, the humanist, or the New Age worldviews. Like the proverbial frog in the kettle that doesn't realize it is slowly being cooked to death, we can gradually accommodate ourselves to subtle changes in thinking until we eventually succumb without much protest. The Bible is the only authoritative source for the biblical-Christian worldview to which we as Christian counselors subscribe. We must stay true to the process of being transformed by the renewing of our minds with the truth of God's Word.

PURSUIT OF SPIRITUAL DISCIPLINES

In general, spiritually mature therapists can more effectively facilitate growth and development in their clients than those who are spiritually immature. Maturity is a process, not an event. Maturity can be delayed, disrupted, or halted if the mind is so deceived or so damaged by strongholds and bondages that God's truths are not able to be perceived.

Because Christian therapists have adopted the biblical-Christian world-view, a knowledge of spiritual formation and the spiritual disciplines is critical for spiritual maturity. Citing spiritual formation professors Richard Foster and Dallas Willard, psychology professor Siang-Yang Tan states:

> From a Christian perspective, the following spiritual disciplines are helpful for developing mature faith and deep Christlike spirituality: the inward disciplines of meditation, prayer, fasting and study; the outward disciplines of simplicity, solitude, submission, and service; and the corporate disciplines of confession, worship, guidance, and celebration.[7]

We would add another spiritual discipline, namely, to put on the armor of God and to take captive every thought to make it obedient to Christ (see Ephesians 6:10–18; 2 Corinthians 10:5). In order to stay free in Christ, we must appropriate all that God has provided for us. As Christian counselors we need to be familiar with principles of spiritual warfare, including the ability to recognize demonic harassment and confusion. The level of deception in our clients is increasing with the rise of postmodernism and New Age philosophy. False messiahs, prophets, and teachers will increase in the latter days, according to the teachings of Scripture, and many of our clients seem to be paying greater attention to "deceiving spirits" (1 Timothy 4:1). Good people can be deceived, and, like any other Christian, therapists are vulnerable. We all stand in need of the encouragement shared by Paul in his letter to the Ephesians: "Finally, be strong in the Lord and in his mighty power. Put on the full armor of God so that you can take your stand against the devil's schemes" (Ephesians 6:10–11).

Dr. McMinn believes that in order to counsel from a biblical-Christian worldview the therapist must be competent theologically, psychologically, and spiritually. The integration of these three components is not accomplished by the credential approach used in theology and psychology, namely, completion of X number of classes leads to a degree, which leads to the right to practice your particular specialty. Rather, it is only personal interaction with the Lord that creates a mature spiritual life.[8]

Piano teachers cannot instruct students if they themselves don't know how to play. An overweight and out-of-shape aerobics instructor unable to perform his or her own routine would soon lose the class to others who demonstrate competency. So it is for therapists in the counseling relationship, as Dr. McMinn explains:

A counselor cannot simply walk into the office and "put on" an effective counseling demeanor even if using prayer, Scripture, or other religious interventions during the session. The substance of spiritually sensitive counseling goes deeper than technique; the care, disciplined objectivity, trustworthiness, empathy, wisdom, and insight must come from within. . . .

Truth is almost always communicated in embodied form. Most of what we know about grace and salvation is accessible to us because Jesus was incarnated and demonstrated a living theology. . . . We remember movies and stories more than essays because we are quicker to observe and understand truth that is embodied. In the same way, truth is communicated more by who the counselor is than by what the counselor says.[9]

DEPENDENCE ON GOD IN THE COUNSELING SESSION

Counselors are the Lord's servants, channeling his grace and mercy to his children. Mother Teresa is reported to have once said, "We are to be pencils in the hand of God, writing his story in the lives of the people we encounter." Spiritually mature counselors know that they can't do anything apart from Christ. Therefore, the Lord is the central figure in the counseling process, with the Holy Spirit prompting, guiding, convicting, comforting, and revealing. There are three ways to envision the triune God's presence in the counseling process:

God the Father as the Senior Surgeon

Long before we begin, God has plowed the ground. The Senior Surgeon is always present — watching, making sure things go according to plan, providing a sense of security. He expresses his wisdom through us as we relate to and care for the client in our offices. We take great comfort in this truth: "Nothing in all creation is hidden from God's sight" (Hebrews 4:13).

God the Son as the Wounded Healer

Jesus Christ is our co-counselor who is touched by the pains, sorrows, and troubles of others. In Jesus we encounter the Wounded Healer, the God-Man who shared in the problems and sufferings of human life. Not only did he share them, but he took them on himself. He has been to the cross. He knows what suffering is: "Because he himself suffered when he was tempted, he is able to help those who are being tempted" (Hebrews 2:18).

God the Holy Spirit as the Counselor and Revealer

God is present in our lives through the indwelling Holy Spirit, who provides guidance and leads us into all truth. He also is the source of power over the spiritual forces of evil, for "the one who is in you is greater than the one who is in the world" (1 John 4:4).

By way of summary, spiritually mature therapists are those who have

- resolved their own personal and spiritual conflicts in Christ
- involved themselves in an accountability group
- balanced their reading between biblical and technical sources
- pursued the spiritual disciplines
- depended on God in the counseling process

CLIENT COMPREHENSIVE ASSESSMENT

Differentiating between the psychological, physical, and spiritual dimensions of the client's problem poses a difficult challenge when these dimensions intersect at common points. Because of this challenge, Christian therapists assess all domains prior to deciding on interventions. For instance, where is the line of demarcation between the psychological, the physical, and the spiritual in grief therapy? Psychologically, an individual goes through stages of shock, denial, anger, bargaining, and depression to come in the end, one hopes, to acceptance. Physically, the client often experiences fatigue, chest heaviness, sleep disturbance, appetite alterations, and the like. Spiritually, God is the ever-present help in time of need and the only source for overcoming losses and feelings of helplessness and hopelessness. The speed of clients' recovery will vary greatly, depending on whether or not they turn to the God of all comfort and allow themselves to feel the full force of the loss. Jesus said, "Blessed are those who mourn, for they will be comforted" (Matthew 5:4). In analyzing treatment options for a client, interventions exist for the psychological, physical, and spiritual dimensions to assist the client in resolution of the loss.

The marketplace standard for psychological evaluation of the client is the *Diagnostic and Statistical Manual of Mental Disorders*, 4th ed. (DSM-IV), published by the American Psychiatric Association in 1994.[10] This edition includes an important change for Christian counselors: formal acknowledgment that spirituality is a factor both in the diagnosis of mental health problems and in psychological treatment planning. The diagnosis, which is identified as V62.89 Religious or Spiritual Problem, is defined as follows:

> This category can be used when the focus of clinical attention is a religious or spiritual problem. Examples include distressing experiences that involve loss or questioning of faith, problems associated with conversion to a new faith, or questioning of spiritual values that may not necessarily be related to an organized church or religious institution.[11]

This addition to the mental health diagnostic categories is important because greater intentional emphasis may now be placed in graduate education on Christian spiritual health. Most counselors, Christian and non-Christian, have been trained in secular graduate programs in which humanist, utopianist, and New Age worldviews were infused without being identified as religious. Advanced training in the typical graduate program involves little or no appreciation among faculty for religious principles, which blatantly leaves Christianity "out" and the others subtly "in."

For example, Terry received his secular terminal degree as Doctor of Philosophy; Julie's advanced degree is a Master of Science in Psychiatric Nursing (she is also certified as a Clinical Specialist for Advanced Practice by the American Nurses Association). Both were trained to use their education as "scientist practitioners," focusing attention on the observable and measurable. Before Terry became a Christian, the closest he ever came to anything "spiritual" in his graduate work as a psychologist was in his doctoral research on the use of Viktor Frankl's (1905–1998) existential-humanist psychotherapy approach called logotherapy.[12]

Outside of a few Christian universities and colleges, we know of no advanced diploma offered for the study of spiritual health. Psychology professors Edward Shafranske and H. Newton Malony indicate that support for including religious issues in graduate mental health training "appears to be developing in a number of professional associations."[13] In addition, the American Psychiatric Association recommends that "religion be considered in the evaluation and treatment of patients within residency training."[14]

When formal instruction has addressed the issue of spiritual health, the approach has typically been anti-Christian. Generally a humanist worldview is promoted, and counselors are taught that only that which can be seen and rationally explained through scientific study is acceptable. Thus Drs. Shafranske and Malony state, "Our training as social-behavioral scientists has been dominated by a 'methodological atheism' at best and a 'materialistic bias' at worst. Both are understandable. They reflect our scholarly heritage and current understanding of behavioral causation."[15]

Historically, psychology as a discipline has been closely linked with the modern scientific approach. Limiting itself to observable and rationally explicable evidence, psychology has avoided conclusions about human events that could not be applied within an empirical framework. Furthermore, psychology promoted the belief that one could obtain a factual, objective reading of reality through certain scientific procedures. In short, "religious thinking was seen to be anathema to the scientific mind."[16] This view forms part of the perspective represented by the Closed approach discussed in chapter three.

Such an orientation is too inaccurate and incomplete for a Christian counselor to adopt. It leads to a false dichotomy. A Christian therapist must approach the task of diagnostic assessment with a balanced worldview, which requires a therapist to be familiar with the criteria used to differentiate health from illness in both the spiritual and psychological dimensions of the client. As Shafranske and Malony observe, "Elements of religious involvement, including beliefs, practices, and affiliations, should be assessed in terms of their dynamic role in supporting or impeding mental health."[17] This statement defines the Conjoint approach described in chapter three. In order to maintain a healthy balance between the spiritual and psychological realms, a therapist must integrate the definitions of spiritual health and mental health into his or her assessments and treatment choices. When the reality of the spiritual world is accepted as a potential contributor to mental health problems, the explanation for voices being heard in a person's head expands from one to two or more. The symptoms may be the result of paying attention to deceiving spirits or of a psychotic break manifest as auditory hallucinations; both perspectives need to be considered when doing an assessment.

If a Christian therapist discerns or suspects that the client is spiritually deceived, the therapist can now use the DSM-IV category V62.89 Religious or Spiritual Problem in his or her diagnosis. This code supports psychotherapeutic consideration of spiritual issues during a session, even when the session is paid for by insurance. Unfortunately, third-party reimbursement to mental health professionals is not at a stage where payment for counseling services exclusively focused on a religious problem can be routinely expected. Therefore, when insurance companies are being billed, a spiritual diagnosis code should only be noted secondarily as it interfaces with other primary diagnoses. If there is no other legitimate primary diagnosis, then insurance should not be billed, and the client will have to use self-pay (fee for service).

ASSESSMENT OF THE CLIENT'S SPIRITUAL WELL-BEING

For many secularly trained Christian therapists, the idea that clients have problems that need to be assessed and treated in the spiritual as well as the psychological realm is unfamiliar and perhaps even uncomfortable. Fortunately, help is available. For example, the National Institute for Healthcare Research has published four volumes that offer compelling evidence for the need to assess spiritual dimensions.[18] This organization also has a curriculum for introducing spiritual assessment and interventions into psychiatric residency programs.[19] Tools for assessment can be routinely used at intake and then discussed with the client in the first and subsequent sessions.

Assessing clients' spiritual condition can be difficult for a relatively simple reason: The presenting problem is seldom the root issue. Clients may honestly tell their counselors what has happened to them, but they are less likely to share how they feel about it and what they have chosen to believe as a result of it. What the therapist can see rather easily is a barren life; what is out of sight is the *root system* that serves as the foundation for their life. David Ritzenthaler, who founded and directs Victorious Christian Living International, a Christ-centered counseling center in Phoenix, Arizona, developed the Barren Tree diagram (see Figure 7.1) to depict the spiritual condition of struggling clients.

Below the surface in every struggling client lies a faulty root system. No attempt to repair surface issues will produce any lasting benefit unless the root system is dealt with. Utilizing the methodology of behaviorism alone is like trying to glue leaves back on a tree. We must identify what is causing the barren life — which is what we attempt to do as we use the "Steps to Freedom in Christ." It is, however, not the absolute responsibility of the therapist to bring to the surface what is hidden. God knows — and his Word proclaims, "There is nothing concealed that will not be disclosed, or hidden that will not be made known" (Matthew 10:26). Moreover, God is the One who grants "repentance leading [people] to a knowledge of the truth" (2 Timothy 2:25). People are in bondage to the past because of the lies they believe. It is truth that sets us free. The Bible clearly identifies the source of these lies as the world, the flesh, and the devil:

As for you, you were dead in your transgressions and sins, in which you used to live when you followed the ways of this world and of the ruler of the kingdom of the air [the devil], the spirit who is now at work in those who are disobedient. All of us also lived among them at one time, gratifying the cravings of our sinful nature [the flesh] and following its desires and thoughts. Like the rest, we were by nature objects of wrath.

—*EPHESIANS 2:1–3*

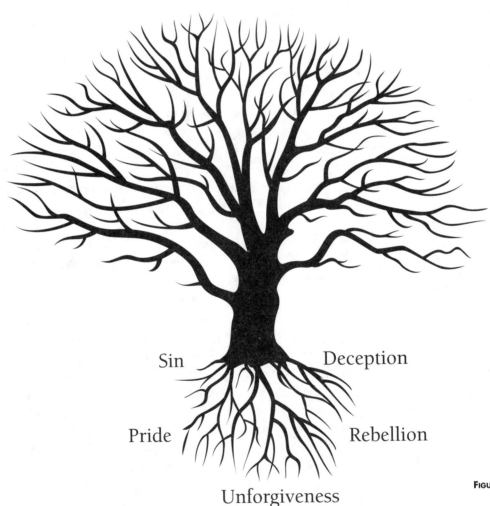

Sin   Deception

Pride   Rebellion

Unforgiveness

FIGURE 7.1

The therapist must assess the extent to which clients have a biblical understanding of Jesus Christ and whether they have a personal relationship with him. If clients are truly born-again children of God, they have been purchased by Christ's blood (see 1 Peter 1:19). They belong to God, and Satan cannot change that. Satan cannot do a thing about their position in Christ, but if he can get them to believe that they are not secure in Christ, they will live as though they are not. Satan will tempt them, accuse them, and try to deceive them, but he cannot separate them from the love of God (see Romans 8:38–39). Yet, a therapist needs to be aware of the various influences that can potentially sabotage the healing process.

Worldly Influences

Nothing has done more damage to the church worldwide than syncretism, the blending of divine revelation with existing cultural beliefs. It is often easier to recognize the problem on the mission field, where Christianity is typically blended with some form of spiritism. It is difficult to recognize our own struggle with syncretism because our Christian beliefs most often get blended in with Western rationalism and materialism. The biblical writer James had strong words for Christians who want the best of both worlds: "You adulterous people, don't you know that friendship with the world is hatred toward God? Anyone who chooses to be a friend of the world becomes an enemy of God" (James 4:4). Paul expressed a similar warning: "What agreement is there between the temple of God and idols? For we are the temple of the living God. As God has said: 'I will live with them and walk among them, and I will be their God, and they will be my people.' 'Therefore, come out from them and be separate, says the Lord'" (2 Corinthians 6:16–17).

We have seen many clients who have been influenced one moment by their church and the next moment by the world. They appear to come to some measure of resolution in therapy, then change their minds the moment they reenter the world. Initial assessment seeks to understand what impact the environment has had on the client and what existing worldly influences might undermine therapy or support it. New Testament professor Clinton Arnold describes these worldly influences as "the ungodly aspects of culture, peer pressure, values, traditions, 'what is in,' 'what is cool,' customs, philosophies, and attitudes. The world represents the prevailing worldview assumptions of the day that stand contrary to the biblical understanding of reality and biblical values."[20]

One example of worldly influences involved a seven-year-old whose divorced parents shared legal and physical custody. The father was a Christian who had remarried; the mother, not a believer, remained single and was cohabiting with a divorced man. The parents sought counseling to resolve a conflict over how their child was to participate in Halloween activities. The father and stepmother wanted the child to attend a costume party at church; the mother and her live-in partner threatened court action if the child was not allowed to dress up as a goblin and go trick-or-treating with neighborhood friends. Clearly, both parties were influenced by their own worldviews. Unfortunately, the mother's worldview was not a Christian one.

Fleshly Influences

The flesh stands in opposition to the Spirit of truth: "For the sinful nature [the flesh] desires what is contrary to the Spirit, and the Spirit what is contrary to the sinful nature. They are in conflict with each other" (Galatians 5:17). They are in opposition because the Holy Spirit operates in a dependent relationship with God the Father, and the flesh always operates independently of God. Before salvation, we had learned to live our lives independently of God. Thus, a proper diagnosis must consider these strongholds, or flesh patterns, which can be deeply ingrained. Galatians 5:19–21 and Colossians 3:5, 8 list these deeds of the flesh. These flesh patterns do not produce a Christlike temperament; rather, they are part of the old Adamic nature described by James:

> What causes fights and quarrels among you? Don't they come from your desires that battle within you? You want something but don't get it. You kill and covet, but you cannot have what you want. You quarrel and fight. You do not have, because you do not ask God. When you ask, you do not receive, because you ask with wrong motives, that you may spend what you get on your pleasures.
>
> —JAMES 4:1–3

Identifying the influence of the flesh is not always easy. For example, consider the case of a middle-aged client who worked as a sales representative. This man struggled with deeply ingrained flesh patterns. He presented with a history of obesity, hatred toward his father and older brother, gambling problems, and a marital separation. His initial reason for coming to therapy was a desire for help with his goal of becoming more financially successful in his job!

Another client came for counseling because she was jealous of and angry about her coworker's promotion to partner in the law firm for which they worked. She presented with symptoms of depression because her efforts to discredit her colleague were being rejected by other employees. She was also upset that a senior partner had confronted her after he heard that she had "joked" about sabotaging the coworker's legal briefs.

In both of these cases, an assessment of the fleshly influences and motivations is crucial in order to identify the root causes and address the root systems of the clients. The fleshly influences of worldly values and emotions will need to be considered when working with clients toward restoration of mental health.

Satanic Influences

Nearly two thousand years ago the apostle Paul observed, "The Spirit clearly says that in later times some will abandon the faith and follow deceiving spirits and things taught by demons" (1 Timothy 4:1). We have seen evidence of this all over the world. Neil makes these comments in his book *Victory Over the Darkness*:

> Satan and his demons are actively involved in trying to distract you from your walk of faith by peppering your mind with his thoughts and ideas. He is relentless in his attempts to establish negative, worldly patterns of thought in your mind which will in turn produce negative, worldly patterns of behavior.[21]

The fact that the father of lies can put thoughts into the minds of believers is evident throughout Scripture: "Satan rose up against Israel and incited David to take a census of Israel" (1 Chronicles 21:1); "Then Peter said, 'Ananias, how is it that Satan has so filled your heart that you have lied to the Holy Spirit and have kept for yourself some of the money you received for the land?'" (Acts 5:3). God struck down Ananias and Sapphira because he wanted to send a message to the early church: If Satan could get us to believe a lie, he could control our lives.

Several examples will illustrate what we mean. A godly wife of a pastor suffered from pneumonia. During the process of removing fluid from her lungs, cancer was discovered, and she became fearful. She confided to Neil doubts about her salvation. When asked why she was questioning her salvation, she said, "I struggle with these foul thoughts, and when I go to church they are blasphemous thoughts." Neil immediately discerned this situation to be a spiritual battle for her mind. Within an hour she was free from those condemning thoughts. This woman's fear had been triggered by the possibility of dying without the assurance of salvation.

A young man sitting in church became overwhelmed with homosexual thoughts toward the pastor. He shared this with his parents, who correctly diagnosed the problem as a spiritual one. Relieved to hear this, the young man was instructed not to pay attention to these thoughts, and they slowly subsided. If he hadn't told his parents, he may have reasoned, "Why am I thinking these thoughts? If I'm thinking these thoughts, then maybe I'm a homosexual." If he had believed the lie, he may have concluded that he must be a homosexual. He shared the battle for his mind, and he was able to overcome.

Sometimes the spiritual battle for the mind is very subtle. Once a theologian told Neil, "Every time I meet a man for the first time, I immediately look at his crotch!" He wasn't struggling with homosexuality; in fact, he abhorred it. Yet this distracting habit was making him insecure and fearful. A therapist had a similar struggle during graduate school. Every time he had a cup of coffee in his hand and happened to meet a person along the way, he was attacked by the thought, "Throw it in his face!" These subtle spiritual attacks on these godly and mature men had no basis in psychology. The thoughts were contrary to their true nature and had no basis of origin except in the spiritual realm.

Likewise, imagine a mother of two just home from the hospital following the birth of her third child. She is extremely tired and vulnerable. Suddenly she has a distinct thought, "Kill your baby!" At first she is shocked that she could have such a thought. Who is she going to share this thought with? Her husband? "Sweetheart, I've been thinking about killing our baby!" In a case like this the diagnosis would probably be postpartum depression, but it may not be the root issue. To immediately consider the problem to be all psychological or even all spiritual would be a mistake; rather, we suggest that a counselor consider a third option. This woman's problem could be a combination of psychological, physical, and spiritual issues. In our experience, a thorough assessment should include all three.

The following testimony Neil received in an e-mail message explains why we must seek to understand this battle for our minds and not neglect a consideration of the spiritual realm:

> I wanted to thank you for showing me how to be mentally free. Ever since I was a teenager (I am now 36), I had "voices" in my head. There were four in particular and sometimes what seemed loud choruses of

them. When the subject of schizophrenia would come up on television or in a magazine, I would think to myself, "I know I am not schizophrenic, but what is this in my head?"

I was tortured, mocked, and jeered; every single thought I had was second-guessed. Consequently, I had zero self-esteem. I often wished the voices would be quiet, and I always wondered if other people had this as well and if it was "common."

I learned from you how to take every thought captive to Christ. When I learned that others struggled with these voices, I came to recognize them for what they were, and I was able to make them leave.

This was an amazing and beautiful thing. To be fully quiet in my mind, after so many years of torment. I don't need to explain further all the wonderful things that come with this freedom of the mind; it is a blessing you seem to know well. I could write volumes explaining all that was before and all that is now.

Separating the client's own thoughts from foreign thoughts is critical for diagnosis. It becomes even harder when dealing with Dissociative Identity Disorders, because these clients can seldom discern whether the thought is demonic or the expression of an alter personality. They cannot tell a fragmented personality, which is a part of themselves, to leave. Thus, it does no good for someone to misdiagnose this as a demon and try to drive it out. A counselor, on the other hand, could misdiagnose a demonic presence as an alter personality and try to integrate its influence into a client's personality.

Examples of Satan's influence can be found in virtually every aspect of our culture. For example, a settlement for $10.6 million was reached between a woman who sued two psychiatrists and the hospital that employed them because she was allegedly led "to recall that she had been a high priestess in a satanic cult."[22] One must ask: Was this a false memory planted by the counselors, or was it an honest attempt on the part of the therapists to set a captive free?

The media, especially in television and film, is another area in which Satan has been able to exert considerable influence. Consider the Disney/ABC-sponsored sitcom *Ellen*, whose main character openly professed to be a lesbian. After the show was removed, the president of ABC admitted that Disney/ABC had done everything possible in promoting the gay theme. Even though ABC was dropping the show, he said the network had been unbelievably supportive of the sitcom's effort to increase people's tolerance of homosexuals.[23] Furthermore, Hollywood film productions have begun to heavily promote the occult, according to evangelist Paul McGuire. Regarding the widespread promotion of New Age thinking in the film and television industry, McGuire writes:

> It's not that a group of Hollywood executives, producers, and stars got together in some dark room to plan a conspiracy. It's simply that Hollywood films and television programs reflect the spiritual beliefs of those who produce them. However, the net result is the same because the power of those films and television shows to influence young minds and shape the belief systems of new generations is staggering. In a very real sense, "evangelism" is occurring and — perhaps unwittingly — many of Hollywood's biggest stars are winning souls for the occult.[24]

Demonic influence often leads to terrible crimes. The recent nation-wide epidemic of school shootings is a clear example. Local pastors in Littleton, Colorado, expressed the belief that the behavior of Eric Harris and Dylan Klebold at Columbine High School was motivated by Satan. In a similar case, Luke Woodham, a Pearl, Mississippi, high school student, killed two students and his mother. At his trial he testified that demons "said I was nothing and I would never be anything if I didn't get to that school and kill those people."[25] The news article further revealed that the student was following instructions from an allegedly satanic mentor.

New Age therapists often incorporate demonic influences into their practices. There is nothing new about what they are doing. Change the names from *medium* to *channeler* and *demon* to *spirit guide* — a gullible public will never know. These psychics are also challenging the field of psychology. Consider the lead article in a 1998 issue of a psychotherapy newsletter. Titled "Practice Issues: Will You Be Competing with Psychics and Philosophers?" the article reads as follows:

> It's not a happy thought, but it's probably true. A lot of people who should be in therapy are paying psychics instead. If you watch late-night television, you've seen commercials for "psychic friends," or "caring psychic families".... It's supposed to be fun. But according to Rita, a woman from New York who called us recently, it's about therapy — not entertainment.
>
> Rita is a student and mother of two who needed some extra cash. She was hired as a telephone psychic after responding to an ad in the newspaper.... "They told me to go out and buy a deck of tarot cards, and I started right away," she said....

Quickly, the job began to get to her. "I was talking to people about their marital problems, drug problems, all kinds of stuff. I'd sometimes tell them to go see a counselor, but mostly they didn't want to". . . .

By the way, though Rita admits she's not a psychic herself, she has a strong belief in the occult. "Psychology and the world of the psychic are closely related. . . . It's just that we're not ready as a society to accept it."[26]

The same issues surface often in our caseloads. For example, Terry worked with a fifty-six-year-old woman with a history of having undergone extensive emotional, physical, and sexual abuse throughout childhood and adolescence. Whenever she went to church she saw images of snakes crawling all over the cross and heard voices telling her to curse the pastor. To do justice to this client assessment and the development of treatment options, it's crucial to drill down to the root issues, and in so doing to consider satanic influences and treat accordingly.

A female client of Julie's struggled with a sense of spiritual emptiness and was emotionally and physically detached from her husband and children. During the intake interview, it was discovered that her father had been extensively involved in the Masons as well as in a local cult. From our years of experience we can determine that part of her problem was spiritual due to the influence of counterfeit religious experiences passed on by her father.

Consider also the case of a nineteen-year-old student who requested counseling after her freshman year at a Christian college. Her presenting problems involved fear as well as confusion about the changes she'd experienced during her year away at school. The history revealed she had become involved with an off-campus occult group, ostensibly formed for the purpose of protecting the environment and saving "Mother Earth." She also had started listening to satanic rock music, wearing a pentagram necklace, and smoking marijuana (though "only recreationally"). Since returning home, she complained of waking up at night with evil spirits taunting her about her decision to seek Christian counseling.

According to most mental health experts, we are mentally healthy if we are in touch with reality and relatively free from anxiety. According to that definition, clients who are being spiritually deceived would fail on both counts. If these clients try to explain the spiritual battle for their minds, many therapists will conclude the clients are out of touch with reality. If truth be told, one person in those sessions could be out of touch with reality — but it may not be the client! The spiritual world is just as real as the natural world, and fear will be the dominant emotion of those who are under spiritual attack. (In Neil's book *Freedom from Fear*,[27] he seeks to resolve anxiety disorders from a wholistic and integrative perspective.)

From a Christian perspective, mental health begins with a true knowledge of God and a true understanding of who we are as children of God. From this perspective, people are mentally ill if they have a distorted concept of God and themselves, which is the case for almost every inpatient in a psychiatric ward. The mentally ill are often religious people, to be sure, but their beliefs about themselves and God are distorted. When secular therapists observe this, some will blame the church for messing up people's minds; most will try to free their clients from their "religious obsessions" by discouraging them from Bible reading or church attendance.

The world, the flesh, and the devil all stand in opposition to our sanctification. It is not always necessary to separate the three when helping a client. Lies are lies, whether they come from the world through the television screen, from mentally ingrained patterns of thought, or from the pit of Satan. In every situation, "we take captive every thought to make it obedient to Christ" (2 Corinthians 10:5). Moreover, no tempting, accusing, or deceiving thought represents our new nature in Jesus Christ. If any thought is inconsistent with who we are as children of God, then do not believe it! As the apostle Paul writes, "Whatever is true, whatever is noble, whatever is right, whatever is pure, whatever is lovely, whatever is admirable — if anything is excellent or praiseworthy — think about such things" (Philippians 4:8).

PSYCHOLOGICAL ASSESSMENT OF THE CLIENT

Professional therapists are expected to use the DSM-IV as a diagnostic frame of reference. As stated in the manual itself, "The purpose of DSM-IV is to provide clear descriptions of diagnostic categories in order to enable clinicians and investigators to diagnose, communicate about, study, and treat people with various mental disorders."[28] To arrive at a diagnosis, the manual uses a multiaxial system involving five domains of clinical information. If you seek greater detail about this system, we would refer you to DSM-IV, pages 25 – 35. For our discussion of the psychological assessment of the client, we will focus on the fifth axis.

The subjective rating by the therapist regarding overall psychological mental health is expressed in the DSM-IV on Axis V, the Global Assessment of Functioning (GAF) scale. Some helpful psychological assessment principles for the clinician to consider when he or she is making a diagnosis are described in detail in James Morrison's book, *DSM-IV Made Easy: The Clinician's Guide to Diagnosis.*[29]

History Is Better Than Cross-sectional Observation

Longitudinal data (repeated observation over time) is more accurate than impressions based on a single incident in the client's life. For example, if a client complained about severe anxiety and a therapist used only the symptom presentation in the office, the client could easily be misdiagnosed without the benefit of additional information from her past. Information gleaned from a client's history helps us make a correct diagnosis. The following situations illustrate this point:

- A pattern of being nervous about one's environment unless accompanied by a companion and a desire to avoid public places where large crowds gather could suggest Agoraphobia.
- A history of excessive fears during severe thunderstorms and extreme efforts to avoid inclement weather could suggest a Simple Phobia, Natural Environment Type.
- A thirty-year history of avoiding firearms and a pattern of detesting "war movies," combined with a record of military service as a combat nurse in Vietnam, might lead to a diagnosis of Post-Traumatic Stress Disorder.

Recent History Benefits from Ancient History

We must remember that people's lives change, and, as James Morrison observes, "often the evolving symptoms of an illness will help you to evaluate it better. A diagnosis that seemed reasonable ten years ago may be untenable in the light of more recent symptoms."[30] Consider the following examples:

- A twenty-eight-year-old man with a diagnostic history of intermittent anxiety attacks marked by expansiveness and distractibility as a teenager was recently diagnosed with Major Depression, Single Episode. When the history was reviewed and the symptom pattern noted, the diagnosis was changed to Bipolar I Disorder, Most Recent Episode Depressed.
- A shy, withdrawn sixteen-year-old girl was diagnosed with a Social Phobia. In college the struggles with low self-esteem, interpersonal avoidance, and hopelessness continued, and she was diagnosed as

Major Depression, Single Episode. Shortly after graduation, she became delusional, accusing her fiancé of being repeatedly unfaithful. In the end she was diagnosed as Schizoaffective Disorder, Depressive Type.

Collateral Information Augments History from the Patient

Even when clients tell us the truth as they describe it from their perspective, chances are good that we have not heard the whole truth. Consider this proverb from the wise King Solomon: "The first to present his case seems right, till another comes forward and questions him" (Proverbs 18:17). This principle applies to children and adolescent clients who do not know their family history. Adults with severe mental disorders of psychotic proportions may also be unable to give a good clinical history of their problems. Julie and Terry apply this principle when working with adult married clients. Routinely, they ask to meet the spouse of a client at least once. They give the client the following rationale: "Others close to us can see more objectively than we can." For example:

- A male client was being seen for an Intermittent Explosive Disorder and was resistant to the diagnosis. The client's wife revealed that a family member had told her that as a child her husband was physically and verbally abused by his stepfather. The client's mother had coerced her son into silence because she would have risked a second failed marriage if he told anyone what had been happening to him. Because the wife broke the silence, the client was eventually able to accept the diagnosis.
- The wife of a client revealed that their son had told her that the client had hidden pornography in the house and had made multiple "hits" on sexually explicit web sites. The client had not disclosed that information in counseling, which, when revealed, suggested a possible sexual addiction.

Signs Are Better Than Symptoms

Signs (what you actually observe a client doing) are more objective than symptoms (what a client tells you about the presenting problem). By observing signs, the therapist is making interpretations that are more accurate because they are not influenced by what the client has said. For example:

- Although a client denies drinking alcoholic beverages, the counselor smells alcohol on his breath.
- An elderly client claims to have an excellent memory but is unable to remember what she had for breakfast that morning.

Objective Assessments Are Better Than Subjective Judgments

Clinical intuition and hunches should be avoided. James Morrison states, "One goal of DSM-IV is to encourage diagnosis that can predict the future course of an illness, its probable response to treatment, and the likelihood of its being passed on to the patient's children."[31] For example:

- At the recommendation of the school counselor, a principal expelled a ten-year-old child from school. The suspension came after repeated warnings to obey classroom rules, stay at his desk during study time, and avoid physical fights with fellow students. After being assessed by an independent psychologist, the child was diagnosed as having Attention Deficit/Hyperactivity Disorder (ADHD) and was able to return to school with ongoing support from outpatient counseling and medication (Ritalin).
- A forty-eight-year-old female client complained of recurring medical problems with no apparent physical basis. The counselor's initial diagnosis was Hypochondriasis. A thorough physical examination revealed the correct diagnosis — which was Multiple Sclerosis.

Crisis-generated Data Are Suspect

Assessment of someone in the midst of a crisis may result in a distorted picture of baseline intellectual and personality functioning of clients such as these:

- A twenty-four-year-old rape victim presented at a crisis clinic but could not remember her home address, telephone number, or where the attack took place. Assessment of limited intelligence based on her poor memory would be inaccurate.
- A seventeen-year-old adolescent female returned home after a long unexplained absence and claimed to have been kidnapped and abused; she was diagnosed as Post-Traumatic Stress Disorder. Later, telephone records revealed she had actually run away to rendezvous with a man she had met on the Internet.

ROLE OF PSYCHIATRY IN SPIRITUAL-PSYCHOLOGICAL ASSESSMENT[32]

Providing a spiritual and psychological diagnosis is not enough if a therapist does not consider a possible physical (biological and neurological) basis for mental illness. We believe the Christian therapist should work closely with both the church and the medical profession. We have physical bodies that suffer from decay and from the effects of living in a fallen world. Christians also have an inner person that is being renewed day by day (see 2 Corinthians 4:16). Thus, we need to keep the hospital and the church in proper balance.

Some problems (a broken leg, for example) can be easily diagnosed as physical in nature, while others (bitterness, for example) can just as easily be diagnosed as spiritual in nature. The struggle comes in the fuzzy space between the two. Twenty years ago everyone who occupied the middle zone was hypoglycemic and was getting glucose tolerance tests. What's happened to hypoglycemia? We don't hear much about it anymore. Then came the Epstein-Barr virus. Now everyone has Attention Deficit Disorder. The tendency in our Western world is to search first for every possible natural explanation; if none is found, there's nothing left to do but pray — or call the counselor or pastor. The Bible proposes a different order: "Seek first his kingdom and his righteousness, and all these things will be given to you as well" (Matthew 6:33). It's a process that begins with genuine repentance and belief in God. In the next chapter we'll demonstrate how these root issues can be resolved in a clinical setting.

8

Resolving Root Issues in the Marketplace

It is one thing to mourn for sin because it exposes us to hell, and another to mourn for it because it is an infinite evil; one thing to mourn for it because it is injurious to ourselves, and another thing to mourn for it because it is wrong and offensive to God. It is one thing to be terrified; another, to be humbled.

GARDINER SPRING

FIVE SPIRITUAL OBSTACLES IN THE MARKETPLACE

The major difference between counseling in a church and in the marketplace is the incredible "mix" of persons seeking help. For the most part, clients of church counselors have decided to seek counseling that is compatible with their Christian worldview. In the marketplace, the client seldom has any prior attachments of worship, relationships, or ministry with the therapist. Here clients come to their first session "cold," meeting therapists who are usually total strangers. The following obstacles may be encountered in the therapeutic marketplace, and they may stand in the way of nonbelievers making a salvation decision or of believers living victoriously and bearing fruit.

OBSTACLE ONE: IDENTITY CONFUSION

Christian psychologist Robert McGee notes that a major obstacle limiting freedom and blocking intimacy with God is the belief that one's self-worth is the sum of one's performance plus the opinions of others: Self-worth = Performance + Others' Opinions.[1]

Unsaved people are often open to embracing this equation, because deep down they may be aware that they are "missing something" and may have a sense of their fallen nature. Often they will conclude that their sense of worth is based on performance and worldly values. Even after we have been reborn through the power of God's Spirit, it can be difficult to accept God's view of us. If we base our worth on performance, we will invariably find ourselves engaged in a frenzy of perfectionism, driven to "do it right" — or we will withdraw for fear of failing and "doing it wrong." This performance mentality is not primarily adopted for our own approval but is usually dependent on others' approval, with its consequent yo-yo effect on our lives. Our sense of worth is then based on the "votes" we perceive others to be directing our way, whether positive or negative. In contrast, Christians who are secure in Christ and who know they are God's children conclude, "It would be nice to have the approval of my parents, my spouse, my boss, my neighbors, my friends, and everyone else, but even if they don't approve of me, I'm still loved and accepted by my heavenly Father."

For example, during her youth from the ages of twelve to sixteen, one client had been repeatedly abused by her stepfather and subsequently placed in a girls' facility by the court. As a young woman she married an alcoholic and physically abusive husband. She presented for therapy at age forty-six with an Axis I dual diagnosis of Major Depression (recurrent, chronic) and Bipolar II, along with an Axis II diagnosis of Antisocial Personality Disorder. In spite of significant trauma, family dysfunction, two suicide attempts, and medication sensitivities, this client now has a rock-solid identity in Christ. She would very likely have taken her life by now if the Lord had not been sustaining her. After going through a Freedom Appointment at her church, she knows who she is in Christ. She has a peace that is supernatural — a peace that, even in the midst of all her turmoil, gives her the strength to endure life's trials without bitterness, doubt, or cynicism and has made it possible to work on other issues that needed attention in her life.

OBSTACLE TWO: EMBEDDED WOUNDS FROM THE PAST

Emotional wounds from the past can damage our intimacy with God and stand in the way of our experience of freedom. Marriage and family counselor Jan Frank made this point when she visited one of Neil's classes at Talbot School of Theology. She brought two baby dolls with her — one had bandaged wounds on various parts of the body and the other was totally covered and bound up with gauze. She explained, "The first baby is wounded and will take time to heal. The other baby is in bondage; it won't take long to set this one free." In all likelihood, when the gauze is removed, it will reveal other wounds, which will now begin to heal.

Strong, perplexing emotions and behaviors that appear to be out of context may in fact be unveiling wounds from the past. Consider these examples:

- A woman recoils in fright when her loving husband (to whom she's been married for ten years) comes up behind her and gives her a gentle hug while she is washing the dishes.
- A man fails to openly support his wife's wise decision simply because his parents have raised an objection.
- A college student flunks his sophomore year even though he earned a 3.5 GPA in high school.

Neil refers to these reactions as primary emotions that are triggered by present events; they reflect prior trauma and embedded lies from the past. In the examples above, the emotional response of the wife was triggered when her husband touched her from behind. She may very well have been sexually abused in the past, which would have led her to believe lies such as, "I'm in danger! I'll get hurt! I'm powerless!" In the second case, lingering in the back of the husband's mind are the controlling expectations of authoritative parents. As a result, he may believe, "I can't make a decision on my own. I'm stupid. I'm incompetent." In the third example, the student might be remembering the words of his father telling him, "You will never succeed on your own!" As a result, he may believe, "I'm a failure."

OBSTACLE THREE: LACK OF GENUINE REPENTANCE

Many clients are locked in a *sin-confess-sin-confess-sin* cycle, and they don't know how to get out of it. Tell an average Christian to repent, and he or she may have no idea what to do. Sin is not simply the discrete behaviors of commission or omission we commit on a daily basis, but it's also the rebellious old nature within us that is hostile to God and doesn't want to submit to him. If a client is deeply grieved over his or her sinful nature, it's usually not hard to get the client out of the *sin-confess* cycle; it's far more difficult to help carnal Christians or nonbelievers who aren't aware of their depravity. The latter are spiritually dead, while the former think they are rich but in reality "are wretched, pitiful, poor, blind and naked" (Revelation 3:17). Expressing only temporal remorse, they soon return to their maladaptive behaviors.

For example, a young Christian couple, married for eight years, was enormously successful financially. Yet their relationship was conflictual and emotionally strained due to the husband's workaholism, pride, narcissism, and denial of trauma from being part of an alcoholic family of origin. The wife contributed to the tension by using perfectionism and compulsivity to cope with the abandonment and isolation she experienced with her family of origin. Both claimed to be committed Christians but could not see their own sins. They could easily pinpoint the speck of idolatry and sin in the other, but they could not see the planks in their own eyes. Counseling helped to a degree through teaching them to communicate more effectively, to set boundaries, and to practice stress-management techniques, as well as through prescribing helpful medication. In the end, however, these individuals did not achieve confession, repentance, and humility before God, nor did they gain a clear understanding of who they were in Christ or how they could employ effective spiritual warfare strategies. They remained stuck in their frustration and their disrupted intimacy with each other and God.

OBSTACLE FOUR: STRUCTURES AND PHILOSOPHY OF THE WORLD

As noted in chapters one and two, every client has been influenced by the competing worldviews of humanism, utopianism, and New Age. For example, as a member of a liberal church, Mary had jumped through all the required religious hoops as she was growing up. But since she was merely "doing religion," she saw nothing wrong with living with her boyfriend prior to marriage. Within weeks after their marriage, however, she found herself unorgasmic and repulsed by sex. This shutdown, a mystery both to her and her husband, was tearing at the fabric of their marriage. How had she come to this point of believing that sex was dirty? In her childhood, a neighbor boy had inappropriately exposed himself to her; furthermore, her mother was sexually promiscuous in her presence. Though willing to go into therapy for a time, she chose not to believe in a forgiving God who ordained sex to be good only within the confines of marriage, and she would not accept his forgiveness for sexual sin. She had felt sexually exploited by others, and this negative experience hindered her ability to enjoy the God-ordained gift of sex within her marriage relationship.

The humanist concept of evolution proved to be the barrier to her coming to the point of understanding and loving the God of the Bible. She had taken college science courses that had presented evolution as fact and negated the teaching of biblical creation. In therapy she was given a reading assignment on creation, which she returned with no comment, and she continued in the pain of guilt and confusion about sexuality. Therapy approaches such as cognitive restructuring, desensitization, and structured exercises met with no success, and she subsequently withdrew from counseling.

Obstacle Five: Unregenerate Spirit

The apostle Paul describes the reality of who we were before Christ:

> As for you, you were dead in your transgressions and sins, in which you used to live when you followed the ways of this world and of the ruler of the kingdom of the air, the spirit who is now at work in those who are disobedient. All of us also lived among them at one time, gratifying the cravings of our sinful nature and following its desires and thoughts. Like the rest, we were by nature objects of wrath.
>
> —*Ephesians 2:1–3*

The natural person is subject to the decay and death of the universe and separated from God. Since God does not force himself on anyone against his or her will, we in the field of Christian counseling certainly would not do so either. Yet we do well to keep in mind that every unregenerate client does not really need a personal therapist; such clients need a personal relationship with the living God.

Frank and Sue were referred by their church for premarital counseling. One of the sessions focused on their spiritual beliefs to see if they were compatible, thus ensuring they would be equally yoked (see 2 Corinthians 6:14). It was apparent that the man was receptive to the gospel, but the woman appeared hostile. A presentation of the gospel was made, and the man wanted to offer a prayer of response, but the woman did not. Fearfulness gripped the man, and he agreed with her not to proceed further. They terminated therapy at that point and subsequently refused to pay for any of the sessions.

PRESENTING THE GOSPEL

Assessment approaches and subsequent methods of resolving root issues serve to distinguish Christian counselors who are using *implicit* integration from those who are using *explicit* integration. The implicit integrator may pray privately for clients and covertly use Judeo-Christian values in counseling (that is, working toward the goal of preserving marriages, promoting a pro-life position, discouraging pornography), while not identifying these strategies as biblical. The implicit integrator will not demonstrate a Christian perspective in written materials or in spoken manner. In some environments, this may be a personal decision or one based on the belief that an explicit approach could be interpreted as a legal or ethical violation. The dictates of governmental, military, school, or other public agencies may prohibit such disclosure. Our hearts go out to counselors who practice in such restrictive settings. These counselors are like the biblical Daniel in the Babylonian court, completely surrounded by the worldview of the environment in which they find themselves. However, Daniel's impact on his culture was significant, for he maintained his personal practices without compromise and his godly life was directly evident to all through his courageous spirit. He had opportunity to proclaim the Lord despite his circumstances. Such may be the influence of those born-again counselors who are implicit integrators.

Explicit integrators, on the other hand, identify themselves as Christians, discuss the role of prayer in counseling sessions, refer to Scripture passages, and in other ways openly express Christian values. A routine part of their initial assessment interview is made up of foundational questions about the client's spiritual background and current practices and beliefs. The initial questions can be as simple as "What kind of religious influences did you have in your childhood?" "What religious beliefs did your family practice in your home?" "How important was religion when you were growing up?" Depending on a client's answer, the therapist can move on to determine the presence of routine religious behavior as opposed to an emphasis on a personal relationship with Jesus as the client was growing up. Questions concerning the current spiritual status of the client can be phrased sensitively as well: "How have you stayed the same or changed from the religious exposure you had as a child?" "How important is religion or church currently in your life?" Here too the therapist can expand to determine the same information with respect to perfunctory religiosity versus a transformed life in the client's life at present.

To digress for just a moment, we note that questions such as these are often acceptable in non-Christian marketplace settings, since they are informational and do not explicitly advance any particular worldview. These kinds of questions can help an implicit therapist identify believers with whom a more explicit type of counseling may indeed be possible, as well as assist the therapist in discerning specific prayer avenues for a non-Christian.

This line of questioning, along with other assessment data used in the interview, can reveal a client's basic worldview. In our experience, clients genuinely seem to appreciate this type of probing and generally are willing to declare their beliefs. If a client is non-Christian, we are clear in stating our own Christian values base, but we verbalize a respect for the client's right to choose; in this way we model Jesus Christ. Jesus did not hesitate, however, to point out people's deep spiritual needs and to give them an opportunity to respond—and so should we. The timing for citing spiritual needs and giving an opportunity to respond to the gospel is crucial. Until we have established rapport with the client, we may be viewed as intrusive and pushy if we probe too deeply and too quickly into questions about their spiritual commitment.

Jesus allowed the rich young man to walk away when the man could not accept the conditions of discipleship (see Mark 10:17–22). In the same way, some of our clients may walk away because they do not accept the principles of our values base or our therapy methods. Don't be surprised but be ready to make a referral to another therapist for treatment rather than abandoning the client. To make a referral as necessary and appropriate is a basic ethical requirement in most states.

When dealing with Christian clients, we acknowledge God's presence and discuss the use of prayer in counseling sessions. Prayer is not "bookended" ritualistically at the start and end of the session. In addition, prayer is rarely offered during the intake session because clients are at such vastly different and varied spiritual places. Any sort of ritualistic prayer could create an emotional-spiritual barrier for those who are struggling with a variety of feelings about and toward God. Until the therapist knows that the client is receptive, prayer will likely be empty and even offensive in the client's experience. Typically we indicate during the first session that the role of prayer in counseling will be specifically addressed in later sessions.

People who come to counseling are at any one of a vast number of stages in their relationship with God. Some feel distant from him, some are angry, some believe he has deserted them, some are convinced they do not want to know him. In a professional clinic, we should not automatically assume that a client wants to pray in a session; obviously we do not hesitate to pray for the client if he or she directly asks for prayer in the intake session or in a subsequent session. Client-initiated prayer is ethical and spiritually sound—and always granted!

The use of the seven "Steps to Freedom in Christ" (see Appendix E), as well as certain other counseling approaches, calls for the direct use of prayer, primarily on the part of the client. If such an approach is indicated during the process of assessment and treatment planning, the client is made fully aware of it and must be in complete agreement with the recommended spiritual methodology before it is undertaken. We always hear the client's story first, and then ask the client if he or she would like to resolve the issues raised.

Because our practice states clearly that we counsel from a Christian perspective, the Professional Counseling Agreement form (see Appendix D) has a place for clients to sign, verifying that they were informed that our counseling is values-based and that prayer and biblical references and principles may be a part of the Christian methodology employed. The signature satisfies the informed consent obligation we have as practitioners to make our values base explicit to our clients.

If a non-Christian counselee elects to work with us, we look for opportunities in the course of the counseling relationship to address spiritual issues and to present the Good News of Jesus Christ. We carefully try to discern the Lord's timing and look for the natural fit of the gospel presentation in the flow of treatment interventions. We use and also recommend the *Evangelism Explosion* method developed by D. James Kennedy, beginning with the two diagnostic questions. These two questions clarify the degree of assurance of salvation clients have and the basis for their assurance.

When the time is right, we will ask a client, "Have you come to the place in your spiritual life where you know that if you were to die tonight you would go to heaven?" and after the client responds the second question is asked: "Suppose you died tonight and stood before God in heaven, and he asked you, 'Why should I let you into my heaven?' What would you say?"[2] He or she may respond with genuine assurance (based on a personal relationship with Jesus Christ), false assurance (based on good works, faithfulness to a denomination, parental faith, infant baptism, and the like), or lack of assurance ("I don't have a clue" or "I wouldn't go to heaven").

There are a number of other gospel presentations therapists can use as well. Surely the Holy Spirit is not limited by our methodology! We simply have the privilege to share the Good News in the power of the Holy Spirit—and then to leave the results to God. If a decision for Christ is made, we as counselors have the responsibility to follow up with new believers — which is another good reason why we believe every Christian therapist should be an active member of a local church, working together with the church body for the good of their people.

THE REALITIES OF MANAGED CARE

We live in an era of managed care, in which our actions in the counseling arena need to be documented, authenticated, relevant, effective, measurable, and cost-effective. Health care providers are under siege to "do more with less"[3] by insurers, employers, and the government in an effort to control spiraling costs. External review mechanisms have been established, and care is being managed by reviewers outside of the clinical setting. Managed care is a reality we all must live with for the present. Clarity in communication is therefore imperative for the Christian counselor who provides mental health services. The necessity of dealing with managed care requires that the external reviewer and the practitioner speak the same language and understand well the process of counseling.

In their helpful book *Managing Managed Care*, Michael Goodman, Janet Brown, and Pamela Deitz explain that "mental health care is a multidisciplinary and therefore a multilingual field." They observe that when you add "the growing and diverse demands of various managed care organizations and third-party payers, the potential for communication difficulties is compounded."[4] Moreover, the reality of the different perspectives of the various mental health disciplines (psychiatry, psychology, social work, psychiatric/mental health nursing, chemical dependency units, marriage and family counseling), funding agencies (insurers, employers, government), and Christian communities (for-profit, nonprofit, church-based, parachurch organizations) sets up an unavoidable collision.

For Christian counselors, the collision point involves not only all the ingredients present in the secular maze but the addition of the biblical perspective as well — which the marketplace often greets with skepticism, ignorance, or downright hostility. To be faithful to our calling as Christians to walk in the light, it is imperative that we communicate what we do clearly and honestly to those who fund our services. The mentality of sneaking prayer into counseling sessions and using biblical resources in a clandestine manner not only smears our integrity but prevents us from demonstrating to our professional colleagues the excellence with which we practice. Our light need not be put under a bowl but can shine brightly for the whole world to see (see Matthew 5:15).

Our New Age counterparts boldly present their methodologies. The preponderance of non-Christian modalities such as visualization, centering, crystals, self-hypnosis, mantras, finding the "god within," to name just a few, are rampant in the field of mental health. By the same token, Christian methodologies should be evident in the marketplace as well. By our silence we have allowed the foxes into the vineyard (see Song of Songs 2:15). Development of terminology that speaks to both the managed care and counseling communities is one part of the process of ending that silence. It provides an opportunity to connect the needs of Christian clinical practitioners with the needs of third-party payers.

Michael Goodman, Janet Brown, and Pamela Deitz share this observation: "We decided to develop a meaningful, serviceable language of treatment and a documentation system for all mental health professionals who provide direct patient care and whose treatment services may be subject to review prior to reimbursement."[5] We believe a meaningful, serviceable language for spiritual intervention services would likewise be helpful for Christian mental health professionals seeking to integrate biblical truths into their work with clients who choose a biblical values base for treatment.

The authors of *Managing Managed Care* further state, "Our method for documenting and communicating the necessity, appropriateness, and effectiveness of mental health care services is the common avenue upon which the practitioner, the external reviewer, and the quality management reviewer can communicate and travel in amicable parallel."[6] This clarification is necessary for issues of practitioner accountability, as well as for an effective proactive response to what counselors with a Christian worldview actually do. Many Christian counselors have not been taught how to address the management of their care by outside reviewers, nor have they been prepared to meet the demand for increased accountability. The fact is that when we resist this accountability or are ignorant about it, we are not living in a way that is consistent with our biblical worldview. As Christians we understand the reality of human depravity, and therefore we ought to welcome the practice of accountability.

Managed care companies have developed specific terminology to identify the client's actual symptoms, the impairments in living that normally exist, the ultimate goal that is desired, the precise treatments required to achieve that goal, and the objective criteria that will signal when healing has occurred. In the medical realm, this is similar to diagnosing pneumonia when a patient experiences fever and pain (the symptoms), identifying that a particular bacteria (the impairment) is causing the fever and pain, and noting that physiological normalcy is desired (the goal), for which penicillin is prescribed (the treatment intervention). The patient is healed when the fever and pain are no longer present (objective criteria for discharge).

Symptoms are the reasons a patient requires treatment. They are neither the reasons for the presence of the disorder nor the actual disorder itself; they are the observable, objective manifestations that necessitate and justify care. Impairments are "behavioral windows" into the biochemical, psychological, and spiritual realities in the client's life that lie behind the symptoms. Treatment interventions for the impairments are chosen for their ability to "repair" the disordered symptoms by correcting the problems.

For example, the *diagnosis* of Intermittent Explosive Disorder, like pneumonia, is not an impairment because it does not relate to specific, measurable behavior; the diagnosis is only a description of a category of symptoms. However, if a client exhibits symptoms of uncontrollable anger and verbal outbursts when a spouse fails to keep the house spotless, the *impairment* is the behavior of *rage reactions*. This measurable behavior impairs or prevents the client from living an emotionally, relationally, and spiritually healthy life. This isolating of the measurable behavior is analogous to isolating the bacteria that is causing the pneumonia.

Treatment could be implemented by the counselor with the following goals for the client:

- increase the ability to appropriately express angry feelings in a controlled and assertive manner
- release the demands of perfectionism to the Lord through confession and repentance
- seek forgiveness from the spouse for controlling and wrathful behavior
- verbalize an understanding of past or current life events that create anger
- utilize the "Steps to Freedom in Christ" to expose the lies that fuel the behavior

Having set these goals, the therapist would then establish objective criteria for discharge. For example, the client will

- demonstrate to the therapist an understanding of the difference between assertion, passivity, and aggression, using assertion skills eighty percent of the time in relating to others
- journal perfectionistic thoughts and behaviors for two weeks, daily confessing and repenting of each occurrence of negative behavior
- request feedback from his or her spouse daily about inappropriate behavior, asking forgiveness when necessary
- demonstrate understanding of key unresolved life conflicts and develop truthful self-talk as a means of handling anger

When the client has achieved all or most of the stated objectives, he or she no longer needs counseling for that particular impairment.

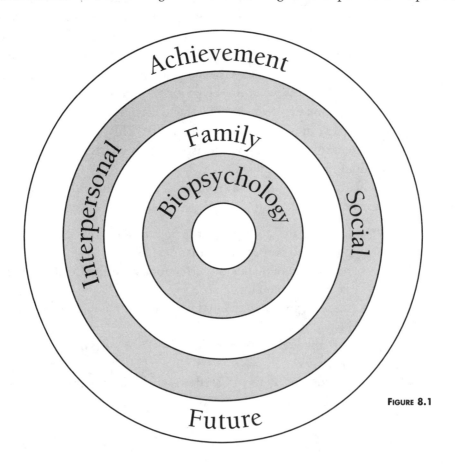

FIGURE 8.1

Impairments are located both in the patient's subjective private world and in the objective action world.[7] In Figure 8.1 the former is represented by the *biopsychology* realm (that is, all that takes place within a person — one's internal world and inner experiences), while the objective action world is portrayed by the remaining spheres, which represent the *family/significant* other realm, the *social/interpersonal* realm, and the *future/achievement* realm.

This model does not take into account the biblical-Christian worldview and therefore does not include the realm of God, angels, and demons. As those who hold to the biblical-Christian worldview, we know the spiritual realm affects and interacts with all four realms. Because many in our culture embrace the humanist worldview, the spiritual realm — the "excluded middle" (see Figure 2.1 on page 49) is consistently and quite predictably ignored.

If we add in the spiritual dimension to accomplish a wholistic approach, the diagram would look like this (see Figure 8.2)[8]:

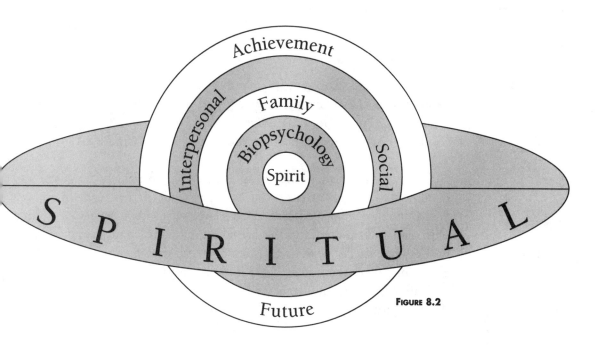

FIGURE 8.2

There are certain "critical impairments" that have the potential to be dangerous to the client and/or to other people. These reflect a level of

Critical Impairments

Assaultiveness	Obsessions
Compulsions	Paranoia
Concomitant medical condition	Phobia
Delusions	Psychomotor agitation
Dissociative states	Psychomotor retardation
Dysphoric mood	Psychotic thought and perception
Dysphoric mood with alexithymia	Psychotic thought, perception,
Eating disorder	and behavior
Fire setting	Rage reactions
Hallucinations	Running away
Homicidal thought/behavior	Self-mutilation
Manic thought/behavior	Substance abuse
Mood lability	Suicidal thought/behavior

Note: Critical impairments are those that have potential on their own to justify more intensive service interventions (for example, inpatient hospitalization).

TABLE 8.1

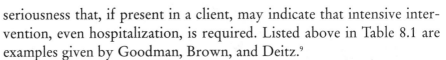

seriousness that, if present in a client, may indicate that intensive intervention, even hospitalization, is required. Listed above in Table 8.1 are examples given by Goodman, Brown, and Deitz.[9]

They also list impairments in the four realms of Figure 8.1 (see Table 8.2).[10]

Knowledge of this kind of assessment and treatment language and documentation system is crucial as we provide patient care in today's environment of managed care. As we have seen, the necessity of dealing with managed care requires that we speak the same language and communicate what we do clearly and honestly to those who fund our services. Knowing where the impairments in living normally exist and what they are will help us communicate well and will benefit our clients as we guide them toward healing.

SUBMITTING TO MANAGED CARE

Since managed care became a clinical reality in the 1980s, documentation skills and requirements in treatment planning have become important

Impairments in the Biopsychology Realm

Altered sleep	Medical risk factor
Compulsions	Medical treatment noncompliance
Concomitant medical condition	Mood lability
Decreased concentration	Obsessions
Delusions	Paranoia
Deficient frustration tolerance	Pathological grief
Dissociative states	Pathological guilt
Dysphoric mood	Phobia
Dysphoric mood with alexithymia	Promiscuity
Gender dysphoria	Psychomotor agitation
Eating disorder	Psychomotor retardation
Encopresis	Psychotic thought and perception
Enuresis	Psychotic thought, perception,
Externalization and blame	and behavior
Fire setting	Rage reactions
Grandiosity	Self-mutilation
Hallucinations	Somatization
Hyperactivity	Stealing
Learning disability	Substance abuse
Manic thought/behavior	Suicidal thought/behavior

Impairments in the Family/Significant Other Realm

Emotional/physical trauma perpetrator	Marital/relationship dysfunction
Emotional/physical trauma victim	Marital/relationship dysfunction with
Family dysfunction	physical abuse
Family dysfunction with substance abuse	Running away

Impairments in the Social/Interpersonal Realm

Assaultiveness	Paraphilia
Egocentricity	Repudiation of adults as helpers
Homicidal thought/behavior	Sexual dysfunction
Lying	Social withdrawal
Manipulativeness	Tantrums
Oppositionalism	Uncommunicativeness

Impairments in the Future/Achievement Realm

Educational performance deficit	School phobia
Hopelessness	Truancy
Inadequate health care skills	Work dysphoria
Inadequate survival skills	

TABLE 8.2

considerations for any counselor dealing with third-party payers and outside accrediting agencies. Behavioral managed care organizations (MCOs) expect mental health providers to work quickly through the intake process of assessment and diagnosis. They also require written documentation that identifies the nature and degree of impaired function, outcome goals, a statement of case formulation, and a plan for treatment implementation. Psychologist Art Jongsma and social worker L. Mark Peterson write, "Treatment plans must be specific as to the problems and interventions, individualized to meet the client's needs and goals, and measurable in terms of setting milestones that can be used to chart the patient's progress."[11] The clinical providers' manual for one MCO states its belief that outpatient treatment must consider time and cost as legitimate parameters of effectiveness and that specific goals for change should be behaviorally referenced. "Medical necessity," reads the manual, "requires treatment be delivered in the most cost-effective manner consistent with quality outcome."[12]

Such expectations and rigorous standards can create considerable difficulty for Christian practitioners who have little experience in the development and expression of spiritual treatment plans. Issues such as symptom identification, determination of behavioral impairments, expression of outcome goals, and establishment of objective criteria for goal attainment are not easily faced by many Christian providers.

At one of our clinical staff meetings some time ago, we talked about the managed care requirements for documentation of spiritual concerns. One therapist made a comment that illustrated the difficult and even discouraging impact these requirements can have on Christian counselors: "It would be easier to work in a secular setting and not have to go to all this work to figure out how to define spiritual problems in a way that satisfies the insurance company." Because of these challenges, the concluding sections of this chapter will clarify and facilitate the integration of the spiritual component into the treatment planning process.

Managed care agencies have different requirements for the authorized use of mental health benefits, so the client and counselor must understand the nature of the client's coverage before any treatment begins. In our clinic, one of our employees is our "insurance specialist." This person (a special person, indeed, given that this is not an easy job to master!) works with the client before the first appointment to define the benefits as comprehensively as possible. Because coverage varies from plan to plan (and, unfortunately, sometimes even from contact person to contact person within the plan's benefits department), final responsibility for determination of coverage is left up to the client. We would maintain that the therapist is responsible for explaining to the insurance carrier that outpatient psychotherapy is "medically necessary" in accordance with the client's benefits plan description or that the client's condition reflects a "serious and persistent illness" that requires authorization for treatment.

Once client and counselor establish the necessity for psychotherapy, the counselor must provide the MCO, either verbally by telephone or in writing, an individualized treatment plan. Some health care plans require this information after the first session, some after a second or third, some after the tenth. In some instances, the MCO will allow ten initial sessions per calendar year before a patient authorization request for further outpatient treatment is needed; the reality is that requirements for outpatient treatment reports vary, depending on the utilization criteria established by the managed care company.

After obtaining initial authorization for treatment for a certain number of sessions, treatment can proceed. In our experience, the initial authorization for treatment usually grants eight to ten sessions. If authorization for counseling beyond the original allotment of sessions is required, a second request must be submitted before counseling may continue. This document, known as a prior authorization (P.A.) request, will be submitted by the counselor before each series of authorized sessions is completed. While each MCO has its own form, we routinely submit the clinic's Individual Treatment Plan (ITP — see Appendix D) along with the P.A. request. By doing so, we decrease the amount of duplication in paperwork for the counselor, since the ITP can be attached to the documentation, with the notation "see attached" in areas of duplication.

Art Jongsma and L. Mark Peterson remind us that the key to managed care reporting is that all the goals, plans, interventions, and criteria for discharge should be objective and behaviorally defined, with a realistic potential for improvement that is measurable. A well-crafted treatment plan that clearly stipulates presenting problems and intervention strategies facilitates the treatment process — and it will hold clinicians accountable in a health care environment where more and more managed care systems are demanding a structured therapeutic contract that has measurable objectives and explicit interventions.[13]

Use of the Goodman, Brown, and Deitz impairment language (see Tables 8.1 and 8.2) helps MCO case coordinators differentiate between what a counselor is doing and what a client is doing.[14] Managed care reviewers of a clinician's treatment approach want to know how clinical decisions are made and what the rationale is for each decision. Clinicians need to articulate and document their own thought processes so that the reviewer understands the purpose for the therapy. As noted above, reviewers want to know why symptoms are "serious and persistent," why treatment is "medically necessary," why a particular level of care (intensity of service) is necessary, and why alternative treatments are not being considered. Treatment language that uses clear, commonly understood, behaviorally focused terms communicates the measurable, objective process and the quality of care to the managed care reviewers. If we view the reviewers' follow-up questions as ways to establish clarity of thought rather than as threats of potential nonpayment, we can respond as colleagues rather than as adversaries.[15]

Using the impairment model as a conceptual framework for treatment planning, we respond by providing the client's managed care reviewer with specific patient outcome objectives selected for each impairment in the profile, based on the patient's ability to complete the defined treatment goals. The date of completion of the resolution of the last remaining impairment, to whatever degree possible, is the duration of treatment. We always refer to these outcome objectives when talking with outside reviewers. To receive continued authorization for care, we must communicate that the treatment plan is working (that is, the patient is getting better), but we must also convey to the reviewer that the patient requires additional treatment at that level of care (that is, the patient is still sick).[16] This is the point in the therapy process where a subsequent P.A. is submitted.

DOCUMENTATION OF SPIRITUAL TREATMENT INTERVENTIONS

Rather prophetically, George Fox University psychology professor Roger Bufford proposed in 1988 to add a spiritual diagnosis to the DSM-IV:

> This dimension would assess spiritual condition. It could address such questions as whether the person professes any religious faith, importance of religion to the individual, frequency of church attendance, frequency of personal devotionals, and any recent changes in the person's religious life.[17]

Dr. Bufford added that the Bible delineates the nature and scope of sin but that it wasn't intended to define the limits of the intellectual and scientific disciplines. He explained that the Bible contains geographic and historic information but that it is not a history book or a geographic text. Similarly, the Bible is not a diagnostic tool for mental disorders. However, the DSM-IV is such a tool, though it is by no means perfect. It is a secular tool counselors must be familiar with in order to communicate with other clinicians as well as with case managers in managed care organizations. Dr. Bufford also stated that mental disorders are too complex to be dismissed as personal sin only, although personal sin (for example, lying, slander, pride), sin in the world as a result of the curse (for example, infections, aging, trauma), and the effects of others' sins (for example, abuse) may indeed result in mental disorders.[18]

The DSM-IV was published in 1994, and it included the V-Code 62.89 Religious or Spiritual Problem diagnosis under the section "Other Conditions That May Be a Focus of Clinical Attention." As Christian counselors, we consider the inclusion of the Religious or Spiritual Problem V-Code as an important step; however, it is only the first step toward increased recognition and legitimization of the need for integrating spiritual and psychological components within the psychotherapy treatment process. As noted previously, use of a V-Code diagnosis alone will not qualify for insurance coverage — even though the DSM-IV reported the new diagnosis as having been added in order "to improve coverage."[19] When a client presents and a DSM-IV diagnosis is established, and when the spiritual issues to be discussed relate to the impairments identified, the V-Code diagnosis is presented only as a secondary diagnosis.

We employ differing modalities to handle the V-Code issues in the therapeutic session. We assign some of the spiritual work to be completed outside of the therapy session, with clients reporting in on their progress. We use lay counselors in the church community to accomplish the interventions in a ministry format. This can take the form of a referral, for example, to a church-based Freedom Ministry, where trained lay volunteers complete the entire seven "Steps to Freedom in Christ" in a single three- to five-hour session with the client. It can also take the form of a two-hour therapy session, where the "medically necessary" interventions are accomplished during the first hour, with the second hour focusing on spiritual issues and paid for by the client as a fee-for-service; yet again it can take the form of interventions similar to "medically necessary" interventions—for example, rage reactions, obsessions, or compulsions being addressed within the session using an interwoven combination of spiritual and psychological interventions. The impairment language table (see Table 8.3) provides examples of the written documentation submitted to the insurance company when spiritual problems are addressed in the counseling hour.

The best alternative is to address the spiritual issues from the biblical-Christian worldview as legitimate interventions for the wide variety of impairments that exist, as do humanist, utopianist, and New Age practitioners. Simply code the issues under the categories of the Impairment Profile that hold true as legitimate interventions of choice. If questioned, defend them as legitimate interventions from the worldview of the client and the therapist, citing the parallel interventions from other worldviews. Only in this way will we begin to influence the field of counseling on behalf of the only worldview based on the truths of the Word of God.

Impairment behaviors, treatment goals, and objective criteria for discharge are used in the Individual Treatment Plan (ITP) when a therapist documents the spiritual component for treatment. These spiritual treatment interventions are presented in the remainder of this chapter and reflect our integration of the Goodman, Brown, and Deitz managed care impairment language with Neil Anderson's "Steps to Freedom in Christ" model, as well as other interventions such as prayer and Ed Smith's model called TheoPhostics (for more on TheoPhostics, see the discussion in chapter nine). When we as Christian clinicians use an integrated language approach to formulate the spiritual dimension of a client's treatment plan, we will be reflecting the spiritual focus of our counseling. To do so will benefit all who are involved in the treatment experience. The client is served because an integrated ITP clarifies all issues that are the focus of the counseling process. Providers benefit from this kind of treatment plan because they are forced to think clearly about client needs from a wholistic perspective. The articulation of spiritual issues eliminates vagueness and helps both the client and counselor focus on specifically stated objectives that use specific interventions. The insurance company benefits as well, because this type of clearly defined treatment program increases treatment efficacy and consistency of documentation on the part of the therapist. Finally, this approach may become the basis for future research in this area—research that will allow us to measure our successes and demonstrate the healing we know is occurring in spiritual intervention cases.

IMPAIRMENT LANGUAGE FOR SPIRITUAL
INTERVENTIONS: THE "STEPS TO FREEDOM
IN CHRIST" AS A TREATMENT INTERVENTION

DESCRIPTION

This model is a method the counselor can use to convert any of the seven major areas of spiritual conflict into impairment language; the model also presents spiritual treatment interventions and recommended goals, and it specifies the objective criteria for discharge that must be met for treatment to be considered complete. The following chart (Table 8.3) adapts the impairment language of Goodman, Brown, and Deitz to any of the seven areas of spiritual difficulties clients exhibit in the "Steps to Freedom in Christ." Use of this practical impairment language, readily understood by case reviewers, has been helpful in submitting written case formulations as well as for gaining authorizations for additional counseling sessions. See Appendix D for samples of the Individual Treatment Plan using impairment language for spiritual interventions.

Impairments in the Wholistic Realm

STEP 1: COUNTERFEIT VERSUS REAL

Participation in traumatic (counterfeit) religious experiences
Dependency on non-Christian spiritual experiences

STEP 2: DECEPTION VERSUS TRUTH

Self-defensiveness	Paranoia
Compulsions	Somatization
Dissociative states	Mood lability
Obsessions	Social withdrawal
Phobia	School phobia
Dysphoric mood	Work dysphoria
Hopelessness	Medical treatment compliance
Lying	Pathological grief
Delusions	Pathological guilt
Hyperactivity	

STEP 3: BITTERNESS VERSUS FORGIVENESS

Bitterness	Rage reactions
Externalization	Blame
Homicidal thought/behavior	Emotional/physical trauma victim
Family dysfunction	Marital relationship dysfunction

STEP 4: REBELLION VERSUS SUBMISSION

Repudiation   Oppositionalism
Rebellion   Manipulativeness
Medical treatment noncompliance   Running away
Tantrums   Uncommunicativeness
Truancy

STEP 5: PRIDE VERSUS HUMILITY

Grandiosity
Pride
Narcissism
Arrogance
Conceit
Egocentricity

STEP 6: BONDAGE VERSUS FREEDOM

Moral law noncompliance   Antisocial behavior
Oppositionalism   Promiscuity
Paraphilia   Homicidal thought/behavior
Assaultiveness   Eating disorder
Fire setting   Suicidal thought/behavior
Substance abuse   Self-mutilation
Stealing   Addictions
Gender dysphoria   Sexual dysfunction

STEP 7: ACQUIESCENCE VERSUS RENUNCIATION

Family of origin spiritual dysfunction
Abusive/maladaptive behaviors
Marital relationship dysfunction
Emotional/physical trauma perpetrator
Spiritual assignments/curses
Family dysfunction
Emotional/physical trauma victim

Note: All impairments can be genetically, environmentally, and spiritually transmitted through the family line. Impairments that may be due to physical causes include a concomitant medical condition, hallucinations, manic thought or behavior, psychomotor agitation and retardation, psychotic symptoms, encopresis, enuresis, hyperactivity, learning disability, and sexual dysfunction.

TABLE 8.3

WHOLISTIC IMPAIRMENT LANGUAGE FOR USE IN
INDIVIDUAL TREATMENT PLANS

DESCRIPTION

   The following outline is an aid to be used when the counselor sub-
mits a written treatment plan. Each of the specific "Steps to Freedom in
Christ" is followed by the symptoms expected to be seen and the impairments observed, along with the treatment intervention, the treatment
goals, and the objective criteria for discharge.

STEP 1: COUNTERFEIT VERSUS REAL

   Symptoms

   - Demonstrates distortions in thoughts, feelings, and behavior cre-
     ated by participation in traumatic (counterfeit) religious experi-
     ences or by exposure to and dependency on non-Christian spiri-
     tual experiences
   - Exhibits active, passive, or abusive current involvement in mystic,
     occultic, or cultic non-Christian rituals and practices
   - Reports active, passive, or abusive early-childhood exposure to
     mystic, occultic, or cultic non-Christian rituals and practices

   Impairments

   - Participation in traumatic (counterfeit) religious experiences;
     dependency on non-Christian spiritual experiences

   Treatment Intervention

   - Complete Step 1: Counterfeit Versus Real

   Treatment Goals

   - Identifies all non-Christian contacts and experiences
   - Places trust in the absolute authority of the written Word of God
     and in no other religious system

Objective Criteria for Discharge

- Checks off the "Non-Christian Spiritual Experience Inventory" to identify false religious experiences (see Appendix E)
- Demonstrates the ability to verbally confess and renounce past practices with minimal emotional affect
- States several positive alternatives for adhering to an identity in Christ alone, including belief in being accepted, secure, and significant
- Reads the special renunciations for satanic ritual involvement with the absence of anxiety and mind blocking (see Appendix E)

STEP 2: DECEPTION VERSUS TRUTH

Symptoms

- Exhibits dishonesty over own motives and behaviors on a consistent basis, leading to conflict with and alienation from others
- Uses defense mechanisms consistently, even when they are self-defeating and debilitating and they compromise healthy adaptation to life and limit emotional and spiritual freedom (denial, fantasy, emotional insulation, regression, displacement, projection, rationalization, and the like)
- Uses self-deception in such a manner that results in hearing God's Word but not implementing it, denying sin, being proud, assuming personal wisdom, feeling exempt from consequences, believing the unrighteous will be saved, thinking that peers will not create a negative influence, and so forth

Impairments

- Self-defensiveness and lying, compulsions, delusions, dissociative states, hyperactivity, obsessions, paranoia, phobia, somatization, dysphoric mood, mood lability, hopelessness, social withdrawal

Treatment Intervention

- Complete Step 2: Deception Versus Truth

Treatment Goals

- Examines own behavior thoroughly for self-deception and self-defense

- Bases behavior on the truth of God and the Bible
- Achieves freedom from the bondage of fear and conducts life only from the perspective of faith in God

Objective Criteria for Discharge

- Confesses the presence of self-deception, self-defense, and fear when these are identified
- Verbalizes and takes responsibility for personal motives and behaviors
- States an integrated sense of self and relies on Christ as the only defense needed
- Recites the "Doctrinal Affirmation" with the absence of disturbing thoughts or strong emotional reactions (see Appendix E)

STEP 3: BITTERNESS VERSUS FORGIVENESS

Symptoms

- Maintains mental list of persons believed to have wronged, offended, or hurt the self and toward whom current resentment, bitterness, or revenge is directed
- Demonstrates self-criticism, self-condemnation, and self-accusation for past thoughts, feelings, and behaviors
- Verbalizes anger toward self and God for life circumstances that impact personal life

Impairments

- Bitterness, rage reactions, externalization, blame, homicidal thought/behavior, emotional/physical trauma victim, family dysfunction, marital relationship dysfunction

Treatment Intervention

- Complete Step 3: Bitterness Versus Forgiveness

Treatment Goals

- Chooses an attitude of forgiveness toward persons who have been offensive in the past

- Releases the bitterness and anger that may have occurred as a result of the offenses of others against the self and chooses not to retaliate

Objective Criteria for Discharge

- Lists all persons toward whom bitterness and resentment have been held
- Verbally releases to God all persons listed, forgiving every person, including oneself and God, for every painful memory or attributed shortcoming
- Verbalizes the choice to abandon bitterness and anger
- Asks God to heal the damaged emotions from the past and to give peace in the present

Step 4: Rebellion Versus Submission

Symptoms

- Refuses to appropriately submit to established lines of authority (for example, employers, parents, husbands, civil government, church leaders, therapist, and God)

Impairments

- Repudiation, oppositionalism, rebellion, manipulativeness, medical treatment noncompliance, running away, tantrums, uncommunicativeness, truancy

Treatment Intervention

- Complete Step 4: Rebellion Versus Submission

Treatment Goals

- Exhibits appropriate submission, deference, and respect for persons and institutions in authority over the self
- Seeks appropriate assistance when those in authority are abusive or inappropriate in their behaviors

Objective Criteria for Discharge

- Verbally examines each area of authority and asks God to forgive the self for each distinct time submissiveness has been lacking
- Verbally declares the choice to be submissive and appropriately obedient to those in appropriate authority over oneself
- Lists the abusive behaviors of others and identifies the steps necessary to protect the self

STEP 5: PRIDE VERSUS HUMILITY

Symptoms

- Lives independently of others and God and relies solely on own strengths and resources
- Centers life around self and regards self as more important than others

Impairments

- Grandiosity, arrogance, pride, conceit, narcissism, egocentricity

Treatment Intervention

- Complete Step 5: Pride Versus Humility

Treatment Goals

- Transfers overreliance on own accomplishments and abilities to a commitment to live humbly before God

Objective Criteria for Discharge

- Completes a rigorous self-examination of pridefulness
- Verbally recognizes the behaviors of pridefulness as self-defeating
- Lists situations in which to apply appropriate humility and verbally declares a commitment to place confidence in God for empowering a humble attitude in relationships with others

STEP 6: BONDAGE VERSUS FREEDOM

Symptoms

- Habitually disobeys the moral law of God as outlined in the Bible (see Exodus 20:1 – 17; Galatians 5:19 – 21)
- Consistently behaves in ways that are unrighteous and sinful, with obvious legal, social, occupational, and physical consequences
- Demonstrates a disturbed fellowship with God by a decrease in prayer, Bible study, and worship involvement
- Demonstrates a disturbed fellowship with other people by the presence of guilt (conscious or unconscious) that results from breaking the moral law prescribed in the Bible

Impairments

- Moral law noncompliance, antisocial behavior, oppositionalism, promiscuity, paraphilia, homicidal thought/behavior, assaultiveness, eating disorder, fire setting, suicidal thought/behavior, substance abuse, self-mutilation, stealing, addictions, gender dysphoria, and sexual dysfunction

Treatment Intervention

- Complete Step 6: Bondage Versus Freedom

Treatment Goals

- Identifies past and present sins that are acts of rebellion against God
- Seeks forgiveness from others where possible
- Verbalizes freedom from the continued control and dominance of moral failure in life

Objective Criteria for Discharge

- Renounces specific disobedient behaviors as listed in Galatians 5:19 – 21 and asks forgiveness for each one
- Agrees with God about the severity of the wrongdoing (that is, confesses)

- Asks forgiveness from all who have been directly affected by the wrongdoing
- Turns away from the wrongdoing and no longer engages in it (that is, repents)
- Resumes or begins the disciplines of prayer, Bible reading, fellowship, and worship involvement
- Demonstrates absence of self-justification and of a prideful attitude (that is, demonstrates humility)
- Confesses wrongdoing to one or more Christian friends and asks for prayer and accountability
- Engages emotionally in the steps of the grief process
- Verbally accepts the Bible's promises of forgiveness, the presence of spiritual cleansing, and the healing of emotions

STEP 7: ACQUIESCENCE VERSUS RENUNCIATION

Symptoms

- Shows a predisposition to certain problems by known or unknown influences from the willful ancestral disobedience of the moral law
- Shows a predisposition to negative occurrences and conditions from curses directed by past or present satanic forces

Impairments

- Family of origin spiritual dysfunction, spiritual assignments/curses, repeated abusive/maladaptive behaviors, family dysfunction, marital relationship dysfunction, emotional/physical trauma victim and/or perpetrator (all impairments can potentially be transmitted through the family line by familiar spirits)

Treatment Intervention

- Complete Step 7: Acquiescence Versus Renunciation

Treatment Goals

- Identifies sins that are characteristic of one's family
- Breaks any patterns of their influence by prayer and repentance

Objective Criteria for Discharge

- Declares out loud the personal rejection and disavowal of all willful disobedience of God's precepts by ancestors and specifically names the known transgressions
- Humbles self in prayer before God, asks him to renew the mind, and pledges submission to him alone
- Verbally declares the cancellation of all satanic curses and assignments directed against oneself, one's family, and one's ministry

Counseling Assistance Tool Kit

On the assumption that modern knowledge renders unintelligible the scriptural formulation of the Gospel, the secular theologians eliminate the invisible, transcendent, absolute God of the Bible. The most obvious defect of this contemporary theological faddism is its mislocation of the problem of modern man. The modern problem is not the transcendent God but rebellious man — not modern man in some peculiar way but man as fallen.

CARL F. H. HENRY

We have practiced in the field of mental health for many years, first as non-Christians in secular settings, then as born-again Christians in both secular and Christian settings. Along the way, we have acquired certain skills, competencies, and tools that have been effective in client management. As we stated earlier, the secular intervention techniques we have retained are passed through the refining grid of Scripture before we tuck them into our tool kit of interventions.

As we look at the tools we find useful in our clinical practice, we're impressed with the number of them we used in our years of secular practice that have come to life now that we can identify the biblical basis for their effectiveness! We are now able to identify the Scripture verses on which the concepts were based — even though the originators may not have known the true source of the wisdom they were imparting. We encourage clients to meditate, memorize, and utilize these truths from the Bible as they work through their particular instructional area. Other methodologies, which we used before we became Christians, we now recognize as being humanistic, utopianist, or New Age; we have discarded these methodologies and encourage all therapists to do the same.

Before we open the tool kit to share the treasures inside, we want to discuss briefly two ways in which we move into these tool kit areas of focus. The first is with clients who have already had in-depth Freedom Appointments and present for additional counseling assistance; the second is with clients who come to us from a variety of referral sources. Typically the latter are clients who don't know anything about the Freedom Appointment; they are often nominal Christians or non-Christians seeking help, who have given informed consent to receive biblical counsel.

CONTEXT OF A POST–FREEDOM APPOINTMENT

As stated above, some clients are referred to us after they complete a Freedom Appointment. The component of aftercare is always considered at the end of this kind of ministry appointment, and referrals are recommended if additional counseling at a professional level is needed. In the course of the Freedom Appointment, issues such as sexual abuse, chemical dependency, chronic dysfunctional relationships, major mood disturbances, anxiety disorders, marital discord, dissociative disorder, and the like may have been uncovered. These may call for treatment beyond what is available through the Freedom Appointment, because these clients often have many layers of unresolved conflicts.

When a client comes to us out of this context, we know that major spiritual interventions leading to clarity concerning one's identity in Christ and the removal of principal spiritual strongholds have been accomplished through the Freedom Appointment. As a part of the professional differential diagnosis and treatment plan, however, the need for further counseling on boundary clarification, assertiveness, anger management, and the like may become evident. The therapist would then use relevant tools to specifically address the appropriate issues. If additional work is needed on a particular spiritual impairment area, the therapist may ask the client to do it as a homework assignment or may elect to work on it with the client in session.

CONTEXT OF REGULAR THERAPY

The second kind of clinical situation presents itself when a non-Christian seeks help. The tools would be utilized in the context of the treatment plan but would not necessarily have the biblical references identified. If a client identifies himself or herself as one who was raised in a Christian church and is nominally Christian, and if informed consent is discussed and agreed on, even though the individual does not have a personal relationship with Christ, the tools and the treatment approach would include biblical references. To do so can be very helpful in paving the way for the Holy Spirit to act in drawing the person to the Truth. The Christian counselor is ready to draw in the spiritual dimension when God's timing is right to discuss the necessity of making a personal decision and then to pray with the client for salvation.

In the case of a client who does not give informed consent and does not welcome Christian spiritual references in counseling, the appropriate tools would be presented nonetheless — but biblical references would not be made. Nevertheless, the biblical worldview is represented, and God's truths are given. For example, Julie has consistently found this operational in her use of the "Bonding" tool (see the discussion of this tool later in this chapter). With no reference to the Bible, she has presented to many non-Christians the principles of sexual chastity before and marital fidelity after marriage. Her presentation rings true because it is based on truth!

Consider also the case of a Christian client who is seeking professional help directly for a personal, family, or marital issue but who has not experienced the "Steps to Freedom in Christ." If in the course of the diagnostic workup it becomes evident that the treatment plan needs to include interventions in these tool kit areas, we utilize in-session teaching and assign the client outside reading and behavioral practice of the concepts. As we identify spiritual impairments that exist surrounding these areas, we either incorporate the assignment of a particular Step as a homework assignment to repeat privately, or we may work on it in session. Because this client will be unfamiliar with the "Steps to Freedom in Christ," whichever approach to the Steps we choose to use will be explained and assigned. Often we will refer the client to a church with Freedom Ministry resources to go through the Steps with a trained two-person team. This experience can be accomplished outside of therapy during the course of counseling, and we have found that the earlier in the course of treatment, the better.

In summary, spiritual interventions and tool kit interventions are woven together in the total treatment intervention. The list of tools is not exhaustive but is offered in summary fashion, especially to give the beginning professional counselor, lay counselor, or pastoral counselor practical, hands-on resources ready for immediate application. The Christian community has been so prolific in publishing materials to assist counselors that it can sometimes seem overwhelming to the novice practitioner — and even to seasoned ones! We hope these little "bites" will be helpful.

THE TOOL KIT

We have structured this section as follows:

Indications for Use, where we note the general client conditions that exist when instruction in the particular tool area may be beneficial.

Resources, where we identify primary sources that either client or counselor can read to increase familiarity within this area (these are the primary Christian resources we've found helpful in delineating the treatment approach).

Presentation to Client and/or Therapist, written as though either a client is being addressed and taught verbally in session by the counselor, or as though a therapist is being addressed instructionally by the writer. We chose to simplify the content in this way so as to highlight the essential points. We teach the material in session at a level that can be easily grasped by the client, because sometimes the background material comes in such theoretical, intellectual, and technical language that it's difficult for the practitioner to interpret it for the client. A novice therapist could even attach the tool kit material to a clipboard and use it to guide the teaching session with the client the first few times a particular tool is used.

We have asked experienced Christian counselors to contribute to this section; each is knowledgeable and skilled in the particular area about which they write. Since we personally use these particular tools in our counseling sessions, we asked our contributors to summarize the main points and we then embellished their contributions based on our own experiences.

COGNITIVE-BEHAVIORAL THERAPY

TERRY E. ZUEHLKE, PH.D., L.P.

INDICATIONS FOR USE

Primarily when biblical untruths and irrational beliefs are preventing clients from living a free and productive life. The basic premise is that Satan's lies are cognitive distortions of reality. A true understanding of God and a righteous relationship with him are thus blocked. This approach to spiritual and psychological problems helps to transform clients' minds and assists them in learning how to manage their emotions and to be set free from the strongholds of the world, the flesh, and the devil.

RESOURCES

Anderson, Neil T. *Victory Over the Darkness.* Ventura, Calif.: Regal, 1990.

Backus, William, and Marie Chapian. *Telling Yourself the Truth.* Minneapolis: Bethany House, 1980.

Burns, David. *Feeling Good: The New Mood Therapy.* New York: Signet, 1980. (A classic secular resource.)

Pakkala, Alaine. *Taking Every Thought Captive: Spiritual Workouts to Help Renew Your Mind in God's Truth.* Colorado Springs: Lydia Press, 1994.

Thurman, Chris. *The Lies We Believe.* Nashville: Nelson, 1989. Also, *The Lies We Believe Workbook.* Nashville: Nelson, 1995.

———. *The Truths We Must Believe.* Nashville: Nelson, 1991.

PRESENTATION TO CLIENT AND/OR THERAPIST

This counseling experience is similar to the game of baseball (see Figure 9.1 on page 227). There are three bases to pass if one is to touch home plate and accomplish the goal. We are going to move through three bases in our therapy together to help you learn why you are having problems and what to do about them. This process will help you learn how to take thoughts captive and make them obedient to Christ.

FIRST BASE: NEW ATTITUDES

Proverbs 23:7 is the foundational Scripture for First Base: "As he thinketh in his heart, so is he" (King James Version). Peter tells us to prepare our minds for action and to be self-controlled (1 Peter 1:13). These verses show that our feelings and behaviors are largely controlled by the way we think. We can look at this process by using the acrostic A-B-C. The letter "A" represents the *activating event* (behavioral psychologist B. F. Skinner called this the "stimulus"). The stimulus is the person or event that seems to be causing our stress. The letter "C" is the *consequence* ("response") to that stimulus. It occurs on two levels: as a behavioral manifestation (or a physiological response such as blushing, headache, or muscle tension) and as an emotional manifestation (for example, anger, anxiety, or depression).

Secular society believes that A causes C. To each stimulus we have a response. If the telephone rings we answer it. Clearly, sponsors of television commercials would like us to believe that if we use a certain product we will get the results they promise.

A biblical counseling technique known as cognitive-behavioral therapy, however, has a different perspective—one that is based on how our brains really function. This approach emphasizes the importance of the "B" component, which refers to your *belief system*. Attitudes, expectations, interpretations, perceptions, values, thoughts, and self-talk are other names for your belief system. The mind is not just a black box that lacks control over our responses. It is the source of our reactions. Unless we are talking about a reflex action, we do not act or feel anything without first thinking about it. This process is subliminal and rapid. Therefore, to change negative behaviors or feelings, we need to look at what we are thinking or telling ourselves that is leading to our behavioral and emotional consequences.

It's helpful to keep a journal of what is bothersome to you. This is your "Diary of Discontentment." Instead of doing this in an A-B-C sequence, do it in a C-A-B format, because it is easier to identify first a negative *c*onsequence (a feeling and/or behavior) and then write down the *a*ctivating event (circumstances) with which these negative consequences are associated. Then write a paragraph that lists your *b*eliefs (thoughts) in that situation. Bring your journal to the sessions, and we'll examine your self-talk to see if it is biblical and appropriate for you. We'll use the A-B-Cs to help you understand *why* you are having trouble. Then we will add D and E to help you decide *what* to do about the problem. When we review your journal, we will take a thought you have recorded and *d*iscern, *d*ispute, *d*ebate, and *d*ecide if the thought is based on biblical truth. If such is the case, you can keep it. But, if you discover a misbelief, *e*fforts will be made to restructure or stop the thought so that you can behave and feel differently.

SECOND BASE: PREDICT THE PATTERN

At Second Base you have the opportunity to review your journal entries and locate patterns of predictable perceptions that lead to negative feelings and counterproductive behavior. Here you will try to find common denominators that will help you see that your thoughts are not random and chaotic. This process will give you a sense of empowerment because your problems no longer seem to be unpredictable and beyond your control.

Once you can see that your unbiblical and irrational thinking follows a particular pattern, we can begin to look for triggers or cues that led up to these lies. For example, "Suppose my journal reveals I have a problem with anger when I believe I am being ordered around unfairly and no one is listening to me. Suppose also that I know I have a meeting with my boss next week and that some difficult decisions — ones about which she and I disagree — need to be made. Because my journal review has allowed me to realize this approaching event could be troublesome, I can focus on my thoughts about dealing with authority before I am in the situation. As a result, I am able to take captive unbiblical thoughts and restructure them to a more realistic perspective."

Your Scripture reference for Second Base is Romans 12:2: "Do not conform any longer to the pattern of this world, but be transformed by the renewing of your mind."

THIRD BASE: NEW BIBLICAL BEHAVIORS

Third Base is focused on the decision to develop new biblical behavior patterns where they are needed in your life. Identification of your thought processes (First Base) and the ability to understand the patterns of your thinking (Second Base) are not sufficient for healing. The third step in the therapy process is to develop new biblical behaviors and support systems (Third Base) that will enhance recovery. This is the real-life application of the biblical principle that the truth sets you free to lead a more satisfying and fulfilling life. This brings you to the stage where you choose activities to support and strengthen new beliefs. This is also the point where you are challenged to drop any "I can't" or "yeah, but ..." attitudes. As a Christian, you are reminded of what the Bible says to all believers in Philippians 4:13: "I can do everything through him who gives me strength." We also read in 1 Corinthians 10:13 that believers are never tested or tempted beyond their limit and that God will always provide a way to help them make it through their trials. So, I challenge you to substitute the word "won't" for "can't." You must also stop "yeah, but ..." thinking, because the real meaning of such a phrase is "no."

Examples of new behavioral experiences will include daily devotions, Scripture memorization, fasting, a weekly Bible study, participation in an accountability group, continuation of journaling, developing church relationships, shared prayer with a spouse or close companion, increased volunteer activities at church or in the community, increased Christian fellowship, and perhaps continuation of psychotherapy. Other changes for you might include watching what you eat and developing an exercise program, taking psychotropic medication, and undergoing a thorough physical examination.

Your scriptural references for this phase of therapy include:

Make plans by seeking advice; if you wage war, obtain guidance.

—*PROVERBS 20:18*

May the words of my mouth and the meditation of my heart be pleasing in your sight, O LORD, my Rock and my Redeemer.

—*PSALM 19:14*

No temptation has seized you except what is common to man. And God is faithful; he will not let you be tempted beyond what you can bear. But when you are tempted, he will also provide a way out so that you can stand up under it.

—*1 CORINTHIANS 10:13*

We demolish arguments and every pretension that sets itself up against the knowledge of God, and we take captive every thought to make it obedient to Christ.

—*2 CORINTHIANS 10:5*

And my God will meet all your needs according to his glorious riches in Christ Jesus.

—*PHILIPPIANS 4:19*

> Do not conform any longer to the pattern of this world, but be transformed by the renewing of your mind. Then you will be able to test and approve what God's will is — his good, pleasing and perfect will.
>
> —ROMANS 12:2

HOME PLATE: KINGDOM COME

Once you have successfully applied the activities at First, Second, and Third Bases, Home Plate represents the fruit of the Spirit, which removes anger, depression, and anxiety (the "big three" negative emotions in mental health) and replaces them with love, joy, and peace. Remember, we "score a point" for ourselves and the body of Christ when we practice these biblically and psychologically sound principles. Home Plate represents the experience of Christian growth and maturity that results when we seek first God's kingdom and his righteousness (Matthew 6:33). This biblical truth is the cornerstone of reaching Home Plate through the process of Christian psychotherapy. It points out that we cannot serve two masters. Reaching Home Plate by appropriating the three bases of Christian cognitive-behavioral therapy allows you to reprogram your mental computer. Your double-mindedness is dissolved. Philippians 4:6–7 tells us, "Do not be anxious about anything, but in everything, by prayer and petition, with thanksgiving, present your requests to God. And the peace of God, which transcends all understanding, will guard your hearts and your minds in Christ Jesus."

The Game

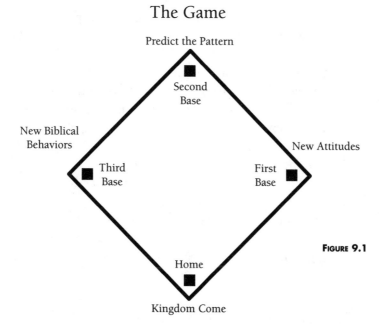

FIGURE 9.1

BONDING

JULIANNE S. ZUEHLKE, M.S., R.N., C.S.

INDICATIONS FOR USE

When premarital or extramarital sexual behavior is part of a client's history. The biblical prohibition of such behavior is the expression of truth and is verified by current research in this area.

RESOURCES

Anderson, Neil. *A Way of Escape*. Eugene, Ore.: Harvest House, 1994.

Focus on the Family, audiotape on bonding, available through Focus on the Family, Colorado Springs, Colorado.

Joy, Donald. *Bonding: Relationships in the Image of God*. Dallas: Word, 1985, 36–53. Now available in a revised edition, published by Word, 1999.

Morris, Desmond. *Intimate Behavior*. New York: Random House, 1971, 74–79.

PRESENTATION TO CLIENT AND/OR THERAPIST

Sexuality is a very powerful, God-given drive that has been distorted and misused, often unknowingly. Most people marry with the intention of staying married for life and expect their spouses to be sexually faithful throughout the relationship. Did you know there are prior behaviors that can weaken the relationship if not renounced and new behavior announced? These prior behaviors have to do with *bonding*.

Bonding is an invisible but powerful emotional and spiritual connection between two people. It is the cementing of an emotional tie that says, "we are knit together." In the biological realm of the animal kingdom, this can be seen in what is called *imprinting*. For example, at six weeks of age goslings who are taken from the mother goose and placed with a dog, hen, or a farmer become bonded to the new "mother," following it around as loyally as if it were the mother goose herself. This imprinting occurs in humans with the act of intercourse. One researcher feels strongly that one of the reasons the divorce rate is so high is that millions of people are frantically searching for the person they bonded with in the backseat of the car at age sixteen!

Marriage and family expert Donald Joy has taken the research of Desmond Morris, a secular anthropologist and author of *The Naked Ape* and other texts, and found that the secular research agrees with the biblical injunctions of monogamy and fidelity. Genesis 2:24 states, "For this reason a man will leave his father and his mother and [cling] to his wife; and they will become one flesh." Morris studied numerous cultures around the world for the factors that make for a lifetime conjugal union. A factor had to be present in eighty-five percent of the cultures to make his list. Figure 9.2 illustrates the successive presence of twelve bonding sequences that have to occur, one after the other, over a significant period of time, in order for lifelong, exclusive, one-flesh pair bonding to occur. Once a couple is appropriately bonded, they can think of nothing *short of death* that can disturb their bond.

Pair Bonding *What God joins together, let no one separate!* (see Matthew 19:6)

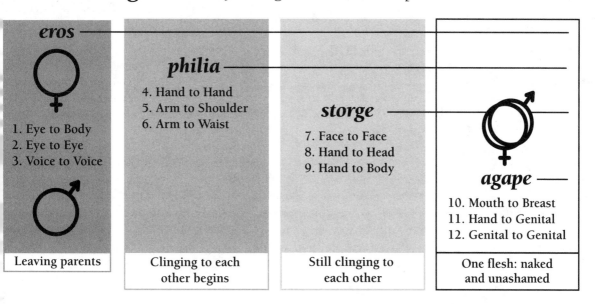

eros
1. Eye to Body
2. Eye to Eye
3. Voice to Voice

Leaving parents

philia
4. Hand to Hand
5. Arm to Shoulder
6. Arm to Waist

Clinging to each other begins

storge
7. Face to Face
8. Hand to Head
9. Hand to Body

Still clinging to each other

agape
10. Mouth to Breast
11. Hand to Genital
12. Genital to Genital

One flesh: naked and unashamed

Adapted from Donald Joy, *Bonding: Relationships in the Image of God* (Nashville: Word, 1999). Used by permission of the author.

FIGURE 9.2

Phase 1 in pair bonding is described as follows:
Leaving: No physical contact. Attraction is private, nonpublic.

- Step 1: *Eye to Body:* Eureka stage: "Where have YOU been all my life!"
- Step 2: *Eye to Eye:* Gazing stage: one- or two-sided, heartbeat quickening.
- Step 3: *Voice to Voice:* Introductions, trivial talk, getting to know you.

Phase 2 is described as follows:
Clinging begins: First touches, but not directly sexual. Attraction becomes publicly declared.

- Step 4: *Hand to Hand:* Making the first social statement — "We belong together."
- Step 5: *Arm to Shoulder:* Not yet a hug, but a gesture of ownership.
- Step 6: *Arm to Waist:* The couple pulls close, but their faces are still "forward" physically — still looking at the outer world. Deep questions posed and answered confidentially. Last exit on the pair-bonding freeway before termination will cause grief and pain.

Phase 3 is described as follows:
Still Clinging: Intimate contact with no direct sexual contact. Unprotected intimacy here exposes the relationship to high levels of anxiety.

- Step 7: *Face to Face:* Mouth-to-mouth, intimate kissing; intense gazing face to face; decrease in communication verbally but increase in nonverbal messages.
- Step 8: *Hand to Head:* Denotes absolute trust. The head is the most vulnerable part of the body, and few have permission to touch it.
- Step 9: *Hand to Body:* Ultimate appreciation for the way the person occupies space, excluding the genitals. It is the *person* who is known and respected, not some phantom of perfection.

At this step, the couple comes to the final point before the bond needs absolute legal protection lest emotional trauma occurs. It is critical to "get them to the church on time" and to provide the resources of families and community to guarantee safe passage into the ultimate intimacy.

The bond needs protection in much the same way as people do not leave an expensive sports car unlocked with the key in the ignition in a high-crime area but lock it up inside a garage. Likewise, people do not toss an expensive ruby stone into a dresser drawer but rather place it into a gold or silver jewelry setting. The pair bond is even more valuable than the previous examples, and it both needs and deserves protection! The legality of marriage is the cultural way of protecting the value of the emotional bond. The marriage certificate is not just a piece of paper, but a protective instrument necessary for the preservation of both of the individuals involved as well as for the sake of the culture.

Phase 4 is described as follows:

One Flesh: Naked and unashamed.

- Step 10: *Mouth to Breast*
- Step 11: *Hand to Genital*
- Step 12: *Genital to Genital*

These three steps in Phase 4 are the different *phases of sexual intercourse.* This stage deserves the absolute privacy to match the absolute intimacy that legal marriage guarantees.

Unfortunately, couples who adopt nonbiblical worldviews often will enter a relationship with the figure inverted, beginning, for example, at Phase 4, with no prior bonding experiences. The sexual intensity obscures temporarily the reality that bonding has not occurred, and marriage ends up being based on a fragile (or perhaps even nonexistent) bond that is easily broken. In another vein, couples will begin living together without the protection of marriage, with resulting exploitation physically, socially, financially, and emotionally—an exploitation usually of the woman. If multiple Phase 4 relationships have been carried out, multiple bonds exist that have been fractured. This in turn creates an unsettled internal emotional environment that is confusing and unstable. The expensive sports car gets trashed or the ruby is lost, so to speak—and grief, suffering, and pain result.

Bonding not only occurs prior to marriage, but it also needs to be continually nurtured in sequence within the marriage to keep the ties strong. When this does not happen, wives in particular feel as though "all my husband wants is sex." That feeling is a red flag that the bonding sequence is not being renewed day by day.

If bonding has occurred with other parties, the spiritual ties have to be broken by the prayerful confessing, renouncing, and repenting of each illegitimate bond; the breaking of those ties is accomplished verbally and preferably with a witness present, such as the therapist (see James 5:16). Steps 3 and 6 in the "Steps to Freedom in Christ" are excellent tools for accomplishing this breaking of ties. The correct bonding sequence (see again Figure 9.2) then needs to be initiated in the authentic relationship, even if it means forgoing intercourse in a marriage for a time until the bonding sequence is followed, enjoyed, and completed.

EARLY RECOLLECTIONS

KRISTIN KYTTA, M.A.

INDICATIONS FOR USE

When clients' beliefs about themselves, others, the world, and/or God are being applied to every situation, no matter what the truth of the belief in a particular circumstance. The basic premise is that distorted beliefs are not based on the truth. This technique assists the client in uncovering the lies or distorted beliefs and gives him or her the opportunity to challenge those beliefs in light of reality and biblical truth.

RESOURCES

Carlson, Randy, and Kevin Leman. *Unlocking the Secrets of Your Childhood Memories.* New York: Pocket Books, 1989.

Cloud, Henry. *Changes That Heal: How to Understand Your Past to Ensure a Healthier Future.* Grand Rapids: Zondervan, 1990.

Johnson, Mark. *Spiritual Warfare for the Wounded.* Ann Arbor, Mich.: Vine Books, 1992.

Seamands, David A. *Healing of Memories.* Wheaton, Ill.: Victor, 1985.

Smith, Ed. *Beyond Tolerable Recovery.* 2d ed. Campbellsville, Ky.: Family Care Ministries, 1997.

PRESENTATION TO CLIENT AND/OR THERAPIST

You've heard it said that our past affects both our present and our future. While this is a truth we may know logically, much of the time we are unaware of the extent to which our current thoughts and behaviors are influenced by past experiences. At times, the influence of the past can have a positive effect on our present situation. For instance, my mother has the gifts of encouragement and hospitality. While I was growing up, I would observe her reaching out in a variety of ways to help people in need. She prepared meals, assembled Christmas and birthday baskets for people who wouldn't otherwise receive them, and visited those who were lonely. Now, while I cannot claim to have her gifts, I do see the influence of her actions in my life. By modeling this behavior, she taught me to be aware of needs and to respond in love.

Unfortunately, the majority of people who seek counsel do so because of the negative effect of experiences in their lives. For example, a child may have been neglected by her parents, whom she could not rely on to meet her needs for shelter, food, safety, security, and the like. She may have unconsciously summarized her belief about her parents as follows: "Parents are unpredictable and untrustworthy." It is quite possible that this belief about her parents could have been expanded to people in general and to authority figures in particular. She could also have formulated negative beliefs about herself, which in turn would strongly influence how she relates to others.

Suppose this child, now a young wife and mother, enters counseling because she feels her husband is unpredictable and untrustworthy. It may be premature in the initial sessions to help her cognitively pursue whether or not this is factual (that is, by exploring her husband's positive and negative qualities, examining their marital relationship, and so forth). This is especially true if she is working from the premise of a distorted belief that *all* people are unpredictable and untrustworthy. She may not be able to look objectively at her own unique situation. It may be helpful at this point to determine the beliefs, developed early in life, by which she is presently living; these may include beliefs about herself, others, the world, and God.

One way to uncover the beliefs that help form and inform a person's worldview is to have him or her share some early recollections, which in essence are simply early memories that assist us in uncovering the possible hidden hurts, unmet needs, and suppressed emotions that can include lies we believe about ourselves and the world around us. These beliefs, which are often distorted and unknown to us, are powerfully shaping our reactions to current life experiences. Obviously, we cannot undo the reality of what has occurred in our lives, but we do have the power, with the Lord's help, to change the effect that the past may be having on us in current situations.

As you present to the client, you may want to ask him or her to do the following:

Please give me four or five of the earliest memories you have, preferably before the age of eight. *(The following "memories" are inserted for illustrative purposes.)*

Memory One

Age: 6

My family was having dinner, and my dad was in a very bad mood. I think we were eating meatloaf with applesauce and corn. Anyway, I didn't like it when my dad was in a bad mood, so I tried to make everyone, including Dad, forget about his bad mood by telling jokes and trying to keep the attention off of him and his bad mood.

Feeling: Nervous

Memory Two

Age: 4

My sister was in her crib, and I was in bed with the pretty pink comforter on it. We were supposed to be sleeping. My mom and dad were downstairs watching TV. Something must have happened, because they both started yelling and then my mom started crying. My sister climbed into bed with me.

Feeling: Scared

Memory Three

Age: 5

It was fall and really pretty outside. Dad took us for a drive. We stopped at an apple orchard. We got to pick big red apples and drink apple cider. It was a great day.

Feeling: Happy, content

Memory Four

Age: 5

My dad's brother, my uncle, lived in another state. He would come to visit us now and then. My sister and I would always get a toy from him when he came. He brought me a Barbie one time. One day when he was at our house, he came to my room at night to read me a story. When the story was over, he touched me and I didn't like it.

Feeling: Scared

From these four memories you've shared with me, I have a few observations or hunches about the type of beliefs your worldview might consist of. Can I share them with you? Please let me know what you think fits your situation, and what doesn't fit.

With respect to your view of *self,* here are some beliefs you may or may not hold:

- I am not safe.
- I am a detailed person.
- I notice things that are pretty.
- I am bad.
- I am artistic.
- I am a people person.
- I have to make things better for everyone.
- If I keep things under control, nothing bad will happen.
- If I do the right thing, nothing bad will happen.
- I have to take care of others.
- I have to take care of myself.
- I can't trust anybody.

With respect to your view of *others and the world,* here are some beliefs you may or may not hold:

- People can do nice things for me.
- People can confuse me.
- The world is not a safe place.
- People are unpredictable.
- Life can be scary.

With respect to your view of *God*, here are some beliefs you may or may not hold:

- God can't be trusted.
- God is not around.
- There is no God.
- God does not protect me.

Now that we've discussed the statements that reflect what you believe, how do you think these beliefs might be affecting your marriage, both in helpful and unhelpful ways? Which beliefs do you want to keep, and which do you want to try to change? Which do you think are contrary to what the Bible teaches? (Uncovering hidden beliefs in this manner will help identify the beliefs behind the client's behavior. It may also give you the opportunity to challenge those beliefs in light of reality and the Bible's teaching.)

The following Scripture references will be helpful for you as you begin this journey of uncovering the lies or the distorted beliefs that are negatively affecting your life:

Then we will no longer be infants, tossed back and forth by the waves, and blown here and there by every wind of teaching and by the cunning and craftiness of men in their deceitful scheming. Instead, speaking the truth in love, we will in all things grow up into him who is the Head, that is, Christ.

—*EPHESIANS 4:14–15*

Though my father and mother forsake me, the LORD will receive me. Teach me your way, O LORD; lead me in a straight path because of my oppressors.

—*PSALM 27:10–11*

When I was a child, I talked like a child, I thought like a child, I reasoned like a child. When I became a man, I put childish ways behind me.

—*1 CORINTHIANS 13:11*

In the same way, the Spirit helps us in our weakness. We do not know what we ought to pray for, but the Spirit himself intercedes for us with groans that words cannot express.

—ROMANS 8:26

We demolish arguments and every pretension that sets itself up against the knowledge of God, and we take captive every thought to make it obedient to Christ.

—2 CORINTHIANS 10:5

Jesus said, "If you hold to my teaching, you are really my disciples. Then you will know the truth, and the truth will set you free."

—JOHN 8:31B – 32

Trust in the LORD with all your heart and lean not on your own understanding; in all your ways acknowledge him, and he will make your paths straight.

—PROVERBS 3:5 – 6

Be strong and courageous. Do not be afraid or terrified because of them, for the LORD your God goes with you; he will never leave you nor forsake you.

—DEUTERONOMY 31:6

"For I know the plans I have for you," declares the LORD, "plans to prosper you and not to harm you, plans to give you hope and a future."

—JEREMIAH 29:11

The LORD is faithful to all his promises and loving toward all he has made.

—PSALM 145:13B

It's important to remember that uncovering the lies and distorted beliefs and challenging them is a lifelong process. As Paul says in Philippians 3:14, "Press on toward the goal to win the prize for which God has called [you] heavenward in Christ Jesus."

EATING DISORDERS

MARTHA HOMME, M.A., L.P.

INDICATIONS FOR USE

When bondage to food-related deceptions and behaviors is part of a client's history. The biblical commands to "have no other gods before me" and to "not make for yourself an idol" (Exodus 20:3, 4) prohibit placing priority on one's relationship with food or on making an idol of one's body.

RESOURCES

Boone O'Neill, Cherry, and Dan O'Neill. *Living on the Border of Disorder*. Minneapolis: Bethany House, 1992.

Bray-Garretson, Helen, and Kaye V. Cook. *Chaotic Eating: A Guide to Recovery*. Grand Rapids: Zondervan, 1992.

Garner, David M., and Paul E. Garfinkel. *Handbook of Treatment for Eating Disorders*. 2d ed. New York: Guilford, 1997.

Homme, Martha W. *Seeing Yourself in God's Image*. Chattanooga, Tenn.: Turning Point Ministries, 1999.

Siegel, Michele, Judith Brisman, and Margot Weinshel. *Surviving an Eating Disorder: Strategies for Family and Friends*. New York: HarperPerennial, 1997.

Thurman, Chris. *The Lies We Believe*. Nashville: Nelson, 1989. Also, *The Lies We Believe Workbook*. Nashville: Nelson, 1995.

— — —. *The Truths We Must Believe*. Nashville: Nelson, 1991.

Vath, Raymond E. *Counseling Those with Eating Disorders*. Waco, Tex.: Word, 1986.

Vredevelt, Pam, Deborah Newman, Harry Beverly, and Frank Minirth. *The Thin Disguise*. Nashville: Nelson, 1992.

PRESENTATION TO CLIENT AND/OR THERAPIST

The primary purpose of food is to satisfy physical hunger. God created all food to be good food. He did not, however, intend for food, or our attitude toward it, to become our God. Nor is he pleased when we place inappropriate focus on our body image, making our body in essence an idol.

The Bible states, "You shall have no other gods before me. You shall not make for yourself an idol in the form of anything in heaven above or on the earth beneath or in the waters below" (Deuteronomy 5:7–8).

Chaotic eating occurs when we let eating (or *not* eating) dominate our lives and when we worry more about our physical shape than we do about our spiritual and emotional worth and well-being. The A-B-Cs of chaotic eating are *a*norexia, *b*ulimia, and *c*ompulsive overeating. The focus of this client presentation is primarily on anorexia and bulimia, since they tend to be more popularly identified as eating disorders. However, the principles of bondage to food apply to compulsive overeating; hence, it should not be ignored as an eating disorder.

Anorexia and bulimia are characterized by a compulsive need to control weight, to be perfect, always to be the best, and to excel at everything one tries. Ten major factors contribute, in varying degrees for each individual, to the emotional and perceptual makeup of the eating-disordered personality:

1. distorted body image and denial
2. irrational beliefs and reckless thinking
3. perfectionism
4. low self-esteem
5. depression (especially the depression of masked anger and unresolved grief or loss)
6. control
7. dependency
8. distorted sexual identity
9. dysfunctional family system patterns of enmeshment, rigidity, overprotection, conflict avoidance/detouring, inconsistent atmosphere, and/or excessively high expectations
10. sociocultural distortion of the importance of physical appearance via peer pressure and media influence

God created each of us to have an "identity." His positive identity plan pertains to both physical and spiritual life and includes significance, worth, safety/security, and belongingness. Unfortunately, the impact of the Fall, even for the Christian, has left us vulnerable toward the dominant negative emotional effects of rejection, shame, guilt, hopelessness, and powerlessness.

Instead of claiming our identity in Christ, we too often seek significance, worth, safety/security, and belongingness in the wrong places.

Thinness, performance, and control do not equal significance and wholeness. When we fail to recognize that we are unconditionally loved and regarded by our heavenly Father, we set ourselves up for rejection, shame, guilt, hopelessness, and powerlessness.

The positive attributes of our position in Christ are replaced by the eating-disordered distortions with their need to *perform*, *please*, or *control*. Eating-disordered behaviors (for example, restricting, bingeing, and purging) are typically a cover for these underlying problems. Medical management is critical to restoring physical well-being; psychological, emotional, and spiritual management is essential for restoration of significance, worth, safety/security, and belongingness. The following two Scripture verses provide encouragement for individuals with eating disorders to address their inappropriate, unhealthy relationship with food:

> Don't you know that you yourselves are God's temple and that God's Spirit lives in you? If anyone destroys God's temple, God will destroy him; for God's temple is sacred, and you are that temple.
>
> —1 CORINTHIANS 3:16–17

> "Don't you see that nothing that enters a man from the outside can make him 'unclean'? For it doesn't go into his heart but into his stomach, and then out of his body." (In saying this, Jesus declared all foods "clean.")
>
> —MARK 7:18–19

Addressing the psychological, emotional, and spiritual issues of anorexia and bulimia is a task that is both complex and simple; the most basic truths (the most profound yet simple truths) that must be internalized are obedience to God (see Deuteronomy 5:6–8), the unconditional love of God (see John 3:16), and God's plan for and faithfulness to each of his children (see Psalm 139:13–14a; Jeremiah 29:11). Clients are in a position to address the issues of performance, pleasing others, and control only when they are willing to accept these basic truths as possibilities for themselves personally to experience.

Misplaced management of the individual's need to belong and contribute productively has led to inferiority, discouragement, and misbehavior (which is both avoidant and aggressive). Assuming the only way to belong and contribute is through performance, the eating-disordered individual adopts either a pleasing and/or control personality priority.

The "pleasers" strive to belong by achieving success in relationships through being friendly, keeping the peace, and steering clear of competition. They avoid anger and hide their feelings to avoid rejection. They battle with food rather than expressing themselves to others (that is, they stuff, or restrict, food and feelings).

The "controllers" strive to belong by maintaining maximum self-control and/or by controlling others. (Usually there is a perceived lack of ability to do the latter; however, they may indeed control others through the attention being focused on the "illness.") Controllers avoid feelings of powerlessness, humiliation, being out of control, and embarrassment. Any act of speaking up to ask for what they need is construed as loss of control.

Eating disorders paint a picture of people striving to "stay small" so neither needs nor imperfections will be noticed. Recovery begins when clients acknowledge the reality of their worth in Christ and the lack of any necessity to perform: "Christ died for me because I am not perfect; because he died for me, I do not need to be perfect. God's desire is that I function as a healthy member of the body of Christ in relationship, not in isolation, and that I nurture and nourish my physical body, which is the temple of the Holy Spirit."

Spiritual deception is an often overlooked dimension in eating disorders, and clients are seldom aware of why they binge, purge, or defecate. The apostle Paul says, "So I find this law at work: When I want to do good, evil is right there with me" (Romans 7:21). The evil that is present in those who struggle with eating disorders cannot be eliminated by bingeing, purging, and defecating. In Step 6 of the "Steps to Freedom in Christ," we have clients renounce the lie that defecating (or bingeing or purging) is a means of cleansing themselves; they are to trust only in the cleansing work of Jesus Christ.

GRIEF AND LOSS

Linda S. Wismer, M.A., L.P.

INDICATIONS FOR USE

When depression, anxiety, posttraumatic stress, and varying somatic complaints are part of clients' present experience and/or history. Initial intake information will often uncover intense events that have resulted in compounded grief and loss. A biblical approach to suffering instills hope.

RESOURCES

Anderson, Neil. *Finding Hope Again*. Ventura, Calif.: Regal, 1999.

Campbell, Brian M. *Pearls: Scriptures to Live By*. Lake Mary, Fla.: New Horizons, 1993.

Skinner Cook, Alicia, and Daniel S. Dworkin. *Helping the Bereaved*. New York: Basic, 1992.

Tournier, Paul. *Creative Suffering*. New York: Harper & Row, 1981.

Worden, William J. *Grief Counseling & Grief Therapy*. New York: Springer, 1991.

Wright, H. Norman. *Recovering from the Losses of Life* (Grand Rapids: Revell, 1991), 121, diagram.

PRESENTATION TO CLIENT AND/OR THERAPIST

A biblical approach to suffering allows a personal, creative, and unique response to loss. Physician Paul Tournier suggests in *Creative Suffering* that in tragedy, deprivation, and trial we must react, and in that reaction the mesh of old routines is broken, our usual models of behavior no longer serve effectively, and we must turn to our own innate creativity. Although suffering is not beneficial in and of itself, our personal response has potential to develop the person. Meaningful therapeutic intervention at the right moment may contribute to emotional and spiritual growth and healing.

A grief and loss assessment will be followed by moving through a series of tasks related to the recovery process. Each individual's experience and time frame is specific to him or her. Sensitivity to the uniqueness of the process facilitates healing. The following grief and loss assessment is to be used by the therapist as a general outline as he or she interviews the client. The gathering of this information may take up to four sessions or longer, depending on managed care time allotments or financial constraints. A church-based grief and loss group can serve as an important adjunct to individual therapy.

GRIEF AND LOSS ASSESSMENT

A. LOSS HISTORY
1. Previous losses inventory
2. Successful strategies

B. SUPPORT SYSTEM
1. Family
2. Friends
3. Community

C. TELLING THE STORY
1. Recounting circumstances
2. Nature of the loss
3. Unfinished business

D. SECONDARY LOSSES
1. Resulting role changes
2. Loss of dreams and expectations
3. Change of routine
4. Physical touch
5. Social adjustments

E. DEVELOPMENTAL ISSUES
1. Compounding life issues
2. Understanding of death
3. Facing own mortality

F. EXPRESSION OF EMOTIONAL PAIN
1. Grief and loss reaction, feeling

2. Adaptations

3. Gender differences

4. Coping skills

G. PHYSICAL ASPECTS

1. Compromised health

2. Physician's care

3. Physical and emotional risk factors

H. SPIRITUALITY

1. Beliefs related to death, the hereafter, and suffering

2. Relationship with Jesus Christ

3. Understanding of Scripture

I. THERAPEUTIC CONSIDERATIONS

1. Family and cultural norms

2. Client goals

3. Treatment goals

4. Therapist's own grief and loss

5. Collaborative effort

GRIEF AND LOSS TASKS

Recovery from grief and loss can be facilitated by systematically addressing four major tasks:

1. accepting the reality of the loss
2. working through emotional pain
3. adjusting to life without whatever has been lost
4. reinvesting emotionally

Task 1: Accepting the Reality of the Loss

Although clients may accept the reality of certain losses, such as health or aging, it is of paramount importance that they use all available resources to slow the process and possibly even reverse it. However, many losses are not reversible and are permanent in nature. Help the client to identify and discern the difference between losses that can be battled and those that must be accepted as permanent.

Psychologist Georgia Witkin, author of *The Female Stress Syndrome*,[1] adapted Thomas Holmes's and Richard Rahe's 1967 "Social Readjustment Rating Scale"[2] to reflect new point values derived from a survey of 2,400 women in 1990. Holmes and Rahe postulated that those experiencing losses in the past year with combined scores over 300 would have an eighty percent chance of contracting a major illness, having an accident, or becoming depressed. Those with a score of 150 to 300 would have a fifty percent risk of falling ill within two years. Using this inventory therapeutically will assist the client in identifying compounding losses and validating resulting feelings of sadness and confusion. Administer the "Season of Loss" inventory at this point (see Table 9.1).

Task 2: Working Through Emotional Pain

During this phase the therapist guides the client through the identification and expression of feelings. A daily journaling of feelings will help a client embrace the loss. A state of confusion or upheaval is often felt and frequently results in anger at God or inability to understand his master plan. A sense of isolation from God may be present, even in those clients who have experienced a close personal relationship with him. Encourage clients to share with God through journaling and prayer the entire range of their feelings. Also encourage clients to enlist other believers to pray for and with them during this time of confusion, as we are encouraged to "carry each other's burdens" (Galatians 6:2). The goal is to allow the client to feel the full force of the loss, because, as Jesus taught, "Blessed are those who mourn, for they will be comforted" (Matthew 5:4).

Receiving spiritual nourishment is critical for moving through emotional pain. Clients may resist the intentional choosing of Christian music, quiet time, church attendance, and fellowship with other believers. It is important to gently challenge this resistance. Clients who connect behaviorally and spiritually with others and the Lord find that their feelings move toward adjustment more quickly.

The reality is that some day we shall lose everything we now have. The recovery time is directly related to the degree we were attached to whatever was lost. The ultimate expression of Christian maturity is to be able to say with the apostle Paul, "I consider everything a loss compared to the surpassing greatness of knowing Christ Jesus my Lord, for whose sake I have lost all things" (Philippians 3:8).

Season of Loss

Life event	New Point Value	Old Point Value
Death of spouse	99	100
Divorce	91	73
Marital separation	78	85
Jail term	72	63
Death of close family member	84	63
Personal injury or illness	68	53
Marriage	85	50
Fired at work	83	47
Marital reconciliation	57	45
Retirement	88	45
Change in health of family member	58	44
Pregnancy	70	40
Sex difficulties	53	39
Gain of new family member	51	39
Business readjustment	50	39
Change of financial state	61	38
Death of close friend	68	37
Change to a different line of work	48	38
Change in number of arguments with spouse	48	35
Mortgage over $10,000	48	31
Foreclosure of mortgage or loan	55	30
Change in responsibilities at work	46	29
Son or daughter leaving home	41	29
Trouble with in-laws	43	29
Outstanding personal achievement	38	28
Spouse begins or stops work	58	26
Begin or end school	45	28
Change in living conditions	42	25
Revision of personal habits	44	24

LIFE EVENT	NEW POINT VALUE	OLD POINT VALUE
Trouble with boss	45	23
Change in work hours or conditions	36	20
Change in residence	47	20
Change in school	38	20
Change in recreation	26	19
Change in church activities	26	19
Change in social activities	26	18
Mortgage or loan less than $10,000	27	17
Change in sleeping habits	27	16
Change in number of family get-togethers	15	15
Change in eating habits	29	15
Vacation	43	13
Christmas	56	12
Minor violations of the law	30	11

TABLE 9.1

Task 3: Adjusting to Life Without Whatever Has Been Lost

Adjustment requires the establishment of a "new normal," the building of a new support structure that incorporates parts of the past. Some activities and relationships from the past will change, but some will surely be retained.

A new identity will be forged, recognizing that this experience has and will bring about change. The individual will behave in new ways. Traditions and rituals will be established to assist the client in healthy and appropriate development of a different perspective toward the loss.

Examination of strategies that have proved successful during past times of stress and trial will help shape a present plan. Include clients in the development of specific, tangible goals. Encourage them to identify those forces in their lives that keep them moving toward reaching their goals and those forces that hold them back from achieving their goals.

Task 4: Reinvesting Emotionally

A client can emerge from the grief and loss experience, having developed creative skills, diverse relationships, an expansion of roles, increased compassion and insight, and spiritual growth. As the individual takes initiative in all areas of his or her life, a sense of hope, confidence, and optimism about the future will develop. Reinvestment includes a spirit of willingness to try new activities, to build relationships, to make plans, to take risks, to explore, and to remain flexible. The result will be a new sense of meaning, focus, and direction in life, along with an understanding of and greater communion with the God of all comfort.

Use the following Scripture references for grief and loss therapy:

There is a time for everything, and a season for every activity under heaven: . . . a time to weep and a time to laugh, a time to mourn and a time to dance.

—*ECCLESIASTES 3:1, 4*

The eternal God is your refuge, and underneath are the everlasting arms.

—*DEUTERONOMY 33:27A*

I waited patiently for the LORD; he turned to me and heard my cry. He lifted me out of the slimy pit, out of the mud and mire; he set my feet on a rock and gave me a firm place to stand.

—*PSALM 40:1–3A*

"For I know the plans I have for you," declares the LORD, "plans to prosper you and not to harm you, plans to give you hope and a future."

—*JEREMIAH 29:11*

Praise be to the God and Father of our Lord Jesus Christ, the Father of compassion and the God of all comfort, who comforts us in all our troubles, so that we can comfort those in any trouble with the comfort we ourselves have received from God.

—*2 CORINTHIANS 1:3–4*

Come to me, all you who are weary and burdened, and I will give you rest. Take my yoke upon you and learn from me, for I am gentle and humble in heart, and you will find rest for your souls. For my yoke is easy and my burden is light.

—*MATTHEW 11:28–30*

Find rest, O my soul, in God alone; my hope comes from him. He alone is my rock and my salvation; he is my fortress, I will not be shaken.

—*PSALM 62:5–6*

PHYSICAL, EMOTIONAL, AND SEXUAL ABUSE

JEANETTE VOUGHT, PH.D., L.P.

INDICATIONS FOR USE

When the effects of past abuse cause emotional pain that hinders the practice of positive daily living skills. Nearly everyone has been affected to some degree by past physical, emotional, and/or sexual abuse. The counselor's task is to discover the core beliefs and emotional pain that have resulted from these experiences. Through prayer, the Holy Spirit reveals the lies that reside within clients' core beliefs and heals the pain embedded in their memories.

RESOURCES

Parker, Ken. *Reclaiming Your Inner Child* (Nashville: Nelson, 1993), 5–6.

Seamands, David A. *Putting Away Childish Things* (Wheaton, Ill: Victor, 1986), 5, 28.

Smith, Ed. *Beyond Tolerable Recovery*. 2d ed. (Campbellsville, Ky.: Family Care Ministries, 1997), 40–41, 119.

Vought, Jeanette, and Lynn Heitritter. *Helping Victims of Sexual Abuse* (Minneapolis: Bethany House, 1989), 147, 198–99.

PRESENTATION TO CLIENT AND/OR THERAPIST

Those who have been abused in childhood and/or adolescence may still be suffering many spiritual and emotional wounds. Although they may have biblical or intellectual knowledge about how to deal with these wounds, they don't know how to put their knowledge into practice. Pastor David Seamands states in *Putting Away Childish Things*, "Many people who are chronological adults are still emotional and spiritual children. Their quantity of birthdays may reveal their age in life, but their quality of behavior reveals their stage in life — childhood."[3]

The apostle Paul wrote, "When I was a child, I talked like a child, I thought like a child, I reasoned like a child. When I became a man [woman], I put childish ways behind me" (1 Corinthians 13:11). When we still carry with us the wounds of this child, it seems very difficult to "put childish ways" behind us. The wounded adult has built his or her core beliefs on the emotional pain of the wounded child. But God wants us to "grow up in every way into Christ" (Ephesians 4:15 Phillips). As counselors, we need to help clients identify these childish patterns and beliefs and see how Christ can bring growth, truth, freedom, and healing.

Often those who have been abused struggle with feelings of betrayal. How could someone they thought really cared about them treat them this way? Developmentally (especially if the abuse came from a parent), the trust they should have learned in childhood has been fractured. They have a secret they cannot share. They may feel abandoned by their family, even by God, and left alone in their pain. Even as adults, they fear what the perpetrator may do to them if they tell someone about the abuse. That fear may be transferred to all authority figures, making it difficult to share the secret even when the abuser can no longer hurt them.

Their sense of dignity and worth has been stolen from them. They struggle with a tremendous sense of guilt and feel responsible for the abuse that was perpetrated on them. Their shame makes them feel confused, unsure of who they are, convinced they are "bad" people.

Because their boundaries have been violated, they cannot protect themselves. They often feel uncomfortable with who they are as male or female and may use layers of clothing to cover their bodies. Their huge need to be loved clashes with a greater fear of intimacy and being hurt again. Love and hate feelings become difficult to distinguish.

The victims of abuse may project their anger on to others around them. They often choose abusive relationships and may abuse themselves or their own children. Anger and fear consume their waking hours, and nightmares disrupt their sleep. The wounded person may use work, food, drugs, or sex to deaden the pain for a little while.

Based on Ken Parker's analysis in *Reclaiming Your Inner Child,* we can help the abused person understand his or her symptoms by asking the following questions:

- Do you have times of depression or unhappiness that come and go without any logical reason? Do you find yourself more unhappy than happy? Has there been a family history of depression, or have you yourself suffered from recurrent depression?
- Do you have lots of ups and downs in your moods? Do you have difficulty controlling or dealing with your anger?

- Do you have difficulty sleeping? Do you have excessive anxiety about how you perform in your family, work, or church?
- Do you have feelings of fear or panic that interrupt everyday functioning? Are you struggling with compulsive behaviors regarding cleaning, food, drugs, gambling, or sex?
- Have you had trouble maintaining stable relationships? Are you overly dependent on others? Do you feel as though you can't live with them or without them?
- Does everything have to be perfect in your everyday activities? Do you expect perfection from others? Do you feel you have to control everything and everyone around you?
- Do you struggle with self-destructive behavior and thoughts? Have you struggled with thoughts of committing suicide, or have you actually made suicide attempts?

Having identified the symptoms, we can look for the core beliefs and emotional pain these symptoms reflect. Core beliefs are the foundational beliefs on which we build our lives. These beliefs can be divided into five categories:

1. How we see ourselves: I'm worthless. I'm stupid (or ugly). I can't protect myself.
2. How we see others: Nobody is trustworthy. People want to control me. All men think about and want is sex, or all women want to do is use me.
3. How we think others see us: I have to be perfect. I'm not as good as others. Nobody wants to be with me.
4. How we see God: God is an angry God. God is my judge. God is powerless to help me.
5. How we think God sees us: I am unlovable. I am a failure. I am insignificant.

Generally these core beliefs come from perceived or real events in childhood or adolescence. Because children believe the world revolves around them, they often feel they are responsible for terrible things that happen in the family: Dad dying or leaving the home; Mom and Dad getting a divorce; or abuse that was perpetrated on them.

In *Helping Victims of Sexual Abuse*, Jeanette Vought and Lynn Heitritter use the roots of a tree to depict the roots of our lives. These roots illustrate where our shame messages (negative core beliefs) come from:

- We experience shame when our basic needs of childhood go unmet — the needs to be loved unconditionally, to be valued, and to feel secure.
- Parents, siblings, or other authority figures can directly or indirectly relay shaming messages concerning our bodies, feelings, and needs.
- Some of the lies embedded in our core beliefs come from sexual and physical violations of the body.

Our wounds from the past are encoded in the brain through visual, emotional, and physical/sensory memories. These past wounds can be called up at any time by a similar sensory or emotional event; even a certain date or time of the year or a person with similar characteristics can trigger an emotional response from a past wound. In *Beyond Tolerable Recovery* Dr. Ed Smith urges us to look for the historical memory event that feels the same way or matches the emotions we are currently feeling (Dr. Smith calls these *echo emotions*).

In this search for core beliefs and embedded emotional pain, it's important to invite the "Wonderful Counselor" (Isaiah 9:6) to guide and direct the process. We need to pray, "Search me, O God, and know my heart; test me and know my anxious thoughts. See if there is any offensive way in me, and lead me in the way everlasting" (Psalm 139:23 – 24). God knows where the hidden pain and anxiety are located, even though the hurting person may not be aware of it. He sees the lies embedded in the core beliefs and can show us where in our memory the healing needs to take place. Satan, who is the father of lies, deceives abuse victims and can keep them in darkness for years. We need to pray that God will "open their eyes and turn them from darkness to light, and from the power of Satan to God" (Acts 26:18). We need to pray in the power and authority that we have in the risen Lord Jesus to bind Satan from interfering in any way.

As God brings to mind a memory connected to a core belief, we ask him to reveal any lies in that memory. The person may or may not regress to the age of the memory's trauma, feeling the pain the six-year-old felt and expressing the lies the child believes, but it is important for the "wounded child" to identify the lies and fully express his or her painful emotions.

As counselors, we repeat back to the wounded child the lies and pain he or she is expressing. Then we can pray and ask Jesus to reveal the truth and heal the pain of the child. The wounded child can also pray and ask Jesus to come into that specific memory and to reveal truth. In therapy, many of these hurting people have said they see Jesus come into the memory—revealing truth, comforting them, and demonstrating acts of love and protection. Sometimes they see an image of light in the memory and sense it is Jesus. Other times, they hear the Holy Spirit whispering truth to them in their minds.

One way to determine whether the pain has been released from the memory is to take hurting clients back to the memory and see if any other lies or pain remain. If they say they feel peaceful and the pain in the memory is gone, then you can thank God for what he has done. If not, there may be other lies within the memory that need to be identified and replaced with truth. Then ask God to lead you to any other memories that need healing. Many times the same lie is embedded in other memories, and when the truth is revealed and pain healed in one memory, similar memories also are affected.

In *Putting Away Childish Things*, David Seamands encourages us to "remember that Christ is alive. He is here now. And because He transcends time, He is also back at that painful experience. Confess to Him, turn over to Him each experience, each emotion, each attitude. Let Him love and comfort and forgive you. Let Him cleanse your hates and comfort your hurts and disinfect your lusts and remove your fears. Don't be in a hurry. Allow plenty of time for undisturbed, unhurried prayer."[4]

This approach to addressing core beliefs is very helpful when we can trust Jesus and those around us, but some people find it very difficult to get in touch with memories or to hear truth from Jesus. Some of the difficulties we've seen include:

- *Fear of getting in touch with the pain in the memory.* The fear of feeling and experiencing again the past painful event seems overwhelming, and some will do almost anything to avoid approaching it.
- *Fear of letting go of defense mechanisms.* The child had to build such a wall of defenses (such as denial, rationalization, projection, and disassociation) to protect himself or herself from the pain that now the client may find it difficult to knock the walls down.
- *Holding on to anger and bitterness to protect themselves.* Many abuse victims feel that if they let go of these feelings and forgive the abuser, they may be hurt again or forget what this person did to them. Holding on to the anger is their way to exact revenge on the abuser.

- *Intellectualism.* Victims may feel they have all the answers; they do not want to give up control and trust anyone besides themselves.
- *Demonic interference.* Demonic forces are drawn to the darkness by the lie in the memory. Once the lie is dispelled, we have the authority to bind the demonic in the name of Jesus Christ. Use the Non-Christian Spiritual Experience Inventory in the "Steps to Freedom in Christ" to determine occult involvement (see Step 1 in Appendix E) and lead the hurting person through the seven Steps, especially Step 3 on Bitterness Versus Forgiveness (see Appendix E).
- *Unconfessed sin.* The apostle John writes, "If we confess our sins, he is faithful and just and will forgive us our sins and purify us from all unrighteousness" (1 John 1:9).

Another source of interference in the work of dealing with memories is the difficulty some people have in trusting Jesus. Because adults have traumatized them, they cannot and will not trust adults — and they see Jesus as an adult who cannot be trusted. Jesus will not force himself on anyone, but the counselor can pray that Jesus will give the client the faith to trust him. Those struggling with the issues mentioned above will need to address these concerns before they can proceed further in getting in touch with their memories.

Once clients have examined their memories, they must take responsibility for making good decisions and changing the behaviors that are binding them. In *Helping Victims of Sexual Abuse*, Vought and Heitritter identify several areas for which the abuse victim needs to take responsibility:

- stop blaming themselves for the abuse
- make healthy choices for themselves, work to create a safe environment, and set boundaries in abusive relationships
- replace shame messages about themselves with new messages of truth
- continue to seek Christ-honoring behavior patterns
- replace their shame-identity with a Christ-centered identity, actively seeking God's strength in their healing
- ask for forgiveness and/or make restitution where necessary
- let go of controlling behaviors and stop assuming personal responsibility for things that are not their fault
- forgive the perpetrator of the abuse
- seek therapy when necessary to work through future conflicts

The goal is to help the client be free from his or her past. The abuse itself is not what keeps people in bondage; what keeps us in bondage are the lies we have believed as a result of the abuse. That is why it is *truth* that sets us free, and the process is brought forward to completion when we forgive our abusers. We do not heal in order to forgive; we forgive in order to heal. How will we know when healing has taken place? Healing is a process that takes time, but when we see the fruit of the Spirit in a person's life — living in the light and in truth — we know he or she has found freedom. John writes, "Let us not love with words or tongue but with actions and in truth. This then is how we know that we belong to the truth, and how we set our hearts at rest in his presence" (1 John 3:18–19).

PARENTING

PATTI BROWN, M.S., R.N., C.S.

INDICATIONS FOR USE

When there are behavioral problems that may be resolved through purposeful parenting.

RESOURCES

Anderson, Neil, and Rich Miller. *Leading Teens to Freedom in Christ*. Eugene, Ore.: Harvest House, 1997.

Anderson, Neil, and Steve Russo. *The Seduction of Our Children*. Eugene, Ore.: Harvest House, 1991.

Anderson, Neil, and Peter and Sue Vander Hook. *Spiritual Protection for Your Children*. Eugene, Ore.: Harvest House, 1996.

Campbell, Ross. *How to Really Love Your Child*, rev. ed. Wheaton, Ill.: Scripture Press, 1992.

Scott, Buddy. *Relief for Hurting Parents*. Nashville: Tommy Nelson, 1989.

PRESENTATION TO CLIENT AND/OR THERAPIST

Parenting is fraught with both awesome highs and discouraging lows. You are to model God's love, grace, mercy, and call to obedience. Often this becomes especially trying when your child is in rebellion. This rebellion may stem from your child's disobedience, your ineffective discipline of the child, or a combination of the two. We often parent our children without thought or a plan, yet it is important to have both. To parent reactively and without a clear purpose or vision often results in the child receiving mixed messages; it may also result in a rebellious child who continues to gamble on whether or not a parent or any authority figure will ever follow through on consequences.

Parenting must be practiced intentionally and with authority. A family is not a democracy; it is a hierarchy. The parents, not the child, should be in control. Your words and your deeds must be carefully thought through. Consistently ask yourself the question, "What message am I conveying to my child?" While not every moment of every day is an exercise in self-analysis, there are moments where you can and should be able to identify the message you are relaying to your children. By saying, "I mean it this time.... You need to get off that counter ... right now! Get off! ... I'm getting angry.... Get off! This is your last warning.... I mean it this time ...," you are conveying that you don't back up your words with immediate, clear, and consistent consequences. Hence, your child will very likely continue to "roll the dice" when in a confrontation with you. The issue will not be over until he or she decides that it is over — with the result that you are no longer in control of the situation.

One way to provide clear and consistent discipline is to know your and your partner's values and philosophy on parenting. It is of supreme importance for you and your spouse to be intentional about the values and behaviors you want to instill in your children. It would be helpful for each of you to write out those values and approaches and to compare them. At the same time discuss the moral reason why some behaviors are right and some are wrong. The moral reason should be shared with your child at times of correction because it helps to give them an internal moral compass. Include in this plan and discussion with your spouse issues related to the child's role in household responsibilities — and the consequences for failing to perform those duties. What about punctuality for activities and for getting to school? How much responsibility falls on the child, and how much on the parent? Those areas that cause you the most difficulties are the ones to work on and to come to a consensus on with your spouse. Children learn quickly to divide and conquer in an atmosphere where there is not consistency among the parents.

FAMILY MEETING

A helpful habit that can build unity and facilitate useful feedback is a family meeting. Family meetings provide an opportunity to make your expectations clear, to show your appreciation for improvements in character, and to point out good deeds. Initially the meetings should be weekly and have a distinct agenda — and attendance is mandatory. All members can contribute to the agenda, and, as appropriate, leadership of the meeting may shift. Minutes should be kept and reviewed. Look for ways to apply a lighthearted tone to the meetings. You may want to take turns stating one thing someone did that you particularly appreciated. The secretary would record these on scraps of paper, and at the end of the meeting you would conduct a drawing of the good deeds. The person selected could receive a special treat (a favorite meal or a choice of family activity, for example).

YELLING AND AVOIDANCE

During times of high stress, it's tempting either to yell at your children or to try to avoid the conflict altogether. Yelling displays to children a lack of control and conveys to them that they can control you. Often we yell because we feel pushed and yelled at by others. When you are at the yelling point, it's helpful to take time away — not to run to the nearest room, but to explain to your child that you feel yourself losing control and you need to take some time apart to regain your composure. Once your thoughts and your voice are under control, go back to your child and discuss the situation and administer consequences as appropriate.

Avoiding the conflict often consists of ignoring unacceptable behavior — which may allow for temporary peace in the house but can undermine consistent discipline. If you catch yourself ignoring a behavior, especially a behavior that you and your spouse have identified as important, go to your child and admit that you were aware of the offensive behavior and that you were wrong not to correct it. This reinforces that you *were* aware of your child's behavior and puts him or her on alert that you will not let the lapse happen again. Moreover, it will serve as a model of confession and repentance.

You do not simply want to punish or condemn your child, but you want to restore your child to right behavior. You also want to be able to discern those behaviors that are the result of immaturity and those that are the result of rebelliousness; each of these behaviors would be disciplined differently. For those actions that are a result of a child's immaturity, a discussion of why that behavior is wrong or inappropriate may be sufficient. For those behaviors that are the outcome of rebellion or defiance, the disciplinary approach may consist of a time-out, an allowing for natural and logical consequences, or a spanking.

NATURAL AND LOGICAL CONSEQUENCES

Let's look for a moment at natural and logical consequences. The age of the child and the context of the situation are important factors in determining the consequence. Was this a rare occurrence, or one that is becoming a common pattern? If an elementary-age child is having problems being kind to peers, then the natural consequence would be suspending the privilege of going over to a friend's house or having a friend come over to your house. Let your child know that in choosing to behave poorly toward friends, he or she has lost the privilege of playing with friends until he or she can demonstrate kinder behavior. This consequence can be for whatever time period seems appropriate to you and your spouse.

Be sure to relay to the child that the choice to behave in a wrongful way brings appropriate consequences. What's more, in setting these consequences, you must be prepared to fulfill them. Take, for example, the consequence of restricting your child to the home for a week. Can *you* stand firm and "endure" the sentence? Can your child? If you think your child cannot fulfill the consequence without creating additional problems, such as incessant whining or complaining, then state in advance what the additional penalty will be for those behaviors.

Parenting is an awesome responsibility filled with heartache and happiness. You are not your child's parent by accident. You were chosen by almighty God to parent this child, and you can do it successfully. It's helpful to have a vision of just what it is you want to convey to your child as important. What will your child say about you as a parent ten or twenty years from now? That you were firm but fair, and that the love of God and his Word were evident in your parenting? Or will your child say that you were inconsistent and didn't seem to possess a clear moral compass? Parenting that is purposeful gives your children a richness and security that they will be able to transfer to many areas of life.

THEOPHOSTICS

JULIANNE S. ZUEHLKE, M.S., R.N., C.S.

INDICATIONS FOR USE

When clients demonstrate the prevalence of lies from childhood wounds that are embedded in their memories. This form of therapy is effective when emotions in a current situation far exceed the appropriate level of feelings that should exist due to the current stimuli. It can be used with all mental health conditions that are not primarily organic in nature. It has been found to be especially effective in the integration of clients who have a diagnosis of Dissociative Identity Disorder. Many counselors use TheoPhostics in conjunction with the "Steps to Freedom in Christ" to take aim at major mental strongholds.

RESOURCES

Smith, Ed. *Beyond Tolerable Recovery.* 2d ed. Campbellsville, Ky.: Family Care Ministries, 1997.

PRESENTATION TO CLIENT AND/OR THERAPIST

You are here seeking therapy because you have strong, negative emotions that are creating pain in your life. You want to have victory over these emotions and be able to live in peace and victory. Emotions do not occur in a vacuum but rather have their origin in our current and past experiences. Emotions are the result of thoughts, beliefs, and understandings about events in our lives. Thoughts create emotions, which in turn trigger behaviors. This works just fine when the thoughts are creating light and happy emotions and healthy behaviors. However, when the thoughts are based on lies that were believed during traumatic events, the feelings are heavy and the behavior maladaptive.

These wounds from the past are encoded in the brain through visual, emotional, and physical/sensory memories. If your father was verbally abusive and called you stupid when you brought home a low grade on an assignment, you may have believed him to be truthful and accurate in his estimation of your intelligence. As a child, your abstract reasoning was not developed enough to refute such an authority figure's opinion of you. This lie or false assessment is like a computer chip deeply embedded in your mind. Old tapes recorded in early childhood are played again and again in our minds and can truly hinder our progress in understanding who we now are in Christ. Dr. Ed Smith states, "If we have lies stored in our experiential knowledge we will have little choice but to act out accordingly or else live a life of constant struggle and self-effort.... Mental darkness cripples the spirit; since we can only act as far as we can think, our spirit person (our real self) cannot live out its righteousness until the mind is free from unrighteous lies."[5] Only to the extent that we are free of lies can we live out a victorious Christian life.

Dr. Smith believes that deeply embedded lies generally cause a person to feel fearful, abandoned, shamed, tainted, powerless, hopeless, invalidated, and confused. These emotional responses can be triggered in the present, but they are *rooted* in the past. He refers to these as "echo emotions" from previous trauma. Realizing that the source of many strong emotions may lie in the past rather than in the present changes the way we resolve conflicts. Smith encourages us to look for the *historical memory event* that feels the same way or matches the emotions we are currently feeling. In this search for core beliefs and embedded emotional pain, it is important that you (the client) be led by the Holy Spirit. The Holy Spirit will guide you into all truth—and that truth will set you free.

COMMENTS TO THE THERAPIST

We find this approach to be a combination of David Seamands's "healing of damaged emotions" and Richard Foster's "authoritative prayer." Describing it in this way makes it initially understandable for the client. The following is a description of the steps Julie and Terry use in a session (only experienced and trained counselors can use these steps).[6] Be sure the client is comfortable; you'll want a tissue box nearby for the client to use during the session. Instruct the client to keep his or her eyes closed in prayer during the session, which will allow the client to block out awareness of the room or the therapist and focus solely on the Lord Jesus.

- Ask the client where he or she wants to start the session, that is, either by going to a specific memory or focusing on an important feeling, either recent or distant past, where emotional pain is known to exist, or by allowing Jesus to take the client wherever he chooses to take him or her. Once the starting place is determined, proceed to the next step.

- Open in prayer (only the therapist praying). Worship the Lord Jesus for who he is, thank him for the time you will have with him as he enters the client's memories to bring about healing, and ask for his wisdom in every part of the session. Exercise the authority you have in Christ by binding Satan and all of his evil workers to silence. End your prayer in Jesus' name. We have found that paraphrasing the opening prayer and statement of declaration from the "Steps to Freedom in Christ" can be helpful (see Appendix E).[7]

- Ask Jesus to take the person to a memory he wants the client to work on today or to the specific memory selected, for example, "Lord Jesus, take Sue to a memory you want to deal with today. You are in complete control, and we welcome you." Then instruct the client, "Let yourself go where Jesus takes you. Don't try to select a memory yourself. Just be aware of the first picture or body sensation or sensory experience you have, then briefly let me know so I can be aware of what is happening." Be careful not to encourage clients to adopt a passive state of mind, which could set them up for deception. Be reminded that these are real memories the client is dealing with, and that God will not bypass the client's mind — and remember too that the Holy Spirit will lead the client into all truth.

- Within five to ten seconds the client will usually report a specific memory. The memory will be in the present tense, since experientially the client is in the memory. It will go something like this (actual example from a client of Julie's): "I'm very young, and my daddy is coming in the door from being gone to the war. He picks me up and hugs me, and I am so happy to see him. He loves me. But he is putting me down! He is turning to Mommy, and he is hugging her. He put me down!"

- The therapist knows there is trauma in this memory because the client is showing strong negative emotions. She is weeping because her daddy put her down. The pain in the memory comes from the lie that she believes. At this point the therapist assists the client to determine the emotions (pain) and the lie causing the pain. The therapist says, "How did that make you feel when your daddy put you down?" The client may share several thoughts and feelings, such as, "I felt so alone, so surprised, so unhappy, so left out." The therapist then asks, "Which of these experiences feels the strongest — 'I'm alone; surprised; unhappy; left out'?" The therapist may refer to the Eight Categories of Lies[8] to help the client identify the lie that matches the feelings being experienced.

- Julie's client knew without a doubt that the feeling "I'm left out; I don't count" (invalidation) was her strongest emotion. Julie asked her to "scale" the intensity of the pain, whether it felt like a zero or a ten or somewhere in between — zero being not painful and ten being intensely painful. She indicated it was a strong ten.

- At this point, direct the client to get in touch with the painful emotions as intensely as possible by experiencing the memory, seeing the scene play out, and repeating the false belief in his or her mind. Because our feelings result from what we believe, the emotions typically intensify during this part of the prayer time.

- After allowing several moments of strong emotional awareness on the part of the client, ask the Lord Jesus to come into the memory and touch (minister to) this memory in any way he desires. The therapist may say, "Lord Jesus, come into this memory. What would you want this little one to know?" Experientially, the client is the young child, and the pain of invalidation is being lived once again.

- The Lord shows up in a variety of ways. He may appear visually in the client's mind. He may impress a truth in the person's mind through thoughts, or he may give a sensory experience of warmth or light. In this particular client's situation, Jesus gave her a picture of him picking her up in his arms, hugging and comforting her. When he did that, she was raised to the height of her parents, enjoying the experience of all being together again. Jesus told her, "You count. Your daddy loves you and your mommy, and he is telling your mommy, just like he told you, that he loves her too." When Jesus gave her this visual picture and this specific truth of her daddy's love, her face broke out in a broad smile, her tears ended, and she was praising the Lord for the father who loved her. She had experienced the healing touch of the Lord Jesus Christ, who deployed his truth against the deceptions in her memory. (Bear in mind that on some occasions Jesus does not "show up." A likely reason for this is "clutter" — that is, barriers to Jesus' grace, which can include client carnality or demonic interference. Carnality can be unconfessed sin, unrenounced vows, reliance on intellectual reasoning, fear of exposure, or a desire to look good in the presence of the therapist. When these barriers appear, the therapist and client must discuss them and work toward resolution.)

- Julie then asked her client to go back in her memory of when her daddy had put her back down on the ground. She asked the client to "look" into any other parts of that memory where there could be pain, and the client indicated that the memory was calm and peaceful. Julie then asked her how true it was that she did not count. She stated without hesitation that it was a zero—absolutely not true.
- The therapist then praises the Lord for his grace and mercy in shedding light on the painful episode in the client's life. The Lord is asked to strengthen the client in the days ahead and to protect the client until we again meet to seek his healing touch.
- The client is then asked to open his or her eyes and process with the therapist the prayer time they have just had. Processing is important in order to confirm what has happened. Julie's client had not remembered until the therapy session this scene that had happened over fifty years ago. As she looked over her life, she confirmed she had gone through her life feeling inferior to others—as someone who did not matter. We discussed how that lie had permeated all of her relationships and that she could now experience release from its grip.

The therapist should be prepared for spiritual warfare interventions if the demonic or a counterfeit Christ enters the memory. Julie once worked with a client who had "Jesus" show up on the sidelines of a sports event in which the client was being ridiculed by the other kids. In the client's memory this counterfeit Jesus turned his back on the client and looked over his shoulder with an angry look. By the power of the Lord Jesus, Julie commanded the false Christ to leave the memory—and immediately the real Jesus appeared with the compassion we know he possesses, and he brought healing to that memory. Similar negative impressions occur when guardian or demonic spirits stand in the way of the memory or feelings, cast a darkness over the memory, or manifest themselves as confusing voices in the mind. Each time this happens the authority of Jesus Christ is proclaimed, and the already-defeated interfering spirit leaves.

The process is repeated often throughout the course of therapy. As the Lord reveals painful feelings and memories, we use the TheoPhostic process to remove the darkness of the particular lie and replace it with the light of God's truth. This "laser" approach is woven in with the more general areas covered in the "umbrella" approach of Neil Anderson's seven "Steps to Freedom in Christ."

For example, using the methodology described above, Terry worked with a client who possessed a low sense of worth and significant perfectionistic tendencies. During a TheoPhostic procedure the Lord revealed a stronghold of bitterness toward her parents because they had moved frequently when she was little. As these issues surfaced, the client did the necessary work on forgiveness by completing Step 3 (Bitterness Versus Forgiveness).

When we receive Jesus Christ into our lives, we receive eternal life — past, present, and future. The omnipresent life of Christ within us was present at every event in our past. A theological basis for TheoPhostic counseling is given in John 16:13 – 15: "But when he, the Spirit of truth, comes, he will guide you into all truth. He will not speak on his own; he will speak only what he hears, and he will tell you what is yet to come. He will bring glory to me by taking from what is mine and making it known to you. All that belongs to the Father is mine. That is why I said the Spirit will take from what is mine and make it known to you." As Dr. Smith observes, "When you heal the past, you redeem the present."[9]

ANXIETY DISORDERS

NEIL T. ANDERSON, M.A.C.E., M.DIV., ED.D., D.MIN.

INDICATIONS FOR USE

When the client exhibits panic attacks, excessive worry, and debilitating fear. These anxiety disorders are keeping the client from living a responsible life.

RESOURCES

Anderson, Neil T. *Freedom from Fear*. Eugene, Ore.: Harvest House, 1999.

Bourne, Edmund J. *Healing Fear*. Oakland, Calif.: New Harbinger, 1998.

Jeffers, Susan. *Feel the Fear and Do It Anyway*. New York: Fawcett Columbine, 1987.

Wilson, R. Reid. *Don't Panic*. New York: HarperCollins, 1996.

PRESENTATION TO CLIENT AND/OR THERAPIST

Have you ever been so anxious about the uncertainties of tomorrow that you felt keyed up, fatigued, and irritable? You may have found it difficult to sleep, and you just couldn't relax because your mind was racing and your muscles were tense. Have you ever been paralyzed by fear to the extent that you couldn't carry out your heart's desire? You knew what was right, and you wanted to do the right thing, but some unknown fear kept you from doing it. Have you ever had a sudden episode of acute apprehension or intense fear that appeared out of the blue? You had a shortness of breath and felt like you were being smothered. Your heart pounded, causing you to sweat profusely. You began to tremble with feelings of unreality, as though you were going crazy. You may have felt chest pains and numbness or tingling in your hands and feet.

These are the symptoms of anxiety, fear, and panic attacks, which cripple a large percentage of our population. Perhaps you can relate to one or more of the symptoms I just described. Are such mental, physical, and emotional reactions to life always wrong? Shouldn't we be concerned about things we care about? Isn't it appropriate to fear those things that threaten our lives? A life totally devoid of fear and anxiety would be boring at best and debilitating to our own productivity and self-preservation at worst.

When does legitimate concern become stifling anxiety, and when does a rational fear become an incapacitating phobia? Is there a scriptural answer to these blights of the soul? What is the difference between anxiety, fear, and panic attacks? In order to live a healthy productive life, every child of God needs adequate answers to these critical questions. Let's start by defining the terms.

WHAT IS FEAR?

Fear is the natural response when our physical safety and psychological well-being are threatened. Rational fears are learned, and they are vital for our survival. Falling off a chair at an early age helps us develop a healthy respect for heights. *Phobias*, however, are irrational fears that compel us to do irresponsible things or inhibit us from doing that which is responsible. Fear differs from anxiety and from panic attacks, because legitimate fears have an object. In fact, fears or phobias are categorized by their object as follows:

- acrophobia ....fear of high places
- agoraphobia ....fear of marketplaces
- claustrophobia ....fear of enclosed places
- gephydophobia ....fear of crossing bridges
- hematophobia...................fear of blood
- monophobia ....fear of being alone
- pathophobia ....fear of disease
- pyrophobia.......................fear of fire
- toxophobia ....fear of being poisoned
- xenophobia.......................fear of strangers
- zoophobia.........................fear of animals

The list goes on and on. In order for a fear object to be legitimate, it must possess two attributes: It must be perceived as both *imminent* (present) and *potent* (powerful). For instance, most of us have been taught to believe that poisonous snakes are legitimate fear objects. But right now, I sense no fear of snakes because there are none present (potent but not imminent). Now what if someone threw a rattlesnake into the room and it landed at our feet (both imminent and potent)? We would probably be terrorized. Finally, suppose a dead snake is thrown at our feet (imminent but not potent). We wouldn't feel any fear, provided we were sure it was dead! The fear object is no longer legitimate when just one of its attributes is removed.

The core of most phobias can be traced to the fear of death, humans, or Satan. The reality of physical death is always imminent, but the *power* of death has been broken. The apostle Paul teaches that Christ's resurrection has rendered physical death impotent: "'Death has been swallowed up in victory.' 'Where, O death, is your victory? Where, O death is your sting?'" (1 Corinthians 15:54–55). Paul also observed, "For to me, to live is Christ and to die is gain" (Philippians 1:21). The person who is free from the fear of death is free to live today.

Many of our phobias are rooted in the fear of other humans, such as the fears of rejection, failure, abandonment, and even death. But Jesus taught, "Do not be afraid of those who kill the body but cannot kill the soul. Rather, be afraid of the One who can destroy both soul and body in hell" (Matthew 10:28). Peter added, "Do not fear their intimidation, and do not be troubled, but sanctify Christ as Lord in your hearts, always being ready to make a defense to everyone who asks you to give an account for the hope that is in you, yet with gentleness and reverence" (1 Peter 3:14–15 New American Standard Bible). The purpose for these verses is obvious if you have ever taught evangelism. The number one reason Christians don't share their faith is the fear of others — more specifically the fear of rejection and failure.

Both of these Scripture passages teach that it is *God* whom we should fear. Two of God's attributes make him the ultimate fear object in our life: He is both *omnipresent* (always present) and *omnipotent* (all powerful). To worship God is to acknowledge and ascribe to him his divine attributes. We do this for our own sakes; to do so keeps fresh in our minds the truth that our loving heavenly Father is always with us and is more powerful than any enemy. The fear of God is the one fear that can dispel all other fears, because God rules supreme over every other fear object, including Satan. Even though "your enemy the devil prowls around like a roaring lion looking for someone to devour" (1 Peter 5:8), he has been defeated (imminent but not potent). Jesus came to earth for the very purpose of destroying the works of the devil (1 John 3:8). In fact, "having disarmed the powers and authorities, he made a public spectacle of them, triumphing over them by the cross" (Colossians 2:15). Notice the ancient wisdom recorded by the prophet Isaiah:

> Do not call conspiracy everything that these people call conspiracy; do not fear what they fear, and do not dread it. The LORD Almighty is the one you are to regard as holy, he is the one you are to fear, he is the one you are to dread, and he will be a sanctuary.
>
> —ISAIAH 8:12–13

Fear of any object other than God is mutually exclusive to faith in God. Irrational fears either compel us to do that which is irresponsible or prevent us from doing that which is responsible. I'd like to take you through the following Phobia Finder to see if we can bring some resolution to this problem of debilitating fear.

PHOBIA FINDER

A. ANALYZE YOUR FEAR UNDER GOD'S AUTHORITY AND GUIDANCE
   1. Identify all fear objects (that is, what are you afraid of?)
   2. Determine when you first experienced the fear
   3. Identify the events that preceded the first experience
   4. Determine the lies behind every phobia

B. ANALYZE HOW YOU HAVE BEEN LIVING UNDER THE CONTROL OF FEAR RATHER THAN BY FAITH IN GOD
   1. How has fear
      a. prevented you from doing what is right and responsible?
      b. compelled you to do what is wrong and irresponsible?
      c. prompted you to compromise your witness for Christ?
   2. Confess any active or passive way in which you have allowed fear to control your life
   3. Commit to God that you will live a righteous and responsible life

C. PRAYERFULLY WORK OUT A PLAN OF RESPONSIBLE BEHAVIOR

D. DETERMINE IN ADVANCE WHAT YOUR RESPONSE WILL BE TO ANY FEAR OBJECT

E. COMMIT YOURSELF TO CARRY OUT THE PLAN OF ACTION IN THE POWER OF THE HOLY SPIRIT

WHAT IS ANXIETY?

Anxiety is different from fear in that it lacks an object or adequate cause. People are anxious because they are uncertain about a specific outcome or don't know what is going to happen tomorrow. It is normal to be concerned about things we value; to not do so would demonstrate a lack of care.

It's important to distinguish between a temporary state of anxiety and an anxiety trait that persists over time. A *temporary state of anxiety* exists when concern is shown before a specific event. One can be anxious about an examination yet to be taken, attendance at a planned function, or the threat of an incoming storm. Such concern is normal and should ordinarily move one to responsible action. A *generalized anxiety disorder* exists when an individual exhibits an anxiety trait over a long period of time; to be diagnosed as such, the obsessive worrying must occur more days than not for at least a six-month period. Those who struggle with a generalized anxiety disorder experience persistent anxiety and worry, and they fret over two or more stressful life circumstances, such as finances, relationships, health, or ability to perform. Usually they struggle with a large number of worries and spend a lot of time and energy doing so. The intensity and frequency of the worrying are always out of proportion to the actual problem. In fact, the worrying is usually more detrimental than the negative consequences they were initially concerned about. The vast majority of our fears and anxieties are never realized.

In the Bible, the Greek word for *anxiety* comes from two root words, meaning "divide" and "mind." An anxious person is double-minded. James says that "a double-minded man [is] unstable in all he does" (James 1:8). Jesus said, "No one can serve two masters. Either he will hate the one and love the other, or he will be devoted to the one and despise the other. You cannot serve both God and Money. Therefore, I tell you, do not worry [be anxious] about your life" (Matthew 6:24–25).

Peter urges us to cast all our anxieties on Christ because he cares for us (1 Peter 5:7). In light of these truths, I want to guide you through the Anxiety Worksheet (see page 273):

- We need to begin with prayer. Prayer is the first step in casting all our anxiety on Christ. As Paul reminded us, "Do not be anxious about anything, but in everything, by prayer and petition, with thanksgiving, present your requests to God" (Philippians 4:6). The first thing a Christian should do about anything is pray; turning to God in prayer demonstrates our reliance on him.

- The second step is to resolve any personal and spiritual conflicts you may have. We need to humble ourselves before God and resist the devil—in other words, make sure our hearts are right with God. James says, "Submit yourselves, then, to God. Resist the devil, and he will flee from you" (James 4:7). You must seek to get radically right with God and eliminate any possible influences of the devil on your mind. Remember, "The Spirit clearly says that in later times some will abandon the faith and follow deceiving spirits and things taught by demons" (1 Timothy 4:1). You will be a double-minded person if you pay attention to a deceiving spirit. The "Steps to Freedom in Christ" will help you submit to God and resist the devil. Moreover, "the peace of God, which transcends all understanding, will guard your hearts and your minds in Christ Jesus" (Philippians 4:7).

- The third step is to attempt to state the problem. A problem well stated is a problem half-solved. In anxious states of mind, people typically can't see the forest for the trees. Put the problem in perspective: Will this thing about which I'm anxious matter for eternity? Generally speaking, the process of worrying takes a greater toll on a person than the negative consequences of what is being worried about. Many anxious people find tremendous relief by simply having their problems clarified and put into perspective.

- The fourth step is to separate the facts from the assumptions. People may be fearful of the facts, but *not* anxious. We become anxious when we don't know what is going to happen tomorrow. Since we don't know, we make assumptions. A peculiar trait of the mind is its tendency to assume the worst. If the assumption is accepted as truth, it will begin to drive the mind toward its anxiety limits. If you are presumptuous about tomorrow, you will undoubtedly suffer some negative consequences. Therefore, as best as possible, verify all your assumptions.

- The fifth step is to determine what you have the right or the ability to control. You are only responsible for that which you have the right and the ability to control. Your sense of worth is tied only to that for which you are responsible. If you aren't living a responsible life, you *should* feel anxious! Don't try to cast *your* responsibility on Christ; he will throw it back. But do cast your anxiety on him, because his integrity is at stake in meeting your needs if you are living a responsible and righteous life.

- The sixth step is to list everything related to the situation that is your responsibility. When people don't assume their responsibilities, they turn to temporary cures for their anxiety. The Bible teaches us that "the fruit of righteousness will be peace" (Isaiah 32:17). Turning to an unrighteous solution will only increase the anxiety in the future. So you need to commit yourself to be a responsible person and fulfill your calling and obligations in life.
- The seventh step is to declare that once you are sure you have fulfilled your responsibility, the rest is God's responsibility, except for your commitment to pray and focus on the truth, in accordance with Philippians 4:6–8. Any residual anxiety may well be due to your assuming responsibilities that God never intended you to have.

ANXIETY WORKSHEET

A. GO TO GOD IN PRAYER

B. RESOLVE ALL KNOWN PERSONAL AND SPIRITUAL CONFLICTS

C. STATE THE PROBLEM

D. SEPARATE THE FACTS FROM THE ASSUMPTIONS
   1. Facts relating to the situation
   2. Assumptions relating to the situation
   3. Verify the above assumptions

E. DETERMINE WHAT YOU HAVE THE RIGHT OR ABILITY TO CONTROL
   1. What you can control as a matter of personal responsibility
   2. What you have no right or ability to control

F. LIST EVERYTHING RELATED TO THE SITUATION THAT IS YOUR RESPONSIBILITY

G. THE REST IS GOD'S RESPONSIBILITY, EXCEPT FOR YOUR CONTINUING WALK WITH GOD IN PRAYER, IN ACCORDANCE WITH PHILIPPIANS 4:6–8

WHAT ARE PANIC ATTACKS?

People can experience *panic attacks* when they become physically and emotionally aware of the symptoms of hypothyroidism, hypoglycemia, heart palpitations, or other physical abnormalities. Many who struggle with the heart condition known as mitral valve prolapse have panic attacks. They suddenly experience a heart flutter that can cause them to panic. Although it may feel like it, the problem is typically not life threatening. Once these individuals are properly diagnosed, they usually return to a normal life, often without the need for medication.

Panic attacks occur spontaneously and unexpectedly without any apparent reason. They may or may not occur with any existing phobias. Agoraphobia (the fear of marketplaces, or open places) is often the result of panic attacks, because a person fears that an attack may happen in a public setting. Somewhere between one and two percent of the American population suffer from panic attacks, but five percent suffer from panic attacks complicated by agoraphobia. Of that category, eighty percent are women.

Such episodes are labeled "attacks" because the panic is not preceded by any abnormal thinking or any warning of approaching danger. Could some part of a panic attack be a spiritual attack? Have you ever been suddenly awakened in a paralyzing grip of fear — feeling a pressure on your chest or experiencing the sensation of choking or being choked. When you tried to respond physically, you couldn't seem to move or even to speak. You may have experienced a spiritual attack. You can stop that attack by first submitting to God inwardly, because he knows the thoughts and intentions of your heart. Then you will be able to resist the devil verbally, and he will flee from you.

DEPRESSION

Neil T. Anderson, M.A.C.E., M.Div., Ed.D., D.Min.

INDICATIONS FOR USE

When the client presents physical and emotional symptoms of depression. Depression is so prevalent that it has been called the "common cold" of mental illness. It is a body, soul, and spirit problem that requires a wholistic solution.

RESOURCES

Anderson, Neil T. *Finding Hope Again*. Ventura, Calif.: Regal, 1999.
Hart, Archibald. *Counseling the Depressed*. Waco, Tex.: Word, 1987.
Papolos, Demitri, and Janice Papolos. *Overcoming Depression*.
New York: HarperPerennial, 1992.

PRESENTATION TO CLIENT AND/OR THERAPIST

Depression is both an agony of the body and of the soul. There can be a biochemical or a biological basis for depression, and we surely want to explore that possibility. The more common psychological bases for depression are related to our mental stability and to losses in our lives. Many people are depressed because they have a learned sense of helplessness or hopelessness. Entire cultures can exhibit depressive symptoms because of oppressive circumstances. In this kind of situation, people are depressed because they have a negative view of themselves, their immediate circumstances, and the future. *Reactionary depression* to losses is the most common form of depression. Those losses can be real, threatened, or imaginary. There is a well-documented response pattern to losses: first denial, then anger, bargaining, depression, and finally resignation or recovery. Let's begin by having you take a simple test to determine the extent of your depression.

Depression Diagnosis

1. Low energy	1	2	3	4	5	High energy
2. Difficulty sleeping, or sleeping all the time	1	2	3	4	5	Uninterrupted sleeping patterns

3. No desire to be involved in activities	1	2	3	4	5	Very involved in activities
4. No desire for sex	1	2	3	4	5	Healthy sex drive
5. Aches and pains	1	2	3	4	5	Feel great
6. Loss of appetite	1	2	3	4	5	Enjoy eating
7. Sad (tearfulness)	1	2	3	4	5	Joyful
8. Despairing and hopeless	1	2	3	4	5	Hopeful and confident
9. Irritable (low frustration tolerance)	1	2	3	4	5	Pleasant (high frustration tolerance)
10. Withdrawn	1	2	3	4	5	Involved
11. Mental anguish	1	2	3	4	5	Peace of mind
12. Low sense of worth	1	2	3	4	5	High sense of worth
13. Pessimistic about the future	1	2	3	4	5	Optimistic about the future
14. Perceive most circumstances as negative and as harmful to self	1	2	3	4	5	Perceive most circumstances as positive and as opportunities for growth
15. Self-destructive (I and others would be better off if I weren't here)	1	2	3	4	5	Self-preserving (glad I'm here)

If you predominantly circled 3s, 4s, and 5s in this survey, you are not struggling with depression. Individual temperament and personality can affect some of the individual items on the test. For a *rough* determination of your level of depression, add up all the circled answers and compare them to the following key:

45–75   Likely not depressed

35–44   Mildly depressed

| 25 – 34 | Depressed |
| 15 – 24 | Severely depressed |

Overcoming depression requires a commitment, and I'm committed to working with you until we see this mood pass. I'll ask you to work through the following commitments with my help — a process that may take several weeks, or maybe even months.

COMMIT YOURSELF TO COMPLETE RECOVERY

Over fifty percent of those who struggle with depression never ask for help or seek treatment. If you have the desire to get well and if you are willing to assume your responsibility for your own attitudes and actions, then I believe there is hope for you. There are adequate answers for depression, but you have to want it more than anything else in the world and be willing to do whatever it takes to be free. The key to any cure is *commitment.*

COMMIT YOURSELF TO PRAY FIRST ABOUT EVERYTHING

I'm not asking you to get tough and try harder. That kind of advice and attitude could itself lead to more burnout and depression. Human effort alone cannot be an adequate solution. I am encouraging you to trust God by submitting yourself to him and his ways and by seeking a wholistic answer. Jesus tells us, "But seek first his kingdom and his righteousness, and all these things will be given to you as well" (Matthew 6:33). The first thing a Christian should do about anything is pray.

COMMIT YOURSELF TO AN INTIMATE RELATIONSHIP WITH GOD

The "Steps to Freedom in Christ" are intended to help you resolve, through repentance and faith, any conflicts that may exist between you and your heavenly Father. Essentially, the process helps you submit to God and resist the devil (see James 4:7) — eliminating the influence of the devil in your life and connecting you with God in a personal and powerful way. You will then be able to experience the peace of God that guards your heart and mind (see Philippians 4:7), and you will sense the Holy Spirit testifying with your spirit that you are a child of God (see Romans 8:16). Then, by the grace of God you will be able to process the remaining issues.

COMMIT YOURSELF AS A CHILD OF GOD

God loves you because God is love and you are his child. It is his nature to love you; he couldn't do anything other than that. . God is omnipotent; therefore, you can do all things through Christ who gives you strength (see Philippians 4:13). God is omniscient; therefore, he knows the thoughts and intentions of your heart (see Hebrews 4:12 – 13). He knows what you need, and he is able to meet that need. God is omnipresent; therefore, you are never alone, and he will never leave you or forsake you. You have become a partaker of his divine nature (see 2 Peter 1:4) because your soul is in union with God. That is what it means to be spiritually alive in Christ. He has defeated the devil, forgiven your sins, given you eternal life, and you are now his child, if you have received him into your life.

COMMIT YOUR BODY TO GOD

Depression is a multifaceted problem that affects the body, soul, and spirit. Consequently, a comprehensive cure for depression will require a wholistic solution. If your depression is truly endogenous (neurological), then you should seek out a medical doctor or psychiatrist who can administer the appropriate medication.

Some forms of biological depression can be diagnosed and treated relatively easily. A disorder of the endocrine system can produce depressive symptoms. The endocrine system includes the thyroid, parathyroid, thymus, pancreas, and adrenal glands. They produce hormones, which are released directly into the blood system. The thyroid gland controls metabolism. An underactive thyroid (hypothyroidism) will cause changes in mood, including the onset of depression. The right treatment in this case is to prescribe a thyroid hormone, *not* antidepressants. The metabolism of sugar is especially important for maintaining physical and emotional stability. Hypoglycemia (low blood sugar) is known to produce emotional instability. The pituitary gland in the brain produces adrenocorticotropic hormone (ACTH), which stimulates the adrenal glands. The malfunctioning of either gland will produce lethargic behavior and depression. The fact that women suffer from depression more than men do may be due to their biological nature. The hormones (estrogen and progesterone) associated with female reproductive organs appear to contribute significantly to mood swings in women.

COMMIT YOURSELF TO THE RENEWING OF YOUR MIND

Our minds can quickly become programmed to think negatively about ourselves, our circumstances, and the future. These negative thoughts and lies can be deeply ingrained. Thousands and thousands of mental rehearsals have added to the feelings you are experiencing right now. The natural tendency is to go over these negative thoughts repeatedly. The answer is to *know* and *choose* the truth.

COMMIT YOURSELF TO GOOD BEHAVIOR

It takes time to renew our minds, but it doesn't take time to change our behavior, which, when we do change it, actually facilitates the process of renewing our minds as well as positively affects how we feel. When Cain and Abel brought their offerings to the Lord, the Lord was not pleased with Cain's: "So Cain was very angry, and his face was downcast. Then the LORD said to Cain, 'Why are you angry? Why is your face downcast? If you do what is right, will you not be accepted? But if you do not do what is right, sin is crouching at your door; it desires to have you, but you must master it'" (Genesis 4:5–7). In other words, you don't feel your way into good behavior; you behave your way into a good feeling. If you wait until you *feel* like doing what is right, you will likely never do it.

Schedule appointments and activities that pull you out of your negative mood. Force yourself to work, even though you may not feel like getting out of bed. Plan an activity and stick to it. Get plenty of exercise and commit yourself to follow through. Start with a low-impact aerobic program or take walks with friends and family members. Continue routine duties even when you feel as though you don't have the energy to carry on. These behavioral interventions or activities are only a start, but a very important one, in developing a lifestyle that is healthy.

COMMIT YOURSELF TO MEANINGFUL RELATIONSHIPS

A major symptom of depression is withdrawal from meaningful relationships, which would be number two on the list of destructive behaviors. Isolating yourself to the point where you are alone with your negative thoughts will certainly contribute to the downward spiral. You may feel like you need to be alone, but in reality you need to stay in contact with the right people. A good church will have many meaningful activities, as well as provide small discipleship groups where you can get the prayer and care you need in order to keep going.

COMMIT YOURSELF TO OVERCOME EVERY LOSS

The losses in your life can be real, threatened, or imagined. Here are some steps to follow in evaluating your losses:

Identify and understand each loss. Many losses are easy to recognize, while some are not. Changing jobs or moving to a new location can precipitate a depression. Although both could result in an improved social status or lifestyle, the reality is that something important was lost in the move — the loss of an attachment to old friends, familiar places, or comfortable working conditions. Many losses are multifaceted. For instance, the loss of a job may also include the loss of wages, the loss of social status, the loss of respect, and so forth.

Separate concrete losses from abstract losses. Concrete losses can be seen, touched, measured, and clearly defined. Abstract losses refer to personal goals, dreams, and ideas. Overcoming a concrete loss is typically easier because it is more definable.

Separate real, imagined, and threatened losses. You cannot process an imagined or threatened loss in the same way you can a real one. In a real loss, you can face the truth, grieve the loss, and make the necessary changes that enable you to go on living in a meaningful way.

Convert imagined and threatened losses into real-loss terms. Imagined losses are distortions of reality and are generally based on suspicions or lies we have believed or presumptions we have made. Threatened losses have the potential for being real losses. They include such things as the possibility of a layoff at work or a spouse who threatens to leave you. These kinds of threats can precipitate a depression.

Facilitate the grieving process. You cannot bypass the grieving process, but you can shorten it by allowing yourself to feel the full force of the loss. The fact that certain losses are depressing is reality. It hurts to lose something that holds value for you. Remember that Jesus said, "Blessed are those who mourn, for they will be comforted" (Matthew 5:4).

Face the reality of the loss. Only after you have faced its full impact are you ready to deal with the reality of the loss. This is the critical juncture: Are you going to resign from life, surrender to the depression, and drop out — or are you going to accept what you cannot change and let go of the loss? We can feel sorry for ourselves for the rest of our lives, or we can decide to live with our losses and learn how to keep going in a positive and meaningful way.

Develop a biblical perspective on the loss. The trials and tribulations of life are intended to produce proven character (see Romans 5:3–5; James 1:2–4). Suffering can be for the sake of righteousness. We can potentially come through any crisis a better person than we were before. Losses are inevitable, and they don't destroy you — but they do reveal who you are.

Renew your mind to the truth of who you really are in Christ. This is the final step in evaluating your loss. Be sure to review the description of who you are in Christ (see pages 94–95 or pages 305–306 at the end of this chapter).

BOUNDARIES

JULIANNE S. ZUEHLKE, M.S., R.N., C.S.

INDICATIONS FOR USE

When clients demonstrate difficulty with assertiveness regarding their time, energy, property, and relationships and choose a passive or passive-aggressive response. These difficulties can cause them to feel used or manipulated, leading them to become resentful. These tools are also useful for clients who demonstrate classic codependency traits, which emphasize relentless overresponsibility for the problems and behaviors of significant others. Codependents assume responsibility for a primary dependent person while repressing their own needs (physical, emotional, social, or spiritual), and in the end they feel burned-out, stressed, and overwhelmed. Both the unassertive and the codependent categories of people are unclear about their preferences, live reactively, do more and more for less and less, feel hurt and victimized, act out of compliance and compromise, do favors they inwardly resent doing, and feel as though they are living a life that is not their own and that seems unalterable.

RESOURCES

Cloud, Henry, and John Townsend. *Boundaries: When to Say Yes, When to Say No.* Grand Rapids: Zondervan, 1992.

Koch, Ruth, and Kenneth Haugk. *Speaking the Truth in Love.* St. Louis: Stephen Ministries, 1992.

Moon, Sheryl Baar. *Boundaries Leader's Guide.* Grand Rapids: Zondervan, 1994.

PRESENTATION TO CLIENT AND/OR THERAPIST

Boundaries are the invisible but powerful demarcations between yourself and another person, an assignment, a task, or a responsibility; there are even dimensions of personal boundaries within yourself. We are familiar with boundaries in the realm of geography. For instance, a map in city hall records the exact dimensions of the lot on which my home is built. I have a sense of the boundary line by means of visual markers, such as the telephone pole at the back and the big bush at the front, with the invisible property line running between the two. I know I don't have the right to plant a tree three feet across the boundary into my neighbor's yard. That action would be violating my neighbor's boundaries, and he could rightfully protest. With regard to my yard, I can set up boundaries of different types to control access to it. If I want to severely restrict access to my property, I can put up a huge stone wall around the perimeter, along with a locked gate. Persons on the outside could not see inside, nor could they enter without having made prior arrangements. I can put up a picket fence with a swinging gate that has a latch to release it. This prevents casual entry, but a guest can make a decision to enter without prior permission, unlatch the gate, and come to the front door of the house. At that point, we can decide to answer the door and admit the guest or not. I can also put up a small wire edging to keep people from entering my flower gardens but leave the majority of the yard wide-open. People can wander into the yard by mistake or enter it by intent, since there is no barrier whatsoever. They could even smash my tulips if they weren't being careful or if they were being vengeful. There would be minimal barriers present to protect my yard, warn intruders against entering, or control their access.

In a similar way, we can erect personal boundaries. Some people develop rigid and exacting boundaries with their time and their person. All access to them has to be scheduled and is tightly controlled; they do not self-disclose (let others see into their yard). Others allow easier access to themselves personally, but those who approach them realize there is a structure that needs to be addressed before access is granted. The guest needs to stop, take stock, and then negotiate the boundary. Finally, others set up no delineation between themselves and others, allowing free access at all times, with the risk that there may be some damage rendered by those who are thoughtless, careless, or malicious.

The Lord teaches us about boundaries in his Word. After the Flood, the waters "went down into the valleys, to the place you assigned for them. You set a boundary they cannot cross; never again will they cover the earth" (Psalm 104:8–9). In this passage God is promising to protect us by erecting an impenetrable barrier. Jesus had boundaries, but they were more of the picket-fence variety. He allowed structured access and was careful to reserve time for himself: "Very early in the morning, while it was still dark, Jesus got up, left the house and went off to a solitary place, where he prayed" (Mark 1:35). After healing the invalid, Jesus "slipped away into the crowd that was there" (John 5:13). Jesus removed himself regularly from the press of people and the demands around him for times of personal contemplation and recharging.

Psychologists Henry Cloud and John Townsend have written a superb book called *Boundaries: When to Say Yes, When to Say No*. In their book they discuss these main ideas about boundaries:

- Boundaries are a "property line." Their purpose is to help us know what we are responsible for and what we are not responsible for.
- The functions of a boundary are to keep good in and bad out, to act as an alarm system, to help us to withdraw, and to protect our freedom.
- Examples of boundaries include skin/body, words (truth), geographical distance, time, emotional distance, and other people.[10]

Cloud and Townsend explain that we can have problems and symptoms in three main areas.[11] These difficulties serve as red flags to indicate that our boundaries are weak or nonexistent (that is, our yard is wide-open to intruders). In the first area, poor boundaries can show up in clinical symptoms such as depression, resentment, rage or anger, and obsessive and compulsive behavior. Scripture teaches, however, that we are to realize, "It is for freedom that Christ has set us free. Stand firm, then, and do not let yourselves be burdened again by a yoke of slavery" (Galatians 5:1).

The second area involves a sense of loss of freedom and loss of love in our relationships. Failing to set boundaries leads to fearing the lengths to which others will go in order to use us, resenting the requests others make of us, even actively avoiding others for fear of being taken advantage of. The Bible states that "there is no fear in love. But perfect love drives out fear, because fear has to do with punishment. The one who fears is not made perfect in love" (1 John 4:18). Therefore, it is loving to set appropriate limits, which in turn frees us up to love others.

Finally, Cloud and Townsend state that the third area of boundary difficulty involves symptoms that show up in functional areas such as being unable to reach a goal or finish a task and manifesting a high degree of disorganization, feeling low energy levels, and having problems with concentration. Boundaries appropriately give us a sense of purpose, direction, and worth. The apostle Paul asks, "Who serves as a soldier at his own expense? Who plants a vineyard and does not eat of its grapes? Who tends a flock and does not drink of the milk?... 'Do not muzzle an ox while it is treading out the grain.'... because when the plowman plows and the thresher threshes, they ought to do so in the hope of sharing in the harvest" (1 Corinthians 9:7, 9 – 10).

Cloud and Townsend delineate Ten Laws of Boundaries that are crucial to understand as you work on establishing good boundaries in your life:

- *Law 1: The Law of Sowing and Reaping.* We are personally responsible for our own actions and the consequences of those actions.
- *Law 2: The Law of Responsibility "for" and "to."* We are responsible for our own feelings, actions, and behaviors. When we take responsibility for someone else, we keep them in an immature state.
- *Law 3: The Law of Power and Powerlessness.* We cannot change anyone else, but we can change ourselves, with God's help.
- *Law 4: The Law of Receiving Others' Boundaries.* We need to learn to hear when other people say no.
- *Law 5: The Law of Motivation.* Boundaries help us gain control of our own lives and fulfill what we were created for — to love. When we have the proper motivation, we experience freedom and appropriate expressions of responsibility.
- *Law 6: The Law of Evaluating the Pain Caused by Your Boundaries.* There is a difference between hurt and harm.
- *Law 7: The Law of Proactive Versus Reactive Boundaries. Proactive* means freely choosing to love, enjoy, and serve one another; *reactive* means letting someone else define and direct who we are and what we do.
- *Law 8: The Law of Envy. Envy* is seeing the good as that which we do not have.
- *Law 9: The Law of Activity.* Boundaries are created in our lives when we do something. We must take the initiative and accept the responsibility for our feelings, attitudes, and behaviors.
- *Law 10: The Law of Exposure.* Internal boundaries need to be visible and communicated to others.[12]

DISSOCIATIVE IDENTITY DISORDER
KAREN SACKETT, M.A., L.P., R.N.
WITH JULIANNE S. ZUEHLKE, M.S., R.N., C.S.

INDICATIONS FOR USE

When clients present with a lack of connection in their thoughts, feelings, actions, or sense of identity. In this type of situation, dissociation is suspected. These individuals may also tell about internal voices, unexplained episodes of extreme rage, ongoing states of anxiety, inability to trust people or God, an overwhelming sense of helplessness, or a desire to self-injure. Dissociation can also include the presence of two or more distinct identities or personality states, each with its own manner of perception, thinking, speech, conduct, or styles. These personality states switch back and forth with respect to taking control of the person's actions. Also noted is an extensive amount of memory loss of events, the memory loss being too great to be attributed to normal forgetfulness.[13] Other clusters of symptoms that may be the result of trauma and dissociation include eating disorders, migraine headaches, sexual dysfunction, and seizures.

RESOURCES

Friesen, James G., E. James Wilder, Anne Bierling, Rick Koepcke, and Maribeth Poole. *The Life Model: Living from the Heart Jesus Gave You.* Van Nuys, Calif.: Shepherd's House, 1999.

Hawkins, Tom R. *Breaking the Demonic Network: What is the Core? Pre-counseling Questionnaire, Boundaries for the Therapist, Restoring Shattered Lives.* www.shieldoffaith.org: Restoration in Christ Ministry, 1998.

Herman, Judith. *Trauma and Recovery.* New York: HarperCollins, 1992.

McGee, Robert. *The Search for Significance,* rev. ed. Nashville: Word, 1998.

Ritchie, Bill. *A Dad Who Loves You: Experience the Joy of a Perfect Father.* Sisters, Ore.: Multnomah, 1992.

Smith, Ed. *Advanced Studies in TheoPhostic Ministry.* Campbellsville, Ky.: Alathia Equipping Center, 1999.

Wilder, E. James. *Life Passages for Men.* Eugene, Ore.: Wipf & Stock, 1997.

PRESENTATION TO CLIENT AND/OR THERAPIST

Dissociation is a coping mechanism that is present at birth and is used to manage the experiences of everyday life, as well as many events that are experienced as traumatic. Children learn to associate and develop an internal sense of self through normal developmental processes when they are parented in a healthy manner on a daily basis. If healthy parenting did not occur or if you experienced a trauma such as physical or sexual abuse, rape, or severe neglect, then dissociation is the coping mechanism that protected you from pain. If you demonstrate dissociative symptoms, you have experienced events that have involved threats to your life or to your bodily integrity and that have evoked extreme helplessness in you as a child. In her landmark book *Trauma and Recovery,* psychiatrist Judith Herman explains that traumatic events are those experiences that overwhelm your coping skills.

In dissociation, the mind builds a wall around the trauma so as to separate the memory from conscious awareness. The dissociated part of the mind holds these visual images, body memories, belief systems, and neurological materials that were present when you experienced the traumatic event. As children, we do not have the mental and emotional structures to make sense of experiences that threaten our lives. Consequently, as a defense against terror, we dissociate, or close off, the part of our mind that contains the painful material. Included in the closed-off part are lies that were programmed intentionally into your mind by a cult or by evil persons, or lies that were the interpretation you placed on the event that seemed "logical" to believe. For example, the threat that "you'll die if you tell anyone" is believed, and the dissociated part resists disclosing the experience later in life because the lie remains active.

Recovery is a process of repairing and reorganizing the memory material that will once again restore wholeness to the mind and body. This process is accomplished by accessing and healing the lie that is believed. This lie is what holds the traumatic material in place and maintains the dissociation. The threat may have been true in the past (that is, the cult or evil person had the ability and intention to implement the threat) but is no longer true for the adult (who was the child in the past). Hence, it is now a lie that simply maintains the dissociation.

The mind is like a house with many rooms. One large room could represent the Host Personality, which is the dominant part of the person. That room could be completely cleaned up — while the other rooms may not be. Some rooms are co-conscious with other rooms (that is, several rooms can be present to one's consciousness at the same time). Every room represents a period of time in the person's life. To be whole, each room would have to be cleaned up and the walls separating them torn down — a process that takes a lot of time, because some rooms could be hostile to the other rooms (loyal to the cult) and to the process of integration. To clean up a room, something will always have to be renounced (for example, a lie, pledge, vow, or sinful activity) and someone forgiven. These rooms are like files on a computer screen. What we want to do is click on each personality and drag it over to the other healthy ones.

Dissociation as a disorder brings with it a vulnerability to demonic attack. Your ability to take captive every thought to make it obedient to the Lord Jesus Christ (see 2 Corinthians 10:5) is absent in dissociation because the lies are inaccessible to the conscious mind. Therefore, Satan takes advantage of this vulnerability.

There are four main steps involved in this recovery process.

First, *grow close to Jesus.* If you have a consistent and close relationship with the Lord Jesus, you will find your recovery process much easier and quicker. Therefore, this is an important part of your treatment plan. It is preferable to have both an intercessor and a discipleship person from your church involved. If that is not possible, then you need to go through the study of *The Search for Significance,* which can be facilitated by volunteers. At the same time, you will learn about conflict management and your internal world — and how to communicate with your internal world. If you do not fit into this type of study, work with *Life Passages for Men* or *A Dad Who Loves You* in order to utilize your therapy more completely.

Second, *experience authentic praise and worship.* A significant step in the recovery process is to discover the awesome power of praise and worship that allows you to walk in greater freedom. You will also be trained to utilize your authority in Jesus Christ in order to stand against the raging attacks of the enemy that come as your healing begins. You will explore your beliefs about yourself and about God, as well as seek to clarify what happens physically and spiritually when you praise the Lord. You may be tortured by the demonic whenever you pick up a Bible or you open your mouth to sing praises. These attacks can be dealt with through spiritual warfare techniques and through the involvement of your intercessors.

Third, *uncover lies and see Jesus replace them with truth.* The third phase involves uncovering the hidden lies and demonic structures that are keeping you from knowing reality. This phase is what psychology has traditionally called *memory work.* In the secular treatment world, the painful reliving of memories has been considered to be the norm. However, with the power of Jesus Christ to usher in his healing presence, a gentle healing can now become the norm. You will remain much more stable while you assimilate traumatic or painful material and are able to hear Jesus replace the lie with the truth and then to experience his wonderful healing.

Fourth, *connect with the body of Christ in the true church.* This fourth and final phase of recovery is of paramount importance in the healing process. God has planned for you to reestablish a sense of connectedness with the human race after being traumatized. Scripture teaches us to comfort others with the comfort with which we have been comforted (see 2 Corinthians 1:3–4). We are privileged to see this expression of comfort at work in fellowship groups and in Bible studies. You will give testimony about God's grace as you return to your church body, and eventually as you are able to reach out and minister to others.

PRETHERAPY THOUGHTS AND CONSIDERATIONS

Although the treatment of Dissociative Identity Disorder entails a complex process, it is very rewarding to watch the Lord set prisoners free and bind up the brokenhearted. It is not too complex for him. If this is a new area of treatment for you, don't be afraid to get in-depth training. Several training sites are noted in the resource list above.

This is an area of great need and great spiritual reward. Be prepared to explore your own personal weaknesses, which God will reveal to you. This type of therapeutic work often causes the hidden wounds of the therapist to surface. The work is fruitful only if the Holy Spirit leads it and the Lord is allowed to set the pace and direction of the session. Does that mean you'll simply sit there and do nothing? Hardly! Be actively involved in conversation with the Lord as he directs by means of the questions and interventions he desires. Abandon a strong desire to rescue or save clients. They generally have a strong survivor mechanism in place, or they would not be sitting in therapy. To attempt to save is an easy trap to fall into, yet it's one that can be costly to your own health while also failing to aid the client's genuine recovery. If a client appears not to be safe, get consultation immediately rather than move into a rescue mode. Encourage clients to stay involved in their world and not to focus exclusively on therapy in their recovery.

Clients in treatment have most likely never had a safe place to talk about their pain, which makes your provision of an atmosphere of trust and safety crucial. Survivors of incest, molestation, or ritual abuse have an intense need to have their reality validated. As small children, they were told by the cult or evil persons that they were crazy and were inventing stories that could not possibly be true. As they grew older, they may have courageously shared something of their story with someone in a church setting and may have been told to forget the past. They may have been told that "all things are made new" and that what they are remembering does not count, no matter how horrific and heinous the memories may be.

In order for clients to unwrap their pain, they need to know how the therapist views dissociation. If you believe it is a rare psychiatric disorder and that those who have it are psychotic, then they will likely tell you very little of what is happening in their reality. Clients thrive when we honor and respect them for their ability to survive and encourage them to respect themselves. It is difficult emotionally for clients to handle the sense of betrayal they feel when they realize that those whom God had ordained to care for and protect them relinquished their authority over them. They turned the client over to one who wants them dead, namely, their adversary Satan. Our responsibility as we walk the road of healing with our clients is to listen with God's heart for the lies they believe, for these are what hold the trauma in place.

As therapists, we must be aware that the inner fragments of the psyche that have been walled off are a part of a real person. Even though chronologically a client may be fifty years of age, the thought process may be that of a two-year-old with respect to a specific memory. Be aware of how you would respond to a small child of that age, and proceed accordingly. Be courteous and introduce yourself to the "child" who does not know you. You may need to have toys and art materials at hand. Begin immediately to ask the Lord what he wants to give this little one and how he wants to heal. This process will lead to the discovery of the lie and will open the way for Jesus to bring truth. As you guide, you seek answers to the questions "What is the source of the trauma that caused the mind to dissociate?" and "What does the mind believe has happened?" At this juncture, you are likely to encounter double binds of conflicting messages, such as, "I will die or explode, or our 'children' [the fragmented parts] will be killed if we reunite [into one person]." This is the juncture where much deeper training is required.

Healing becomes in the end a journey to uncover what is hidden in the darkness of dissociation in order to please the Father and to obey him no matter what is discovered. Those clients who make *their healing* the focus typically do not progress, while those who remember that *Jesus Christ has already won the victory* over Satan experience the most healing. In the case of those who were ritually abused, they heal when they embrace the truth that what the cult teaches about Satan's dominion over Christ is a bald-faced lie. These are the ones who are walking a path of sanctification and restoration; they understand what it means to stand in the presence of the Lord. They see their pain and the conflicts in the world through the eyes of God.

MARRIAGE COMMUNICATIONS

TERRY E. ZUEHLKE, PH.D., L.P.

INDICATIONS FOR USE

When clients have problems in their marriage relationship, particularly in the area of communication. These techniques supply basic elements for use in marriage counseling when a couple's interaction is the primary concern. Taking the role of a "teacher/coach," the therapist helps the couple develop new skills to better understand each other and resolve disagreements.

RESOURCES

Anderson, Neil T., and Charles Mylander. *The Christ Centered Marriage*. Ventura, Calif.: Regal, 1996.

Stanley, Scott, Daniel Trathen, Savanna McCain, and B. Milton Bryan. *A Lasting Promise: The Christian Guide to Fighting for Your Marriage*. San Francisco: Jossey-Bass, 1998.

Worthington, Everett L., Jr., and Douglas McMurry. *Marriage Conflicts*. Grand Rapids: Baker, 1994.

PRESENTATION TO CLIENT AND/OR THERAPIST

People usually go to a doctor with two questions in mind: First, "Why am I having problems?" and second, "What are you going to do about it?" If the doctor is a physician, the treatment will typically follow the medical model and involve some kind of pharmaceutical or surgical intervention carried out by a specialist. However, if the doctor is a mental health professional (other than a psychiatrist), the emphasis of treatment will be directed internally at your personal responsibility as the client. During our time together I'm going to help you learn practical ideas that can protect your marriage relationship and make it better. Each of you will be the "doctor" for your marriage. The material we'll be using is based on solid biblical principles and on years of research about what makes marriages healthier and happier. The help you'll be getting is not going to teach you how to avoid marital disagreement but what to do on those occasions when you disagree.

The treatment program involves two fundamental phases. First, you will learn how to discuss your issues better. The goal is that you would learn to present clearly your position and to understand the position of your partner accurately. Using speaker-listener techniques, you will learn how to "diagnose" why you are having an argument. Second, if mutual understanding does not lead to an agreement on the issues, you will learn what to do to resolve the conflict. The goal of conflict resolution is to enable you to win together as a team. If there is a winner and a loser, then the marital relationship ends up being a loser — because a minus times a plus is still a minus.

PROBLEM DISCUSSION

This phase separates communication into "process" and "content" components. The *process* component refers to your style of communication; it is about how you treat each other. The *content* component deals with the issues and topics in the conversation. *Process* refers to the way you communicate, *content* to what is communicated. Because you'll always have issues in your marriage and probably don't want someone else to tell you what is right and wrong regarding each issue, we're going to spend our time concentrating on how to communicate more effectively.

The process of communication can be broken down into two roles: speaker and listener. Each of these roles has particular rules. When you are the speaker, you need to speak for yourself using "I" statements. You'll want to tell your partner what you are thinking, how you are feeling, and what solution you would like regarding the issue. These are the three components of an assertive statement: "I think ..., I feel ..., and I want [or propose] ...." It is crucial that you include information on what you would like to have happen so that, if your partner does not agree with your position on the issue, he or she will have an idea of how to resolve the disagreement through compromise. As the speaker you must remember that all you can do is invite your partner to understand you accurately; you cannot expect or require agreement. The difference between invitation ("would you?") and expectation ("you must!") is important to remember when you are the speaker. The difference between advice (trying to fix) and support (listening) is also important to remember.

When you are in the listener role, you must pay attention. Put the newspaper down or turn off the television set when your partner is speaking. The listener's responsibility is to understand the position of the speaker; remember, however, that *understand* does not mean that you must *agree*. After the speaker has spoken for a brief time, the listener is to paraphrase and echo back what has been said. Accurate paraphrasing demonstrates to the speaker that the listener understands the points being made. The speaker should continue with brief statements that the listener paraphrases until the speaker is finished, and then the roles are reversed.

When each partner has had a chance to speak and to listen, the question is asked, "Do we agree?" If the answer is yes, then for all practical purposes the discussion is over. If you use the speaker-listener procedures, you will find that many of your issues can actually be easily resolved. I have often heard a partner say, "Well, now that you put it that way, I agree with you." However, there will be times when your discussion clearly reveals that you do *not* agree and that a negotiated solution is required. At this point it becomes necessary to move to the conflict resolution phase.

CONFLICT RESOLUTION

The conflict resolution phase begins by one partner stating, "Since we agree that we don't agree, let's work out a compromise." At this point there are four steps to follow:

1. *Agenda Setting:* Make it as clear as you can what you are trying to solve at this time. Mutually agree about what to focus on.

2. *Brainstorming:* Use this time to propose various solutions to the disagreement. Be creative and have fun. Remember that no idea is a bad idea. You simply want to get possibilities on the table.

3. *Agreement and Compromise:* Narrow the proposals to specific solutions that could be tried. Your goal here is to identify a specific solution or combination of solutions that both of you would agree to try out. If each of you is willing to budge a little bit on your position, it's typically possible to find some middle ground in order to resolve the disagreement.

4. *Follow-up:* This is an extremely important part of the conflict resolution process. It is the grease that helps a compromise become successful. If you know that what you are agreeing to is only a trial solution, you will be more willing to compromise. So once the agreement has been reached, set a specific time (in a week, in two weeks, in a month) to sit

down and talk about how well the compromise is working. At that time you can discuss any small changes that might be needed to make the agreement work better. Follow-up is also important because it will hold you accountable for your end of the agreement.

One other important technique in marital communication that I want to teach you is *Time-Out*. It is an intervention that either partner may use in order to prevent a "meltdown" when an argument occurs. The following rules should be agreed on if Time-Out is used as a communication process option:

- Either partner may call a Time-Out.
- Person A may call a Time-Out whenever he or she feels the conversation (fight) is headed toward a "meltdown."
- The only thing Person B can say at that time is "okay, when can we continue?"
- Person A sets a specific time to resume—within twenty-four hours. However, the meeting may not be scheduled after 10:00 P.M. or before 6:30 A.M.—we need our sleep!
- Since Person A called the Time-Out, he or she must go to Person B at the appointed time and restart the conversation.
- Remember: If the Time-Out was too short to have achieved its objective, either person can call another Time-Out and restart the process.

The book *The Christ Centered Marriage* contains steps for "Setting Your Marriage Free," a process husband and wife can work through on their own in the presence of God. To do so would require a willingness on the part of both spouses to assume their own personal responsibility before God. The study guide for the book contains a similar process for those who are engaged.[14]

SEXUAL ADDICTION

TERRY E. ZUEHLKE, PH.D., L.P.

INDICATIONS FOR USE

When clients suffer from habitual sexual sins and are caught in the vicious cycle of *sin-confess-sin-confess-sin*.

RESOURCES

Anderson, Neil T. *A Way of Escape*. Eugene, Ore.: Harvest House, 1994.

Arterburn, Stephen. *Addicted to Love*. Ann Arbor, Mich.: Servant, 1991.

Carnes, Patrick. *The Sexual Addiction*. Minneapolis: CompCare, 1983.

Hemfelt, Robert, Frank Minirth, and Paul Meier. *We Are Driven*. Nashville: Nelson, 1991.

Laaser, Mark. *Faithful and True*. Grand Rapids: Zondervan, 1996.

— — —. *Faithful and True: Sexual Integrity in a Fallen World Workbook*. Nashville: LifeWay, 1996.

Weiss, Douglas. *101 Freedom Exercises: Christian Guide for Sex Addiction Recovery*. Fort Worth, Tex.: Discovery, 1997.

Weiss, Douglas, and Dianne DeBusk. *Women Who Love Sex Addicts*. Fort Worth, Tex.: Discovery, 1993.

PRESENTATION TO CLIENT AND/OR THERAPIST

Bondage to sexual sin is the result of a combination of influences from the world, the flesh, and the devil. This bondage may have been the result of a traumatic event such as childhood sexual abuse or a rape that you experienced. More commonly, it may have developed as a result of your gradual surrender to sexual temptations, such as sexual fantasy, masturbation, and use of pornography. Our vulnerability to these temptations is one of the results of the Fall, when Adam and Eve were deceived by Satan. Since that time sexual impurity has been a primary weapon of the evil one used to ruin relationships and attack the body of Christ.

Because you suffer from the sin of sexual addiction, you most likely have the following core personality beliefs:[15]

- Low self-image: "I am personally unattractive and a failure."
- Poor relationships: "Nobody wants to be around me."
- Unmet needs: "I cannot depend on God or on others for love and acceptance. I must figure out a way to take care of my own needs."
- Sex will give me love: "Sexual pleasure will help me feel acceptable, loved, and complete."

Patrick Carnes, renowned expert on addiction and recovery issues, has described a typical pattern of sexual bondage as involving a series of progressively deteriorating stages.[16] These include:

1. *Preoccupation.* In order to contend with the core personality beliefs described above, you focus on sexual fantasies as a way to cope with your painful feelings of not being loved.

2. *Ritualization.* You develop special patterns to lead to sexual gratification. Rituals such as compulsive masturbation in certain surroundings, elaborate preparations for extramarital trysts, and scheduled visits to a massage parlor are examples of your attempts to reduce the spiritual and psychological pain of loneliness and insignificance: "Cruising, watching, waiting, preparing are part of the mood alteration."[17]

3. *Compulsive sexual behavior.* Your expression of sexual addiction "may range from the seemingly 'normal' sexual encounter with another consenting adult, to illegal and abusive behavior, such as rape or incest."[18]

4. *Despair.* The failure of the above activities to remove your pain for more than a short time results in an increased sense of helplessness and hopelessness. Consequently, you may feel self-pity or self-hatred; you may have, or have had, thoughts of suicide as well as a repetition of the *sin-confess-sin-confess-sin* cycle.

Your recovery from sexual addiction will require tremendous resolve on your part, full disclosure, and the grace of God. Your recovery may also require family and group psychotherapy. I will not contribute to the guilt and shame you are already feeling. I believe there is no condemnation for those who are in Christ Jesus. The first step in the change process must focus on your spiritual maturity and the establishment of a plan to enhance spiritual discipline. Neil Anderson's book *A Way of Escape* is an excellent resource for helping with this process. More help can be found in Mark Laaser's *Faithful and True* workbook. The section on "The Spiritual Dimension" addresses your religious history, shame experiences, magical thinking, and spiritual discipline, as well as the central importance of faith in your life.[19] The "Steps to

Freedom in Christ" will help you break the bondage, which then makes the rest of your treatment possible. This bondage is twofold: physical and mental. The apostle Paul says, "In the same way, count yourselves dead to sin but alive to God in Christ Jesus. Therefore do not let sin reign in your mortal body so that you obey its evil desires. Do not offer the parts of your body to sin, as instruments of wickedness, but rather offer yourselves to God, as those who have been brought from death to life; and offer the parts of your body to him as instruments of righteousness" (Romans 6:11–13).

No one can commit a sexual sin without using his or her body as an instrument of wickedness. Therefore, if we commit a sexual sin we will allow sin to reign in our mortal bodies. To resolve this, we ask the Lord to reveal to our minds every sexual use of our bodies as an instrument of wickedness. When he does, we renounce those uses of our bodies and then submit our bodies to God as instruments of righteousness. We are urged, in view of God's mercy, to present our bodies to him as living sacrifices, and then we will be able to renew our minds (see Romans 12:1–2). During sessions using the TheoPhostic approach, Jesus will uncover and correct the original lies you have learned.

Your belief in God's provision is the key to beginning the process of breaking sexual addiction. The answer is not what you do as a result of *your own understanding* of what you need. Demolishing sexual strongholds starts with the above steps and leads to your appreciation of the gift of Christ's resurrection. After you have submitted to God, confessed, repented, and experienced forgiveness, you must go on the offensive and start to act responsibly by resisting the temptation.

The following suggestions will help you in your resistance efforts. At the family level, you need to seek an understanding of the family dynamics that contributed to your emotional wounds. Sexual sobriety will require the awareness, understanding, and support of others—including your spouse or other members of your immediate and extended family. Accountability with a mature Christian peer as well as in a Christian recovery group is important. Sexual sobriety will require exercising behavioral discipline and following a specific plan. Therapist and sexual addiction expert Douglas Weiss recommends that you develop an Action Plan and follow it for ninety consecutive days.[20] Schedule fifteen to thirty minutes each day to work on the material in the Action Plan. Examples of daily exercises include the following:

- praying in the morning
- reading recovery literature daily
- calling someone in recovery daily
- attending Christian recovery meetings regularly
- praying in the evening and thanking God for your day of sobriety

CHEMICAL ADDICTIONS

NEIL T. ANDERSON, M.A.C.E., M.DIV., ED.D., D.MIN.

INDICATIONS FOR USE

When a client is unable to manage his or her life due to chemical addiction. The addictive behavior is negatively affecting the client's life, family, friends, and career.

RESOURCES

Anderson, Neil, Mike Quarles, and Julia Quarles. *Freedom From Addiction*. Ventura, Calif.: Regal, 1996.

Anderson, Neil, and Julia Quarles. *Freedom From Addiction Workbook*. Ventura, Calif.: Regal, 1997.

— — —. *One Day at a Time*. Ventura, Calif.: Regal, 2000.

Bartosch, Bob, and Pauline Bartosch. *Overcomers Outreach: A Bridge to Recovery*. Goose Creek, S.C.: Meister, 1994.

Bustanoby, Andre S. *The Wrath of Grapes*. Grand Rapids: Baker, 1987.

Johnson, Vernon. *I'll Quit Tomorrow*. San Francisco: Harper & Row, 1980.

Van Cleave, Stephen, Walter Byrd, and Kathy Revell. *Counseling for Substance Abuse and Addiction*. Waco, Tex.: Word, 1987.

PRESENTATION TO CLIENT AND/OR THERAPIST

We are all needy people, and we are driven to meet those needs in a variety of ways. We all need to be loved and accepted for who we are, and we are all looking for some affirmation in life. For various reasons, people turn to alcohol and drugs to assist them with the problems of life. Some people experiment with alcohol and drugs for social reasons; it becomes a means to get rid of inhibitions or to be a part of the crowd. Others turn to alcohol and drugs as a means to cope with or to stop the pain — a pain that can be either physical or emotional. The temporary high or the relief from pain is only short-lived, however. If people continue using chemicals as a means of partying, escaping, or coping, the result is fairly predictable as follows (see Figure 9.3):[21]

The Addiction Cycle

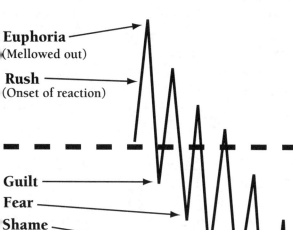

Euphoria
(Mellowed out)

Rush
(Onset of reaction)

Addiction:
1. Habituation
2. Dependency
3. Tolerance
4. Withdrawal

Baseline experience

Guilt
Fear
Shame

Occasional drinking

Increase in tolerance

Memory blackouts

Excuses increase

Grandiose, aggressive behavior

Efforts to control fail repeatedly

Tries geographical escapes

Family and friends avoided

Loss of ordinary willpower

Tremors and early morning drinks

Decrease in ability to stop drinking

Onset of lengthy intoxication

Moral deterioration

Impaired thinking

Drinking with inferiors

Unable to initiate actions

Obsession with drinking

All alibis exhausted

Surreptitious drinking

Increased dependency

Persistent remorse

Promises fail

Loss of interest

Work, money troubles

Resentments pile up

Neglect of food

Physical deterioration

Irrational fears

Obsessions

Physical illness

Complete defeat

Death or recovery

Alcohol and drugs work not so much by stepping on the accelerator as by releasing the brake. Inhibitions are overcome, and the person feels a certain euphoria. For those looking for a good time, getting high can be fun for the moment. The *baseline experience* is different for those who are looking for a temporary reprieve from the pressures of life. They could be a bundle of nerves or depressed about their circumstances; they are looking for a high to lift their spirits or something to calm their nerves. Melancholy people just want to drown their sorrows. Drinking will help them mellow out. It works! Within a matter of minutes they feel better. The same is true for those who want to stop the pain. They can't wait for the rush to take effect — for when it does, they'll feel better.

Unfortunately, the effects wear off. The morning after is a different deal. You wake up feeling just a little bit lower than your baseline experience. Reality sets in. You have a headache, and you may hardly recognize the person in the mirror. You have to go to work or to school, and all the pressures and responsibilities of life come rushing right back at you. There could be a stab of guilt, shame, or fear, depending on your moral and social conscience.

The first step toward addiction is *habituation.* Alcohol and drugs become the means to having a good time or to coping with life. A habit is a knee-jerk response. You feel a pain, so you reach for the pills. You feel down, so you do something that will pick you up. You feel stressed-out, so you do something that will calm your nerves. You have trained yourself to depend on chemicals to pick you up, to stop the pain, to soothe your nerves, to help you feel good. Occasional drinking has become a habit, a means of emotional support, a crutch to lean on.

When the effects wear off, however, the guilt, fear, and shame become more and more pronounced. With each successive use, you are getting further and further away from your original baseline experience. You are the king of the hill when you are on a high; you are filled with grandiose ideas and often become aggressive in your behavior. On the down side, you begin to experience memory blackouts, and efforts to regain control of your life fail repeatedly. "How did I get home last night?" "What happened?" "I better get a grip on myself; I'm starting to lose control!" You become more and more *dependent* on chemicals (the second step) to get you through the day, but your *tolerance* has increased (the third step). You need more and more in order to get high. You feel guilty about your behavior, so you begin to drink furtively — leaving familiar surroundings to go where people don't know you. You can't live with the shame, so you begin to *withdraw* (the fourth step).

How can you know when you are addicted to alcohol? John Hopkins University Hospital in Baltimore, Maryland, uses the following test questions to help their patients recognize the warning signs:

1. Do you lose time from work due to drinking?
2. Is drinking making your home life unhappy?
3. Do you drink because you are shy with other people?
4. Is drinking affecting your reputation?
5. Have you ever felt remorse after drinking?
6. Have you gotten into financial difficulties because of drinking?
7. Do you turn to lower companions and an inferior environment when drinking?
8. Does drinking make you careless of your family's welfare?
9. Has your ambition decreased since drinking?
10. Do you crave a drink at a definite time daily?
11. Do you want a drink the next morning?
12. Does drinking cause you to have difficulty in sleeping?
13. Has your efficiency decreased since drinking?
14. Is drinking jeopardizing your job or business?
15. Do you drink to escape from worries or trouble?
16. Do you drink alone?
17. Have you ever had a complete loss of memory as a result of drinking?
18. Has your physician ever treated you for drinking?
19. Do you drink to build up your self-confidence?
20. Have you ever been to a hospital or institution on account of drinking?

According to John Hopkins University Hospital, if you answer yes to any one of these questions, there is a definite warning sign that you may be an alcoholic. If you answer yes to any two, the chances are pretty good that you're an alcoholic. If you answer yes to three or more, you are undoubtedly an alcoholic.

THE PATH TO RECOVERY

To overcome your addiction, you have to admit you have a problem and be willing to walk in the light and speak the truth in love with me, your family, and friends. This addiction has not only affected you, but it has affected everyone you've been in touch with. Abstinence is not the primary goal we're trying to achieve. To take away your drug of choice would only leave you a dry drunk. We have a far bigger and more ambitious goal. We want to help you resolve your psychological and spiritual conflicts so as to establish you alive and free in Christ. You need to know who you are in Christ and what it means to be a child of God. You need to understand the battle for your mind and how to take captive every thought to make it obedient to Christ, because you have been and are continuing to be overwhelmed with tempting and accusing thoughts. Then we're going to learn how Christ can meet all your needs according to his riches in glory. Remember, you have legitimate needs, but you have attempted to meet them in the wrong ways.

Chemical addictions are long-established habits. They are not easy to break because there is a fleshly craving for your drug of choice. You also have certain, well-established mental flesh-patterns that we are going to flush out in therapy and learn to overcome. To overcome the flesh will require total dependence on God as well as the support of family and friends. You need to set up an accountability group you can meet with regularly and find at least one person you can call when the temptation to drink or to use drugs becomes overwhelming. Then we're going to have to meet with your family, who have also suffered because of your addiction. They will have to work through their own issues of shame, guilt, bitterness, and codependency. By the grace of God, you can overcome your addiction and learn to live a victorious life in Christ. Throughout the period of treatment, I want you to dwell on the following description of who you are in Christ and on the pledges that are found in "The Overcomer's Covenant in Christ."

WHO I AM IN CHRIST

I AM ACCEPTED IN CHRIST

I am God's child (John 1:12)

I am Christ's friend (John 15:15)

I have been justified (Romans 5:1)

I am united with the Lord and one with him in spirit (1 Corinthians 6:17)

I have been bought with a price; I belong to God (1 Corinthians 6:20)

I am a member of Christ's body (1 Corinthians 12:27)

I am a saint (Ephesians 1:1)

I have been adopted as God's child (Ephesians 1:5)

I have direct access to God through the Holy Spirit (Ephesians 2:18)

I have been redeemed and forgiven of all my sins (Colossians 1:14)

I am complete in Christ (Colossians 2:10)

I AM SECURE IN CHRIST

I am free forever from condemnation (Romans 8:1 – 2)

I am assured that all things work together for good (Romans 8:28)

I am free from any condemning charges against me (Romans 8:33 – 34)

I cannot be separated from the love of God (Romans 8:35, 38 – 39)

I have been established, anointed, and sealed by God (2 Corinthians 1:21 – 22)

I am confident that the good work God has begun in me will be perfected (Philippians 1:6)

I am a citizen of heaven (Philippians 3:20)

I am hidden with Christ in God (Colossians 3:3)

I have not been given a spirit of fear, but of power, love, and a sound mind (2 Timothy 1:7)

I can find grace and mercy to help me in time of need (Hebrews 4:16)

I am born of God, and the evil one cannot touch me (1 John 5:18)

I AM SIGNIFICANT IN CHRIST

I am the salt and light of the earth (Matthew 5:13–14)

I am a branch of the true vine, a channel of his life (John 15:1, 5)

I have been chosen and appointed to bear fruit (John 15:16)

I am a personal witness of Christ (Acts 1:8)

I am God's temple (1 Corinthians 3:16)

I am a minister of reconciliation (2 Corinthians 5:17–20)

I am God's coworker (2 Corinthians 6:1)

I am seated with Christ in the heavenly realms (Ephesians 2:6)

I am God's workmanship (Ephesians 2:10)

I may approach God with freedom and confidence (Ephesians 3:12)

I can do all things through Christ who gives me strength (Philippians 4:13)

The Overcomer's Covenant in Christ

1. I place all my trust and confidence in the Lord. I put no confidence in the flesh, and I declare myself to be dependent on God.
2. I consciously and deliberately choose to submit to God and resist the devil by denying myself, picking up my cross daily, and following Jesus.
3. I choose to humble myself before the mighty hand of God in order that he may exalt me at the proper time.
4. I declare the truth that I am dead to sin, freed from it, and alive to God in Christ Jesus, since I have died with Christ and have been raised with him.
5. I gladly embrace the truth that I am now a child of God who is unconditionally loved and accepted. I reject the lie that I have to perform in order to be accepted, and I reject my fallen and natural identity, which was derived from the world.
6. I declare that sin shall no longer be master over me, because I am not under the law but under grace, and that there is no more guilt or condemnation, because I am spiritually alive in Christ Jesus.
7. I renounce every unrighteous use of my body, and I commit myself to no longer be conformed to this world but rather to be transformed by the renewing of my mind. I choose to believe the truth and walk in it, regardless of my feelings or circumstances.
8. I commit myself to take captive every thought to make it obedient to Christ and choose to think about that which is true, honorable, right, pure, and lovely.
9. I commit myself to God's great goal for my life to conform to his image. I know that I will face many trials, but God has given me the victory. I am not a victim but an overcomer in Christ.
10. I choose to adopt the attitude of Christ, which means that I will do nothing out of selfishness or empty conceit, but with humility of mind I will regard others as more important than myself. I will not merely look out for my own personal interests but also for the interests of others. I know that it is more blessed to give than to receive.

10

Professional Christian Therapy and the Church Community

Consecration is not wrapping one's self in a holy web in the sanctuary and then coming forth after prayer and twilight meditation and saying, "There, I am consecrated." Consecration is going out into the world where God Almighty is and using every power for His glory. It is taking advantages as trust funds—as confidential debts owed to God. It is simply dedicating one's life, in its whole flow, to God's service.

HENRY WARD BEECHER

As Christians we carry our faith into our homes, communities, and workplaces—wherever we are, day after day. There is to be no fragmentation of our lives into Sunday "church" behaviors and carnality the other six days of the week. We do not take off our Christian hats when we walk through the door of our clinic. We continue at all times to be members of the body of Christ—children of God who are saved and sanctified by faith and empowered by the Holy Spirit. We are not therapists; we are children of God who have been called to practice Christ-centered therapy.

The integration of Christian counseling practices with local churches as partners in ministry should be a natural occurrence. Both the church and the Christian counselor should be committed to a Christlike ministry of healing the sick, binding up the brokenhearted, bringing unity and wholeness where there is division, and restoring individuals to their full God-given potential. However, as we have seen in chapter three, diverse strategies in Christian counseling can threaten the unity we have in Jesus

Christ. Being Conjoint therapists, we are committed to work together with the local church; hence the wounded suffer when there is a lack of cooperation and unity between the church and the Christian counselor. The following sections will address both the mutual and unique responsibilities of the professional Christian counselor and the church.

MUTUAL RESPONSIBILITIES OF THE CHURCH AND THE COUNSELOR

In this collaborative partnership, both the church and the counselor must share certain basic understandings in order for mutual trust and confidence to exist:

First, *we must recognize the power of prayer.* The church and the counselor should be praying for each other and for the people they are trying to help. There are multiple venues for prayer. The church prays corporately for the needs of their people during small groups, other meeting times, and at staff times. Prayer should be the first thing a Christian does about anything. It's hard to be at odds with a brother or sister in Christ if you are petitioning God together. Our corporate prayer life reveals our dependency on God as a church (or our lack of dependency). Prayer is the "oxygen of the spiritual life" and "the way the life of God is nourished in us."[1] Likewise, counselors need to pray in small groups, at other meetings, and at staff times for the wounded ones in their caseloads — and they do so for essentially the same reason. Praying with clients in actual sessions in the marketplace requires wise assessment of the timing and implementation, but it ought not be neglected. Private prayer by the therapist for clients before, during (as silent prayers to God), and after sessions is always appropriate, even if the client refuses to endorse prayer with the therapist in session.

Second, *we must develop mutual concern for the hurting.* Both the church and the counselor need to recognize their interdependence in binding up the brokenhearted. The government has taken over the care of the ill, an area in which the church historically reigned. As the private sector is increasingly urged by the government to assume greater responsibility, opportunities for the church and the Christian mental health clinician are opening up once again. Healthy community experiences, biblical values, wholesome activities, and caring friendships are seen as available for clients within the wider church community; the secular mental and physical health systems cannot come close to providing these kinds of benefits.

One example of a partnership between the church and the private health care sector is clearly demonstrated in the development of the REACH program (Responding with Empathy and Care at Home). This program is the brainchild of Ruth Bolton, a medical doctor and founder of the Soteria Family Health Center in Robbinsdale, Minnesota. Dr. Bolton founded a Christian nonprofit family practice clinic to provide Christ-centered medical care to patients. She had become dismayed by the proabortion attitudes, the teen counseling that advocated contraceptives rather than abstinence, the bias toward euthanasia, and the other unbiblical mind-sets so prevalent in the secular domain in which she was providing medical care.

While providing patient care at Soteria, Dr. Bolton began to realize that, once medical treatment came to an end, she was sending many patients back into family systems that were unhealthy, isolated, and spiritually bankrupt. Her heart was led to seek partnership with the church in order to try to correct this tragic reality. She now works with two churches that train certain of its members in basic communication skills, appropriate evangelism, boundaries issues, referral making, and discipleship. Through a triage nurse, the Soteria physician refers an appropriate candidate to the program. One of the REACH volunteers from one of the churches will observe and befriend this patient on a regular basis. Since patients are assigned by matching their zip code with the zip code of the nearest church with a REACH program volunteer, there is a wonderful opportunity to enfold the patient into a healthy church community by means of the volunteer's invitation.

In the process, as the Spirit leads, a decision for Jesus Christ may also become a reality. Many patients who would otherwise never step foot into a church are being led in through the love and compassion of the healthy relationships provided by this partnership. The REACH model certainly has applicability to the clients we serve in our Christian mental health practices. We believe it is a foretaste of what we can accomplish when we focus on partnership with the church, rather than on isolationism and territoriality.

Third, *we must have a biblical worldview.* Both the church and the Christian therapist must overcome our tendency to adopt Western rationalism and naturalism. In reality, there is no "excluded middle" between the heavenly realms and the earth (see Figure 2.1 on page 49). The god of this world prowls around like a hungry lion looking for someone to devour (see 1 Peter 5:8). We have to overcome the syncretism — the combining of different forms of belief — that exists between the secular and the sacred. Humanist and utopianist philosophies are promoting self-sufficiency and state-sufficiency, while the New Age offers counterfeit spirituality. Surely to all appearances we are engaged in a cultural war of epic proportions.

Fourth, and finally, *we must work toward a wholistic answer.* The Christian mental health counselor and the church coexist in a delicate balance. Believers benefit from the *coordination* of interventions from the church and the professional Christian counselor in the marketplace. Both elements are needed if the Christian is going to be productive physically and spiritually in Christ. Understanding the battle for the mind as physical, psychological, *and* spiritual calls for the church and the Christian therapist to work together collaboratively.

THE COUNSELOR'S RESPONSIBILITIES

There are several responsibilities Christian mental health professionals should assume in order to advance their partnership with the local church:

First, *approach local churches humbly.* It's crucial for the counselor to realize that he or she does not have all the answers to the mental health needs of individual. Psychological practitioners are relative newcomers on the scene, while churches have been the healers for centuries and continue to possess significant resources to offer hurting people.

Second, *provide clear mission statements.* It is advantageous for the Christian counseling clinic with which the clinician associates to devise a clear mission statement for its marketplace practice. This statement clarifies for the client, the third-party payer, and the church the values base on which the practice rests. Inherent in a partnership is the full knowledge of the other party. Churches need to know the clinician's main interest — whether it is for profit or for people, for simply executing a job or for carrying out a service, for implicit or for explicit therapy, to blend in with the eclectic, secular mix of therapy values or to take a stand for the Lord in the marketplace. The mission statement Terry and Julie use to guide their practice can be found in Appendix D. In all of their materials they describe their counseling approach as one that represents "the Christian perspective." To feature this phrase prominently is congruent with their belief that it is preferable for counselors to be explicit with respect to their values base. We understand that Christian counselors in secular settings may not have the opportunity to advance such a mission statement, yet their own disclosure of worldview in clinical sessions can in essence serve as their "mission statement."

Third, *vigorously reject nonbiblical worldviews.* Christian counselors will want to demonstrate to the church that they are able to discern deviations from biblical truths in treatment modalities and psychological theories, especially the subtleties of the New Age philosophy. They will want to communicate to church leaders the Christian modalities they use (prayer, the "Steps to Freedom in Christ," repentance, identification of sin, biblical views on divorce and homosexuality, and the like), as well as the ones they reject (mantras, meditation, higher consciousness, imagery, unbiblical morals, absence of absolutes, and the like).

Fourth, *be an active member of a local church.* It's important for Christian counselors to share professional, noncompensated time in teaching, consultation, or responding to emergency situations and to volunteer time in regular ministry opportunities (for example, ushering, teaching a church school class, singing in the choir) in their own church. To be a good steward, the Christian counselor will want to be involved in the church community.

Fifth, *seek to partner with churches in a spirit of cooperation.* Christian counselors would do well to recognize referrals from pastors or church leaders with a written note of appreciation (omitting the client's name unless they have a signed Release of Information). It would also be good to secure a Release of Information and share a midpoint summary with the referral source, either in writing or verbally. If possible, counselors may want to make available in their waiting room publications that announce church conferences, ministries, music programs, support groups, vacation Bible school classes, and the like. Secular barriers may hinder this, but Christian counselors ought not to be afraid to ask. Whenever possible, it is always beneficial to visit personally with pastors and interested staff, sharing their own integration work and asking for input.

Sixth, *demonstrate competence in spiritual integration.* Christian counselors are in a unique position to integrate into counseling sessions spiritual components and teachings about a Christian's identity in Christ. Clients often give testimony to this need as they speak with their pastors and church leaders, and to be intentional about this integration will at least indirectly foster confidence among church leaders toward this approach. It is good also to take part with an open mind in any training opportunities that deal with spiritual issues such as evangelism, spiritual warfare, our identity in Christ, and authoritative prayer. Fellow Christians who attend these training sessions will take note of the counselor's presence and willingness to learn, thereby fostering confidence in his or her practice among those in the church community who hear the comments of those who observed their involvement.

Seventh, and finally, *frequently refer clients to church ministries.* Christian counselors will want to view the church as a resource and a valuable adjunct to therapy — familiarizing themselves with the various church programs and referring clients to the appropriate ones. Every client can profit, for example, by attending church support groups and Bible studies and by becoming part of lay ministry and marriage mentoring opportunities. It is good to encourage clients to become involved in ministries themselves, as they are physically, mentally, emotionally, and spiritually able to do so. Christian counselors may also want to invite clients to make appointments with their pastor, with an open heart to sharing their difficulties and seeking spiritual guidance.

THE CHURCH'S RESPONSIBILITY

There are several responsibilities the church should assume in order to advance its partnership with Christian mental health professionals:

First, *develop a Christlike heart of compassion.* Jesus amazed others by touching hurting people, even "untouchable" lepers. Strugglers in every conceivable area of human experience sit in the pews of every church. Church leaders will do well to avoid the kind of self-righteousness that says, "We have no problems like that in this church," but instead to humbly see their church as a cross section of the culture and of what it means to be human. We would encourage church members to roll up their sleeves, smell the reality of the stench of death at "Lazarus's tomb" (see John 11), and resolve to remove the stench through applying the healing touch of Christ. What a message it sends when churches are willing to give equal budgeting allocations, equipment, office space, and staff support to their "care ministries" department as they do to other ministries.

Second, *provide ministries and structures for the hurting.* Effective churches enlist lay leaders and mobilize them for compassionate ministry. This will lead churches toward becoming balanced churches, carrying out all the functions that are important biblically for eternal purposes. We believe that when churches show us their structure, we will see their heart. Is your church balanced or out of balance? Ask yourselves the following questions:

- Are you a *social* church — lots of bazaars, craft projects, and fellowship suppers?
- Are you an *evangelizing* church — lots of door-to-door witnessing, seeker services, and altar calls?
- Are you a *missions* church — lots of international maps in prominent places, speakers, fund-raising and awareness-raising drives, and short-term overseas projects?
- Are you a *teaching* church — lots of Bible studies, expository preaching, and Scripture memorization?
- Are you a *caring* church — lots of lay counseling, hospital visitation by laypeople, food and clothing drives, prison ministry, and freedom ministry? (See Appendix C for a sampling of the kinds of care ministries available at Crystal Evangelical Free Church.)

Third, *avoid viewing woundedness as unspiritual.* It's important for churches to develop compassion for brokenness rather than to treat it with shame and condemnation. We would urge churches to avoid fault-finding like that expressed by the disciples toward the man blind from birth: "Who sinned, this man or his parents?" (John 9:1) and to avoid calling emotional difficulties sin unless they are doubly sure they are; there may be biological reasons for emotional difficulties, as well as circumstances of abuse, poverty, and neglect foisted on individuals due to no sin of their own.

Fourth, *recognize the complex needs of clients as valid and worthy of professional help.* If churches cannot provide needed ongoing interventions, they should refer to qualified Christian counselors; at the same time they should develop referral sources for specific areas of professional assistance, both medical and psychological. When the church views itself as a partner with Christian counselors, not as an adversary, unity can occur with a common purpose of caring for those who hurt.

Fifth, and finally, *collaborate with genuinely Christian counselors.* Professional Christian counselors are committed to study and learn about the wide range of psychological problems, while sincere laypersons may be equipped in one specific area of spiritual intervention. Stephen ministers are equipped to provide prayer support, listening, and caring in a weekly structural format. Freedom Encouragers (those who are trained to take people through the "Steps to Freedom in Christ") provide three- to five-hour sessions. Marriage mentors can teach basic communication skills and be an example through positive role modeling. Persons who receive lay assistance at the church may need a more comprehensive approach, and a referral may be important. The science of psychology is relatively new, and sincere Christian counselors are committed to identifying harmful untruths, fads, and corrupt psychology, as well as to applying truths from Scripture in their work. The church can and should assist them in this process.

MODEL FOR INTEGRATION

The diagram on the next page (see Figure 10.1) illustrates one way to visualize the interrelationship between the church and the Christian counselor. Both the church and counselor work together to minister to the needs of individuals and families struggling with emotional and relational pain in their lives.

RESOLUTION AND SERVICE

In this model, a client with personal or spiritual conflict in his or her life contacts the local church or a Christian therapist — or both. In the church track, the contact person(s) identifies the need, such as assurance of salvation, feelings of inferiority, anxiety about the future, negative thought patterns, loneliness, or bitterness. An initial plan is instituted; this plan could involve a Freedom Appointment with the church's Freedom Ministry team as a baseline of spiritual freedom and resolution. In other cases, the church may address needs through involvement in a lay counseling assignment, through evangelism or discipleship experiences, or through referral to a support group within the church (for example, divorce recovery, grief and loss, and the like).

If a Freedom Appointment appears to be the best initial option, the ministry team and/or church contact person(s) will then consider the appropriateness of referral for ongoing growth and discipleship — perhaps to a church ministry for sanctification work in discipleship, to a Bible study group, to various support groups, to lay counseling, to involvement in personal service or ministry, to marriage mentoring, to an accountability relationship, or to other resources that are available. If the problems are more pervasive, long term, complex, or biological in nature, the client may be referred to a Christian professional practitioner.

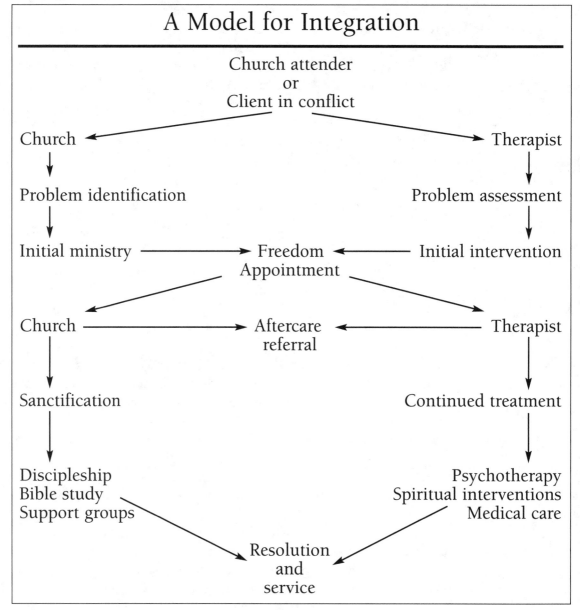

A Model for Integration

Church attender
or
Client in conflict

Church ← → Therapist

↓ ↓

Problem identification   Problem assessment

↓ ↓

Initial ministry ⎯→ Freedom ← ⎯ Initial intervention
Appointment

Church ⎯→ Aftercare ← ⎯ Therapist
referral

↓ ↓

Sanctification   Continued treatment

↓ ↓

Discipleship   Psychotherapy
Bible study   Spiritual interventions
Support groups   Medical care

Resolution
and
service

FIGURE 10.1

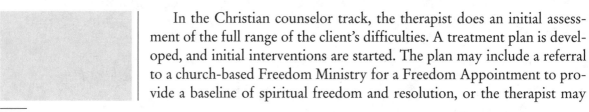

In the Christian counselor track, the therapist does an initial assessment of the full range of the client's difficulties. A treatment plan is developed, and initial interventions are started. The plan may include a referral to a church-based Freedom Ministry for a Freedom Appointment to provide a baseline of spiritual freedom and resolution, or the therapist may decide to incorporate various individual "Steps to Freedom in Christ" during the course of the counseling experience. If a Freedom Appointment does occur, the ministry team and/or therapist will make recommendations as to the modes of ongoing growth and discipleship. The client may be referred to church ministries for the many resources available but also may continue in a therapy relationship according to the treatment plan. In the latter case, the client may benefit from available psychotherapy modalities, some of which are outlined in the tool kit in chapter nine.

The ultimate goal is the client's spiritual and psychological health. Eventually, we want the client to be involved in a fruitful ministry where he or she can be actively serving others with internal peace and personal joy. Once the goals are accomplished, the client will be restored or introduced to full worship, prayer, praise, fellowship, ministry, and accountability in the local church.

The importance of the church community in this process cannot be overestimated, for it possesses such potent resources. There is nothing like the local church for strengthening persons in Christ. Paul says, "So then, just as you received Christ Jesus as Lord, continue to live in him, rooted and built up in him, strengthened in the faith as you were taught, and overflowing with thankfulness" (Colossians 2:6–7). The church functions in the role of "community counseling" because it offers an array of preventative, psychoeducational, and counseling interventions that seek to prevent mental health problems, promote positive mental health, and treat mental health problems through the various resources of the church community. In light of that definition, pastoral activities such as sermons, premarital counseling, educational groups, and even discipleship or Bible study groups might be legitimately considered community counseling.

In partnership with the church, professional counselors can confidently include referrals of clients to church-based "community counseling services" as an important part of the overall treatment or discharge plan. As the church and professional Christian counselor work in concert with each other, the body of Christ will be built up for service and ministry in the local community and the world.

HOW TO ESTABLISH A FREEDOM MINISTRY IN YOUR CHURCH

Terry and Julie's church (Crystal Evangelical Free Church in New Hope, Minnesota) has a well-established Freedom Ministry, which Julie oversees. In our experience this may be the best way for Christian therapists to work with their own church and other churches in the community. Crystal Evangelical Free Church has invited other churches to participate in its lay counselor training, and it networks with many other churches in the Minneapolis area. Ninety-five percent of its trained encouragers are laypeople who can lead people through the "Steps to Freedom in Christ." Equipping lay Christians must take place if we are to see our churches and ministries come alive, because there are not enough professional pastors or counselors in our country to help more than five percent of the population—even if that were the only thing pastors and counselors did. We must equip the saints to do the work of ministry if we are going to multiply ourselves.

Suppose your church carefully chose twenty people and trained them as outlined in Tables 10.1 and 10.2. Now suppose that each person agreed to help just one other person every other week. By the end of one year, your church would have helped 520 people—and the ministry would not stop there. These people who have been helped will become witnesses without even trying. Your church will become known in the community as the place that really cares for its people and communicates an answer for the problems of life. What kind of witness do Christians have if they are living in bondage? But if children of God are established alive and free in Christ, they will naturally (or, better to say, supernaturally) be a witness as they glorify God by bearing fruit. (Don't worry. Working *with* your church will not cut into your counseling business; it will greatly increase it. Terry and Julie are booked for months in advance.)

BASIC LEVEL AND ADVANCED LEVEL TRAINING OPPORTUNITIES

Freedom in Christ Ministries has developed the resources described in Tables 10.1 and 10.2 for training encouragers—including books, study guides, and tape series (both video and audio). The tape series all have syllabi that complement the teaching. The best training takes place when the trainees watch the videos, read the books, and complete the study guides. The study guides will greatly enhance the learning process and help trainees personalize and internalize the message. We recommend allowing a period of sixteen weeks for the basic training, which is divided into four-week segments. The basic training material is presented in the order in which it should be taught:

Basic Level Training

	First Four Weeks	Second Four Weeks	Third and Fourth Four Weeks
PURPOSE	To understand who we are in Christ, how we can walk by faith and win the battle for our minds, what our emotions are, and the means by which we relate to one another	To understand the nature of the spiritual world and to know the position, authority, protection, and vulnerability of the believer	To understand the theological foundations and the practical means by which we can help others find freedom in Christ with a discipleship/counseling approach
VIDEO/ AUDIO SERIES	"Resolving Personal Conflicts"	"Resolving Spiritual Conflicts"	"Discipleship Counseling" and "How to Lead a Person to Freedom in Christ"
READING	*Victory Over the Darkness* and *Victory Over the Darkness Study Guide*	*The Bondage Breaker* and *The Bondage Breaker Study Guide*	*Helping Others Find Freedom in Christ* and *Helping Others Find Freedom in Christ Study Guide.* This study guide details how your church can establish a discipleship/counseling ministry and provides answers for commonly asked questions.
YOUTH EDITION	*Stomping Out the Darkness* and *Stomping Out the Darkness Study Guide*	*The Bondage Breaker Youth Edition* and *The Bondage Breaker Study Guide*	*Leading Teens to Freedom in Christ*
SUPPLEMENTAL READING	*Living Free in Christ*: The purpose of this book is to establish us complete in Christ and to show how he meets our critical needs for identity, acceptance, security, and significance.	*Released From Bondage*: This book has chapter-length personal testimonies of finding freedom in Christ from depression, incest, lust, panic attacks, eating disorders, and the like, with explanatory comments by Neil Anderson.	*Daily in Christ*— a one-year devotional for individuals as well as families to use over the course of an entire year. Dave Park, Rich Miller, and Neil Anderson have completed four forty-day devotionals for youth: *Ultimate Love; Awesome God; Extreme Faith;* and *Reality Check.*

Basic Level Training

	First Four Weeks	Second Four Weeks	Third and Fourth Four Weeks
NOTES		*Breaking Through to Spiritual Maturity* is an adult curriculum for teaching the above material. *Busting Free* is the corresponding youth curriculum.	To successfully complete the basic training, trainees should also have gone through the "Steps to Freedom in Christ" with an encourager, have participated in two or more Freedom Appointments as a prayer partner, and be recommended by the director of the Freedom Ministry and meet the qualifications established by your church. Also it should be made clear that, although the basic training meetings are open to all who will make the time commitment, attendance at the seminars does not automatically qualify one to participate in the ministry.

TABLE 10.1

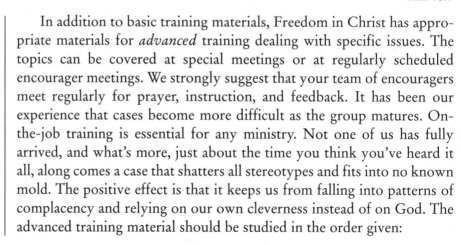

In addition to basic training materials, Freedom in Christ has appropriate materials for *advanced* training dealing with specific issues. The topics can be covered at special meetings or at regularly scheduled encourager meetings. We strongly suggest that your team of encouragers meet regularly for prayer, instruction, and feedback. It has been our experience that cases become more difficult as the group matures. On-the-job training is essential for any ministry. Not one of us has fully arrived, and what's more, just about the time you think you've heard it all, along comes a case that shatters all stereotypes and fits into no known mold. The positive effect is that it keeps us from falling into patterns of complacency and relying on our own cleverness instead of on God. The advanced training material should be studied in the order given:

Advanced Level Training

First Four Weeks	Second Four Weeks	Third Four Weeks
PURPOSE To discern counterfeit guidance from divine guidance, how to pray in the Spirit, and how to walk by the Spirit	**PURPOSE** To understand the culture our children are being raised in, what is going on in their minds, how to be the parent they need, and how to lead them to freedom in Christ	**PURPOSE** To understand how people get into sexual bondage and how they can be free in Christ
READING *Walking in the Light*	**VIDEO/AUDIO SERIES** "The Seduction of Our Children"	**READING** *A Way of Escape*
YOUTH EDITION *Know Light, No Fear*	**READING** *The Seduction of Our Children, The Seduction of Our Children Workbook,* and *Spiritual Protection for Your Children,* which includes "Steps to Freedom in Christ" for children	**YOUTH EDITION** *Purity Under Pressure*

Fourth Four Weeks (can include one of the following)

BOOKS AND VIDEO SERIES

Freedom From Addiction; Freedom From Addiction Workbook; and "Freedom From Addiction" video series

One Day at a Time is a 120-day devotional for those who have addictive behaviors. Subjects include the nature of substance abuse and how the bondage can be broken in Christ.

BOOKS AND VIDEO SERIES
The Christ Centered Marriage; The Christ Centered Marriage Study Guide; and
"The Christ Centered Marriage" video series

BOOK AND VIDEO SEMINAR
Finding Hope Again (overcoming depression) and "Finding Hope Again"
video seminar

BOOK AND AUDIOPAGES
Freedom from Fear (overcoming anxiety disorders) and *Freedom from
Fear* audiopages

BOOK AND STUDY GUIDE
The Common Made Holy (comprehensive study on sanctification,
explaining who we are in Christ and how we mature in Christ) and
The Common Made Holy Study Guide

TABLE 10.2

SCHEDULES FOR BASIC LEVEL TRAINING

A sixteen-week format would require meeting one night each week for two to three hours. Viewing two video lessons each night, it will take about twelve weeks to view the first three video series. The last four weeks you would use the "How to Lead a Person to Freedom in Christ" video. It has four segments, each one hour long. You would show one hour of the video each evening, which allows ample time for discussion. This schedule does not include much time for discussing the book or doing inductive studies of the content of the video series. A summary of the schedule is as follows:

Schedule for Basic Level Training: Sixteen-Week Format

Weeks 1-4	Weeks 5-8	Weeks 9-16
Resolving personal conflicts	Resolving spiritual conflicts	Spiritual conflicts and counseling, and how to lead a person to freedom in Christ

Two video lessons each night	Two video lessons each night, the last tape has the "Steps to Freedom in Christ," which can be done as a group in class or separately with an encourager	Two video lessons each night for four weeks, then one hour per night for four weeks	

TABLE 10.3

Another way to schedule basic training sessions is to present one video series on a Friday night/Saturday format each month. To do so would require only one facilitator to give one weekend each month—and you would still cover all the material in four weekends (The fourth session could be done just on a Saturday, using the video series "How to Lead a Person to Freedom in Christ." The schedule in Table 10.4 assumes that you will choose to do three Friday/Saturday sessions and one Saturday-only session.) There is generally less time for discussion of the videos in this schedule, but you could meet on another occasion each week to discuss the books and the inductive studies.

Schedule for Basic Level Training: Four-Weekend Format

Weekend #1	Weekend #2	Weekend #3	Weekend #4
Resolving personal conflicts	Resolving spiritual conflicts	Spiritual conflicts and counseling	How to lead a person to freedom in Christ
Friday night: video lessons 1-2; Saturday: video lessons 3-8	Friday night: video lessons 1-2; Saturday: video lessons 3-7 and the "Steps to Freedom in Christ"	Friday night: video lessons 1-2; Saturday: video lessons 3-8	Saturday: video series "How to Lead a Person to Freedom in Christ"

TABLE 10.4

323

All the above resources for basic and advanced training materials may be purchased from:

FREEDOM IN CHRIST MINISTRIES
491 EAST LAMBERT ROAD
LA HABRA, CA 90631
PHONE: (562) 691-9128
FAX: (562) 691-4035
E-MAIL ADDRESS: INFO@FICM.ORG
WEB SITE: WWW.FICM.ORG

11

Professional Accountability Relationships with Authority

"You hypocrites, why are you trying to trap me? Show me the coin used for paying the tax." They brought him a denarius, and he asked them, "Whose portrait is this? And whose inscription?" "Caesar's," they replied. Then he said to them, "Give to Caesar what is Caesar's, and to God what is God's." When they heard this, they were amazed. So they left him and went away.

MATTHEW 22:18–22

This well-known passage of Scripture regarding temporal and heavenly authority accurately pictures the dual nature of the professional accountability of a Christian counselor. Not only do we hold ourselves accountable to God and what he has to say in his Word, but we must also comply with secular expectations for professional conduct. Our first alliance is to God, but we must submit to the authority of the state as well. As the apostle Paul explains, "Everyone must submit himself to the governing authorities, for there is no authority except that which God has established. The authorities that exist have been established by God. Consequently, he who rebels against the authority is rebelling against what God has instituted" (Romans 13:1–2).

Counselors and legal experts George Ohlschlager and Peter Mosgofian explain why the responsibility for counselors' professional behavior is controlled by state licensure, certification, and registration statues: "The central justification by states for this regulatory scheme is protection of the public from incompetent and unethical clinicians and counselors."[1] However strongly Christian therapists may argue that secular regulation is unnecessary because God's law is our guiding directive, we must submit to the law of the land. This obligation applies to those who are formally licensed by the state to practice mental health as well as to lay ministry and pastoral counselors. Those who counsel from a lay ministry position, though not formally licensed, must follow the counseling and ethical guidelines established by the church with whom they are affiliated. Psychology professor Siang-Yang Tan, citing W. W. Becker, points out that a lay counselor "should also provide accurate and sufficient information on his or her qualifications, training, and values, as well as the process, goals, and possible consequences of counseling so that the client can make educated choices."[2]

Likewise, someone who is familiar with both biblical and secular requirements must offer adequate supervision of pastoral and lay counseling providers. That individual is called to balance the goal of the effective administration of the church (see Romans 12:4, 8; 1 Corinthians 12:27–29) with the biblical and legal mandate to protect the flock from harm (see Matthew 18:10–14). In this context, the "flock" would include both members and nonmembers who participate in a particular pastor's church fellowship.[3]

State regulation of pastoral counselors is still relatively uncommon at this point, but this present reality does not mean clergy liability is something to be ignored. The high visibility of the California case of *Nally v. Grace Community Church of the Valley* taught us that even Christian counseling in a church setting is subject to judicial accountability. Even though the ultimate outcome of that case was the protection of pastoral counseling from excessive malpractice liability, many people predict that the security of clergy counseling will decline.

Therefore, we need to be aware of the issues of dual accountability and make every effort to comply with both sets of standards. Competent Christian counseling requires familiarity with the mandates of God's law *and* the law of the state.

PROFESSIONAL AND CHRISTIAN ETHICS: THE VALUE OF INFORMED CONSENT

Just as accountability and liability issues are important considerations that exist in both the biblical and secular realms, so also do *ethical* considerations. There are always professional as well as biblical guidelines to process when we discuss a case at our staff conferences. While we acknowledge the different dimensions of ethical issues, to this day we have not had a conflict arise between the professional and ethical expectations of our licensing boards and our approach to the integration of

Christian and psychological counseling principles. We agree with and accept dual accountability, and we do not view biblical and secular perspectives as rivals. It is not necessary to pick between "the world" and Christ. In our view, Christian ethical principles include professional ethical standards. We agree with psychologist Alan Tjeltveit, who wrote:

> Christian ethics undergirds professional ethics, so a therapist engaged in professionally ethical behavior, (e.g., upholding clinical confidentiality) is engaged in fully Christian behavior. Although Christian ethics does sometimes limit the Christian's behavior, careful thinking and responsible professional behavior (especially centered around informed consent) will usually, though not always, result in a satisfactory resolution of dilemmas arising from conflicts between professional and Christian ethics.[4]

We have found that a careful discussion with our clients leading to their informed consent to work with us in the context and on the content we have described in their Individual Treatment Plan (ITP) has prevented conflicts between our Christian worldview and our professional code of ethical conduct. We stress with our clients our desire to avoid any hint of manipulation, not only because manipulation is disrespectful and unethical but also because change accomplished under any kind of false pretense is unlikely to last. Without thorough, clear, honest, and easily understandable discussion with the client regarding procedures and outcome goals of therapy, the potential for misunderstanding and causing disappointment for the client increases dramatically. Thus Dr. Tjeltveit states, "To avoid the peril, Christian mental health professionals need to act in concord with professional ethics and provide therapy fully informed by Christian ethics only when clients give their free, full, and informed consent."[5]

Although we have responsibilities to the state and its licensing boards, as well as to our employers, as Christians we must keep in mind that our primary allegiance is to the Lord and to the authority of the Bible. As psychologist Gary Collins has noted, "Christians who work in any field have a commitment and obligation to their secular employers or to their professions, but they have a higher commitment to their God."[6] Speaking from the perspective of a Christian military officer and psychologist, Dr. Richard Price states, "The most common temptation for me is to overvalue the approval of senior officers. When I do this, I lose sight of my primary allegiance to God. I think it is important for us as Christians in the military to show respect for our superiors — tempered with an inner awareness that our ultimate commander is Jesus."[7]

CHRISTIAN ETHICS AND THE UNSAVED CLIENT

An important consideration regarding the interface of secular and Christian ethical guidelines involves the issue of a presentation of the gospel to an unsaved client. There is a difference of opinion as to the acceptability of sharing the Good News of Jesus Christ as Savior in the context of a psychotherapy relationship. Those opposed to such a spiritual goal and procedure base their opinion largely on the issue of the unethical imposition of values on the client. As Alan Tjeltveit notes, the concern is that the therapist is "using coercive methods to indoctrinate or influence clients, especially concerning therapy session content that is not relevant to the disorder or problem being treated."[8] Addressing this issue, P. Scott Richards and Allen Bergin make the following observation:

> One form of religious value imposition occurs when therapists attempt to preach, teach, or otherwise persuade clients that their own particular religious or spiritual ideology, denomination, cause, or worldview is the most correct, worthwhile, moral, or healthy.... Such religious proselytizing is clearly unethical. Therapists should not use therapy as a vehicle for promoting their particular religious or spiritual ideology or cause.[9]

A different perspective is summarized by Siang-Yang Tan, who supports the suggestions of A. A. Nelson and W. P. Wilson:

> It is ethical for therapists to use or share their religious faith in therapy (a) if they are dealing with clinical problems that would be helped by spiritual or religious intervention, (b) if they are working within the client's belief system (as long as they do not impose their own religious values on the client), and (c) if they have carefully defined the therapy contract or informed consent agreement to include the use of religious or spiritual interventions and resources.[10]

We agree with this perspective, and when these parameters are in place, we proceed accordingly.

In our practice, the goal with clients is twofold. First, we desire to help Christian clients realize their freedom in Christ and become mature in their faith so they may become increasingly healthy, both mentally and spiritually. Second, for those who do not have a personal relationship with Jesus Christ, we hope eventually to have the opportunity to share the gospel, if we are given permission by the client to explain the issues of eternal life. The key word is *opportunity*. We do not intend to compel a salvation decision; that is a choice only the client can make with the help of the Holy Spirit. In this sense we agree with Allen Bergin, I. Reed Payne, and P. Scott Richards, who declare that there should be no indication whatsoever that therapists are applying pressure to convert the client to their own biblical perspective.[11] However, as we said before, we approach our counseling work from a biblical-Christian worldview not merely with the goal of alleviating symptoms of mental distress, but also with the deeper goal to give others the opportunity to come into a personal relationship with Jesus. We then help clients resolve conflicts in their struggles with the world, the flesh, and the devil. These ultimate goals do exist for us as therapists — and we address them in counseling when we are invited to do so by the client. When the specific conflicts for which counseling originated include a spiritual problem, and when a natural opening for the consideration of spiritual matters occurs, we proceed with a spiritual intervention.

DOCUMENTATION

Professional accountability is important for the Christian counselor. We should do all things heartily and with excellence (see Colossians 3:23). Every Christian therapist should exemplify integrity, honesty, forthrightness, and godly character. This responsibility is especially important with respect to the written and spoken words of a psychotherapist. The Lord spoke creation into existence (see Genesis 1:3 – 27; Hebrews 11:3). His Word is "God-breathed" (2 Timothy 3:16). Every word and punctuation mark in Scripture is intentional and crucial (Matthew 5:18). Thus, since we are to follow our Lord's example, we regard the written materials generated during the course of a counseling relationship as very significant. Even the omission, or addition, of a comma can completely alter the meaning of a sentence for or about a client.

Every therapist is tempted to see paperwork as busywork — annoying, frustrating, endless, seemingly irrelevant, time consuming, and unnecessary. While there are times when it is frustrating and does seem irrelevant and unnecessary, when it comes to professional documentation of services promised and services rendered, it can mean the difference between a successful counseling ministry and one that ends up in failure, between a legal authority making a judgment in your favor or against you. Paperwork is a visible trail that outside reviewers can use to verify actions taken or neglected, safeguards employed or abandoned, agreements sealed or not negotiated, values stated or left ambiguous, finances accounted for or mismanaged. The list can be endless. Psychologists Edward Zuckerman and Irvin Guyett note, "As therapists, our best defenses against malpractice are offering high quality and thoughtful care, rational and effective procedures, and the thorough documentation of our decisions and reasoning."[12] As the saying goes, "If it's not documented, it didn't happen."

As professionals in the marketplace of mental health practitioners, we need to let our lights shine as we follow Christ's example in all we do. It is true that God looks at the heart and not the outward appearance (see 1 Samuel 16:7), but this is not an issue of the heart. It concerns the manner in which we present ourselves to those in our culture as we "ply our trade." The psalmist implores God to examine him and see if there is any offensive way in him (see Psalm 139:24). We are to present ourselves so no one takes offense, for if others are offended, it would discredit the gospel that has been entrusted to us.

"BEST PRACTICES" IN DOCUMENTATION

The Christian professional counselor is responsible to produce documentation that is excellent. Several important areas will be delineated, although these are by no means exhaustive. Samples of many of these documents can be found in Appendix D.

1. *Professional brochure.* This well-designed and carefully crafted presentation should outline a practice's worldview as well as the credentials of the practitioner(s) and any specialty areas.

2. *Professional Counseling Agreement.* This document delineates the practice's business procedures and includes a statement announcing the worldview and differentiating it from others in our culture. The client signs this agreement after it has been verbally explained.

3. *Prayer in Session.* After discussion of the role of prayer in session, the therapist documents in the progress notes whether the client has agreed to this practice.

4. *Individual Treatment Plan (ITP).* Although the format will vary, all professional counselors must create a working document that describes the mental and physical condition of the client and outlines a plan for treating the impairments. As we have pointed out, Christian counselors typically add the dimension of a "religious diagnosis"[13] to their analysis of the client's condition. Documentation of therapy needs

and procedures is an ever-present reality to those who operate in a third-party payer environment. While frustrating to deal with at times, the current requirements for documentation of efficacy and course of therapy have done much to improve the quality of psychotherapeutic care provided by professional mental health practitioners. Intuitive or subjective formulations of a diagnosis and treatment plan are no longer adequate if a therapist desires insurance-based reimbursement for clinical services rendered. Psychologist Donald Wiger explains, "Effective documentation holds mental health professionals accountable for accurate diagnosis, concise treatment planning, case notes that follow the treatment plan, treatment reflecting the diagnosis, and documentation of the course of therapy."[14]

The particular format we use in our practice to meet the requirements for third-party documentation requirements is an *intake form* called the Individual Treatment Plan (ITP). An example is provided in Appendix D, and the reader is free to use as is or revise as desired. This form assists us in gathering the required information for evaluating and planning our work with a client. Traditional areas reviewed include a description of the presenting problem, any relevant past treatment history, a social and developmental history, a spiritual history, delineation of behavioral dysfunctions (impairments) that present the reasons the client requires psychotherapy, expression of outcome goals, and the objective criteria for discharge from treatment. The ITP is also useful when third-party payers request a prior authorization (P.A.) before approval for continued services is given.

Because there are a number of acceptable formats for meeting the documentation requirements of diagnosis and treatment planning, we won't go into detail on what to do when an intake interview is recorded. Readers are referred to the notes for resources in this area.[15]

Before the third session takes place, the manner in which the client's presenting problems are going to be handled is written on the ITP and subsequently discussed with the client. Some questions we typically ask, especially in the Treatment Goals section of the plan, include these:

- If counseling was really successful, and you got your money's worth from coming, what would happen? If we took a videotape of you in three months, what would look different or better?
- What do you think might prevent you from accomplishing your goals?

- What has not worked for you in the past? What has been particularly helpful?
- Who do you think would be most helpful to you if you are going to work on your goals, and how do you think they could help?
- What role, if any, has church played in your circumstances, either negatively or positively?
- Do you feel that your behavior and lifestyle are consistent with the values you profess?[16]
- Tell me your "wish list" for change. Then put it away for a couple of months before looking at it again. When you do, you'll know if we are making any progress.[17]

When appropriate, the Religious or Spiritual Problem V-Code (62.89) for disclosure of anticipated spiritual interventions is included, along with the other diagnoses, under Axis I (see discussion of the V-Code 62.89 in chapter 8). The client's signature is obtained, indicating that the ITP was discussed and that the client agrees with the therapist's recommendations.

5. *Rights and Information Sheet.* This form delineates the role expectations of both client and therapist in the treatment process. Confidentiality is explained, and the address of the appropriate licensing board is provided in the event that a grievance must be filed.

6. *Progress notes.* These are written during or shortly after a session with the client; these notes include both subjective and objective observations and assessments as well as the plan of action recommended for the period between the current session and the next. In our practice, some therapists use the SOAP (subjective, objective, assessment, plan) format for organizing session notes. The records of clinical contact help us organize our thoughts about a client, document provision of services, establish for the client a record of adaptive or maladaptive functioning (which may be useful if eligibility for a judgment of disability is ever needed), and ensure that we as therapists are complying with ethical guidelines.

As the therapy continues, these plans may be revised or new ones added. The plans in the progress notes relate to the overall Individual Treatment Plan but are much more detailed and specific. For instance, bibliotherapy may be recommended on the initial ITP, while the progress notes document the exact books or articles or portions of Scripture recommended for use as treatment progresses. Each session is dated, and the therapist initials or signs each note. In the notes it is helpful to use direct client quotes, such as, "I have been quite depressed lately and feel like giving up," as well as summary statements by the therapist, such as: "Jane rarely smiled during session and was wearing black clothing." Interpretations or clinical impressions of session content are kept to a minimum and are documented as such when entered in the chart.

7. *Day Sheet.* This form records the date of service, the service code for the treatment rendered, the number of sessions provided, the fee charged, and pertinent information about the type of payment being given, whether self-pay (fee-for-service) or insurance co-payment. This information must agree with the office billing information sent to the insurance company. The therapist keeps this day sheet in the client's chart and is responsible for keeping it current. It must also agree with the progress notes in terms of dates of service.

8. *Miscellaneous additional documents*

a. *Release of Information.* This document is signed by the client and an office "witness" whenever an individual (other than in-house supervisory/consultation persons) is given any information about client contact with the therapist. This document is crucial in protecting the confidentiality of client information, and it assures the client that he or she knows where any information about the counseling process is going.

b. *Informed Consent Agreement.* If counselors work with gay or lesbian clients to orient them to their biological gender identity, a separate informed consent sheet is necessary. The American Psychological Association has approved reparative therapy if it is mutually agreed to by the therapist and the client and if written consent is given; otherwise, this type of therapy is considered unethical in today's cultural state of affairs.

c. *Waiver.* This form is needed if sessions extend longer than one hour. In such cases the client agrees to pay a negotiated out-of-pocket fee for any therapy time beyond the initial insurance-covered session. The waiver is signed by the client, indicating agreement to this "out-of-plan" arrangement for each date of service. Doing so will protect the counselor should the client ever contest the out-of-plan time. Generally the managed care company isn't concerned, but using this form protects the counselor if the client becomes adversarial and maintains that he or she was not aware that insurance did not cover the session.

d. *Statement of Understanding for Freedom Appointments.* If you, as a professional, take part in a Freedom Appointment as a ministry volunteer through a church, be sure this Statement of Understanding is signed. The document states that you are a professional but in this case function only in a spiritual capacity and that the individual keeping the appointment understood this fact.

     e. *Parent/Minor Child Confidentiality Statement.* The prevailing ethic in our society is that minor children have no rights to privacy if parents choose to examine the chart of their child who is receiving treatment. While this is generally not a problem for the minor, there are instances in therapy when issues are disclosed that the child does not want the parents to know; there may also be important clinical issues the minor child will not discuss if it is believed the parents may learn about them.

     In our practice we take the initiative to address this potential dilemma by discussing this parent/minor child confidentiality form with the minor and the parents. We agree with professional counselor and pastor Charles Kollar that "limitations and exceptions to confidentiality need to be given careful consideration. Circumstances surrounding confidentiality are not always easily defined and discretion needs to be demonstrated."[18] In essence, then, the signatures of the therapist, the minor child, and the parents on this form grant permission to the therapist to use clinical judgment as to what is or is not shared with the parents. Attention to this issue in the early stages of therapy has proven most effective in dealing with the right to privacy and discovery on the part of the minor child and the parents.

     9. *Managed Care Documentation.* Required documentation varies from insurance company to insurance company. Complete all documentation required by managed care reviewers, using the language described in chapter six wherever appropriate. The majority of the time simply photocopying the Individual Treatment Plan is sufficient for most reviewers. Instead of recopying information, we attach the ITP to the insurance form and write "see attached copy" when items from the treatment plan will suffice.

CLINICAL COMPETENCY

     It isn't easy to get a handle on the issue of clinical competency, the last of the professional issues we'll address in this book. Standards and definitions vary from state to state, so a unified explanation is essentially impossible to provide; moreover, heated discussion often occurs when standards are set. Whether a standard is a *realistic* determinant of a limitation of competency or whether that standard is actually more of an *intrusive restriction* on therapeutic technique is not always unequivocal.

In a general sense, most mental health professional organizations will set guidelines to prohibit their practitioners from practicing outside the boundaries of identified areas of professional competence.[19] In our experience, however, these guidelines are generous and nonrestrictive. For example, as a psychologist in the state of Minnesota, Terry can declare the areas of his professional competency and register them with the Board of Psychology. Moreover, initial acceptance of submitted declarations of competency by that licensing agency is straightforward. However, if a complaint is filed against him in a particular area of competency, it would be his responsibility to defend the declaration of his competencies to the satisfaction of a peer review committee.

Considerable latitude for interpretation and application of these guidelines by the therapist remains. As a result of this ambiguity in understanding specific standards, the risk of malpractice allegations has risen steadily in recent years. With regard to pastoral provision of psychotherapy, for example, George Ohlschlager and Peter Mosgofian note that "unquestioned public confidence in the pastor as a counselor has eroded over the past thirty years, with a steady increase in the number of lawsuits against clergy in the last decade."[20]

Despite these limitations and ambiguities, it is indisputable that Christian counselors must be sure to obtain adequate training before spiritual counseling procedures are introduced into a session. At the same time a word of caution must be shared about the trap of deception regarding skills acquired in post-graduate education. As psychologist and professor Richard Butman points out, "Advanced degrees alone don't confer, nor does the process of credentialing or licensing necessarily guarantee, specific clinical skills and sensitivities."[21] Based on our review of the literature and our experience with fellow counselors, we have found that the training programs for many professional therapists are deficient in their provision of training in spiritual resources and therapy skills to be used in an integrated counseling setting. Happily, this gap is closing, as evidenced by the growing body of professional literature "that provides insight into the relationships among religion, spirituality, mental health, and psychotherapy."[22] A recently published manual for psychiatrists seeks "to enhance psychiatrists' ability to more adequately assess and address the religious/spiritual practices, beliefs, and attitudes as well as the influence of religious/spiritual factors on their patients' clinical status."[23]

Those Christian counselors who incorporate religious concepts and procedures into a therapy session must recognize their own particular strengths and weaknesses. Where clinical settings do not provide consultation in integration, continuing education and supervision should be pursued. Another source of valuable self-monitoring can come through participation in an accountability group of Christian colleagues. By doing so, we equip ourselves with increased skill and confidence, thereby benefiting our clients as well.

It's a sad truth that one advantage we receive when we pay attention to the boundaries of our clinical competencies is the *reduced risk of possible legal action.* As we've already stated, professional Christian counselors are accountable to God and to other people for their behavior in therapy. We must use "sober judgment" (Romans 12:3) and test our own actions (see Galatians 6:4) when we consider our suitability for providing Christian counseling. Psychologist George Ohlschlager comments on the teaching of Scripture: "In fact, Paul's instructions in Galatians are set in a helping context, indicating that humble self-assessment that respects the limits of one's abilities is essential to the task of restoring the erring brother or sister in Christ."[24] Writing about the challenges of ethical failure for a pastoral counselor, church leader Jim Smith put it well: "Ironically, the best defense against failing ethically in counseling is to remind myself daily that I am a fallible human being, with the same capacity for self-deception and hidden motivation as those who come to me for counseling."[25]

We've chosen to conclude this section on clinical competency, and this chapter on professional accountability, by sharing the "Ten Guidelines for Improving the Competence of Christian Counselors," written by psychology professor Richard Butman. We've listed only the summary of each guideline, and the reader is urged to review the detailed discussion in the reference listed in the notes.

1. Seek rigorous training in one of the major mental health disciplines.
2. Become exposed to diversity in initial training and beyond.
3. Make a commitment to careful supervision and regular consultation.
4. Pursue legitimate credentials and professional licensure.
5. Develop good treatment plans and use them as a basis for peer review.

6. Regularly participate in continuing education.
7. Understand and use Scripture wisely.
8. Develop a strong link with a local church.
9. Become actively involved in a support group of Christians who are not therapists.
10. Take up the challenge of personal and spiritual growth.[26]

SPIRITUAL CONFLICT INTEGRATION IN PSYCHOTHERAPY: A PERSONAL TESTIMONY

JUDITH KING, M.S.W., A.C.S.W.

Judith King is a social worker in private practice in Grand Rapids, Michigan. She has been integrating Neil Anderson's "Steps to Freedom in Christ" in her private counseling practice for several years. Based on this experience, she shares in this article her impressions and integrations. We've also included the research Judith is conducting concerning the effectiveness of this spiritual approach in resolving the conflicts clients present.

INTRODUCTION

Over the past few years I've had the privilege of learning the value of Dr. Neil Anderson's "Steps to Freedom in Christ" from three different perspectives. First, as a therapist in private practice I have been actively integrating the Steps with clients in the professional therapy setting. It has been a continual learning process. God encourages us to ask for his wisdom; I have done so as I have sought to integrate this material into individual sessions in a variety of ways with over a hundred clients. I'm thankful that in my counseling sessions I have seen many people healed and set free by Jesus' healing power. I have experienced the truth of James 1:5: "If any of you lacks wisdom, he should ask God, who gives generously to all without finding fault, and it will be given to him."

The second area of my experience relates to the research I have conducted and am still conducting with an increasing sample of people who have been led through the seven Steps by lay counselors in area churches. These lay counselors received training prior to and during Dr. Anderson's "Living Free in Christ" conference. A brief questionnaire was initially given to about eighty persons going through the Steps with local lay counselors. The questionnaire is a checklist for symptom pathology — a self-rated scale measuring depression, anxiety, tormenting thoughts, or voices, and habits over which we have little control, on a scale from one to ten. People are also asked to rate levels of inner conflict or distress, daily functioning skills, tools of spiritual warfare, the reality of God in their life, the quality of their devotional life, and their experience of Christian fellowship.

Two to three months after the initial appointment, participants were sent the same questionnaire and asked to rate themselves again. A sample of sixty-eight people responded to the follow-up questionnaires, with results that were really quite astounding but not surprising to me, since I have personally seen the results of the Steps work with many people. They are as follows (see Table A.1):

Follow-up Results on Self-rated Scale

Complaint	Average Improvement
Depression	47%
Anxiety	44%
Tormenting thoughts or voices	58%
Uncontrolled habits	43%
Inner conflict or distress	51%

TABLE A.1

I made no attempt to isolate or correlate individual-specific problems. Thus, a forty-seven percent improvement in manifesting the symptom of depression seems even more remarkable, since some of the counselees may not have even been previously depressed. It's interesting to note that the greatest help from the Steps was in the area of tormenting thoughts or voices, a fifty-eight percent improvement.

Of course, we must keep in mind that this is soft, subjective, merely descriptive data—it represents just a beginning attempt to get some indications about outcomes. Over the last year, several of the centers in our area have continued to use the questionnaire. If the recipients of the Freedom Appointment were organized according to the presenting problem, and the results tabulated accordingly, our study would undoubtedly be more solid. We did not do this in the preliminary study above; each was tabulated as an average improvement overall. It would be helpful to conduct a double-blind study with a larger "n." Expanding and implementing the research nationally would give us the larger sample; however, the notion of a control group with a placebo effect is another challenge—one we will need to address.

Based on my experience and the results of this research, I recommend using Dr. Anderson's Steps as a therapeutic spiritual tool. It is proving to be helpful for the Christian therapist who wants to integrate prayer into the therapeutic process, resolve root issues, and eliminate any spiritual interference. It also provides the client with a spiritual tool for ongoing maintenance of spiritual health and freedom.

The third perspective is from my experience as a consultant to other therapists. Here I think particularly of the time I was asked to lead another therapist's client—a woman on permanent mental disability (diagnosis of DID—Dissociative Identity Disorder)—through the "Steps to Freedom in Christ" in one session. In this case, the client's therapist and another therapist sat in as prayer partners during the entire session that lasted for seven hours.

As fellow members of the body of Christ, we are challenged to call on the name of Jesus Christ, who is our liberator and our source of power, and to ask him to walk beside us as we seek to help our clients. I find Isaiah 42:6–7 especially meaningful as I ponder our mission: "I, the LORD, have called you in righteousness; I will take hold of your hand. I will keep you and will make you to be a covenant for the people and a light for the Gentiles, to open eyes that are blind, to free captives from prison and to release from the dungeon those who sit in darkness." I believe this is what we are called to do in our professions as servants of Jesus Christ. Dr. Anderson's approach to spiritual conflict integration has been helpful to me as I've sought to fulfill this mission.

NEIL ANDERSON'S WORLDVIEW

Most readers will believe, as I do, in the importance of addressing the spiritual components of our clients. We believe there is a connection between the body, soul, and spirit, and we work with these issues in many ways. There are, of course, many questions that arise: Should we leave the spiritual component to pastors and chaplains? What about spiritual warfare and the demonic? More and more we are seeing clients who have been involved in New Age religions and occult activities. There is a hunger for spiritual reality in our world as never before.

There is abundant scriptural basis to support Dr. Anderson's approach, and I do not hesitate to teach these Scriptures to my clients where appropriate. As Christians, we are in a spiritual battle, and we must possess the spiritual armor and weapons to fight against the enemy:

> Your enemy the devil prowls around like a roaring lion looking for someone to devour. Resist him, standing firm in the faith.
>
> —*1 Peter 5:8–9*

> Submit yourselves, then, to God. Resist the devil, and he will flee from you.
>
> —*James 4:7*

> The weapons we fight with are not the weapons of the world. On the contrary, they have divine power to demolish strongholds.
>
> —*2 Corinthians 10:4*

> Put on the full armor of God so that you can take your stand against the devil's schemes.
>
> —*Ephesians 6:11*

Part of this armor is the truth, which can come against the lies of the enemy. Another weapon in our spiritual arsenal is forgiveness. We are admonished to forgive "in order that Satan might not outwit us" (2 Corinthians 2:11). Truth and forgiveness form the foundation for the seven "Steps to Freedom in Christ."

Spiritual Warfare: The Enemy's Deception

God   **Satan**

Equal & Opposite
forces?

NO!
(That's the lie, the
deception of the enemy)

FIGURE A.1

Spiritual Warfare: The Reality

FIGURE A.2

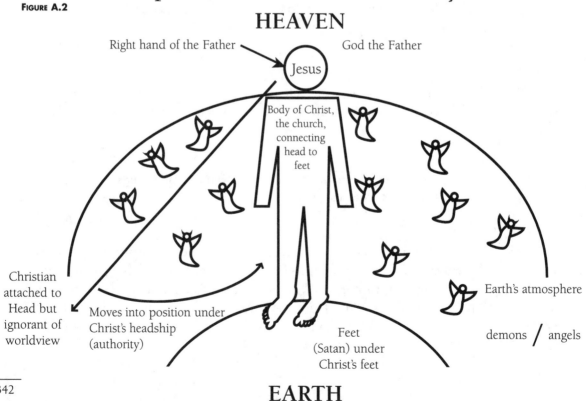

HEAVEN

Right hand of the Father   God the Father

Jesus

Body of Christ,
the church,
connecting
head to
feet

Christian
attached to
Head but
ignorant of
worldview

Moves into position under
Christ's headship
(authority)

Feet
(Satan) under
Christ's feet

Earth's atmosphere

demons / angels

EARTH

Renowned British apologist C. S. Lewis says in *The Screwtape Letters* that the devil would like us to believe one of two extremes: either that he does not exist at all, or that he exists under every bush. Both of these positions keep us from dealing with the problem in a wholistic, balanced way.

INTEGRATION OF DR. ANDERSON'S WORLDVIEW IN MY THERAPY

I use simple drawings to illustrate two different conceptions of our relation to God and Satan (see Figures A.1 and A.2 on previous page).

Many people believe the misconception that God and Satan are equal and opposite forces by which we are pulled back and forth. This teaching is a lie and a deception of the enemy.

In fact, Jesus sits at the right hand of the Father interceding for us (see Romans 8:34). Jesus' death on the cross has overcome all the works of the enemy, and all things are under his feet (see Ephesians 1:19–23). We, as we realize our identity in Christ, are the body of Christ and have a position in spiritual places, in the heavenly realms (see Ephesians 2:6). If we are lined up correctly under the headship of Christ, if we, the body, are attached to him, the Head, then Satan is under our feet in the name of Jesus. It is only in the name of Jesus and in our position in Christ that we have this authority and thus have the power to fight the enemy in the spiritual warfare that is a part of every Christian's life (see Ephesians 6:10–18).

THERAPEUTIC ADVANTAGES OF THE "STEPS TO FREEDOM IN CHRIST"

The Steps provide a useful tool for therapist and client to address this reality of spiritual warfare. It is a comprehensive inventory to identify the various strongholds that are keeping people in bondage. Each Step examines a different issue or potential stronghold.

As I have used the Steps in my work, I've discovered many positive therapeutic advantages:

- The Steps encourage personal responsibility; the client is responsible to do the work, not the therapist for the client (akin to William Glasser's Reality Therapy).
- The Steps empower the client (akin to Cognitive-Behavioral Therapy).

- The Steps point to the healing power of Jesus Christ, which is accessed through confession, prayer, forgiveness, and the granting of salvation (see James 5:16). Because the Word of God is the foundation on which the Steps are built, there is great power in the use of these Steps.
- The Steps help strengthen the client's personal identity and sense of worth.
- The Steps help solidify object constancy and boundaries.
- The Steps help build up a client's faith.
- The Steps help the client quickly identify defense mechanisms.
- The Steps open the way for a spiritual inventory that will identify problem areas quickly.
- The Steps provide a comprehensive tool that encompasses all areas of life and can be readily utilized in psychotherapy, with an expectation that comprehensive disclosure and subsequent healing will take place.
- The Steps help the client make verbal renunciations and thus solidify the healing.
- Because of the structured approach in the "Steps to Freedom in Christ," the session can be rather easily controlled — a great comfort for the therapist who is inexperienced or reluctant to confront the demonic.

CASE STUDIES

In my experience of integrating the Steps into the therapeutic setting, I have found that the process can differ from client to client, especially as it relates to issues of when to introduce the Steps, how much to try to accomplish in a session, when to slow down and explore more deeply, and in what order the Steps should be used. In all of these areas we need the guidance of the divine Counselor (see John 14:16) — the Holy Spirit. Some people may go through the Steps in two to three sessions; others may take months. Some of my case studies include

- problems of addictions (sexual, alcohol, and drugs)
- eating disorders
- severe to mild depressions
- severe to mild anxiety disorders
- issues of unresolved rage

- stress
- burnout in professional caregivers
- compulsive disorders
- Dissociative Identity Disorders
- character pathology
- victims of abuse, including occult abuse

POTENTIAL DIFFICULTIES

I have encountered some difficulties as I have used the "Steps to Freedom in Christ" in my practice. There is the possibility of regression if you move too quickly. The session *must* be orchestrated by the Holy Spirit; when God is there, he shows you what to do and when to do it. Some clients need a great deal of relationship building and other types of healing before getting into the Steps. It is also important to assess the level of ego strength in a particular client. In these situations we tread gently, always using our therapeutic skills in partnership with the Holy Spirit.

BASIC PREMISES

In order for the therapist to utilize the Steps as effective tools, there are two foundational premises that must be understood and accepted:

First, if someone opens up himself or herself to the oppression of the enemy, giving place to the devil through dabbling in the occult — even if done innocently or merely out of curiosity — or through continued patterns of unconfessed sin (bitterness, unforgiveness, sexual immorality, rebellion), demonic spiritual entities have somehow attached themselves to this person to torment him or her and feed him or her lies. The influence of these entities can cause many physical and emotional symptoms. The solution is confession and renunciation on that individual's part, with the result that an actual spiritual entity leaves the person and he or she becomes free from this demonic control. This result is based on the individual's identity as a professing Christian, as one who is united with Christ, who has already defeated the enemy through his work on the cross. I have seen these results time and time again with well-integrated, Bible-believing Christians; there is a visible change that can be seen and felt. Something is there, it is commanded in the name of Jesus to leave, and it leaves, to be disposed of by the Lord himself.

Second, ingrained strongholds and patterns of thought can continue to defeat Christians, robbing them of their victory in Christ on a practical, daily level. This premise seems less overt than the previous case, but it may be the same phenomenon; at any rate, it seems a bit more subtle. These people have been listening to lies about themselves and others, directly fed to them by the enemy. If a person continues to listen to and accept the lies of the enemy, then no amount of therapy will help. The lies must be recognized as coming from Satan, and they must be renounced. When lies are recognized, exposed, and renounced, the enemy's influence is halted. The key is to recognize the lie. The enemy is the deceiver par excellence. He does not show himself outfitted with horns and a red cape, but his methods are pure deception. If we believe that a thought or idea is coming from our own mind or even from God but it is really a lie from the enemy, then the deception is complete. I counsel people to listen to their thoughts and to judge if those thoughts are truths or lies; this is what we are instructed to do in taking captive every thought to make it obedient to Christ (see 2 Corinthians 10:5).

STRATEGY FOR USE

I have developed a strategy that I generally follow in using the Steps in therapy, but each therapist will need to figure out what is comfortable and workable. Remember that clients come to us for therapy, not for the "Steps to Freedom in Christ." The Steps are a tool we use in therapy as appropriate. My customary procedure is as follows:

1. Establish a trusting therapeutic relationship.
2. Hear the client's story and take a brief social history.
3. Make a clinical diagnosis and assess the degree of ego strength. A client must be motivated for change and possess a reasonably intact ego. A severely abused client must be taken through the Steps very slowly. A fragile ego usually needs more work within the therapeutic relationship.
4. Assess for medical needs and consider whether medical intervention is necessary. Sometimes the decision is made to hold off on medication until after the Steps have been completed; the outcome will depend on the degree of organic dysfunction and the presenting level of distress.

5. Introduce the idea of the Steps at an appropriate time, as the Lord leads. Have the client read the books *Victory Over the Darkness* and *The Bondage Breaker*. Give the client a Steps booklet to read and review at home. I instruct the client to put the book or booklet aside until the time of the appointment if it becomes too distressing.

6. Schedule a two-hour appointment if possible in which to work on the Steps.

7. Start each session with the beginning Prayer and Declaration (see Appendix E).

8. Finish each session with the Daily Prayer in the Steps or the Doctrinal Affirmation (see Appendix E).

9. Make notes of issues to explore further in therapy, or as the Lord leads continue to work on a particular issue in the midst of the Steps, incorporating inner healing.

10. Eventually complete all of the Steps. (Sometimes people can gain enough benefit from working through the Steps on their own at home.)

11. Encourage the client to take personal responsibility to maintain his or her own spiritual health and freedom by using the Steps as a way of doing an ongoing spiritual inventory. I believe it would be beneficial for every one of my clients to go through this experience in some way as part of my intervention repertoire for them. I have come to understand that if a client is suffering from demonic oppression, a spiritual solution is necessary; a spiritual problem requires a spiritual intervention. As therapy progresses, individual issues can be sorted out, lies identified and resisted, traumas healed, and truth embraced.

APPENDIX B

THE ROLE OF PSYCHIATRY IN MANAGED CARE

STEPHEN KING, M.D.

Stephen King is a practicing psychiatrist in Grand Rapids, Michigan. Prior to coming to Grand Rapids, Dr. King served as a missionary doctor and then went on to complete his residency in psychiatric medicine.

INTRODUCTION

The words "I would like you to see a psychiatrist," when spoken by a family doctor, a counselor, or a pastor, evoke feelings of fear, dread, and failure for many people. One is only referred to a psychiatrist, so the thinking goes, when one is "crazy,' a "total basket case," or needs to be admitted to an insane asylum. Such are some of the misconceptions of the role the psychiatrist plays on the mental health team. The images of a man or woman lying on a couch, session after session, replaying dreams to a blank-screen bearded male muttering, "Very interesting," long stays in locked units in aging hospitals, truth serums, straitjackets, and aides in white coats are by and large ancient history in the field of psychiatry. Unfortunately, these are still the images many people have when they think of seeing a psychiatrist.

WHAT IS PSYCHIATRY?

Psychiatry is the medical branch of behavioral health care. A psychiatrist is a medical doctor (M.D. or D.O.) with specialized training and expertise in the neurological and psychological problems of human beings. Most psychiatrists, like other professionally trained counselors, are trained in a bio/psycho/social model of human development and life experience. Many psychiatrists, if they are Christians, would add a *spiritual* dimension to their understanding of what makes us healthy and well-adjusted individuals; some would also investigate why clients are not functioning spiritually in a healthy way.

Psychiatry of the 1980s and 1990s has elected to sink its roots into the medical model and concentrate mostly on the biological aspects of the bio/psycho/social/spiritual paradigm, leaving other professional disciplines such as psychology, sociology, pastoral care, and theology to examine and enlarge our therapeutic understanding of the other spheres of human functioning. God is a trinity (three in one), and he has created humans as trinities — spirit, mind, body — three entities that make up a unified whole. If there is any malfunction in any one area, the whole entity suffers and does not function to its fullest capacity. The role of the psychiatrist is to address the *body* part of the whole, that is, the physical, organic, biological parts and how this functioning or malfunctioning relates to the well-being of the whole person.

Psychiatry, like all branches of science and medicine, is constantly changing and gaining new knowledge for the relief of human suffering and pain. Just as the treatment of cancer and heart disease has radically progressed in the last twenty to thirty years, psychiatric care has similarly advanced into an age of greater enlightenment and understanding. Most mental and emotional illnesses are now treated on an outpatient basis, with minimal use of hospital stays. Even in situations of extreme loss of impulse control in which danger to self or others is present, hospital stays are relatively brief and predominantly crisis-oriented.

The dominant theory in modern psychiatry is that human behaviors and adaptive functioning or malfunctioning are biochemically based, with neurochemical imbalance in certain brain areas causing symptoms and resulting illness. Thus, symptoms of anxiety, depression, insomnia, irrational thinking, mood swings, and the like can be traced to a deficiency in the brain cells of important chemicals such as serotonin, dopamine, and norepinephrine. Modern medications are prescribed to remedy these deficiencies or imbalances as specifically as possible in order to relieve the symptoms of the illness. Unfortunately, brain chemistry research is still in the early stages and not as precise as would be desired. On a clinical level, medical labs cannot measure and analyze

The Role of Psychiatry in Managed Care

brain chemicals (such as is possible with blood sugar, cholesterol, and the like), so the psychiatrist cannot pin down the neurochemical status with specific accuracy.

STRATEGIES IN PSYCHIATRIC TREATMENT

Despite these limitations, modern psychiatry has much to offer the present-day emotional sufferer. Indeed, most of the medications used today have only been available in the last twenty years, many in the last five to ten years. All the new antidepressants (for example, Prozac, Zoloft, Paxil, Celexa, Serzone, Effexor, Remeron), antipsychotics (for example, Clozaril, Risperdal, Zyprexa, Seroquel), and mood stabilizers (for example, Depakote, Tegretol, and others) are all relatively recent interventions to control behavioral distress and alleviate symptoms.

The psychiatrist is the mental health team member who is responsible to evaluate the overall physical status of the patient. Not all cases of abnormal behavior, such as anxiety and depression, are caused by faulty brain chemistry, traumas to the psyche, or insults and assaults on the spirit. Behavioral symptoms secondary to many other organic etiologies must be ruled out by screening for thyroid and other metabolic dysfunctions, anemia and other blood diseases, brain lesions, medication side effects, and neurological illnesses. A psychiatrist will either complete or make a referral for completion of a thorough physical and neurological examination, with appropriate laboratory and X-ray tests as indicated, before medications specific to the behavioral symptoms are prescribed.

Most referrals to psychiatrists such as myself come from excellent clinical therapists. They may have conducted a number of therapeutic sessions dealing with psychological and spiritual issues — with various spiritual, cognitive, and behavioral interventions compassionately given. Their clients may now have been referred because the following symptoms have not abated: panic attacks, obsessions, compulsions, constant worry, inner agitation, depression, irritability, low energy, reduced motivation and pleasure, reduced concentration, or sleep and appetite changes. Quite possibly, these symptoms could be lingering because of a biochemical cause that has not been remedied by psychological or spiritual interventions.

I often use the analogy of a runner participating in a race while wearing a plaster cast on his leg. He's still in the race, running to the best of his ability, but he cannot keep up due to the weight and hindrance of the cast. Another analogy is that God has given us an eight-cylinder brain, but we sometimes function on just five or six cylinders. We can still make forward movement on the highway of life, but we cannot push it up to the speed limit and we struggle to go up hills that used to pose no problem whatsoever. In both illustrations, the person hasn't quit functioning but is working under a handicap that may be able to be medically corrected. Many times this is where appropriate medications fit in, namely, to balance the brain chemistry back to normal functioning, thus overcoming the physically constraining handicap and releasing the person back into the flow of life with full efficiency.

Many Christians have difficulty giving themselves permission to take a pill to help them feel or function better. They may struggle with the guilt of not having enough faith or of having weak faith or with the fear that they'll let God down by choosing a more passive, "secular" route to healing rather than by choosing to tough out their suffering — relying on God's grace and growing through their misery and turmoil. God must have a reason for this, they reason, and they don't want to disobey him or go against his plan for their life. These same people see no conflict with God's will when they wear corrective eyeglasses for visual defects, visit a dentist for tooth problems, or take antibiotics for a strep infection (or an aspirin for a headache). God is a *healing* God who has made our physical body to heal itself in many situations. Research and science are truth-seeking endeavors with the goal of making the broken whole and the crooked straight. All medications prescribed by a physician attempt to relieve some type of suffering or dysfunction in order to provide healing. God is at work in the healing process — whether through physical (medication, electroconvulsive therapy, and the like), psychological (counseling therapy), or spiritual (prayer, deliverance interventions, and the like) pathways to wholeness.

Certainly, with the newer antidepressants, there is nothing to lose when a trial seems indicated. These medications are safe in all ways: There are few if any side effects (minor, if any); the medications are not habit forming or addicting, and they are compatible with other medications. If a chemical imbalance is present, within several weeks the person will feel remarkably better and be functioning in keeping with his or her usual productive norm. If the symptoms were *not* biochemically induced, no harm will have been done; it is a "trial and see," not a "trial and error." Unfortunately, because we cannot measure an individual's brain chemistry profile to determine which, if any, neurochemicals are low or deficient, our selection of specific medications still is undertaken under somewhat of a trial basis. The first choice of medication is not always the right one for a particular person. A second, or third, antidepressant with a known but different mechanism of action (serotonin versus norepinephrine versus dopamine) can be tried, often with very definite and favorable results.

The medications that a psychiatrist uses (psychotropics, or drugs that act on the mind) basically fall into four groups or classes:

A. Antianxiety
   1. Sedatives: Valium, Xanax, Ativan, Klonopin, Librium (mainly benzodiazepine derivatives)
   2. Hypnotics: Halcion, Restoril, Ambien (better known as sleeping pills; note that both sedatives and hypnotics are meant for short-term use and can lead to habituation and dependence)
   3. Long-term anxiolytic: Buspar (similar to antidepressants; acts slowly, depends on a blood-level concentration, and is nonhabituating)
B. Antidepressants
   1. Older types
      a. Tricyclics: Elavil, Tofranil, Norpramine, Sinequan (possess nuisance side effects and can be lethal in overdose)
      b. Monoamine Oxidase Inhibitors (MAOIs): Nardil, Parnate (need diet and other medication compliance due to potential hypertensive reactions)
   2. Newer types:
      a. Selective Serotonin Reuptake Inhibitors (SSRIs): Prozac, Zoloft, Paxil, Luvox, Celexa (affect the neurochemical serotonin almost exclusively)
      b. Norepinephrine and dopamine reuptake inhibitors (NDRIs): Wellbutrin (dopamine

reuptake inhibitor that has little effect on
serotonin)

   c. Others: Remeron (norepinephrine and
serotonin); Effexor (norepinephrine and
serotonin); Serzone (mixed systems
with serotonin)

C. Mood Stabilizers:

   1. Older Types: Lithium

   2. Newer Types: Depakote, Tegretol
(these two are originally antiseizure
medications; more potential side effects,
blood levels must be closely monitored,
and these medications are more
complicated to manage)

D. Antipsychotics:

   1. Older types: Thorazine, Mellaril, Stelazine,
Haldol, Navane (they have many side effects,
especially neuromuscular, and there is concern
over long-term use)

   2. Newer types:

      a. Clozaril (the only medication requiring a
weekly blood test — a complete blood
count, or CBC)

      b. Zyprexa, Risperdal, Seroquel (fewer side effects,
easier to tolerate)

A treatment used exclusively in psychiatry is electroconvulsive therapy (ECT), a mode of treatment that began in the 1930s, several decades before medications were used in psychiatry. ECT is reserved for severe mood disorders, primarily depressions that do not respond to medications or other treatment interventions. Properly administered, it is safe and has no long-term complications. In many cases, it can help to save lives and work wonders in a patient's recovery. Like medication, it brings improvement gradually (over the course of one to two weeks). It is not a cure for depression, which frequently is a recurrent illness and may be present in the client episodically.

This is a brief overview of the role of a psychiatrist in the mental health treatment team—a role that has become more focused and defined in recent years. Ongoing research and the development of new knowledge and greater understanding of brain function have led to safer and more patient-friendly medications.

Care Ministries Within the Church

The following is one particular church's approach to a full-orbed care ministry. This church targets eleven ministry areas for meeting people's needs in a loving way and pointing them to Jesus, the great Physician and Healer.

In Times of Special Need...

We stand together as the Crystal Evangelical Free Church Family. Care Ministries provides a response in times of personal stress with the following Christ-centered ministries:

Counseling Assessment and Referral

One session of biblically based consideration of difficulties being experienced by individuals, couples, and families in our church family.

Disability Ministries

Offering fellowship and encouragement for adults and children with developmental, physical, or emotional disabilities.

Focus Groups

A variety of ongoing and short-term groups targeting specific areas of need and interests, such as addictions, divorce, chronic illness, weight loss, and the like.

Freedom Ministry

Appointments arranged for individuals wanting to solidify their identity in Christ and to achieve freedom from spiritual bondages.

Funeral Arrangements

Assisting Crystal Church families with church service, food reception, and as a funeral home liaison when experiencing the loss of a loved one.

Health Ministry

Providing education, wellness screening, and referrals for persons with health questions.

Hospital Care

Providing Crystal Church families personal visits, flowers, and cards when hospitalized.

Prayer Chain

Confidential prayer support for both your immediate family and the larger Crystal Church family.

Senior Adult Ministries

Providing ministry opportunities, fellowship, and outreach to older adults.

Stephen Ministry

One-on-one confidential personal support and encouragement for the trying seasons of life.

Times of Financial Crisis

Lord's Pantry for groceries; Care and Love Offering for severe financial emergencies; Cup of Cold Water for maintenance and repair; confidential financial counseling.

PROFESSIONAL FORMS

This appendix contains a variety of forms that should prove helpful in your practice of Christ-centered therapy. We use many of these forms in our professional practice. You may wish to adapt some of the content and format to fit your own particular needs and circumstances.

Professional Counseling Agreement

For the services rendered by_____at *Pathways* Psychological Services, P.A. ("PPS"), I agree to pay all debts for testing, counseling sessions, and other customary charges in accordance with the terms set below.

1. I acknowledge that each 50-minute counseling session will cost $_____. Initial intake sessions will cost $_____.

2. I agree to pay my co-payment, or my deductible, or my fee-for-service charge *before each appointment begins.*

3. I understand that I am personally responsible to know my insurance limits, exclusions, deductibles, and co-payment structures, even though support staff does a preliminary check. I do not hold PPS responsible for insurance company errors or refusals for reimbursements for services rendered. *I understand I am responsible for all services for which my insurance company will not pay.*

4. *I agree to reimburse PPS in full for any session which I cancel or reschedule without 24 hours notice or for which I fail to arrive.* (Insurance companies will not pay for late cancellations or missed appointments.) I understand that if I miss two or more sessions without giving 24 hours notice, PPS and my therapist reserve the right to terminate our therapy relationship by letter or phone call. I also understand that if I am 20 or more minutes late to my counseling sessions two or more times, my therapist or PPS reserves the right to terminate our therapy relationship by letter or phone call.

5. I understand that at no time will an outstanding co-pay or fee-for-service balance of more than $_____ be allowed and that therapy may be temporarily suspended or terminated until sufficient payment is received to place my outstanding balance below this amount.

6. I understand that a collection agency may be employed after my account becomes 60 days past due with the express purpose of collecting any past-due debts that I might owe PPS. I also understand that other reasonable legal action may be taken to secure my payment. I agree to pay for collection costs, including attorney fees and costs, and to release the information needed to collect my past-due bill.

7. I understand that payment for any psychological/legal report prepared is due in full *before* it will be released to me or another party.

8. I understand that my case may be discussed in group supervision for assessment, diagnosis, and evaluation of treatment and progress.

9. I understand that all counseling is values-based, and that among the many values options available, such as secular, humanist, atheist, agnostic, New Age, Eastern, and the like, PPS counselors represent the Christian perspective. Their counseling approach will reflect this values perspective, such as prayer, biblical references and principles, and the spiritual disciplines, and I agree that this approach is acceptable.

10. In the event that the undersigned therapist reasonably believes that I am a danger, physically or emotionally, to myself or another person, I specifically consent for the therapist to warn the person in danger and to contact the following persons, in addition to medical and law enforcement personnel.

11. I have read the above and understand its contents. I agree to abide by the provisions set forth above. I have been given a copy of "Client's Rights and Information," and I agree to read this information before my next counseling session, if I have not already done so.

_____   _____   _____
Client Signature   Therapist   Date

Professional Counseling Agreement   Revised 03/27/00

Mission Statement

Pathways Psychological Services seeks to provide excellent counseling from the Christian perspective to clients in diverse settings by innovative, committed therapists in partnership with the local church and community. *Pathways* Psychological Services provides:

Psychotherapy from the Christian Worldview
in Expanded Locations
for Diverse Clients
by Innovative Therapists
partnering with Churches and the Community

OBJECTIVES

Pathways Psychological Services exists in order to:

- promote client healing of damaged emotions as therapists are used as servants empowered by the Christian perspective
- produce the integration of the Christian worldview in therapy with clients giving informed consent
- pursue excellence in all domains of the practice: administrative, professional, physical setting, vendor relationships
- penetrate underserved geographic areas with psychotherapy services
- provide training for neophyte counselors
- partner with local churches and the community
- prevent financial barriers to receipt of services

CORE VALUES

Excellence: Clinical treatment, Christian principles, professional standards, office decor, business practices and technology, paperwork.

Perseverance: Stay at a task, whether administrative or clinical, until complete or resolved. Work to save marriages, deliver from bondages, maintain hope.

Relationships: Value staff, both administrative and professional. View clients as valuable, made in God's image. Select new staff compatible with the team.

Collaboration: Value partnerships with churches, specialty clinics and professional colleagues, and all therapists and administrative staff at *Pathways*.

Expansion: Increase caseloads to maximum that therapists can effectively handle, providing marketing, education, and affordable fees, and reaching underserved areas through multiple sites.

Discipleship/Mentoring: Train interns regularly, develop new staff therapists, and encourage spiritual growth in staff and clients.

Consent for Counseling from a Christian Worldview

My signature below confirms that I desire psychological counseling from a wholistic perspective involving assessment and interventions in the spiritual, emotional, physical, and social realms from a Christian worldview by my therapist at *Pathways* Psychological Services, P.A. ("PPS").

Since I embrace the Christian spiritual perspective, I desire that my therapist use the language and practices applicable to that worldview. I do not want language and practices used from other worldviews, such as secular, humanist, New Age, atheistic, or Eastern worldviews.

From my Christian perspective, I agree to the use of one or more of eighteen commonly used Christian disciplines described on the back of this page as part of my treatment plan when spiritual issues are being addressed in my sessions with my PPS therapist(s).

I understand that no organized religion or religious denomination is being promoted by my therapist or by PPS in general, but he/she is working solely from a biblical worldview.

I understand also that I may experience spiritual confusion or interference in my thoughts by the interplay of spiritual and psychological realities as described below:

- Distressing, unresolved memories may surface through the use of spiritual conflict procedures.
- Some clients have experienced reactions during the treatment sessions that neither they nor the administering clinician may have anticipated, including a high level of emotion or physical sensations.
- Subsequent to the treatment sessions, the processing of incidents/material may continue, and other dreams, memories, flashbacks, feelings, and the like may surface.

I further understand that the spiritual dimension is focused on as a part of my overall treatment plan and is not exclusively the focus of treatment.

I understand that I will seek support from my own church and pastoral resources for questions and issues that involve specific doctrinal, religious, or personal spiritual questions and practices.

I understand that spiritual interventions are used when they are intertwined with my psychological and social issues.

I further give my permission for my therapist to discuss with me issues of the afterlife.

Client: _____   Therapist: _____

Date: _____   Date: _____

DEFINITIONS AND SCRIPTURE REFERENCES FOR EIGHTEEN CHRISTIAN DISCIPLINES

Meditation: to engage in contemplation or reflection … to focus one's thoughts on reflection or to ponder over

1. Concrete meditation: A focus of thoughts on Scripture (individual words and/or phrases); this may also include concrete objects of God's creation (Psalm 119:15, 99, 148).
2. Abstract meditation: An activity closely related to concrete meditation, encouraging more active use of the imagination, such as a passive focus on one or more of the attributes of God (Psalm 63:6; 143:5).

Prayer: communion and/or conversation with God

3. Intercessory prayer: A form of prayer that involves making our requests known to God, either as they relate to ourselves or others (Ephesians 6:18; Philippians 4:6).
4. Contemplative prayer: A particular type of interpersonal response to God that seeks to create a passive openness to the experience of God through nonanalytical focus of attention. Often contemplative prayer transcends words and images due to the inadequacy of this vehicle to capture the power and majesty of God (Psalm 27:4; 46:10; Isaiah 55:8–9).
5. Listening prayer: A process similar to contemplative prayer, except that the primary focus is on receptivity to communication (words/images) from God (1 Samuel 3:9–10; Psalm 130:5–6).

Scripture: God's written revelation as contained in the scriptural canon

6. Counselor: Proactive didactic use of Scripture involving teaching, discussion, exhortation, and encouragement (Colossians 3:16; 2 Timothy 3:14–17).
7. Client: Proactive encouragement of Scripture study, memorization, and application as a structured homework technique (Psalm 119:9–16; 2 Timothy 2:15).
8. Confession: Taking personal responsibility for transgressions of thought or deed and entering into a process of repentance that involves admitting to God and/or others our sin (Psalm 51:1–3; James 5:16).
9. Worship: Giving to God our praise, thanksgiving, allegiance, honor, and adoration, both individually and in fellowship with other believers (Psalm 9:1–2; Romans 12:1; Hebrews 10:25).
10. Forgiveness: The complete canceling of a debt or penalty for an offense, which generally involves cleansing and freedom from sin and its effects (Matthew 6:14–15; 1 John 1:9).
11. Fasting: Abstaining from normal pleasures for a period of time for the purpose of spiritual growth and insight (Psalm 35:13; Matthew 6:16–18).
12. Truth Encounter: A person taking authority over oppression by evil spirits or demons affecting himself or herself (Matthew 10:1–8).
13. Solitude/silence: Drawing away from distractions in order to meet with God alone; the attitude of inner stillness as one brings the heart and mind into focus on the Lord (Psalm 131:2; Mark 6:31).
14. Discernment: A gift of divine insight for the purpose of rightly distinguishing between good and evil, truth and error (1 Corinthians 12:10; Hebrews 5:14; 1 John 4:1, 6).
15. Journal keeping: A written expression of emotion, thought, experiences, and/or dreams that serves as an outpouring of the soul as well as an encouragement for self or others (all the psalms are useful in the practice of this Christian discipline).
16. Obedience: The giving up of personal autonomy, entering into a life of freely accepted servanthood to God (1 Corinthians 12:1–31; Philippians 2:5–8; 1 John 5:3).
17. Simplicity: A life lived with singleness of desire as expressed in Matthew 6:33, which involves the freedom of being detached from worldly concern (Matthew 6:22–34; Colossians 3:1–5).
18. Spiritual history: A type of case history that involves the structured discussion of one's religious background, spiritual journey, and other specific events pertaining to a relationship with God (1 Thessalonians 3:5–6; 2 Timothy 1:5–6).

Adapted from Everett P. Worthington Jr., *Psychotherapy and Religious Values* (Grand Rapids: Baker, 1993), 195. See also Richard Foster, *Celebration of Discipline* (New York: Harper & Row, 1978).

Client's Rights and Information

Effective communication between the client and the therapist is an important part of the therapy process. The following information covers many of the questions that may arise about therapy and includes a listing of the client's rights and obligations. Any questions you may have that are not covered may be brought to the attention of your therapist.

1. *The Bill of Rights* of clients obtaining psychological services is as follows. It is not a legal bill of rights but a statement of what you can reasonably expect from a therapist.

YOU HAVE THE RIGHT
- to ask questions at any time
- to know when a therapist is available to see you, or if not, how long the waiting period would be
- to be informed of the therapist's areas of specialization and limitations
- to ask questions about issues relevant to your therapy
- to ask questions about written materials regarding your treatment
- to negotiate therapeutic goals and to renegotiate when necessary
- to be informed regarding fees for therapy and method of payment, including insurance reimbursements
- to refuse a specific intervention or treatment strategy
- to discuss aspects of your therapy with others outside the therapy situation, including consulting with another therapist
- to request the therapist to send a written report regarding services rendered to a qualified therapist or organization on your written authorization
- to know the ethics code to which the therapist adheres
- to solicit help from the ethics committee of the appropriate professional organization in the event of doubt or grievance regarding the therapist's conduct
- to terminate therapy at any time

2. *Psychotherapy* can involve some risk for the client in certain situations.

Sometimes the client will not obtain the desired results or goals from psychotherapy in the time period expected. This can result in frustration and dissatisfaction. During the process of the therapy, psychological pain and distress can arise as difficult issues are addressed and worked through. The therapist may recommend referral for supplemental care when appropriate. If adequate progress is not being made in therapy or if it becomes apparent that the therapist does not have the skills necessary to address the client's issues that have emerged during therapy, the therapist may either refer for more specialized care or discontinue therapy and assist with a referral to an appropriate therapist, health care professional or therapy program.

3. *Confidentiality:* Confidentiality is maintained for all clients except in the following cases:

- If *child abuse* is either reported or suspected.
- When the *client is a minor*. The parents/guardians are entitled to know the condition, diagnosis, and progress of therapy. (See Parent/Minor Child Confidentiality Statement on page 378.)
- If the *client poses a "clear and imminent danger"* either to self or someone else. The therapist is required to report such danger to the appropriate parties, including family members, police, or the threatened party.
- If the client is or becomes a *"vulnerable adult."*
- If the *client releases information with a written authorization.*
- If a *court subpoenas your records.*
- When *consultation or supervision with another therapist* is desired in order to provide the best possible therapy. Such discussions will, of course, remain private within the consultation or supervisory relationship.

4. *Second opinion:* If you would like a second opinion regarding your specific problems or condition, this issue should be brought to the attention of the therapist, and the therapist will offer assistance in obtaining an appropriate referral.

5. *Discontinuation of therapy:* You may discontinue therapy at any time. Please feel free to discuss this with your therapist. Your therapist may discontinue therapy if financial conditions stipulated in the Professional Counseling Agreement are not met or if transfer to another therapist is desirable.

6. *Emergency:* We retain an answering service for 24-hour coverage, 7 days a week. We return calls received during nonoffice hours as promptly as possible. If you are in a crisis and need immediate attention, we refer you to *(name of intervention center, hospital, or crisis line in your area).*

7. If a *grievance* with *Pathways* Psychological Services, P.A., is not resolved to your satisfaction, you may file a complaint with *(your state's Department of Human Services, Licensing).*

Individual Treatment Plan

Client Name: _____ Date of Birth: _____

Subscriber Name: _____ Health Plan Name: _____

Presenting Problem:

I.   DSM-IV (5 AXIS)

    Axis I:

    Axis II:

    Axis III:

    Axis IV: Psychosocial stressors:
        Type(s)_____ Severity: _____

    Axis V: Current GAF: _____   Highest GAF past year: _____

II. PRESENT SYMPTOMS SUPPORTING DIAGNOSIS

III. RELEVANT FAMILY AND SOCIAL HISTORY

IV. PREVIOUS MENTAL HEALTH SERVICES   Consulted: Y/N   N/A

IV. CURRENT IMPAIRMENTS ATTRIBUTABLE TO DIAGNOSIS

V.   SPIRITUAL HISTORY

TREATMENT PROCEDURES

Goals Relative to Impairments	Objective Criteria for Discharge	Anticipated Date of Goal Attainment

MODALITIES:

Medications (name, dosage)

Prescribing Physician:_____

Consulted: Y/N   N/A

DURATION/FREQUENCY:

Therapist _____   Date _____

Client _____   Date _____

The client was informed in the following a
___ 1. Assessment of his/her condition
___ 2. Treatment alternative
___ 3. Possible outcomes and side effects
___ 4. Treatment recommendations
___ 5. Approx. length, cost, & hope for ou
___ 6. His/her rights/responsibilities in the treatment process
___ 7. Staff rights/responsibilities in the treatment process
___ 8. Data Practices Act
___ 9. Procedures for reporting grievances
___ 10. Name of therapist's supervisor

Individual Treatment Plan

Client Name: <u>XXXX (Female)</u>   Date of Birth: <u>XX/XX/XX</u>

Subscriber Name: <u>Same</u>   Health Plan Name: <u>XXXX</u>

Presenting Problem: Anxiety / obsessional beliefs about relatives, men. Worries about her physical condition (menopause, pregnancy, although a virgin). Has sleep disturbances, social isolation in relationships, disrespect from family.

I. DSM-IV (5 AXIS)

Axis I: Schizophrenia, Residual Type (by history), (295.60); Religious or Spiritual Problem (V62.89); Rule out Schizoaffective Disorder and Generalized Anxiety Disorder.

Axis II: Deferred (799.9).

Axis III: Good. PMS Sx.

Axis IV: Psychosocial stressors:

Type(s)<u>Primary support group; social environment; occupation</u> Severity: <u>Mod./severe</u>

Axis V: Current GAF: <u>50</u>   Highest GAF past year: <u>62</u>

II. PRESENT SYMPTOMS SUPPORTING DIAGNOSIS

Affect blunt and flattened with giddiness and superficial reactions; episodic derailment; inability to secure employment; transitory relationships with nonrelatives; dependence on family for activities of daily living; odd beliefs / fears about pregnancy and marriage (paranoia about men looking at her, getting her pregnant).

III. RELEVANT FAMILY AND SOCIAL HISTORY

Single, living alone, mother lives in neighborhood and closely supervises her life. Parents divorced when age 16. Three older brothers.

IV. PREVIOUS MENTAL HEALTH SERVICES   Consulted: Y/N   N/A

Hospitalized FVW, 1973 for 3 mo. / psychotic break; outpatient follow-up and maintenance continuing.

IV. CURRENT IMPAIRMENTS ATTRIBUTABLE TO DIAGNOSIS

Obsessions; Psychotic thoughts / perceptions: preoccupation, fantasies, alienation feelings, illogical thinking, loses train of thought.

V. SPIRITUAL HISTORY

Born-again believer age 8; attends evangelical church; family nonbelievers; worships regularly; consistent devotions.

TREATMENT PROCEDURES

Goals Relative to Impairments	Objective Criteria for Discharge
Obsessions Achieve freedom from the bondage of fear, conducting life from the perspective of faith in God.	1. Report thought-stopping 80% of time. 2. Use relaxation methods (e.g., deep breathing, stress card, walking dog) to counteract high anxiety and ruminating thoughts. 3. Confess the presence of fear when it is identified, asking God to strengthen her. 4. Complete Step 2: Deception Versus Truth.
Psychotic Thoughts Develop ability to function at a consistent level with minimal interference from obsessional thoughts.	1. Continue psychiatric care for medications. 2. Recognize illogical thinking and speech, refocusing disordered ideation. 3. Demonstrate focus on reality of external world versus disoriented self-focus. 4. Report decrease in cognitive interferences. 5. Participate in community counseling through church contact. Complete a Freedom Appointment for all seven Steps.
Mood Lability Develop self-regulation skills to normalize mood extremes.	1. Demonstrate increase in affective vocabulary and apply appropriate label to moods. 2. Describe irrational and rational thoughts and role-play in session, demonstrating ability to restructure irrational beliefs.

MODALITIES: Individual; possibly family

Medications (name, dosage)

Trazedone 50 mg. bid, Tranzene, 2 tabs qd, Zyprexa, 5 mg. qd.

Prescribing Physician: Dr. Jane Doe

Consulted: Y/N   N/A

DURATION/FREQUENCY: Bimonthly visits once emotionally and behaviorally stabilized.

Therapist XXX _____ Date XX/XX/XX

Client XXXX _____ Date XX/XX/XX

The client was informed in the following areas
- X 1. Assessment of his/her condition
- X 2. Treatment alternative
- X 3. Possible outcomes and side effects
- X 4. Treatment recommendations
- X 5. Approx. length, cost, & hope for outco[m]
- X 6. His/her rights/responsibilities in the treatment process
- X 7. Staff rights/responsibilities in the treatment process
- X 8. Data Practices Act
- X 9. Procedures for reporting grievances
- X 10. Name of therapist's supervisor

Client B

Individual Treatment Plan

Client Name: XXXX (Male)   Date of Birth: XX/XX/XX

Subscriber Name: Same   Health Plan Name: XXXX

Presenting Problem: Emotional crisis over wife's affair with her boss and her announced intention to divorce. Wife's emotional affair of one year preceded the physical relationship with the boss.

I. DSM-IV (5 AXIS)

Axis I: Major Depressive Disorder, Single Episode (296.22); Religious or Spiritual Problem (V62.89).

Axis II: Deferred (799.9).

Axis III: Generally good; smokes 1 pack/day.

Axis IV: Psychosocial stressors:

Type(s) Primary support group   Severity: Moderate

Axis V: Current GAF: 55   Highest GAF past year: 70

II. PRESENT SYMPTOMS SUPPORTING DIAGNOSIS

Diminished appetite (20 lb. weight loss); obsessional thoughts about wife's sexual relationship; vomiting until recently; wishes life would end (although denies suicidal ideation or plan); decreased concentration / memory; depressed affect; tearful; angry.

III. RELEVANT FAMILY AND SOCIAL HISTORY

Married 10 yrs., boy (7), girls (5, 2)

IV. PREVIOUS MENTAL HEALTH SERVICES   Consulted: Y/N   N/A

None

IV. CURRENT IMPAIRMENTS ATTRIBUTABLE TO DIAGNOSIS

Dysphoric Mood: resigned supervisor position, significant weight loss
Obsessions: repetitive, intrusive thoughts of wife, is tapping her phone
Rage Reactions: verbally abusive to wife, impulse to confront her boss, quotes Bible to her
Marital Dysfunction: explosive arguments, wife moving out in near future
Grandiosity / Pride: centering life around self and own adherence to biblical morality

V. SPIRITUAL HISTORY

Client and spouse raised in Baptist church; believers since childhood. Infrequent worship. Rare devotions.

TREATMENT PROCEDURES

Goals Relative to Impairments	Objective Criteria for Discharge
Dysphoric Mood Develop healthy cognitive patterns and belief about self and the world that lead to alleviation of depressive symptoms.	1. Take prescribed medications. 2. Replace negative, catastrophic self-talk with realistic cognitions; learn ABCs. 3. Grieve losses experienced, identifying stages on grief curve. 4. Find source and origin of historic lies and replace with truth (TheoPhostics).
Obsessions Identify self-talk supporting anxiety and the relationship between obsessive thinking and labile mood. Examine own behavior thoroughly for self-deception and self-defense.	1. List triggers to anxiety and alternative strategies to implement (boundary setting; focus on here and now; taking thoughts captive; relaxation methods). 2. Complete Step 2: Deception Versus Truth. 3. Confess presence of self-deception and fear when identified.
Marital Dysfunction Recognize own role in the conflictual relationship as related to pride, and transfer overreliance on own accomplishments and abilities to a commitment to live humbly before God.	1. List own contributions to marital dissatisfaction. 2. Learn speaker-listener technique for conflict management. 3. Complete Step 5: Pride Versus Humility and Step 7: Acquiescence Versus Renunciation.
Rage Reactions Decrease overall intensity and frequency of angry feelings, increasing ability to appropriately express them using alternative behaviors and increased control.	1. Differentiate among aggression, passivity, assertion; use Time-Out to de-escalate. 2. Identify anger as a secondary emotion and discuss underlying fear, hurt, frustration. 3. Complete Step 3: Bitterness Versus Forgiveness.

MODALITIES: Individual; four videos on conflict resolution; bibliotherapy; Stephen Minister

Medications (name, dosage)

Prozac 20 mg. (refused resumption on XX/XX/XX)

Prescribing
Physician: ___Dr. John Doe___

Consulted: Y/N   N/A

The client was informed in the following ar

  X 1. Assessment of his/her condition
  X 2. Treatment alternative
  X 3. Possible outcomes and side effects
  X 4. Treatment recommendations
  X 5. Approx. length, cost, & hope for outc
  X 6. His/her rights/responsibilities in the
       treatment process
  X 7. Staff rights/responsibilities in the
       treatment process
  X 8. Data Practices Act
  X 9. Procedures for reporting grievances
  X 10. Name of therapist's supervisor

DURATION/FREQUENCY: 8 sessions / weekly

Therapist ___XXX___   Date ___XX/XX/XX___

Client ___XXXX___   Date ___XX/XX/XX___

Individual Treatment Plan

Client Name: <u>XXXX (Male)</u>   Date of Birth: <u>XX/XX/XX</u>

Subscriber Name: <u>Same</u>   Health Plan Name: <u>XXXX</u>

Presenting Problem: Rageful, physically abusive behavior toward spouse.

I. DSM-IV (5 AXIS)

Axis I: Intermittent Explosive Disorder (312.34); Religious or Spiritual Problem (V 62.89).

Axis II: Deferred (799.9).

Axis III: Good. Chronic sinus problems; neck and back muscle tension; asthma.

Axis IV: Psychosocial stressors:
          Type(s) <u>Primary support group</u>   Severity: <u>Severe</u>

Axis V: Current GAF: <u>56</u>   Highest GAF past year: <u>60</u>

II. PRESENT SYMPTOMS SUPPORTING DIAGNOSIS

Decreased frustration tolerance, irritability, hopelessness, diminished concentration, onset insomnia, depressed mood, guilt, remorse.

III. RELEVANT FAMILY AND SOCIAL HISTORY

Second of six children in alcoholic family with physical and verbal abuse by father. First marriage lasted two years - one child. Currently married one year - one stepchild.

IV. PREVIOUS MENTAL HEALTH SERVICES   Consulted: Y/N   N/A
Four sessions with pastoral counselor.

IV. CURRENT IMPAIRMENTS ATTRIBUTABLE TO DIAGNOSIS

Rage / Assault: threw spouse
Mood Lability: emotional instability, locks self in room to control emotions
Dysphoric Mood: sad, guilty, insomnia

V. SPIRITUAL HISTORY

Born-again believer since childhood. Eratic church attendance. No devotional time.

TREATMENT PROCEDURES

Goals Relative to Impairments	Objective Criteria for Discharge
Rage / Assault Increase ability to appropriately express angry feelings, accepting boundary assistance if rageful feelings erupt.	1. Differentiate among assertion, passivity, and aggression. 2. Identify anger as secondary emotion and discuss underlying fear, frustration, hurt. 3. Focus on Step 3: Bitterness Versus Forgiveness and Step 4: Submission Versus Rebellion. 4. Submit to police and / or restraining order if wife initiates action.
Mood Lability Identify cognitions that support mood instability, reducing agitation, impulsivity and internal discomfort.	1. Learn ABCs and demonstrate ability to dispute irrational beliefs. 2. React more slowly verbally and physically to stressors. 3. Use speaker / listener technique to discuss conflictual issues with spouse. 4. Participate in community counseling through church contact. Complete all seven Steps of a Freedom Appointment.
Dysphoric Mood Identify activating events and cognitions preceding depressed mood. Recognize false beliefs that trigger negative feelings.	1. Replace false beliefs with rational thoughts as demonstrated through journaling. 2. Return to normal sleep pattern, maintaining seven hours of uninterrupted sleep. 3. Go to source and origin of historic lies and replace with truth (TheoPhostics). 4. Report experience of optimism and interest in future events.

MODALITIES: Individual; spouse as guest; anger management group

Medications (name, dosage)

Asthma medications

Prescribing Physician:___N/A_____

Consulted: Y/N   N/A

DURATION/FREQUENCY: 8 sessions / weekly

Therapist <u>XXX</u>_____ Date <u>XX/XX/XX</u>

Client <u>XXXX</u>_____ Date <u>XX/XX/XX</u>

The client was informed in the following areas:
<u>X</u> 1. Assessment of his/her condition
<u>X</u> 2. Treatment alternative
<u>X</u> 3. Possible outcomes and side effects
<u>X</u> 4. Treatment recommendations
<u>X</u> 5. Approx. length, cost, & hope for outcome
<u>X</u> 6. His/her rights/responsibilities in the treatment process
<u>X</u> 7. Staff rights/responsibilities in the treatment process
<u>X</u> 8. Data Practices Act
<u>X</u> 9. Procedures for reporting grievances
<u>X</u> 10. Name of therapist's supervisor

Client D

Individual Treatment Plan

Client Name: <u>XXXX (Female)</u>   Date of Birth: <u>XX/XX/XX</u>

Subscriber Name: <u>Same</u>   Spouse Health Plan Name: <u>XXXX</u>

Presenting Problem: Struggling with self-esteem; withdrawal tendencies from spouse; reported early childhood trauma perpetrated by mother.

I. DSM-IV (5 AXIS)

Axis I: Posttraumatic Stress Disorder (309.81); Religious or Spiritual Problem (V62.89).

Axis II: Deferred (799.9).

Axis III: Good. Fibromyalgia diagnosed ten years ago; miscarriage last year.

Axis IV: Psychosocial stressors:
Type(s) <u>Primary support group; parental abuse</u>   Severity: <u>Severe</u>

Axis V: Current GAF: <u>51-60</u>   Highest GAF past year: <u>65</u>

II. PRESENT SYMPTOMS SUPPORTING DIAGNOSIS

Fatigue, low energy; anxiety about sex; angry; sad; low self-esteem; isolation; body image distortion (feels fat); obsessive regarding cleanliness; perfectionistic anxiety as a parent; hypervigilant.

III. RELEVANT FAMILY AND SOCIAL HISTORY

Second of four; alcoholic family system; mother - bipolar; M/F divorced; drug use / sexual promiscuity as teen.

IV. PREVIOUS MENTAL HEALTH SERVICES   Consulted: Y/N   N/A

Treatment as teen; one session for marriage.

IV. CURRENT IMPAIRMENTS ATTRIBUTABLE TO DIAGNOSIS

Compulsions: stringent housecleaning rules
Concomitant Medical Disorder: fibromyalgia
Marital Dysfunction: negative messages about men from mother, causing marital discord
Family Dysfunction: substance abuse, verbal abuse, sexual anorexia

V. SPIRITUAL HISTORY

Client / spouse new Christians; worship regularly; weekly Bible study; regular quiet time.

TREATMENT PROCEDURES

Goals Relative to Impairments	Objective Criteria for Discharge
Compulsions / Obsessions Diminish perfectionism about tasks; resolve key life conflicts causing negative behavior patterns; achieve cessation of fears, conducting life from a faith-in-God perspective.	1. Increase relational desires while reducing performance-based self-worth. 2. Demonstrate ability to use positive self-talk as coping strategy to abate obsessions. 3. Complete Step 2: Deception Versus Truth. 4. States integrated sense of self; relies on Christ as only defense needed.
Concomitant Medical Condition Decrease overall intensity of psychosocial stressors, accepting their role in medical condition.	1. Report emotional effects of medical condition. 2. Apply M.D.'s recommendations for rest; diet as appropriate.
Marital Relationship Dysfunction Resolve emotional trauma underlying depersonalization and sexual anorexia.	1. Report increased comfort with sexual contact with spouse. 2. Demonstrate increased trust in God as the healer of all trauma. 3. Identify lies / misbeliefs in historical memories and replace with the truth (TheoPhostics). 4. Use speaker / listener technique for conflict management. 5. Complete Step 6: Bondage Versus Freedom.
Family Dysfunction Decrease conflict with spouse and parents, forgiving for past treatment and identifying generational causation for family dysfunction.	1. Describe family of origin trauma effect on perceptions of self and others, especially men. 2. Gradually increase healthy contact with parents as evidenced by holiday, birthday celebrations. 3. Demonstrate use of logical and natural consequences with children. 4. Complete Step 3: Bitterness Versus Forgiveness and Step 7: Acquiescence Versus Renunciation.

MODALITIES: Individual; conjoint

Medications (name, dosage)   Prescribing

None   Physician:___N/A_____

                                 Consulted: Y/N   N/A

DURATION/FREQUENCY: 12 sessions / weekly

Therapist XXX_____ Date XX/XX/XX

Client XXXX_____ Date XX/XX/XX

The client was informed in the following are

X 1. Assessment of his/her condition
X 2. Treatment alternative
X 3. Possible outcomes and side effects
X 4. Treatment recommendations
X 5. Approx. length, cost, & hope for out
X 6. His/her rights/responsibilities in the treatment process
X 7. Staff rights/responsibilities in the treatment process
X 8. Data Practices Act
X 9. Procedures for reporting grievances
X 10. Name of therapist's supervisor

Client E

Individual Treatment Plan

Client Name: <u>XXXX (Male)</u>   Date of Birth: <u>XX/XX/XX</u>

Subscriber Name: <u>Same</u>   Health Plan Name:<u>XXXX</u>

Presenting Problem: Repeated episodes of worry about spouse's commitment to marriage; chronic feelings of invalidation and sexual dissatisfaction; social isolation caused by worries, which is distressing to both husband and wife.

I. DSM-IV (5 AXIS)

Axis I: Anxiety Disorder Not Otherwise Specified (300.0); Rule out Depressive Disorder Not Otherwise Specified.

Axis II: Deferred (799.9); Dependent Personality features.

Axis III: High blood pressure.

Axis IV: Psychosocial stressors:

Type(s) <u>Primary social group</u>   Severity: <u>Moderate</u>

Axis V: Current GAF: <u>61-70</u>   Highest GAF past year: <u>61-70</u>

II. PRESENT SYMPTOMS SUPPORTING DIAGNOSIS

Feels "pounded" by spouse; discouraged by lack of attention / cooperation; avoids her sexually because of recurrent rebuffs; worried about prospect of continued unhappiness; his worries interfere with work performance; motor tension; "pounding heart."

III. RELEVANT FAMILY AND SOCIAL HISTORY

M/F divorced, not close to stepfather; only child; insecure about academic / athletic abilities; afraid would not meet M's (one of his teachers) expectations.

IV. PREVIOUS MENTAL HEALTH SERVICES   Consulted: Y/N   N/A

3 individual sessions five years ago.

IV. CURRENT IMPAIRMENTS ATTRIBUTABLE TO DIAGNOSIS

Labile and Dysphoric Mood
Marital Separation
Lack of Clarity on Worldviews

V. SPIRITUAL HISTORY

Raised Lutheran; attends services on holidays; unaware of a personal relationship with God and its implications for his life.

TREATMENT PROCEDURES

Goals Relative to Impairments	Objective Criteria for Discharge
Labile / Dysphoric Mood Learn to recognize excessive worry problems and to deal with them. Learn effective communication skills for positive coping results and to limit discussions about worries. Reduce the frequency of critical, angry expressions that are related to general state of depression.	1. Verbally identify the triggers and symptoms of worry. 2. Work with spouse to learn her perspective on his anxiety problems and avoidance symptoms. 3. Schedule anxiety-reducing activities that can be done with and without his spouse. 4. Communicate worries to spouse and practice brainstorming ways to avoid them.
Marital Separation Reduce conflict, hurt, doubt, and angry feelings between partners. Decide whether to reconcile or divorce.	1. Verbally assess marital relationship and demonstrate his understanding of significant emotional or personality problems that predate their conflicts. 2. Verbally describe the pros and cons of remaining married. 3. Exercise assertive communication skills using speaker / listener and conflict resolution techniques.
Uncertainty About Worldview Recognize and understand particular choice of worldview (e.g., utopianist, New Age, humanist, biblical Christianity, and so forth).	1. Demonstrate understanding of a particular worldview of choice. 2. Describe basic assumptions regarding the meaning of life, the purpose of life, and his outlook for the future, in the context of his chosen worldview.

MODALITIES: Individual; conjoint

Medications (name, dosage)

None

Prescribing
Physician:_____None_____

Consulted: Y/N   N/A

DURATION/FREQUENCY: 8 sessions / weekly

Therapist <u>XXX</u>_____ Date <u>XX/XX/XX</u>

Client <u>XXXX</u>_____ Date <u>XX/XX/XX</u>

The client was informed in the following ar
- <u>X</u> 1. Assessment of his/her condition
- <u>X</u> 2. Treatment alternative
- <u>X</u> 3. Possible outcomes and side effects
- <u>X</u> 4. Treatment recommendations
- <u>X</u> 5. Approx. length, cost, & hope for ou
- <u>X</u> 6. His/her rights/responsibilities in the treatment process
- <u>X</u> 7. Staff rights/responsibilities in the treatment process
- <u>X</u> 8. Data Practices Act
- <u>X</u> 9. Procedures for reporting grievances
- <u>X</u> 10. Name of therapist's supervisor

Informed Consent Agreement

I am initiating psychotherapy willingly to examine my same-sex attractions and/or behaviors. My goal is to recover from said attractions and/or behaviors and to achieve a heterosexual orientation.

Name: _____

(Print)

_____

(Signature)

Date: _____

Therapist: _____

(Signature)

Witness: _____

(Signature)

Day Sheet

PATIENT: _____   THERAPIST: _____

_____   _____   SUPERVISOR: _____

Diagnosis No.   Description

REFERRAL: _____   TYPE OF PAYMENT: _____

Insurance/Private Pay

No. of Visits	Date	Procedure Code	Charge	Prior Auth. if Necessary	Comments
					Insurance Application
					___ P.A. needed before_____sess▮
					Approved procedures:
					___ 90801
					___ 90806
					___ 90847
					___ 96100
					P.A. needed for psych testing
					___ Yes ___ No
					P.A. contact person's telephone # _____

Authorization for Release of Confidential Information

In consideration for furnishing the designated information to the person or organization named below, I hereby release and agree to indemnify *Pathways* Psychological Services, P.A., its agents, and employees from all liability, damages, and costs arising from the acts or omissions of other persons or organizations.

I, _____   _____
          Print Name   Date of Birth

authorize_____of *Pathways* Psychological Services, P.A., to

_____ disclose information to
_____ obtain information from
_____ exchange information with   _____
                                              Name of Person or Agency

_____

_____

Address, Phone and Fax Number

Regarding _____ myself
          _____ my son/daughter _____ _____
                                          Name   Date of Birth

The information to be disclosed is
_____ Discharge/Treatment Summary   _____ Diagnostic Impressions
_____ Progress Notes   _____ Chemical Dependency Evaluation
_____ Academic Records   _____ Medical History
_____ Psychological Testing and Reports _____ Other

The purpose of this disclosure is _____

I understand that I may revoke this consent at any time by written notice. Without an expressed revocation (unless information has been released), it will expire after 12 months from the date of my signature. I also understand that *Pathways* Psychological Services (PPS) only releases records created by PPS personnel.

_____
Signature of Client, Parent, or Guardian

_____   _____
        Date   Signature of Witness

Release—   Revised 8/19/99

Parent/Minor Child Confidentiality Statement

Pathways Psychological Services respects the right of you as a parent to gain access to all information included in the chart of your minor child. However, we believe that in the best interest of the therapeutic relationship, confidentiality should be maintained between your child and the therapist, except in the following cases:

- when child abuse is suspected
- when the child poses a "clear and imminent danger" either to self or another person
- when the therapist believes it is in the best interest of the child to disclose information to the parent

Given the above, *Pathways* requests your permission to maintain a confidential relationship with your child. If you understand and agree, please provide your signature below.

_____
Client

_____
Date

_____
Parent

_____
Date

_____
Therapist

_____
Date

WAIVER

1. REFERRAL TO A NONPARTICIPATING PROVIDER
   This is to inform you that I am referring you to _____, who
   does not participate with _____. This may result in a lesser
   payment from _____, thereby increasing your liability for services
   you receive from this provider. If a nonparticipating provider recommends hospitalization, you must call _____for approval before you are admit-
   ted to the hospital, except for emergency.

2. RECOMMENDATION TO RECEIVE A SERVICE THAT IS CONSIDERED
   INVESTIGATION BY _____.

   This is to inform you that I am recommending you to receive the following service(s)

   _____

   _____

   _____

   that is/are considered therapeutically necessary by _____. YOUR
   SIGNATURE ON THIS WAIVER SERVES AS AN AUTHORIZATION TO HOLD YOU
   FINANCIALLY LIABLE FOR THE NAMED SERVICES, SINCE THEY ARE NOT COVERED
   UNDER YOUR CONTRACT WITH _____.

   If you have any questions concerning your liability with respect to the above, you may
   contact our office.

   _____   _____   _____
   Representative from Provider Office   Clinic Name   Date

   _____   _____
   Patient Signature   Date

Statement of Understanding (Professional Practitioner)

I understand that _____ is a professional person in the state of _____ and that others attending this session, unless otherwise indicated, are not professional or licensed counselors, therapists, or medical or psychological practitioners.

I understand that everything I state during this encouragement experience will be kept confidential and that I alone hold the right to release any information that comes from this time. I am also aware that as a result of his/her profession _____ is mandated by law to intervene if it is suspected that a child (under the age of eighteen) or an elder (over the age of sixty-five) or a vulnerable adult is currently endangered by abuse or if I am a danger to myself or others.

I understand that I am free to leave at any time and am here voluntarily and that I am under no financial obligation.

I deem the persons leading this session to be "encouragers" in the Christian faith who are helping me assume my responsibilities in finding freedom in Christ.

(PLEASE PRINT)

Name _____ Date _____

Address _____

City _____ State _____ Zip _____

Phone (day) _____ (eve) _____

Signed _____

To be completed by encourager:

Issues covered: _____

_____

_____

Encourager: _____

Prayer Partner: _____

Comments: _____

_____

_____

_____

Statement of Understanding (Nonprofessional Encourager)

I understand that _____ is not a professional person and that others attending this session, unless otherwise indicated, are not professional or licensed counselors, therapists, or medical or psychological practitioners.

I understand that everything I state during this encouragement experience will be kept confidential and that I alone hold the right to release any information that comes from this time. I am also aware that _____ is mandated by law to intervene if he/she suspects that a child (under the age of eighteen) or an elder (over the age of sixty-five) or a vulnerable adult is currently endangered by abuse or if I am a danger to myself or others.

I understand that I am free to leave at any time and am here voluntarily and that I am under no financial obligation.

I deem the persons leading this session to be "encouragers" in the Christian faith who are helping me assume my responsibilities in finding freedom in Christ.

(PLEASE PRINT)

Name _____ Date _____

Address _____

City _____ State _____ Zip _____

Phone (day) _____ (eve) _____

Signed _____

To be completed by encourager:
Issues covered: _____

_____

Encourager: _____
Prayer Partner: _____
Comments: _____

_____

_____

_____

3/2/99 Nonprofessional

Early Recollections Session Record

Client Name: _____ Session #_____ Date:_____

Memory Picture	Emotions	Lies	Pre-rating	Truths Understood	Post-rating

Adapted from Ed Smith, *Beyond Tolerable Recovery*, 2d ed. (Campbellsville, Ky.: Family Care Ministries, 1997), n.p.

Lie/Emotional Identification Sheet

CATEGORY	POSSIBLE LIES PRODUCING EMOTIONS
1. Abandonment	"I am all alone. I have been overlooked. I will always be alone. They do not need me. I don't matter. No one even cares. They are not coming back. There is no one to protect me. God has forsaken me too. No one will believe me. I cannot trust anyone. I am afraid they won't come back."
2. Shamefulness	"I am so stupid, ignorant, an idiot. I should have done something to have stopped it from happening. I allowed it. I was a participant. I should have known better. It was my fault. I should have told someone. I knew what was going to happen, yet I stayed anyway. I felt pleasure, so I must have wanted it. It happened because of my looks, my gender, my body, and so forth. I should have stopped this person. I did not try to run away. I deserved it. I am cheap like a slut. I was paid for service rendered. I kept going back. I did it to him/her first. I'm bad, dirty, shameful, sick, nasty."
3. Fear	"I am going to die. He/she is going to hurt me. I don't know what to do. If I tell, they will come back and hurt me. If I trust, I will die. He/she/they are coming back. It is just a matter of time before it happens again. If I let him/her/them into my life, they will hurt me too. Something bad will happen if I tell, stop it, confront it. They are going to get me. Doom is just around the corner."
4. Powerlessness/ trapped	"I cannot stop this. He/she/they are too strong to resist. There is no way out. I am too weak to resist. The pain is too great to bear. I cannot get away. I am going to die, and I cannot do anything about it. I cannot get loose. I am overwhelmed. I don't know what to do. Everything is out of control. I am pulled from every direction. Not even God can help me. I am too small to do anything."
5. Tainted	"I am dirty, shameful, evil, and perverted because of what happened to me. My life is ruined. I will never feel clean again. Everyone can see my shame, filth, dirtiness, guiltiness. I will always be hurt, damaged, broken because of what has happened. I will never be happy. I will always be unclean, filthy, shameful. God could never want me after what has happened to me. My body has parts that are dirty. No one will ever really be able to love me."
6. Invalidation	"I am not loved, needed, wanted, cared for, or important. They do not need me. I am worthless, have no value. I am unimportant. I was a mistake. I should have never been born. I am in the way. I am a burden. I was never liked by them because I was _____. God could never love or accept me. I could never be as _____ as she/he. I could never jump high enough to please him/her. I am not acceptable."
7. Hopelessness	"It's never going to get any better. There is no way out. It will just happen again and again. There is no good thing for me. I have no reason to live. There are no options for me. I just want to die. Nothing good will ever come of this."
8. Confusion	"I don't know what is happening to me. Everything is confusing. This does not make any sense. Why would they do this to me?" (This lie is sometimes confused with demonic interference. Demons will cause confusion in a memory, which will feel much like a *confusion lie*.)

Adapted from Ed Smith, *Beyond Tolerable Recovery*, 2d ed. (Campbellsville, Ky.: Family Care Ministries, 1997), n.p.

STEPS TO FREEDOM IN CHRIST

It is my deep conviction that the finished work of Jesus Christ and the presence of God in our lives are the only means by which we can resolve our personal and spiritual conflicts. Christ in us is our only hope (see Colossians 1:27), and he alone can meet our deepest needs of life—acceptance, identity, security, and significance. The discipleship counseling process on which these steps are based should not be understood as just another counseling technique that we learn. It is an encounter with God. He is the Wonderful Counselor. He is the One who grants repentance that leads to a knowledge of the truth that sets us free (see 2 Timothy 2:24–26).

The "Steps to Freedom in Christ" do *not* set you free. *Who* sets you free is Christ, and *what* sets you free is your response to him in repentance and faith. These Steps are just a tool to help you submit to God and resist the devil (see James 4:7). Then you can start living a fruitful life by abiding in Christ and becoming the person he created you to be. Many Christians will be able to work through these Steps on their own and discover the wonderful freedom that Christ purchased for them on the cross. Then they will experience the peace of God that transcends all understanding, and it will guard their hearts and their minds (see Philippians 4:7).

BEFORE YOU BEGIN

The chances of discovering that wonderful freedom, experiencing God's peace, and maintaining that freedom will be greatly enhanced if you first read *Victory Over the Darkness* and *The Bondage Breaker*. Many Christians in our Western world need to understand the reality of the spiritual world and our relationship to it. Some cannot read these books or even the Bible with comprehension because of the battle that is going on for their minds. They will need the assistance of others who have been adequately trained. The theology and practical process of discipleship counseling is given in my book *Helping Others Find Freedom in Christ* and in the study guide that accompanies it. This book attempts to biblically integrate the reality of the spiritual and the natural world so we can have a whole answer for a whole person. In doing so, we cannot polarize into psychotherapeutic ministries that ignore the reality of the spiritual world or attempt some kind of deliverance ministry that ignores developmental issues and human responsibility.

YOU MAY NEED HELP

Ideally, it would be best if everyone had a trusted friend, pastor, or counselor who would help him or her go through this process, because it is simply applying the wisdom of James 5:16: "Therefore confess your sins to each other and pray for each other so that you may be healed. The prayer of a righteous man is powerful and effective." Another person can prayerfully support you by providing objective counsel. I have had the privilege of helping many Christian leaders who could not process this on their own. Many Christian groups all over the world are using this approach in many languages with incredible results because the Lord desires for all to come to repentance (see 2 Peter 3:9) and to know the truth that sets us free in Christ (see John 8:32).

APPROPRIATING AND MAINTAINING FREEDOM

Christ has set us free through his victory over sin and death accomplished on the cross. However, *appropriating* our freedom in Christ through repentance and faith and *maintaining* our life of freedom in Christ are two different issues. It was for freedom that Christ set us free, but we have been warned not to return to a yoke of slavery, which is legalism in this context (see Galatians 5:1), or to turn our freedom into an opportunity for the flesh (see Galatians 5:13). Establishing people free in Christ makes it possible for them to walk by faith according to what God says is true and to live by the power of the Holy Spirit and not gratify the desires of the flesh (see Galatians 5:16). The true Christian life avoids both legalism and license.

If you are not experiencing freedom, it may be because you have not stood firm in the faith or actively taken your place in Christ. It is every Christian's responsibility to do whatever is necessary to maintain a right relationship with God and humans. Your eternal destiny is not at stake. God will never leave you or forsake you (see Hebrews 13:5), but your daily victory is at stake if you fail to claim and maintain your position in Christ.

YOUR POSITION IN CHRIST

You are *not* a helpless victim caught between two nearly equal but opposite heavenly superpowers. Satan is a deceiver. *Only God* is omnipotent, omnipresent, and omniscient. Sometimes the reality of sin and the presence of evil may seem more real than the presence of God, but that is part of Satan's deception. Satan is a defeated foe, and we are *in Christ*. A true knowledge of God and knowing our identity and position in Christ are the greatest determinants of our "mental health." A false concept of God, a distorted understanding of who we are as children of God, and the misplaced deification of Satan are the greatest contributors to "mental illness."

Many of our illnesses are psychosomatic. When these issues are resolved in Christ, our physical bodies will function better and we will experience greater health. Other problems are clearly physical, and we need the services of the medical profession. Please consult your physician for medical advice and for the prescribing of medication. We are spiritual *and* physical beings who need the services that both the church and the hospital provide.

WINNING THE BATTLE FOR YOUR MIND

The battle is for our mind, which is the control center of all that we think and do. The opposing thoughts you may experience as you go through these Steps can control you only if you believe them. If you are working through these Steps alone, *do not be deceived* by any lying, intimidating thoughts in your mind. If a trusted pastor or counselor is helping you find your freedom in Christ, that person must have your cooperation. You must share any thoughts you are having in opposition to what you are attempting to do. *As soon as you expose the lie, the power of Satan is broken.* The only way you can lose control in this process is if you pay attention to a deceiving spirit and believe a lie.

YOU MUST CHOOSE

The following procedure is a means of resolving personal and spiritual conflicts that have kept you from experiencing the freedom and victory Christ purchased for you on the cross. Your freedom will be the result of what *you* choose to believe, confess, forgive, renounce, and forsake. No one can do that for you. The battle for your mind can only be won as you personally choose truth. As you go through this process, understand that Satan is under no obligation to obey your thoughts. Only God has complete knowledge of your mind because he is omniscient (all-knowing). So we can submit to God inwardly, but we need to resist the devil by reading aloud each prayer and by verbally renouncing, forgiving, confessing, and so forth.

This process of reestablishing our freedom in Christ is nothing more than taking a fierce moral inventory and establishing a rock-solid commitment to truth. It is the first step in the continuing process of discipleship. There is no such thing as instant maturity. It will take you the rest of your life to renew your mind and conform to the image of God. If your problems stem from a source other than those covered in these Steps, you may need to seek professional help.

May the Lord grace you with his presence as you seek his face and help others experience the joy of salvation.

NEIL T. ANDERSON
FREEDOM IN CHRIST MINISTRIES, 1998

PRAYER

Dear heavenly Father,

We acknowledge your presence in this room and in our lives. You are the only omniscient (all-knowing), omnipotent (all-powerful), and omnipresent (always-present) God. We are dependent on you, for apart from you we can do nothing. We stand in the truth that all authority in heaven and on earth has been given to the resurrected Christ, and because we are in Christ, we share that authority in order to make disciples and set captives free. We ask you to fill us with your Holy Spirit and lead us into all truth. We pray for your complete protection and ask for your guidance. In Jesus' name. Amen.

DECLARATION

In the name and authority of the Lord Jesus Christ, we command Satan and all evil spirits to release _____ in order that _____ can be free to know and to choose to do the will of God. As children of God seated with Christ in the heavenly realms, we agree that every enemy of the Lord Jesus Christ be bound to silence. We say to Satan and all your evil workers that you cannot inflict any pain or in any way prevent God's will from being accomplished in _____'s life.

Preparation

Before going through the "Steps to Freedom in Christ," review the events of your life to discern specific areas that might need to be addressed.

FAMILY HISTORY
___Religious history of parents and grandparents
___Home life from childhood through high school
___History of physical or emotional illness in the family
___Adoption, foster care, guardians

PERSONAL HISTORY
___Eating habits (bulimia, bingeing and purging, anorexia, compulsive eating)
___Addictions (drugs, alcohol)
___Prescription medications (what for?)
___Sleeping patterns and nightmares
___Raped or any sexual, physical, or emotional abuse
___Thought life (obsessive, blasphemous, condemning, distracting thoughts; poor concentration; fantasy)
___Mental interference in church, prayer, or Bible study
___Emotional life (anger, anxiety, depression, bitterness, fears)
___Spiritual journey (salvation: when, how, and assurance)

Now you are ready to begin. The following are seven specific Steps to process in order to experience freedom from your past. You will address the areas where Satan most commonly takes advantage of us and where strongholds have been built. Christ purchased your victory when he shed his blood for you on the cross. Realizing your freedom will be the result of what you choose to believe, confess, forgive, renounce, and forsake. No one can do that for you. The battle for your mind can only be won as you personally choose truth.

As you go through these Steps, remember that Satan will only be defeated if you confront him verbally. He cannot read your mind, and he is under no obligation to obey your thoughts. Only God has complete knowledge of your mind. As you process each step, it is important that you submit to God inwardly and resist the devil by reading aloud each prayer—verbally renouncing, forgiving, confessing, and so forth.

You are taking a fierce moral inventory and making a rock-solid commitment to truth. If your problems stem from a source other than those covered in these Steps, you have nothing to lose by going through them. If you are sincere, the only thing that can happen is that you will get very right with God!

STEP 1: COUNTERFEIT VERSUS REAL

The first Step to is to renounce your previous or current involvement with satanically inspired occult practices and false religions. You need to renounce any activity and group that denies Jesus Christ, offers guidance through any source other than the absolute authority of the written Word of God, or requires secret initiations, ceremonies, or covenants.

In order to help you assess your spiritual experiences, begin by asking God to reveal false guidance and counterfeit religious experiences.

Dear heavenly Father,
I ask you to guard my heart and my mind and reveal to me any and all involvement I have had, either knowingly or unknowingly, with cultic or occultic practices, false religions, or false teachers. In Jesus' name, I pray. Amen.

Using the "Non-Christian Spiritual Experience Inventory," carefully check anything in which you were involved. This list is not exhaustive, but it will guide you in identifying non-Christian experiences. Add any additional involvement you have had. Even if you "innocently" participated in something or observed it, you should write it on your list to renounce, just in case you unknowingly gave Satan a foothold.

Non-Christian Spiritual Experience Inventory

(Please check those that apply)

__Astral projection

__Ouija board

__Table or body lifting

__Dungeons and Dragons

__Speaking in trance

__Automatic handwriting

__Magic eight ball

__Telepathy

__Using spells or curses

__Séance

__Materialization

__Clairvoyance

__Spirit guides

__Fortune telling

__Tarot cards

__Palm reading

__Astrology/horoscopes

__Rod and pendulum (dowsing)

__Self-hypnosis

__Mental manipulations
or attempts to swap minds

__Black and white magic

__New Age medicine

__Blood pacts or cut yourself in
a destructive way

__Fetishism (objects of worship,
crystals, good-luck charms)

__Incubi and succubi
(sexual spirits)

Other_____

__Christian Science

__Unity

__The Way International

__Unification Church

__Mormonism

__Church of the Living Word

__Jehovah's Witnesses

__Children of God (Love)

__Swedenborgianism (Church
of New Jerusalem)

__Unitarianism

__Masons

__New Age

__The Forum (EST)

__Spirit worship

Other_____

__Buddhism

__Hare Krishna

__Bahaism

__Rosicrucian

__Science of the Mind

__Science of Creative Intelligence

__Transcendental Meditation

__Hinduism

__Yoga

__Eckankar

__Roy Masters

__Silva Mind Control

__Father Divine

__Theosophical Society

__Islam

__Black Muslim

__Religion of Martial Arts

Other_____

1. Have you ever been hypnotized, attended a New Age or para-psychology seminar, or consulted a medium, spiritist, or chan-neler? Explain.
2. Do you have or have you ever had an imaginary friend or spirit guide offering you guidance or companionship? Explain.
3. Have you ever heard voices in your mind or had repeating and nagging thoughts condemning you or communicating to you things that were foreign to what you believe or feel, like there was a dialogue going on in your head? Explain.
4. What other spiritual experiences have you had that might be considered out of the ordinary?
5. Have you ever made a vow, covenant, or pact with any individual or group other than God?
6. Have you been involved in satanic ritual or satanic worship in any form? Explain.

When you are confident your list is complete, confess and renounce each involvement, whether active or passive, by praying aloud the following prayer, repeating it separately for each item on your list:

Lord,
   I confess that I have participated in _____ and I renounce_____.
Thank you that in Christ I am forgiven.

If there has been any involvement in satanic ritual or in any heavy occult activity, you need to state aloud the following special renunciations that apply (see next page). Read across the page, renouncing the first item in the column on the Kingdom of Darkness and then affirming the first truth in the column on the Kingdom of Light. Continue down the page in this manner.

All satanic rituals, covenants, and assignments must be specifically renounced as the Lord allows you to recall them. Some who have been subjected to satanic ritual abuse may have developed multiple personalities in order to survive. Nevertheless, continue through the Steps in order to resolve all that you consciously can. It is important that you resolve the demonic strongholds first. Every person must resolve his or her issues and agree to come together in Jesus Christ. You may need someone who understands spiritual conflict to help you maintain control and not be deceived into false memories. Only Jesus can bind up the broken-hearted, set captives free, and make us whole.

Kingdom of Darkness	Kingdom of Light
I renounce ever signing my name over to Satan or having had my name signed over to Satan.	I announce that my name is now written in the Lamb's Book of Life.
I renounce any ceremony where I may have been wed to Satan.	I announce that I am the bride of Christ.
I renounce any and all covenants I made with Satan.	I announce that I am a partaker of the new covenant with Christ.
I renounce all satanic assignments for my life, including duties, marriage, and children.	I announce and commit myself to know and do only the will of God and accept only his guidance.
I renounce all spirit guides assigned to me.	I announce and accept only the leading of the Holy Spirit.
I renounce ever giving of my blood in the service of Satan.	I trust only in the shed blood of my Lord Jesus Christ.
I renounce ever eating of flesh or drinking of blood for satanic worship.	By faith I eat only the flesh and drink only the blood of Jesus in Holy Communion.
I renounce any and all guardians and satanist parents who were assigned to me.	I announce that God is my Father and the Holy Spirit is my Guardian by which I am sealed.
I renounce any baptism in blood or urine whereby I am identified with Satan.	I announce that I have been baptized into Christ Jesus and my identity is now in Christ.
I renounce any and all sacrifices that were made on my behalf by which Satan may claim ownership of me.	I announce that only the sacrifice of Christ has any hold on me. I belong to him. I have been purchased by the blood of the Lamb.

STEP 2: DECEPTION VERSUS TRUTH

Truth is the revelation of God's Word, but we need to *acknowledge* the truth in the inner self (see Psalm 51:6). When David lived a lie, he suffered greatly. When he finally found freedom by acknowledging the truth, he wrote: "Blessed is the man ... in whose spirit is no deceit" (Psalm 32:2). We are to lay aside falsehood and speak the truth in love (see Ephesians 4:15, 25). A mentally healthy person is one who is in touch with reality and relatively free of anxiety. Both qualities should characterize the Christian who renounces deception and embraces truth.

Begin this critical step by expressing aloud the following prayer. Do not let the enemy accuse you with thoughts such as: "This isn't going to work" or "I wish I could believe this but I can't" or any other lies in opposition to what you are proclaiming. Even if it is difficult for you to do so, you need to pray the prayer and read the Doctrinal Affirmation found on pages 395–396.

Dear heavenly Father,

I know that you desire truth in the inner self and that facing this truth is the way of liberation (John 8:32). I acknowledge that I have been deceived by the father of lies (John 8:44) and that I have deceived myself (1 John 1:8). I pray in the name of the Lord Jesus Christ that you, heavenly Father, will rebuke all deceiving spirits by virtue of the shed blood and resurrection of the Lord Jesus Christ. By faith I have received you into my life and I am now seated with Christ in the heavenly realms (Ephesians 2:6). I acknowledge that I have the responsibility and authority to resist the devil, and when I do, he will flee from me (James 4:7). I now ask the Holy Spirit to guide me into all truth (John 16:13). I ask you to "search me, O God, and know my heart; test me and know my anxious thoughts. See if there is any offensive way in me, and lead me in the way everlasting" (Psalm 139:23–24). In Jesus' name, I pray. Amen.

You may want to pause at this point to consider some of Satan's deceptive schemes. In addition to false teachers, false prophets, and deceiving spirits, you can deceive yourself. Now that you are alive in Christ and forgiven, you never have to live a lie or defend yourself. Christ is your defense. Consider how have you deceived or attempted to defend yourself according to the following:

SELF-DECEPTION (deceiving ourselves instead of acknowledging the truth)

____ Hearing God's Word but not doing it (see James 1:22; 4:17)
____ Saying we have no sin (see 1 John 1:8)
____ Thinking we are something when we are not (see Galatians 6:3)
____ Thinking we are wise in our own eyes (see 1 Corinthians 3:18–19)
____ Thinking we will not reap what we sow (see Galatians 6:7)
____ Thinking the unrighteous will inherit the kingdom
      (see 1 Corinthians 6:9)
____ Thinking we can associate with bad company and not be corrupted
      (see 1 Corinthians 15:33)

SELF-DEFENSE (defending ourselves instead of trusting in Christ)

____ Denial (conscious or subconscious refusal to face the truth)
____ Fantasy (escaping from the real world)
____ Emotional insulation (withdrawing to avoid rejection)
____ Regression (reverting back to a less-threatening time)
____ Displacement (taking out frustrations on others)
____ Projection (blaming others)
____ Rationalization (making excuses for poor behavior)

For those things that have been true in your life, pray aloud:

Lord,
I agree that I have been deceived in the area of _____. Thank you for forgiving me. I commit myself to know and to follow your truth. Amen.

Choosing the truth may be difficult if you have been living a lie (been deceived) for many years. You may need to seek professional help to weed out the defense mechanisms you have depended on to survive. The Christian needs only one defense—Jesus. Knowing that you are forgiven and accepted as God's child is what sets you free to face reality and declare your dependence on him.

Faith is the biblical response to the truth, and believing the truth is a choice. When someone says, "I want to believe God, but I just can't," that person is being deceived. Of course you can believe God. Faith is something you *decide* to do, not something you feel like doing. Believing the truth does not make it true. It *is* true; therefore, we believe it. The New Age movement is distorting the truth by saying we create reality through what we believe. We cannot create reality with our minds; we *face* reality. It is what or who you believe in that counts. Everybody believes in something, and everybody walks by faith according to what he or she believes. But if what you believe isn't true, then how you live (walk by faith) won't be right.

Historically, the church has found great value in publicly declaring its beliefs. The Apostles' Creed and the Nicene Creed have been recited for centuries. Read aloud the following affirmation of faith, and do so again as often as is necessary to renew your mind. Experiencing difficulty in reading this affirmation may indicate where you are being deceived and undergoing an attack. Boldly affirm your commitment to biblical truth.

DOCTRINAL AFFIRMATION

I recognize that there is only one true and living God (Exodus 20:2–3), who exists as the Father, Son, and Holy Spirit, and that he is worthy of all honor, praise, and glory as the Creator, Sustainer, and Beginning and End of all things (Revelation 4:11; 5:9–10; Isaiah 43:1, 7, 21).

I recognize Jesus Christ as the Messiah, the Word who became flesh and dwelt among us (John 1:1, 14). I believe that he came to destroy the works of Satan (1 John 3:8), that he disarmed the rulers and authorities and made a public display of them, having triumphed over them (Colossians 2:15).

I believe that God has proven his love for me because, when I was still a sinner, Christ died for me (Romans 5:8). I believe that he delivered me from the domain of darkness and transferred me to his kingdom, and in him I have redemption, the forgiveness of sins (Colossians 1:13–14).

I believe that I am now a child of God (1 John 3:1–3) and that I am seated with Christ in the heavenly realms (Ephesians 2:6). I believe that I was saved by the grace of God through faith, that it was a gift and not the result of any works on my part (Ephesians 2:8–9).

I choose to be strong in the Lord and in his mighty power (Ephesians 6:10). I put no confidence in the flesh (Philippians 3:3), for the weapons of warfare are not of the flesh (2 Corinthians 10:4). I put on the whole armor of God (Ephesians 6:10–20), and I resolve to stand firm in my faith and resist the evil one.

I believe that apart from Christ I can do nothing (John 15:5), so I declare myself dependent on him. I choose to abide in Christ in order to bear much fruit and glorify the Lord (John 15:8). I announce to Satan that

Jesus is my Lord (1 Corinthians 12:3), and I reject any counterfeit gifts or works of Satan in my life.

I believe that the truth will set me free (John 8:32) and that walking in the light is the only path of fellowship (1 John 1:7). Therefore, I stand against Satan's deception by taking captive every thought to make it obedient to Christ (2 Corinthians 10:5). I declare that the Bible is the only authoritative standard (2 Timothy 3:15 – 16). I choose to speak the truth in love (Ephesians 4:15).

I choose to present my body as an instrument of righteousness, a living and holy sacrifice, and I renew my mind by the living Word of God in order that I may prove that the will of God is good, pleasing, and perfect (Romans 6:13; 12:1 – 2). I put off the old self with its evil practices and put on the new self (Colossians 3:9 – 10), and I declare myself to be a new creation in Christ (2 Corinthians 5:17).

I trust my heavenly Father to fill me with his Holy Spirit (Ephesians 5:18), to guide me into all truth (John 16:13), and to empower my life that I may live above sin and not gratify the desires of the flesh (Galatians 5:16). I crucify the flesh (Galatians 5:24) and choose to walk by the Spirit.

I renounce all selfish goals and choose the ultimate goal of love (1 Timothy 1:5). I choose to obey the two greatest commandments: to love the Lord my God with all my heart, soul, and mind and to love my neighbor as myself (Matthew 22:37 – 39).

I believe that Jesus has all authority in heaven and on earth (Matthew 28:18) and that he is the head over all rule and authority (Colossians 2:10). I believe that Satan and his demons are subject to me in Christ, since I am a member of Christ's body (Ephesians 1:19 – 23). Therefore, I obey the command to submit to God and to resist the devil (James 4:7), and I command Satan in the name of Jesus Christ to leave my presence.

STEP 3: BITTERNESS VERSUS FORGIVENESS

We need to forgive others in order to be free from our pasts and to prevent Satan from taking advantage of us (see 2 Corinthians 2:10 – 11). We are to be merciful, just as our heavenly Father is merciful (see Luke 6:36). We are to forgive, just as we have been forgiven (see Ephesians 4:31 – 32). Ask God to bring to mind the names of those people you need to forgive by expressing the following prayer aloud:

Dear heavenly Father,

I thank you for the riches of your kindness, forbearance, and patience, knowing that your kindness has led me to repentance (Romans 2:4). I confess that I have not extended this same patience and kindness toward others who have offended me, but instead I have harbored bitterness and resentment. I pray that during this time of self-examination you would bring to my mind those people whom I need to forgive in order that I may do so now (Matthew 18:35). I ask this in the precious name of Jesus. Amen.

As names comes to mind, make a list of only the names. At the end of your list, write "myself." To forgive yourself is to accept God's cleansing and forgiveness. Also write "thoughts against God." Thoughts raised up against the knowledge of God will usually result in angry feelings toward him. Technically, we do not forgive God because he cannot commit any sin of commission or omission, but we do need to specifically renounce false expectations and thoughts about God and agree to release any anger we hold toward him.

Before you pray to forgive these people, stop and consider what forgiveness is, what it is not, what decision you will be making, and what the consequences will be. In the following explanation, the main points are in italic:

Forgiveness is not forgetting. People who try to forget find they cannot. God says he will remember our sins "no more" (see Hebrews 10:17), but God, being omniscient, cannot forget. To remember our sins "no more" means that God will never use the past against us (see Psalm 103:12). Forgetting may be the result of forgiveness, but it is never the means of forgiveness. When we bring up the past against others, we are saying that we have not forgiven them.

Forgiveness is a choice, a crisis of the will. Since God requires us to forgive, it is something we can do. However, forgiveness is difficult for us because it goes against our concept of justice. We want revenge for offenses suffered. However, we are told never to take our own revenge (see Romans 12:19). You say, "Why should I let this person off the hook?" That is precisely the problem. You are still hooked to them, still bound by your past. *You will let them off your hook, but they are never off God's.* He will deal with them fairly—something we cannot do.

You say, "You don't understand how much this person hurt me!" But don't you see?—they are still hurting you! How do you stop the pain? *You do not forgive others for their sake; you do it for your own sake so that you can be free.* Your need to forgive is not an issue between you and the offender; *it is between you and God.*

Forgiveness is agreeing to live with the consequences of another person's sin. Forgiveness is costly; you pay the price of the evil you forgive. You are going to live with those consequences whether you want to or not; your only choice is whether you will do so in the bitterness of unforgiveness or in the freedom of forgiveness. Jesus took the consequences of your sin upon himself. All true forgiveness is substitutionary, because no one really forgives without bearing the consequences of the other person's sin. God the Father "made him who had no sin to be sin for us, so that in him we might become the righteousness of God" (2 Corinthians 5:21). Where is the justice? It is the cross that makes forgiveness legally and morally right: "The death he died, he died to sin once for all" (Romans 6:10).

Decide that you will bear the burdens of others' offenses by not using that information against them in the future. Doing so does not mean that you tolerate sin. You must set up scriptural boundaries to prevent future abuse. There may be times when some may be required to testify for the sake of justice but not for the purpose of seeking revenge from a bitter heart.

How do you forgive from your heart? You acknowledge the hurt and the hate. If your forgiveness does not visit the emotional core of your life, it will be incomplete. Many feel the pain of interpersonal offenses, but they won't, or don't know how to, acknowledge it. Let God bring the pain to the surface so he can deal with it, for this is where the healing takes place.

Do not wait to forgive until you feel like forgiving; you will never get there. Feelings take time to heal after the choice to forgive is made and Satan has lost his foothold (see Ephesians 4:26–27). *Freedom is what will be gained, not a feeling.*

As you pray, God may bring to mind offending people and experiences you had totally forgotten. Let him do it, even if it is painful. Remember, you are doing this for your sake. God wants you to be free. Do not rationalize or explain the offender's behavior. Forgiveness is you dealing with your pain and leaving the other person to God. Positive feelings will follow in time; freeing yourself from the past is the critical issue right now.

Don't say, "Lord, please help me to forgive," because he is *already* helping you. Do not say, "Lord, I want to forgive," because you are bypassing the hard-core *choice* to forgive, which is your responsibility. Stay with each individual until you are sure you have dealt with all the remembered pain—what they did, how they hurt you, and how they made you feel (rejected, unloved, unworthy, dirty, and the like).

You are now ready to forgive the people on your list so you can be free in Christ—with these people no longer having any control over you. For each person on your list, pray aloud:

Lord,
I forgive _____ for (<u>verbally share every hurt and pain the Lord brings to your mind, and how it made you feel</u>).

After you have forgiven every person for every painful memory, finish this step by praying the following:

Lord,
I release to you all these people and my right to seek revenge. I choose not to hold on to my bitterness and anger, and I ask you to heal my damaged emotions. In Jesus' name, I pray. Amen.

STEP 4: REBELLION VERSUS SUBMISSION

We live in rebellious times. Many believe it is their right to sit in judgment on those in authority over them. Rebelling against God and his authority gives Satan an opportunity to attack. As our Commanding General, the Lord, says, "Get into ranks and follow me. I will not lead you into temptation, but I will deliver you from evil" (see Matthew 6:13).

We have two biblical responsibilities with respect to authority figures: to pray for them and to submit to them. The only time God permits us to disobey earthly leaders is when they require us to do something morally wrong before God or when they attempt to rule outside the realm of their authority. Pray the following prayer:

Dear heavenly Father,
You have said that rebellion is as the sin of witchcraft, and insubordination is as iniquity and idolatry (1 Samuel 15:23). I know that in action and attitude I have sinned against you with a rebellious heart. Thank you for forgiving my rebellion, and I pray that by the shed blood of the Lord Jesus Christ all ground gained by evil spirits because of my rebelliousness will be canceled. I pray that you will shed light on all my ways, that I may know the full extent of my rebelliousness. I now choose to adopt a submissive spirit and a servant's heart. In the name of Christ Jesus, my Lord. Amen.

Being under authority is an act of faith. You are trusting God to work through his established lines of authority. There are times when employers, parents, and husbands violate the laws of civil government that are ordained by God to protect innocent people against abuse. In these cases, you need to appeal to the state for your protection. In many states, the law requires such abuse to be reported.

In difficult cases, such as ongoing abuse at home, further counseling help may be needed. And, in some cases, when earthly authorities have abused their position and are requiring disobedience to God or a compromise in your commitment to God, you need to obey God, not humans (see Acts 5:29).

We are all admonished to submit to one another as equals in Christ (see Ephesians 5:21). However, there are specific lines of authority in Scripture for the purpose of accomplishing common goals:

- Civil government (see Romans 13:1 – 7; 1 Timothy 2:1 – 4; 1 Peter 2:13 – 17)
- Parents (see Ephesians 6:1 – 3)
- Husband (see 1 Peter 3:1 – 4) or wife (see Ephesians 5:21; 1 Peter 3:7)
- Employer (see 1 Peter 2:18 – 23)
- Church leaders (see Hebrews 13:17)
- God (see Daniel 9:5, 9)

Examine each area and, using this prayer, confess those times you have not been submissive:

Lord,
  I agree I have been rebellious toward _____. I choose to be submissive and obedient to your Word. In Jesus' name. Amen.

STEP 5: PRIDE VERSUS HUMILITY

Pride is a killer. Pride says, "I can do it! I can get myself out of this mess without God's or anyone else's help." Oh no, we can't! We *absolutely* need God, and we desperately need each other. Paul wrote, "We who worship by the Spirit of God, who glory in Christ Jesus ... put no confidence in the flesh" (Philippians 3:3). Humility is confidence properly placed. We are to be "strong in the Lord and in his mighty power" (Ephesians 6:10). James 4:6 – 10 and 1 Peter 5:1 – 10 reveal that spiritual conflict follows on the heels of pride. Use the following prayer to express your commitment to live humbly before God:

Dear heavenly Father,

You have said that pride goes before destruction and an arrogant spirit before stumbling (Proverbs 16:18). I confess that I have lived independently and have not denied myself, picked up my cross daily, and followed you (Matthew 16:24). In so doing, I have given ground to the enemy in my life. I have believed that I could be successful and live victoriously by my own strength and resources. I now confess that I have sinned against you by placing my will before yours and by centering my life on myself instead of on you. I now renounce the self-life, and by so doing cancel all the ground that has been gained in my members by the enemies of the Lord Jesus Christ. I pray that you will guide me so that I will do nothing out of selfishness or empty conceit, but with humility of mind I will regard others as more important than myself (Philippians 2:3). Enable me through love to serve others and give preference to others in honor (Romans 12:10). I ask this in the name of Christ Jesus, my Lord. Amen.

Having made this commitment, now allow God to show you any specific areas in your life where you have been prideful, such as

___ having a stronger desire to do my will than God's will
___ being more dependent on my own strengths and resources than on God's
___ too often believing that my ideas and opinions are better than others
___ being more concerned about controlling others than about developing self-control
___ sometimes considering myself more important than others
___ having a tendency to think that I have no needs
___ finding it difficult to admit that I was wrong
___ having a tendency to be more of a people pleaser than a God pleaser
___ being overly concerned about getting the credit I deserve
___ being driven to obtain the recognition that comes from degrees, titles, and positions
___ often thinking I am more humble than others
___ these other ways: _____

For each of these that has been true in your life, pray aloud:

Lord,

I agree I have been prideful by _____. I choose to humble myself and place all my confidence in you. Amen.

STEP 6: BONDAGE VERSUS FREEDOM

The next step to freedom deals with habitual sin. People who have been caught in the trap of *sin-confess-sin-confess-sin* may need to follow the instructions of James 5:16: "Confess your sins to each other and pray for each other so that you may be healed. The prayer of a righteous man is powerful and effective." Those of you who are caught in this trap are urged to seek out a righteous person who will hold you up in prayer and to whom you can be accountable; others may only need the assurance of 1 John 1:9: "If we confess our sins, he is faithful and just and will forgive us our sins and purify us from all unrighteousness." Confession is not saying "I'm sorry"; it is saying "I did it." Pray the following prayer — whether you need the help of others or simply the accountability to God:

Dear heavenly Father,

You have told us to put on the Lord Jesus Christ and make no provision for the flesh in regard to its desires (Romans 13:14). I acknowledge that I have given in to fleshly desires that wage war against my soul (1 Peter 2:11). I thank you that in Christ my sins are forgiven, but I have transgressed your holy law and given the enemy an opportunity to wage war in my physical body (Romans 6:12–13; Ephesians 4:27; James 4:1; 1 Peter 5:8). I come before your presence to acknowledge these sins and to seek your cleansing (1 John 1:9), that I may be freed from the bondage of sin. I now ask you to reveal to my mind the ways in which I have transgressed your moral law and grieved the Holy Spirit. In Jesus' precious name, I pray. Amen.

The deeds of the flesh are numerous. Many of the following issues are found in Galatians 5:19–21. Check those that apply to you, as well as any others you have struggled with that the Lord brings to your mind. Then confess each one, using the concluding prayer. *Note:* Sexual sins, eating disorders, substance abuse, abortion, suicidal tendencies, perfectionism, and fear will be dealt with a bit later in this Step, using special prayers for these specific problems.

____ stealing	____ fighting	____ envying
____ complaining	____ lusting	____ gossiping
____ procrastinating	____ greediness	____ divisiveness
____ lying	____ jealousy	____ outbursts of anger
____ criticizing	____ cheating	____ controlling
____ swearing	____ laziness	____ gambling
		____ other

Dear heavenly Father,

I thank you that my sins are forgiven in Christ, but I have walked by the flesh and therefore sinned by _____. Thank you for cleansing me of all unrighteousness. I ask that you would enable me to walk by the Spirit and not gratify the desires of the flesh. In Jesus' name, I pray. Amen.

It is our responsibility not to allow sin to reign in our mortal bodies by refusing to use our bodies as instruments of unrighteousness (see Romans 6:12–13). If you are struggling or have struggled with sexual sins (pornography, masturbation, sexual promiscuity, and the like) or are experiencing sexual difficulty in your marriage, pray as follows:

Lord,

I ask you to reveal to my mind every sexual use of my body as an instrument of unrighteousness. In Jesus' precious name, I pray. Amen.

As the Lord brings to your mind every sexual use of your body — whether it was done *to* you (rape, incest, or other sexual abuse) or willingly *by* you — renounce every occasion:

Lord,

I renounce (<u>name the specific misuse of your body</u>) with (<u>name the person</u>) and ask you to break that bond.

Now commit your body to the Lord by praying:

Lord,

I renounce all these uses of my body as an instrument of unrighteousness, and by so doing I ask you to break all bondages Satan has brought into my life through that involvement. I confess my participation. I now present my body to you as a living sacrifice, holy and acceptable to you, and I reserve the sexual use of my body only for marriage. I renounce the lie of Satan that my body is not clean, that it is dirty or in any way unacceptable as a result of my past sexual experiences. Lord, I thank you that you have totally cleansed and forgiven me, that you love and accept me unconditionally. Therefore, I can accept myself. And I choose to do so — to accept myself and my body as cleansed. In Jesus' name. Amen.

SPECIAL PRAYERS FOR SPECIFIC PROBLEMS

HOMOSEXUALITY

Lord,

I renounce the lie that you have created me or anyone else to be homo-sexual, and I affirm that you clearly forbid homosexual behavior. I accept myself as a child of God and declare that you created me a man [or woman]. I renounce any bondages of Satan that have perverted my relationships with others. I announce that I am free to relate to the opposite sex in the way you intended. In Jesus' name. Amen.

ABORTION

Lord,

I confess that I did not assume stewardship of the life you entrusted to me. I choose to accept your forgiveness, and I now commit that child to you for your care in eternity. In Jesus' name. Amen.

SUICIDAL TENDENCIES

Lord,

I renounce suicidal thoughts and any attempts I have made to take my own life or in any way injure myself. I renounce the lies that life is hopeless and that I can find peace and freedom by taking my own life. Satan is a thief, and he comes to steal, kill, and destroy. I choose to be a good steward of the physical life that you, Lord, have entrusted to me. In Jesus' name, I pray. Amen.

EATING DISORDERS OR SELF-MUTILATION

Lord,

I renounce the lie that my value as a person is dependent on my physi-cal beauty, my weight, or my size. I renounce cutting myself, vomiting, using laxatives, or starving myself as a means of trying to cleanse myself of evil or alter my appearance. I announce that only the blood of the Lord Jesus Christ cleanses me from sin. I accept the reality that there may be sin present in me due to the lies I have believed and the wrongful use of my body, but I renounce the lie that I am evil or that any part of my body is evil. My body is the temple of the Holy Spirit and I belong to you, Lord. I receive your love and acceptance of me. In Jesus' name. Amen.

SUBSTANCE ABUSE

Lord,

I confess that I have misused substances (alcohol, tobacco, food, prescription or street drugs) for the purpose of pleasure, to escape reality, or to cope with difficult situations — resulting in the abuse of my body, the harmful programming of my mind, and the quenching of the Holy Spirit. I ask your forgiveness. I renounce any satanic connection or influence in my life through my misuse of chemicals or food. I cast my anxiety on Christ, who loves me, and I commit myself to no longer yield to substance abuse but to the Holy Spirit instead. I ask you, heavenly Father, to fill me with your Holy Spirit. In Jesus' name. Amen.

DRIVENNESS AND PERFECTIONISM

Lord,

I renounce the lie that my sense of worth is dependent on my ability to perform. I announce the truth that my identity and sense of worth are found in who I am as your child. I renounce seeking the approval and acceptance of other people, and I choose to believe that I am already approved and accepted in Christ because of his death and resurrection for me. I choose to believe the truth that I have been saved, not by deeds done in righteousness, but according to your mercy. I choose to believe that I am no longer under the curse of the law because Christ became a curse for me. I receive the free gift of life in Christ and choose to abide in him. I renounce striving for perfection by living under the law. By your grace, heavenly Father, I choose from this day forward to walk by faith in accordance with what you have said is true by the power of your Holy Spirit. In Jesus' name. Amen.

PLAGUING FEARS

Dear heavenly Father,

I acknowledge you as the only legitimate fear object in my life. You are the only omnipresent (always-present) and omniscient (all-knowing) God and the only means by which all other fears can be expelled. You are my sanctuary. You have not given me a spirit of timidity, but of power and love and self-discipline. I confess that I have allowed the fear of humans and the fear of death to exercise control over my life instead of trusting in you. I now renounce all other fear objects and worship you only. I pray that you would fill me with your Holy Spirit that I may live my life and speak your word with boldness. In Jesus' name, I pray. Amen.

After you have confessed all known sin, pray this prayer:

Dear heavenly Father,

I now confess these sins to you and claim my forgiveness and cleansing through the blood of the Lord Jesus Christ. I cancel all ground that evil spirits have gained through my willful involvement in sin. I ask this in the wonderful name of my Lord and Savior, Jesus Christ. Amen.

STEP 7: ACQUIESCENCE VERSUS RENUNCIATION

Acquiescence is passively giving in or agreeing without consent. The last "Step to Freedom in Christ" is to renounce the sins of your ancestors and any curses that may have been placed on you. When giving the Ten Commandments, God said, "You shall not make for yourself an idol in the form of anything in heaven above or on the earth beneath or in the waters below. You shall not bow down to them or worship them; for I, the LORD your God, am a jealous God, punishing the children for the sin of the fathers to the third and fourth generation of those who hate me" (Exodus 20:4–5).

Familiar spirits can be passed on from one generation to the next if not renounced and if your new spiritual heritage in Christ is not proclaimed. You are not guilty for the sin of any ancestor, but because of your ancestors' sin, Satan may have gained access to your family. This is not to deny that many problems are transmitted genetically or acquired from an immoral atmosphere. All three conditions can predispose an individual to a particular sin. In addition, deceived people may try to curse you, or satanic groups may try to target you. You have all the authority and protection you need in Christ to stand firm against such curses and assignments.

Ask the Lord to reveal to your mind, as you pray the following prayer, the sins and iniquities of your ancestors:

Dear heavenly Father,

I thank you that I am a new creation in Christ. I desire to obey your command to honor my mother and my father; but I also acknowledge that my physical heritage has not been perfect. I ask you to reveal to my mind the sins and iniquities of my ancestors in order to confess, renounce, and forsake them. In Jesus' name, I pray. Amen.

Now claim your position and protection in Christ by making the following declaration verbally, and then by humbling yourself before God in prayer.

DECLARATION

I here and now reject and disown all the sins and iniquities of my ancestors, including (name them). As one who has been delivered from the power of darkness and translated into the kingdom of God's dear Son (Colossians 1:13), I cancel out all demonic working that has been passed on to me from my ancestors. As one who has been crucified and raised with Jesus Christ and who sits with him in heavenly places (Ephesians 2:6), I renounce all satanic assignments that are directed toward me and my ministry, and I cancel every curse that Satan and his workers have put on me. I announce to Satan and all his forces that Christ became a curse for me (Galatians 3:13) when he died for my sins on the cross. I reject any and every way in which Satan tries to claim ownership of me. I belong to the Lord Jesus Christ, who purchased me with his own blood. I reject all other blood sacrifices whereby Satan may claim ownership of me. I declare myself to be eternally and completely signed over and committed to the Lord Jesus Christ. By the authority I have in Jesus Christ, I now command every spiritual enemy of the Lord Jesus Christ to leave my presence. I commit myself to my heavenly Father to do his will from this day forward.

PRAYER

Heavenly Father,

I come to you as your child purchased by the blood of the Lord Jesus Christ. You are the Lord of the universe and the Lord of my life. I submit m body to you as an instrument of righteousness, a living sacrifice, that I may glorify you in my body. I now ask you to fill me with your Holy Spirit. I commit myself to the renewing of my mind in order to prove that your will is good, perfect, and acceptable for me. All this I do in the name and authority of the Lord Jesus Christ. Amen.

Once you have secured your freedom by going through these seven Steps, you may find demonic influences attempting reentry days or even months later. One person shared that she heard a spirit say to her mind, "I'm back" — two days after she had been set free. "No, you're not!" she proclaimed aloud — and the attack ceased immediately. One victory does not constitute winning the war. *Freedom must be maintained.* After completing these Steps, one jubilant lady asked, "Will I always be like this?" I told her that she would stay free as long as she remained in a right relationship with God. "Even if you slip and fall," I encouraged, "you know how to get right with God again."

One victim of incredible atrocities shared this illustration: "It's like being forced to play a game with an ugly stranger in my own home. I kept losing and I wanted to quit, but the ugly stranger wouldn't let me. Finally I called the police (a higher authority), and they came and escorted the stranger out. He knocked on the door trying to regain entry, but this time *I recognized his voice and didn't let him in.*" What a beautiful illustration of gaining freedom in Christ. We call on Jesus, the ultimate authority, and he escorts the enemy out of our lives. Know the truth, stand firm, and resist the evil one. Seek out good Christian fellowship and commit yourself to regular times of Bible study and prayer. God loves you, and he will never leave you or forsake you.

AFTERCARE

You have won a very important battle in an ongoing war. Freedom is yours as long as you keep choosing truth and standing firm in the mighty power of the Lord. If new memories should surface or if you should become aware of lies that you have believed or other non-Christian experiences you have had, renounce them and choose the truth. Some have found it helpful to go through the Steps again. As you do, be sure to read the instructions carefully.

For your encouragement and further study, read *Victory Over the Darkness* (youth version: *Stomping Out the Darkness*), *The Bondage Breaker* (adult or youth version), and *Released From Bondage.* If you are a parent, read *Spiritual Protection for Your Children. Walking in the Light* was written to help people understand God's guidance and discern counterfeit guidance. To maintain your freedom, we also suggest carrying out the following:

1. Seek legitimate Christian fellowship where you can walk in the light and speak the truth in love.
2. Study your Bible daily. Memorize key verses.
3. Take captive every thought to make it obedient to Christ. Assume responsibility for your thought life, reject the lie, choose the truth, and stand firm in your position in Christ.
4. Don't drift away! It is very easy to get lazy in your thoughts and revert back to old habit-patterns of thinking. Share your struggles openly with a trusted friend; you need at least one friend who will stand with you.
5. Don't expect another person to fight your battle for you. Others can help, but they can't think, pray, read the Bible, or choose the truth for you.
6. Continue to seek your identity and sense of worth in Christ. Read the book *Living Free in Christ* and the devotional *Daily in Christ.* Renew your mind with the truth that your acceptance, security, and significance is in Christ by reading aloud the list of "Who I Am in Christ" (see pages 305-306) and the Doctrinal Affirmation (see pages 395–396) every morning and evening over the next several weeks (be sure to look up the verse references as well).
7. Commit yourself to daily prayer. You can pray these suggested prayers often and with confidence.

DAILY PRAYERS

Heavenly Father,

I honor you as my sovereign Lord. I acknowledge that you are always present with me. You are the only all-powerful and wise God. You are kind and loving in all your ways. I love you and thank you that I am united with Christ and spiritually alive in him. I choose not to love the world, and I crucify the flesh and all its passions.

I thank you for the life that I now have in Christ, and I ask you to fill me with your Holy Spirit that I may live my life free from sin. I declare my dependence on you, and I take my stand against Satan and all his lying ways. I choose to believe the truth, and I refuse to be discouraged. You are the God of all hope, and I am confident that you will meet my needs as I seek to live according to your Word. I express with confidence that I can live a responsible life through Christ who gives me strength.

I now take my stand against Satan and command him and all his evil spirits to depart from me. I put on the whole armor of God. I submit my body as a living sacrifice and renew my mind by the living Word of God in order that I may prove that the will of God is good, pleasing, and perfect. I ask these things in the precious name of my Lord and Savior, Jesus Christ. Amen.

BEDTIME PRAYER

Thank you, Lord, that you have brought me into your family and have blessed me with every spiritual blessing in the heavenly realms in Christ Jesus. Thank you for providing this time of renewal through sleep. I accept it as part of your perfect plan for your children, and I trust you to guard my mind and my body during my sleep. As I have meditated on you and your truth during this day, I choose to let these thoughts continue in my mind while I am asleep. I commit myself to you for your protection from every attempt of Satan or his emissaries to attack me during sleep. I commit myself to you as my Rock, my Fortress, and my Resting Place. I pray in the strong name of the Lord Jesus Christ. Amen.

CLEANSING HOME/APARTMENT

After removing all articles of false worship from your home or apartment, pray aloud, in every room if necessary:

Heavenly Father, we acknowledge that you are Lord of heaven and earth. In your sovereign power and love, you have given us all things richly to enjoy. Thank you for this place to live. We claim this home for our family as a place of spiritual safety and protection from all the attacks of the enemy. As children of God seated with Christ in the heavenly realms, we command every evil spirit claiming ground in the structures and furnishings of this place, based on the activities of previous occupants, to leave and never return. We renounce all curses and spells directed against this place. We ask you, heavenly Father, to post guardian angels around this home [apartment, condo, room] to guard it from attempts of the enemy to enter and disturb your purposes for us. We thank you, Lord, for doing this, and pray in the name of the Lord Jesus Christ. Amen.

LIVING IN A NON-CHRISTIAN ENVIRONMENT

After removing all articles of false worship from your room, pray aloud in the space allotted to you:

Thank you, heavenly Father, for my place to live and be renewed by sleep. I ask you to set aside my room [portion of my room] as a place of spiritual safety for me. I renounce any allegiance given to false gods or spirits by other occupants, and I renounce any claim to this room [space] by Satan based on activities of past occupants or based on my own activities. On the basis of my position as a child of God and a co-heir with Christ, who has all authority in heaven and on earth, I command all evil spirits to leave this place and never to return. I ask you, heavenly Father, to appoint guardian angels to protect me while I live here. I pray this in the name of the Lord Jesus Christ. Amen.

Notes

INTRODUCTION

1. Noted in Brenda C. Coleman, "Doctors Prescribing More Antidepressant Medicines," *Denver Post,* 18 February 1998, sec. A, p. 3.

2. Observed in Mark R. McMinn, *Psychology, Theology, and Spirituality in Christian Counseling* (Wheaton, Ill.: Tyndale House, 1996), 8.

3. See Neil T. Anderson and Robert Saucy, *The Common Made Holy* (Eugene, Ore.: Harvest House, 1997).

CHAPTER 1: VALUES AND WORLDVIEW CLARIFICATION

1. American Psychological Association, Ethical Standard 1.08, noted by Siang-Yang Tan, "Religion in Clinical Practice: Implicit and Explicit Integration," in *Religion and the Clinical Practice of Psychology,* ed. Edward P. Shafranske (Washington, D.C.: American Psychological Association, 1996), 367.

2. American Psychiatric Association Board of Trustees, "Guidelines Regarding Possible Conflict Between Psychiatrists' Religious Commitment and Psychiatric Practice," *American Journal of Psychiatry* 147 (1990), 542.

3. Siang-Yang Tan, "Religious Values and Interventions in Lay Christian Counseling," *Journal of Psychology and Christianity* 10 (1991), 173–82, cited in Mark R. McMinn, *Psychology, Theology, and Spirituality in Christian Counseling* (Wheaton, Ill.: Tyndale House, 1996), 121.

4. Noted by Allen E. Bergin, I. Reed Payne, and P. Scott Richards, "Values in Psychotherapy," in *Religion and the Clinical Practice of Psychology,* 298.

5. Conclusions gleaned from Allen E. Bergin, "Psychotherapy and Religious Values," *Journal of Consulting and Clinical Psychology* 48 (1980), 95–105, cited in Bergin, Payne, and Richards, "Values in Psychotherapy," in *Religion and the Clinical Practice of Psychology,* 299.

6. An excellent reference for further study is David B. Larson and Susan S. Larson, *The Forgotten Factor in Physical and Mental Health: What Does the Research Show?* (Rockville, Md.: National Institute for Healthcare Research, 1994).

7. Observed by L. Beutler and J. Bergan, "Value Change in Counseling and Psychotherapy: A Search for Scientific Credibility," *Journal of Counseling Psychology* 38 (1991), 16–24, cited in Bergin, Payne, and Richards, "Values in Psychotherapy," in *Religion and the Clinical Practice of Psychology,* 297–98.

8. P. Scott Richards and Allen E. Bergin, *A Spiritual Strategy for Counseling and Psychotherapy* (Washington, D.C.: American Psychological Association, 1997), 7.

9. Two other important resources for understanding the increased interest by the American Psychological Association in issues of spirituality include P. Scott Richards and Allen Bergin, *A Spiritual Strategy for Counseling and Psychotherapy* (Washington, D.C.: American Psychological Association, 1997); and William R. Miller, ed., *Integrating Spirituality into Treatment* (Washington, D.C.: American Psychological Association, 1999).

10. G. Owen, "Ethics of Intervention for Change," *Australian Psychologist* 21 (1986), 211–18, cited in Bergin, Payne, and Richards, "Values in Psychotherapy," in *Religion and the Clinical Practice of Psychology,* 316.

11. Bergin, Payne, and Richards, "Values in Psychotherapy," in *Religion and the Clinical Practice of Psychology,* 316–17.

12. See W. Bevan, "Contemporary Psychology: A Tour Inside the Onion," *American Psychologist* 26 (1991), 475–83; W. O'Donohue, "The (Even) Bolder Model: The Clinical Psychologist as Metaphysician-Scientist-Practitioner," *American Psychologist* 44 (1989), 1460–68; J. Olthuis, "On Worldviews," *Christian Scholars Review* 14 (1985), 153–64; and N. Wolterstorff, *Reason Within the Bounds of Religion,* 2d ed. (Grand Rapids: Eerdmans, 1984).

13. Observed by Bergin, Payne, and Richards, "Values in Psychotherapy," in *Religion and the Clinical Practice of Psychology,* 316.

14. See discussion in David M. Wulff, "The Psychology of Religion: An Overview," in *Religion and the Clinical Practice of Psychology,* 47–52.

15. Cited in Tom Prichard, Minnesota Family Council Newsletter (Minneapolis: Minnesota Family Council, November 1999).

16. Wendell W. Watters, "Christianity and Mental Health," *The Humanist* (November/December 1987), 10, cited in David A. Noebel, *Understanding the Times* (Colorado Springs: Association of Christian Schools International and Summit Ministries, 1995), 167. This is an abridged version of Noebel's *Understanding the Times: The Religious Worldviews of Our Day and the Search for Truth* (Eugene, Ore.: Harvest House, 1994). Unless otherwise indicated, references to *Understanding the Times* are to the abridged version of the book.

17. Albert Ellis, "The Case Against Religiosity," in "Testament of a Humanist," *Free Inquiry* (spring 1987), 21, cited in Noebel, *Understanding the Times,* 19.

18. Reported in Larson and Larson, *The Forgotten Factor,* 32, 34.

19. Edward P. Shafranske, "Introduction: Foundation for the Consideration of Religion in the Clinical Practice of Psychology," in *Religion and the Clinical Practice of Psychology*, 1.

20. Statistics cited in Shafranske, "Foundation for the Consideration of Religion," in *Religion and the Clinical Practice of Psychology*, 1.

21. Statistics cited in Stanton L. Jones, "A Constructive Relationship for Religion With the Science and Profession of Psychology: Perhaps the Boldest Model Yet," in *Religion and the Clinical Practice of Psychology*, 113.

22. Noted in Jones, "A Constructive Relationship," in *Religion and the Clinical Practice of Psychology*, 131.

23. L. Rebecca Propst, "The Comparative Efficacy of Religious and Nonreligious Cognitive-Behavioral Therapy for the Treatment of Clinical Depression in Religious Individuals," *Journal of Consulting and Clinical Psychology* 60 (1992), 94–103, cited in Jones, "A Constructive Relationship," in *Religion and the Clinical Practice of Psychology*, 140.

24. T. Kelly and H. Strupp, "Patient and Therapist Values in Psychotherapy: Perceived Changes, Assimilation, Similarity, and Outcome," *Journal of Clinical and Consulting Psychology* 60 (1992), 34–40, cited in Jones, "A Constructive Relationship," in *Religion and the Clinical Practice of Psychology*, 140.

25. Noted by Shafranske, "Foundation for the Consideration of Religion," in *Religion and the Clinical Practice of Psychology*, 2–3.

26. Conclusions cited in Bergin, Payne, and Richards, "Values in Psychotherapy," in *Religion and the Clinical Practice of Psychology*, 300; and in Jones, "A Constructive Relationship," in *Religion and the Clinical Practice of Psychology*, 140.

27. Conclusions cited in Bergin, Payne, and Richards, "Values in Psychotherapy," in *Religion and the Clinical Practice of Psychology*, 300.

28. Observed by Warren Brookes, "The Key to Well-being," *The Washington Times*, 25 December 1989, sec. D, p. 1, cited in Noebel, *Understanding the Times*, 15.

29. Noebel, *Understanding the Times*, 2.

30. Taken from Noebel, *Understanding the Times*, 24. Reproduced by permission.

31. Quoted in Noebel, *Understanding the Times*, 16.

32. Discussed in Stephen P. Goold, "New Age Deception: 'No Other Gods,'" Part 4 (sermon at Crystal Evangelical Free Church, New Hope, Minnesota, 4 October 1998), message tape #98.

33. Noebel, *Understanding the Times*, 171.

34. Ibid., 165–66.

35. Cited in Noebel, *Understanding the Times*, 170.

36. Richard A. Baer, "They Are Teaching Religion in Public Schools," *Christianity Today* (17 February 1984), 15, cited in Noebel, *Understanding the Times*, 18.

37. Francis A. Schaeffer gives examples in his book, *A Christian Manifesto* (Westchester, Ill.: Crossway, 1981), 54, cited in Noebel, *Understanding the Times*, 16.

38. Noted by Schaeffer, *A Christian Manifesto*, 55, cited in Noebel, *Understanding the Times*, 17.

39. Cal Thomas, "Turner's Takeover Tender," *The Washington Times*, 6 November 1989, sec. F, p. 2, cited in Noebel, *Understanding the Times*, 7.

40. Noebel, *Understanding the Times*, 181.

41. Asserted by Vera Alder, *When Humanity Comes of Age* (New York: Samuel Weiser, 1974), 82, cited in Noebel, *Understanding the Times,* 186.

42. Asserted by Shirley MacLaine, *Out on a Limb* (Toronto: Bantam, 1984), 96, cited in Noebel, *Understanding the Times,* 187.

43. Noted by Kathleen Vande Kieft, *Innersource: Channeling Your Unlimited Self* (New York: Ballantine, 1988), 114, cited in Noebel, *Understanding the Times,* 187.

44. Noebel, *Understanding the Times,* 13–15.

CHAPTER 2: RECLAIMING A BIBLICAL PSYCHOLOGY

1. Noted by David A. Noebel, *Understanding the Times* (Colorado Springs, Colo.: Association of Christian Schools International and Summit Ministries, 1995), 192. This is an abridged version of Noebel's *Understanding the Times: The Religious Worldviews of Our Day and the Search for Truth* (Eugene, Ore.: Harvest House, 1994). Unless otherwise indicated, references to *Understanding the Times* are to the abridged version of the book.

2. Quoted in Noebel, *Understanding the Times,* 194–96.

3. Cited in Frank S. Mead, *The Encyclopedia of Religious Quotations* (Westwood, N.J.: Revell, 1965), 11.

4. Noebel, *Understanding the Times,* 18.

5. Observed in Noebel, *Understanding the Times,* 18.

6. See discussion in Allen E. Bergin, I. Reed Payne, and P. Scott Richards, "Values in Psychotherapy," in *Religion and the Clinical Practice of Psychology,* ed. Edward P. Shafranske (Washington, D.C.: American Psychological Association, 1996), 300–301.

7. Stanton L. Jones, "A Constructive Relationship for Religion With the Science and Profession of Psychology: Perhaps the Boldest Model Yet," in *Religion and the Clinical Practice of Psychology,* 140.

8. Bergin, Payne, and Richards, "Values in Psychotherapy," in *Religion and the Clinical Practice of Psychology,* 314.

9. Andy Rowan, quoted in "Christian Counselors in Secular Settings: A Panel Response by Miriam Neff, Andy Rowan, and Steven J. Sandage," *Christian Counseling Today* 5, no. 4 (1997), 15.

10. Statistics cited in David B. Larson and Susan S. Larson, *The Forgotten Factor in Physical and Mental Health: What Does the Research Show?* (Rockville, Md.: National Institute for Healthcare Research, 1994), 24.

11. Larson and Larson, *The Forgotten Factor,* 19.

12. Summarized in Larson and Larson, *The Forgotten Factor,* 33.

13. Cited in Bergin, Payne, and Richards, "Values in Psychotherapy," in *Religion and the Clinical Practice of Psychology,* 311.

14. Gary R. Collins, "What Is Christian Counseling?" in *Case Studies in Christian Counseling,* ed. Gary R. Collins (Dallas: Word, 1991), 14–15.

15. For an example, see Albert Ellis, "Psychotherapy and Atheistic Values: A Response to A. E. Bergin's Psychotherapy and Religious Values," in *Journal of Consulting and Clinical Psychology,* 48 (1980), 635–39.

16. Gerald Corey, Marianne Schneider Corey, and Patrick Callanan, *Issues and Ethics in the Helping Professions,* 4th ed. (Pacific Grove, Calif.: Brooks/Cole, 1993), 13.

17. Ibid., 98.

18. Asserted by Edward P. Shafranske and H. Newton Malony, "Religion and the Clinical Practice of Psychology: A Case for Inclusion," in *Religion and the Clinical Practice of Psychology,* 561.

19. Allen E. Bergin, "Psychotherapy and Religious Values," *Journal of Consulting and Clinical Psychology* 48 (1980), 95–105, cited in Bergin, Payne, and Richards, "Values in Psychotherapy," in *Religion and the Clinical Practice of Psychology,* 298.

20. Bergin, Payne, and Richards, "Values in Psychotherapy," in *Religion and the Clinical Practice of Psychology,* 317.

21. See Edward P. Shafranske, ed., *Religion and the Clinical Practice of Psychology* (Washington, D.C.: American Psychological Association, 1996); P. Scott Richards and Allen E. Bergin, *A Spiritual Strategy for Counseling and Psychotherapy* (Washington, D.C.: American Psychological Association, 1997); and William R. Miller, ed., *Integrating Spirituality into Treatment* (Washington, D.C.: American Psychological Association, 1999).

22. Observed in Jones, "A Constructive Relationship" in *Religion and the Clinical Practice of Psychology,* 139.

23. Observed by David G. Benner, *Psychotherapy and the Spiritual Quest* (Grand Rapids: Baker, 1988), cited in Siang-Yang Tan, "Religion in Clinical Practice: Implicit and Explicit Integration," in *Religion and the Clinical Practice of Psychology,* 378.

24. W. O'Donohue, "The (Even) Bolder Model: The Clinical Psychologist as Metaphysician-Scientist-Practitioner," *American Psychologist* 44 (1989), 1460–68, cited in Jones, "A Constructive Relationship," in *Religion and the Clinical Practice of Psychology,* 130.

25. Cited in Neil T. Anderson, *The Bondage Breaker* (Eugene, Ore.: Harvest House, 1990), 29.

26. See the discussion in Anderson, *The Bondage Breaker,* 28–29.

27. Richards and Bergin, *A Spiritual Strategy for Counseling and Psychotherapy,* 10.

28. Observed in Richards and Bergin, *A Spiritual Strategy for Counseling and Psychotherapy,* 10.

29. Noted in W. I. Trattner, *From Poor Law to Welfare State: A History of Social Welfare in America* (New York: The Free Press, 1994), 2.

30. James C. Coleman and William E. Broen Jr., *Abnormal Psychology and Modern Life* (Glenville, Ill.: Scott Foresman, 1972), 27.

31. Quoted in Coleman and Broen, *Abnormal Psychology and Modern Life,* 27.

32. Theodore Millon, *Modern Psychopathology* (Philadelphia: W. B. Saunders, 1969), 7.

33. Discussed in Millon, *Modern Psychopathology,* 7.

34. Quoted in Coleman and Broen, *Abnormal Psychology and Modern Life,* 42.

35. Discussed in Thomas S. Szasz, *The Myth of Mental Illness: Formulation of a Theory of Normal Conduct* (New York: Dell, 1961).

36. Summarized from the discussion in Millon, *Modern Psychopathology,* 21.

37. See the discussion in Mark R. McMinn, *Psychology, Theology, and Spirituality in Christian Counseling* (Wheaton, Ill.: Tyndale House, 1996), 129.

38. Ibid., 130–132.

39. Millard J. Erickson, *Christian Theology* (Grand Rapids: Baker, 1985), 578.

40. McMinn, *Psychology, Theology, and Spirituality in Christian Counseling*, 134.

CHAPTER 3: DIVERSE STRATEGIES IN CHRISTIAN COUNSELING

1. Noted in E. L. Worthington Jr., and S. R. Gascoyne, "Preferences of Christians and Non-Christians for Five Christian Counselors' Treatment Plans: A Partial Replication and Extension," *Journal of Psychology and Theology* 13 (1985), 29–30.

2. Larry J. Crabb, *Effective Biblical Counseling* (Grand Rapids: Zondervan, 1977), 31.

3. K. N. Lewis and D. L. Epperson, "Values, Pre-therapy Information, and Informed Consent in Christian Counseling," *Journal of Psychology and Christianity* 10 (1991), 113–31, cited in Allen E. Bergin, I. Reed Payne, and P. Scott Richards, "Values in Psychotherapy," in *Religion and the Clinical Practice of Psychology*, ed. Edward P. Shafranske (Washington, D.C.: American Psychological Association, 1996), 313. See also Siang-Yang Tan, "Religion in Clinical Practice: Implicit and Explicit Integration," in *Religion and the Clinical Practice of Psychology*, 369.

4. K. E. Kudlac, "Including God in the Conversation: The Influence of Religious Beliefs on the Problem-Organized System," *Family Therapy* 18 (1991), 281, cited in Bergin, Payne, and Richards, "Values in Psychotherapy," in *Religion and the Clinical Practice of Psychology*, 301.

5. American Psychological Association, "Ethical Principles of Psychologists and Code of Conduct," *American Psychologist* 41 (1992), 1597–1611.

6. Observed in Edward P. Shafranske and H. Newton Malony, "Clinical Psychologists' Religious and Spiritual Orientations and their Practice of Psychotherapy," *Psychotherapy* 27 (1990), 72–78. See also Edward P. Shafranske and H. Newton Malony, "California Psychologists' Religiosity and Psychotherapy," *Journal of Religion and Health* 28 (1990), 219–31; and K. Derr, "Religious Issues in Psychotherapy: Factors Associated With the Selection of Clinical Interventions" (doctoral diss., Los Angeles: University of Southern California, 1991), both cited in Edward P. Shafranske, "Religious Beliefs, Affiliations, and Practices of Clinical Psychologists," in *Religion and the Clinical Practice of Psychology*, 157.

7. Everett L. Worthington Jr., "Psychotherapy and Religious Values: An Update," *Journal of Psychology and Christianity* 10 (1991), 211–23, cited in David B. Larson and Susan S. Larson, *The Forgotten Factor in Physical and Mental Health: What Does the Research Show?* (Rockville, Md.: National Institute for Healthcare Research, 1994), 14.

8. Crabb, *Effective Biblical Counseling*, 34.

9. Ibid., 36.

10. Ibid., 47.

11. Ibid., 40.

12. Ibid., 47.

13. W. Henry, J. Sims, and S. L. Spray, *The Fifth Profession* (San Francisco: Jossey Bass, 1971), cited in Larson and Larson, *The Forgotten Factor*, 49.

14. Crabb, *Effective Biblical Counseling*, 48.

15. See Crabb, *Effective Biblical Counseling*, 49–50. Note that Dr. Crabb's most recent books reflect striking changes in his views on the integration of theology and psychology.

16. Crabb, *Effective Biblical Counseling*, 52.

17. Frank B. Minirth and Walter Byrd, *Christian Psychiatry* (Old Tappen, N.J.: Revell, 1977), 23 – 25, citing Gary Collins, "The Pulpit and the Couch," *Christianity Today* (19 August 1975), 5 – 9.

18. Hendrika Vande Kemp, "Historical Perspective: Religion and Clinical Psychology in America," in *Religion and the Clinical Practice of Psychology*, 87.

19. Observed in Minirth and Byrd, *Christian Psychiatry*, 24.

20. Minirth and Byrd, *Christian Psychiatry*, 24.

21. Observed in Minirth and Byrd, *Christian Psychiatry*, 25.

22. Tan, "Religion in Clinical Practice," in *Religion and the Clinical Practice of Psychology*, 368.

23. Observed in Tan, "Religion in Clinical Practice," in *Religion and the Clinical Practice of Psychology*, 368.

24. Mark R. McMinn, *Psychology, Theology, and Spirituality in Christian Counseling* (Wheaton, Ill.: Tyndale House, 1996), 26.

25. Jay E. Adams, *The Christian Counselor's Manual* (Grand Rapids: Baker, 1973), 13.

26. Ibid., 33.

27. John MacArthur, Jr., *Our Sufficiency in Christ* (Dallas: Word, 1991), 66.

28. Crabb, *Effective Biblical Counseling*, 34.

29. See Gary R. Habermas, "Psychological Versus Biblical Counseling: A House Divided?" *Christian Counseling Today* 1, no. 4 (1993), 32 – 35.

30. Habermas, "Psychological Versus Biblical Counseling," 33.

31. Cited in Habermas, "Psychological Versus Biblical Counseling," 33.

32. Habermas, "Psychological Versus Biblical Counseling," 33.

33. Ibid.

34. Jim D. Owen, *Christian Psychology's War on God's Word: The Victimization of the Believer* (Santa Barbara, Calif.: Eastgate, 1993), 136.

35. Ibid., 195.

36. Habermas, "Psychological Versus Biblical Counseling," 33.

37. Jay E. Adams, *Competent to Counsel* (Grand Rapids: Baker, 1970), 51.

38. Ibid., 51 – 52.

39. MacArthur, *Our Sufficiency in Christ*, 30.

40. Ibid.

41. Edward P. Shafranske and H. Newton Malony, "Clinical Psychologists' Religious and Spiritual Orientations and their Practice of Psychotherapy," *Psychotherapy* 27 (1990), 72 – 78, cited in Tan, "Religion in Clinical Practice," in *Religion and the Clinical Practice of Psychology*, 366.

42. Allen E. Bergin and J. P. Jensen, "Religiosity of Psychotherapists: A National Survey," *Psychotherapy* 27 (1990), 3 – 7, cited in Tan, "Religion in Clinical Practice," in *Religion and the Clinical Practice of Psychology*, 366.

43. Larry J. Crabb, "Struggling Without a Shepherd," *Christian Counseling Today* 4, no. 4 (1996), 15.

44. Dan Allender, "Are We Winning the Battle?" *Christian Counseling Today* 6, no. 1 (1998), 9.

45. Kenneth I. Pargament, "Religious Methods of Coping: Resources for the Conservation and Transformation of Significance," in *Religion and the Clinical Practice of Psychology*, 233.

46. MacArthur, *Our Sufficiency in Christ*, 70.

47. Ibid.

48. Ibid., 70–71.

49. American Psychological Association, "Ethical Principles of Psychologists and Code of Conduct," *American Psychologist* 41 (1992), 1597–1611.

50. Crabb, *Effective Biblical Counseling*, 32.

51. Neil T. Anderson and Robert L. Saucy, *The Common Made Holy* (Eugene, Ore.: Harvest House, 1997), 162.

52. Pargament, "Religious Methods of Coping," in *Religion and the Clinical Practice of Psychology*, 233.

53. Ibid.

54. MacArthur, *Our Sufficiency in Christ*, 70.

CHAPTER 4: THE INTEGRATION OF THEOLOGY AND PSYCHOLOGY

1. Robert Jewett, *Paul's Anthropological Terms* (Leiden: Brill), 313.

2. Discussed by Neil T. Anderson and Robert Saucy, *The Common Made Holy* (Eugene, Ore.: Harvest House, 1997), 42.

3. Sinclair Ferguson, "The Reformed View," in *Christian Spirituality*, ed. Donald L. Alexander (Downers Grove, Ill.: InterVarsity Press, 1988), 60. See also James D. G. Dunn, *The Theology of Paul the Apostle* (Grand Rapids: Eerdmans, 1998), 630–31.

4. John Stott, *Romans: God's Good News for the World* (Downers Grove, Ill.: InterVarsity Press, 1994), 187.

5. Neil T. Anderson, *Living Free in Christ* (Ventura, Calif.: Regal, 1993), 278.

6. See Neil Anderson's book on depression, *Finding Hope Again* (Ventura, Calif.: Regal, 1999). Neil credits two other sources that merit attention: Martin Seligman, *Learned Optimism* (New York: Pocket, 1990); and Demitri Papolos and Janice Papolos, *Overcoming Depression* (New York: HarperPerennial, 1992).

7. See William Backus, *Telling Yourself the Truth*, 2d ed. (Minneapolis: Bethany House, 2000), William Backus, *The Healing Power of a Christian Mind* (Minneapolis: Bethany House, 1998), and David Stoop, *Self-Talk*, 2d ed. (Grand Rapids: Revell, 1996) for more on this topic.

8. Albert Ellis, "Can Rational Counseling Be Christian?" *Christian Counseling Today* 5, no. 1 (1997), 13.

9. Edmund J. Bourne, *The Anxiety & Phobia Workbook*, 2d ed. (Oakland, Calif.: New Harbinger, 1995). First edition published in 1990.

10. Edmund J. Bourne, *Healing Fear* (Oakland, Calif.: New Harbinger, 1998), 2.

11. Ibid., 3.

12. Ibid., 5.

CHAPTER 5: GOD, CLIENT, AND THERAPIST IN CHRISTIAN COUNSELING

1. Neil T. Anderson and Robert Saucy, *The Common Made Holy* (Eugene, Ore.: Harvest House, 1997), 143.

CHAPTER 6: A BIBLICAL STRATEGY FOR CHRISTIAN COUNSELING

1. Discussed in Neil T. Anderson, *Victory Over the Darkness* (Ventura, Calif.: Regal, 1990), 230–31.
2. Cited in Neal T. Anderson and Robert Saucy, *The Common Made Holy*, (Eugene, Ore.: Harvest House, 1997), 361.
3. *Diagnostic and Statistical Manual of Mental Disorders*, 4th ed. (Washington, D.C.: American Psychiatric Association, 1994).
4. Neil T. Anderson, *Helping Others Find Freedom In Christ* (Ventura, Calif.: Regal, 1995).
5. For a more comprehensive explanation, see Neil T. Anderson, *A Way of Escape* (Eugene, Ore.: Harvest House, 1994).

CHAPTER 7: PRACTITIONER AND CLIENT ASSESSMENT

1. Mark R. McMinn, *Psychology, Theology, and Spirituality in Christian Counseling* (Wheaton, Ill.: Tyndale House, 1996), 12.
2. McMinn, *Psychology, Theology, and Spirituality in Christian Counseling*, 13.
3. See the discussion in McMinn, *Psychology, Theology, and Spirituality in Christian Counseling*, 155.
4. Siang-Yang Tan and Douglas H. Gregg, *Disciplines of the Holy Spirit* (Grand Rapids: Zondervan, 1997), 104.
5. Discussed in Stanton L. Jones, "A Constructive Relationship for Religion With the Science and Profession of Psychology: Perhaps the Boldest Model Yet," in *Religion and the Clinical Practice of Psychology*, ed. Edward P. Shafranske (Washington, D.C.: American Psychological Association, 1996), 140–41.
6. Noted in McMinn, *Psychology, Theology, and Spirituality in Christian Counseling*, 157.
7. Siang-Yang Tan, "Religion in Clinical Practice: Implicit and Explicit Integration," in *Religion and the Clinical Practice of Psychology*, 378, citing R. J. Foster, *Celebration of Discipline* (San Francisco: Harper & Row, 1988); and D. Willard, *The Spirit of the Disciplines* (San Francisco: Harper & Row, 1988).
8. Discussed in McMinn, *Psychology, Theology, and Spirituality in Christian Counseling*, 11.
9. McMinn, *Psychology, Theology, and Spirituality in Christian Counseling*, 15, 116.
10. *Diagnostic and Statistical Manual of Mental Disorders*, 4th ed. (Washington, D.C.: American Psychiatric Association, 1994).
11. Ibid., 685.
12. See Terry E. Zuehlke and John T. Watkins, "Psychotherapy with Terminally Ill Patients," *Psychotherapy: Theory, Research, and Practice* 14 (1977), 403–10.

13. Edward P. Shafranske and H. Newton Malony, "Religion and the Clinical Practice of Psychology: A Case for Inclusion," in *Religion and the Clinical Practice of Psychology,* 581.

14. Cited in Shafranske and Malony, "Religion and the Clinical Practice of Psychology," in *Religion and the Clinical Practice of Psychology,* 581.

15. Shafranske and Malony, "Religion and the Clinical Practice of Psychology," in *Religion and the Clinical Practice of Psychology,* 577.

16. Ibid. See also G. W. Albee, "Opposition to Prevention and a New Creedal Oath," *The Scientist Practitioner* 1, no. 4 (1991), 30–31; and Albert Ellis, "Psychotherapy and Atheistic Values: A Response to A. E. Bergin's 'Psychotherapy and Religious Values,'" *Journal of Consulting and Clinical Psychology* 48 (1980), 635–39.

17. Shafranske and Malony, "Religion and the Clinical Practice of Psychology," in *Religion and the Clinical Practice of Psychology,* 568.

18. *The Faith Factor Bibliography Series,* four volumes (Rockville, Md.: National Institute for Healthcare Research, 1993, 1994, 1995, 1997). This series includes more than 350 published studies on the impact of spirituality on various aspects of mental, physical, and social health. See also David B. Larson, James P. Swyers, and Michael E. McCullough, *Scientific Research on Spirituality and Health: A Consensus Report* (Rockville, Md.: National Institute for Healthcare Research, 1998).

19. David B. Larson, Francis G. Lu, and James P. Swyers, *Model Curriculum for Psychiatric Residency Training Programs: Religion and Spirituality in Clinical Practice* (Rockville, Md.: National Institute for Healthcare Research, 1996).

20. Clinton E. Arnold, *3 Crucial Questions about Spiritual Warfare* (Grand Rapids: Baker, 1997), 34.

21. Neil T. Anderson, *Victory Over the Darkness* (Ventura: Calif.: Regal, 1990), 159.

22. "Professional Notes," *Psychotherapy Finances* 24, no. 1 (January 1998), 10.

23. Reported in the *American Family Association* Journal (July 1998), 3.

24. Paul McGuire, "Hollywood Religion," *Christian American* (November/December 1997), 58.

25. Reported in the *Minneapolis Star and Tribune,* 6 June 1998, sec. A, p. 13.

26. "Practice Issues: Will You Be Competing with Psychics and Philosophers?" *Psychotherapy Finances* 24, no. 5 (May 1998), n.p.

27. Neil T. Anderson and Rich Miller, *Freedom from Fear* (Eugene, Ore.: Harvest House, 1999).

28. *Diagnostic and Statistical Manual of Mental Disorders,* 4th ed., xxvii.

29. See James Morrison, *DSM-IV Made Easy: The Clinician's Guide to Diagnosis* (New York: Guilford, 1995), 544–46.

30. Morrison, *DSM-IV Made Easy,* 545.

31. Ibid., 546.

32. Our good friend Dr. Stephen King, a practicing Christian psychiatrist, is intimately familiar with our ministries and methods. His specific comments about the role of the psychiatrist in the comprehensive assessment of the client can be found in Appendix B.

CHAPTER 8: RESOLVING ROOT ISSUES IN THE MARKETPLACE

1. Observed in Robert S. McGee, *The Search for Significance* (Houston: Rapha, 1990), 27.
2. D. James Kennedy, *Evangelism Explosion* (Wheaton, Ill.: Tyndale House, 1970), 16.
3. Michael Goodman, Janet Brown, and Pamela Deitz, *Managing Managed Care: A Mental Health Practitioner's Survival Guide* (Washington, D.C.: American Psychiatric Press, 1992), xiii.
4. Noted in Goodman, Brown, and Deitz, *Managing Managed Care*, xiii.
5. Goodman, Brown, and Deitz, *Managing Managed Care*, xiv.
6. Ibid.
7. Discussed in Goodman, Brown, and Deitz, *Managing Managed Care*, 31.
8. Model found in Goodman, Brown, and Deitz, *Managing Managed Care*, 32.
9. Taken from Goodman, Brown, and Deitz, *Managing Managed Care*, 79.
10. Ibid., 34–37.
11. Arthur E. Jongsma, Jr., and L. Mark Peterson, *The Complete Psychotherapy Treatment Planner* (New York: Wiley, 1995), 1.
12. Value Behavioral Health, *Clinical Manual*, 1995, sec. E, p. 1.
13. Gleaned from Jongsma and Peterson, *The Complete Psychotherapy Treatment Planner*, 3.
14. Observed in Goodman, Brown, and Deitz, *Managing Managed Care*, 145.
15. Ibid., 24.
16. Ibid., 105.
17. Roger K. Bufford, *Counseling and the Demonic* (Dallas: Word, 1988), 95.
18. Observed in Bufford, *Counseling and the Demonic*, 100.
19. *Diagnostic and Statistical Manual of Mental Disorders*, 4th ed. (Washington, D.C.: American Psychiatric Association, 1994), 788.

CHAPTER 9: COUNSELING ASSISTANCE TOOL KIT

1. Georgia Witkin, *The Female Stress Syndrome* (New York: Newmarket, 1991).
2. Thomas Holmes and Richard Rahe, "The Social Readjustment Rating Scale," *Journal of Psychosomatic Research* 11 (1967).
3. David A. Seamands, *Putting Away Childish Things* (Wheaton, Ill.: Victor, 1986), 5.
4. Ibid., 28.
5. Dr. Edward M. Smith, *Beyond Tolerable Recovery*, 2d ed. (Campbellsville, Ky.: Family Care Ministries, 1997), 30, 32.
6. Note that TheoPhostic counseling cannot be conducted unless the facilitator (professional or layperson) has attended a Basic Training Seminar (in person) or has viewed the video training sessions of the Basic Training Seminar and has read the 300-plus pages in the Training Manual. Call TheoPhostic Ministries (1-270-465-3757) for information.
7. See also Neil Anderson, *Helping Others Find Freedom In Christ* (Ventura, Calif.: Regal, 1995), 276.
8. Discussed in Smith, *Beyond Tolerable Recovery*, 18.
9. Smith, *Beyond Tolerable Recovery*, 17.

10. Principles summarized in Sheryl Baar Moon, *Boundaries Leader's Guide* (Grand Rapids: Zondervan, 1994), 8.

11. Discussed in Moon, *Boundaries Leader's Guide*, 13.

12. Ibid., 18, 24.

13. Described in *Diagnostic and Statistical Manual of Mental Disorders,* 4th ed. (Washington, D.C.: American Psychiatric Association, 1994), 487.

14. See Neil T. Anderson and Charles Mylander, *The Christ Centered Marriage* (Ventura, Calif.: Regal, 1996), and Neil T. Anderson and Charles Mylander, *The Christ Centered Marriage Study Guide* (Ventura, Calif.: Regal, 1997). The workbooks *Setting Your Marriage Free* and *Beginning Your Marriage Free* can be purchased from Freedom in Christ Ministries.

15. Discussed in Patrick Carnes, *The Sexual Addiction* (Minneapolis: CompCare, 1983), 126.

16. Ibid., 10.

17. Carnes, *The Sexual Addiction,* 12.

18. Mark Laaser, *Faithful and True: Sexual Integrity in a Fallen World* (Grand Rapids: Zondervan, 1996), 30.

19. Mark Laaser, *Faithful and True: Sexual Integrity in a Fallen World Workbook* (Nashville: LifeWay Press, 1996), 94–111.

20. Discussed in Douglas Weiss, *101 Freedom Exercises: Christian Guide for Sex Addiction Recovery* (Fort Worth, Tex.: Discovery, 1997).

21. See Neil Anderson, Mike Quarles, and Julia Quarles, *Freedom From Addiction* (Ventura, Calif.: Regal, 1996), 205.

CHAPTER 10: PROFESSIONAL CHRISTIAN THERAPY AND THE CHURCH COMMUNITY

1. Siang-Yang Tan and Douglas H. Gregg, *Disciplines of the Holy Spirit* (Grand Rapids: Zondervan, 1997), 66.

CHAPTER 11: PROFESSIONAL ACCOUNTABILITY RELATIONSHIPS WITH AUTHORITY

1. George Ohlschlager and Peter Mosgofian, *Law for the Christian Counselor* (Dallas: Word, 1992), 23.

2. Siang-Yang Tan, "Lay Counselor Training," in *Christian Counseling Ethics: A Handbook for Therapists, Pastors & Counselors*, ed. Randolph K. Sanders (Downers Grove, Ill.: InterVarsity Press, 1997), 240. See also W. W. Becker, "The Paraprofessional Counselor in the Church: Legal and Ethical Considerations," *Journal of Psychology and Christianity* 6 (1987), 78–82.

3. Discussed in Ohlschlager and Mosgofian, *Law for the Christian Counselor*, 263.

4. Alan C. Tjeltveit, "Psychotherapy and Christian Ethics," in *Christian Counseling Ethics*, 28.

5. Ibid., 35.

6. Gary R. Collins, "Excellence in Christian Counseling," ed. Gary R. Collins, *Excellence and Ethics in Counseling* (Dallas: Word, 1991), 16.

7. Quoted in Randolph K. Sanders, "Ethical Issues in Special Settings: An Interview with Stephen H. Allison & Richard L. Price," in *Christian Counseling Ethics*, 255–56.

8. Tjeltveit, "Psychotherapy and Christian Ethics," in *Christian Counseling Ethics*, 27.

9. P. Scott Richards and Allen E. Bergin, *A Spiritual Strategy for Counseling and Psychotherapy* (Washington, D.C.: American Psychological Association, 1997), 154.

10. Siang-Yang Tan, "Religion in Clinical Practice: Implicit and Explicit Integration," in *Religion and the Clinical Practice of Psychology*, ed. Edward P. Shafranske (Washington, D.C.: American Psychological Association, 1996), 369, citing A. A. Nelson and W. P. Wilson, "The Ethics of Sharing Religious Faith in Psychotherapy," *Journal of Psychology and Theology* 12 (1984), 15–23.

11. Discussed in Allen E. Bergin, I. Reed Payne, and P. Scott Richards, "Values in Psychotherapy," in *Religion and the Clinical Practice of Psychology*, 314

12. Edward L. Zuckerman and Irvin P. R. Guyett, *The Paper Office 1* (Pittsburgh: The Clinician's Toolbox, 1992), 1.

13. H. Newton Malony, "The Relevance of 'Religious Diagnosis' for Counseling," in *Psychotherapy and Religious Values*, ed. E. L. Worthington Jr. (Grand Rapids: Baker, 1993), 105.

14. Donald E. Wiger, *The Clinical Documentation Sourcebook* (New York: Wiley, 1997), xi.

15. See Wiger, *Clinical Documentation Sourcebook*; Edward L. Zuckerman, *The Clinician's Thesaurus 3* (Pittsburgh: The Clinician's Toolbox, 1993); S. Richard Sauber, ed., *Managed Mental Health Care* (Bristol, Pa.,: Brunner/Mazel, 1997); Michael Goodman, Janet Brown, and Pamela Deitz, *Managing Managed Care: A Mental Health Practitioner's Survival Guide* (Washington, D.C.: American Psychiatric Press, 1992); James Morrison, *The First Interview* (New York: Guilford, 1995); James Morrison, *DSM-IV Made Easy* (New York: Guilford, 1995); and Randolph K. Sanders, ed., *Christian Counseling Ethics: A Handbook for Therapists, Pastors & Counselors* (Downers Grove, Ill.: InterVarsity Press, 1997).

16. We ask this question as a result of our reading of P. Scott Richards, John M. Rector, and Alan C. Tjeltveit, "Values, Spirituality, and Psychotherapy," in *Integrating Spirituality into Treatment*, ed. W. R. Miller (Washington, D.C.: American Psychological Association, 1999), 153.

17. We make this request as a result of our reading of David Dillon, *Short-Term Counseling* (Dallas: Word, 1992), 150.

18. Charles A. Kollar, *Solution-Focused Pastoral Counseling* (Grand Rapids: Zondervan, 1997), 99.

19. See, for example, American Association of Christian Counselors, *Code of Ethics* (Forest, Va.: American Association of Christian Counselors, 1998); American Association for Marriage and Family Therapists, *Code of Ethical Principles for Marriage and Family Therapists* (Washington, D.C.: American Association for Marriage and Family Therapists, 1985); American Counseling Association, *Code of Ethics and Standards of Practice* (Alexandria, Va.: American Counseling Association, 1995); American Psychiatric Association, *Principles of Medical Ethics with Annotations Especially Applicable to Psychiatry* (Washington, D.C.: American Psychiatric Association, 1986); American Psychological Association, "Ethical Principles of Psychologists and Code of Conduct," *American Psychologist* 47 (1992), 1597–1611; Christian Association for Psychological Studies, *Ethical Guidelines for the Christian Association for Psychological Studies* (New Braunfels, Tex.: Christian Association for Psychological Studies, 1993).

20. Ohlschlager and Mosgofian, *Law for the Christian Counselor*, 253.

21. Richard E. Butman, "Qualifications of the Christian Mental Health Professional," in *Christian Counseling Ethics*, 59.

22. Richards and Bergin, *A Spiritual Strategy for Counseling and Psychotherapy*, 164. The reader is directed to this work for an extensive review of the resources in this area.

23. David B. Larson, Francis G. Lu, and James P. Sawyers, eds., *Model Curriculum for Psychiatric Residency Training Programs: Religion and Spirituality in Clinical Practice* (Rockville, Md.: National Institute for Healthcare Research, 1997), 1.

24. George Ohlschlager, "Liability in Christian Counseling: Welcome to the Grave New World," in *Excellence and Ethics in Counseling*, ed. Gary R. Collins, 61.

25. Cited in Archibald D. Hart, Gary L. Gulbranson, and Jim Smith, *Mastering Pastoral Counseling* (Portland, Ore.: Multnomah Press, 1991), 39.

26. Noted in Butman, "Qualifications of the Christian Mental Health Professional," in *Christian Counseling Ethics*, 61 – 72.

Index

We want to hear from you. Please send your comments about this
book to us in care of the address below. Thank you.

ZondervanPublishingHouse
Grand Rapids, Michigan 49530
http://www.zondervan.com